THE RISE OF
THE GREEK EPIC

THE RISE OF
THE GREEK EPIC

BEING A COURSE OF LECTURES DELIVERED
AT HARVARD UNIVERSITY

BY

GILBERT MURRAY

REGIUS PROFESSOR OF GREEK IN THE UNIVERSITY OF OXFORD

THIRD EDITION

REVISED AND ENLARGED

OXFORD
AT THE CLARENDON PRESS
1924

Oxford University Press

London   Edinburgh   Glasgow   Copenhagen

New York   Toronto   Melbourne   Cape Town

Bombay   Calcutta   Madras   Shanghai

Humphrey Milford Publisher to the UNIVERSITY

PRINTED IN ENGLAND
AT THE OXFORD UNIVERSITY PRESS

PREFACE
TO THE THIRD EDITION

THIS edition contains, besides a good deal of revision in detail, some new material on the historic background of Homeric myths and new illustration of the traditional book by the analogy of stage plays, as well as a small additional appendix. My general attitude towards Homeric problems remains much the same as I have explained in the Preface to the Second Edition, though I hope that, in spite of the War and the League of Nations, I have learnt something more about Homer in the last ten years.

In that period the analysis of the poems has been treated by two acknowledged masters, Wilamowitz and Bethe.[1] It is worth noting that while agreeing in general view and method they differ greatly in their particular conclusions. That result indicates, in my opinion, not that the method is faulty but that the available evidence is insufficient. It can show us, as I have said elsewhere, the kind of thing that must have happened ; it can seldom tell us the exact thing that did happen. Dr. Leaf's *Troy* (1912) and *Homer and History* (1915), though much in both of them fails to convince me, have added greatly to our knowledge of Homeric geography, and show all the lucidity and grip of real life which specially distinguish their author among learned men. From Professor Chadwick I have learnt at last to understand what a 'Heroic Age' really is, an invaluable lesson for Greek scholars. From Professor J. A. K. Thomson I have had real help in the imaginative understanding of Homeric poetry, and in particular of the relations of the bard to the chorus. The ninth and tenth chapters of his *Studies in the Odyssey* appear to me to have brought light into the very heart of what is specially called 'the Homeric Question'. From him also I have adopted the conception of the Achaioi as a north-western tribe, forerunners of the Dorians, and quite distinct from the

---

[1] *Die Ilias und Homer*, by U. von Wilamowitz-Moellendorff (1916, 1920) ; Homer, *Dichtung und Saga*, by Erich Bethe. *Ilias* 1914 : *Odyssee*, &c., 1923.

older Greek civilization, which was the parent of Aeolian and Ionian. This view, based chiefly on the evidence of the three independent groups of Achaean inscriptions, was also suggested by Chadwick and has been adopted by many later writers. It is not in any way essential to my general position, but it seems to me to account for the facts better than any other current hypothesis.

My belief in the importance of the Attic element in the poems is in general, though not in detailed, agreement with the position taken by such writers as Cauer, Bethe, and Mülder, and has lately been confirmed by the striking *Sprachliche Untersuchungen* of Wackernagel (1916).

Among critics who take a radically different view from mine, I have learned most from Drerup (*Das Homerproblem in der Gegenwart*, 1921, being vol. 1 of a large work on *Homerische Poetik*). The masses of interesting material which he has collected and the acuteness of his historical arguments console one for the over-polemical tone of what he openly calls a 'Kriegsbuch'. In this connexion I would fain pay a tribute to the *Grundfragen* of the lamented Paul Cauer, of which the third edition lies before me, a work which, apart from its learning, seems to me to acquire real beauty by its patient candour and reasonableness.

I rejoice to find myself more in agreement with Mr. T. W. Allen's learned and ingenious book, *The Homeric Catalogue of Ships* (1921), than I had expected beforehand. Mr. Allen at least regards the Catalogue as an ancient non-Homeric document, originally composed for another context and, in spite of additions and omissions, still bearing clear marks of its origin, and I see with sympathy that he has brought down upon himself the wrath of a more perfect 'unitarian', Drerup, by these dangerous concessions to human reason. But there is one point of principle on which I think that he has overstated his case. He treats the Catalogue as a legal document, and argues that any alteration in it which may have occurred in the course of ages must be no mere corruption, such as is common in literary texts, but a 'forgery made with a material and quasi-legal purpose'. Such a view appears to me to rest on a misunderstanding, and I have discussed it in Appendix J.

The last few years have produced several new and interesting studies of the peculiarities of Homeric style in narrative, in similes, and in the almost impossible task of describing battles.[1] It would be quite easy, of course, to attribute them all to the personal tastes of a hypothetical individual. One critic, for instance, postulates a poet who knew several dialects and was proud of mixing them, and who also enjoyed making fun of the gods. But, as Jebb emphasized long ago, the thing to be explained is not a personal taste but a tradition. An eccentric Homer is an impossibility. A tradition is a social fact, based on the unspoken agreement of poets and audiences, from which neither can vary widely or abruptly. And the problem to be understood is how and why through many generations the normal Greek public expected its epic poets to speak in a particular artificial dialect, to use a particular type of simile and description, and to obey certain subtle and probably unconscious rules of symmetry. Certainly the artistic instinct implied in both poet and audience by these facts is very remarkable, but perhaps not more so than the exquisite conventions of symmetry and proportion which were traditional in other forms of Greek art, for instance in architecture and the carving of bas-reliefs.

G. M.

Christ Church, Oxford,
July 1924.

---

[1] See the authors quoted in Cauer, *Grundfragen*, iii. 5, to whom may be added Shorey in *Class. Phil.*, July 1922; Fraenkel, *Homerische Gleichnisse*, 1921 (which however I have not seen), and J. T. Sheppard, *The Pattern of the Iliad*, 1923. See also the bibliography by Mülder in Körte's *Jahresbericht über die Fortschritte der kl. Altertumswissenschaft*, Vol. 182 (1920, 1), with his trenchant but over-subjective criticisms.

PREFACE
TO THE SECOND EDITION

In preparing this second edition I should like to thank several friends for notes and suggestions, among them Mr. E. E. Genner, Professor Cruickshank, Mr. J. A. K. Thomson, and Mr. Andrew Lang. I have also derived profit from some of my reviews, both English and foreign.

It was vain, I suppose, to hope that even the most pacific and wary walking would take one far into Homeric territory without rousing the old lions that lie wakeful behind most of the larger stones. I have listened with mixed feelings to their threatening voices. The sportsman within me would like to go gun in hand and bag a few of the most dangerous; the philosopher is resolved to do them no injury, but merely try, gradually and indirectly, to make them friends to man. While still avoiding controversy, therefore, I have tried in this edition to state more clearly or correctly or patiently a number of arguments which seem to have given trouble in the first; I have in many places added or altered a word or two in view of fresh evidence; especially I have added a new chapter on the known history of the Homeric text. The rest of my book proceeds mainly in historical order, and deals largely with regions in which there is no record; this new chapter reverses that order and reaches back, step by step, from the known to the unknown.

I am anxious to find common ground with my unitarian critics. I only differ irreconcilably from those who reject all analysis *ab initio*; who assume as an unquestioned starting-point that, towards the end of the second millennium B.C., when to the best of our knowledge there was no Greek literature, a single miraculously gifted man, of whose life we know nothing, living in the heart of a rich, widespread, and romantic civilization, which no history mentions and all excavation has signally failed to discover, composed for an audience unable to read two poems much too long to be listened to; and then managed by miraculous but unspecified means to secure that his poems should be preserved practically unaltered while flying *viva per ora virum* through some six extraordinarily changeful centuries. These stalwarts do not wish to be persuaded or argued with. But for the rest of us a meeting-ground is possibly within sight. If the *Iliad* is a traditional book, in which old material has been reshaped by later bards—whether we suppose a gradual development of a Trojan story or an Achilles story, or a fictional reshaping of old poetry which had originally nothing to do with Achilles nor yet with Troy, or all these together—the difference between Wolfians and unitarians is really one of degree.

Of course the *Iliad* is a unity. Every successful version of a traditional poem is that. Every new poet who recited and thereby modified the *Iliad* produced or meant to produce a unity. Nay, the very arguments which are used to prove a complex growth in the past will serve to prove a unity in the present. For almost every discrepancy or awkwardness is deliberately smoothed out and reconciled. There are no naked impossibilities, there are no crude and unpalliated contradictions. The poets who worked upon the *Iliad* were too good artists for that. Wherever we can discern the tracks of the ' Diaskeuastês ' we can nearly always discern also the pains he has taken to conceal his tracks.

The original substratum is a *vera causa* : the poem as a whole cannot be conceived without it. The reshaping by later poets or editors is a *vera causa* : it is demonstrated by the history of the text. The task of the unitarian, then, is, somewhere between the first sources of the *Iliad* and the last additions, to find some one poet whose work utterly surpasses that of all who came before or after him. For my own part, I leave that quest to scholars of more confident temper ; the little I have to say about it will be found on pp. 238 ff.

The subject of Homeric language needs a few words to itself, both because of the good recent work done upon it (see p. 168 f.) and because the questions at issue are often misunderstood. The cardinal fact about the language is the extraordinary mixture in it of old and new, in forms, in constructions, in manners of thought. This mixture has, of course, been explained in various ways ; to me it is merely the natural mark and stamp of a Traditional

Book, preserved, renewed, conventionalized, and unconsciously modified—always within the limits of the convention—by many successive generations of reciters.

But the critics of thirty years ago were apt sometimes to go wrong by not recognizing the complexity of the problem before them, and trying by means of the language to determine the comparative date of particular books as wholes, or of the two poems as wholes. It is true that there are differences of style; slight but decided differences, which every good scholar, however he may explain them, feels. But it is impossible to cut out any large section of the poems clean and say: 'Every line of this is written in language of a particular date.' On the hypothesis which I follow, of course, any such expectation would be un-scientific. The mixture of old and new is all-pervasive. The oldest parts have passed through the lips of scores of later poets; the latest parts—even the most confessedly apocryphal additions of the 'wild papyri'—are largely made up of old lines and phrases, and are always composed in the old convention.

Any satisfactory examination of the language statistics must bear these considerations in mind and realize the difficulty of its task. It must never be satisfied with merely counting unanalysed phenomena. It must always dig below the 'surface corruption'. It must never use repeated or inorganic lines as if they were necessarily original or organic in the place where they happen now to stand. It must take full account of differences of subject as naturally producing differences of vocabulary. And it must of necessity, if it is to do much good, practise an extreme deli-cacy of sensitiveness to language. When the whole poem has been uniformly clothed in conventional epic diction, when each rhapsode has deliberately written to the best of his powers in 'Homeric' language, it is only by a delicacy of observation surpassing his that we can hope to detect his deviations from standard. This sounds very difficult; but it has often been done. After all, we scholars have unlimited time: and the rhapsodes, though skilful, were unsuspicious.

As to my own particular views, I am conscious of a slight change, or advance, of opinion on one important question, and it is a pleasure to acknowledge here a debt of gratitude to my famous and inveterate foeman, Mr. Andrew Lang. I only wish the change were one which Mr. Lang were more likely to accept as typical of true repentance.

I speak with diffidence on points of pure archaeology, but in his book on *The World of Homer* [1] Mr. Lang seems to me to have shown that phase after phase of that world, where it is not Mycenaean, agrees with nothing that we know on solid earth before the sixth and fifth centuries. That is, the common opinion which places ' Homer's world ' on solid earth in ' post-Mycenaean ' times, from the tenth to the eighth century, is confronted with greater difficulties than ever. Our archaeological evidence is now fairly abundant, and no such world has been discovered. Of course there are old Mycenaean or ' Achaean ' elements. But, apart from these, Mr. Lang argues in detail that the men's dress, the women's dress, the corslets and armour, are markedly different from those of the earliest vases, and just like those of the sixth and fifth centuries. The dress is that worn by the ' older men of the wealthy classes ' a little before the time of Thucydides (Thuc. i. 6). The same is true, as I rejoice to find Mr. Lang saying, of the Homeric gods. They are, apart from traces of a wilder background, the gods of Pheidias. All our study of Greek religion has long been telling us so. The same, I would say, is true of the moral tone of Homer. Allowing for certain data in the saga, Homeric morals and ' religion ' in the higher sense (see Mr. Lang's excellent remarks on p. 120) are those of pre-sophistic Athens at her best. The expurgations of which I make so much use point on the whole in the same direction. We have no reason to think that the cruelties and indecencies which I believe to have been expurgated were specially objected to in the time, say, of the dipylon vases. The tone of Xenophanes, Thales, and Heraclitus is, I think, enough to show that they would pretty certainly be condemned in Ionia as soon as the great age of Ionia was well established. It is at any rate perfectly easy to show that they were all condemned in fifth-century Athens (see pp. 263 f.).

Of course Mr. Lang and I interpret these facts differently. I take them as confirming the evidence for the Pisistratean recension and the fluid condition of the poems in the fifth and fourth

[1] Chapters viii and ix.

centuries. All this is developed in my new chapter on the history of the text. Mr. Lang supposes that about the year 1000 there was a pure ' Achaean' age uncontaminated by Ionia, very brief and therefore unrecorded, very local and therefore undiscovered, which happened in all the above respects to be surprisingly like the age of Pisistratus, 450 years later, though different from all ages between.

If the corslets are work of the sixth century or later, a much greater part of the elaboration of the *Iliad* than I formerly ventured to suggest must belong to the time of Pisistratus or even of Aeschylus. And I do not shrink from this conclusion. We know for certain of only one great creative age in Greek literature, that which extends, roughly speaking, from Aeschylus to Plato. But doubtless there lived strong men before Aeschylus; the beginning of the great age may confidently be extended to Solon or to Thales. All through this age we know that something called Homer was constantly recited: we have strong evidence to show that, even at the end of it, the text was still fluid and liable to be re-written. Of course we must not forget the old, the very old, substratum. But if we find upon that substratum work of a peculiar architectonic greatness, a peculiar humanity and eloquence and smoothness of diction, a peculiar dramatic form and tragic intensity, is it not reasonable to suppose that it acquired those qualities during the only age in which we know that Greece had them, or something like them, to give?

Mycenae and Cnossus in their prime may conceivably have had such qualities. But the poems are not Mycenaean, much less Minoan. The great age of Greece certainly had them; and during the great age the poems were certainly still being recited and had not yet reached a final form. Between those two ages Greek civilization has little to show that rises above the level of respectable barbarism. One cannot indeed quite suppose that masses of old epic poetry lay completely dead and buried till some sixth-century Kynaethus dug them up. The epic convention is too fixed, the whole style is too intelligible, for that. And our miserable remains of the Rejected Epics illustrate suggestively what the substratum, or the sources, of the *Iliad* may have been like, before they were glorified. There is a separate inquiry there. But it looks as if we must face the probability that a far larger amount of real creative work than we ever suspected was done upon both *Iliad* and *Odyssey* by poets not far removed either in date or in spirit from Pindar and the great Athenians: that the history of Greek literature is after all a great and intelligible *continuum*, not one shining prehistoric island, then centuries of darkness, and then all the rest.

There has been a great output of books on Homer in the last three years; I mention here only a few that may be useful to my readers.[1]   Dealing with the general question, we have to welcome a second edition of Paul Cauer's lucid and fascinating *Grundfragen der Homerkritik* (Leipzig, 1910), to which in my twenties I owed a large debt of gratitude, and an Italian translation of Drerup's well-known and copiously illustrated *Homer*, enlarged and improved.   A new book, Georg Finsler's *Homer* (Berlin, 1908), gives an extraordinarily comprehensive and compressed account of almost all sides of Homeric criticism; Professor Seymour's useful *Life in the Homeric Age* (Macmillan, 1908) is full of minute and sober observation; the short *Probe eines wissenschaftlichen Kommentars zu Homer*, by E. Hermann (Hansaschule-Festschrift, 1908), is particularly promising. I hope it will be carried further.

Dealing with the actual analysis of the poems, Wilamowitz, in a paper on Θ (*Sitzungsber. d. k. Preussischen Akademie*, 1910, xxi), has argued very persuasively that most of that book was probably composed to make room in a connected Iliad for two existing but independent lays, *I* and *K*. Another excellent article is *Hektor's Abschied*, by Erich Bethe (*Abhandlungen der k. Sächsischen Ges. d. Wissenschaften*, xxvii, No. xii), arguing that in the main the author of *Z* was also the author of *Ω*, and, though a late poet, perhaps deserves the name of Homer. There are certainly marked similarities between the two books. Dr. K. Rothe's *Ilias als Dichtung* (Paderborn, 1910) is a very erudite and pleasing restatement of the conservative position. He considers that Homer (1) used old epic material freely, but turned it all to his own artistic ends; (2) that when he had finished the poem he sometimes turned back to it and added pieces; (3) that he lived in a charming court in Ionia, founded by the

---

[1] A very complete bibliography is in Rothe's articles, first in *Bursian's Jahresbericht*, and afterwards in *Zeitschr. f. d. Gymnasialwesen*.

last king of Mycenae, who had fled thither from the Achaeans, and betrayed other personal weaknesses which are reflected in the figure of Agamemnon. This, of course, seems to me like a fairy-story, but much of Rothe's criticism is good. Mr. T. W. Allen's articles on the Homeridae, the Epic Cycle, and the Catalogue are also written from a severely unitarian standpoint (*Classical Quarterly* I (1907), II (two articles); *J. H. S.* xxx. pp. 292–323). Mr. Andrew Lang's *World of Homer* (Longmans, 1910) restates his old views with some interesting modifications in the light of recent literature. Mr. Shewan's *Doloneia* (Macmillan, 1911) is an industrious and gallant attack upon all critics who have either spoken disrespectfully of K or thought its style in any way peculiar. Van Gennep's little *Question d'Homère* has a useful bibliography by A. J. Reinach (Paris, 1910). Dr. Verrall's volume of essays, *The Bacchants of Euripides* (Cambridge, 1910), contains two valuable papers on Homeric subjects : *The First Homer*, showing that in the fifth century ' Homer ' meant much more than ' The *Iliad* and the *Odyssey* ' and suggesting that the first Epic Cycle dates from Pisistratus; and *The Mutiny of Idomeneus,* arguing a harmonization of sources in *Iliad* K–N. Among new attempts at analysis of the poems we have Fick's *Entstehung der Odyssee* (Göttingen, 1910), terse and masterly, like all that Fick writes, though involved with improbable speculations; and Miss Stawell's striking work, *Homer and the Iliad*, a book full of fine observation and poetical understanding. She attempts to reconstruct an ' original Iliad ' (omitting most of B, all H, Θ, I, K, N, Ξ, half O, and much of the later books, but keeping at all costs Z and Ω), and fortifies her results by a further study of the language; this ' original Iliad ', however, probably made free use of older poems.

A somewhat new form of ' unitarianism ' is put forth in Dr. Mülder's vigorous and valuable book, *Die Ilias und ihre Quellen* (Weidmann, 1910). ' An abundance of unassimilated material in spite of a constant effort after uniformity ' is his description of the problem, and he finds its solution in the hypothesis of a single gifted and artificial poet who, by processes of daring fiction, wrought a new poem out of numbers of old ones—the old Thebais, a Meleager epic, a Heracleia, a Pylian epic, an Achilleis, and others. The *Iliad* was thus produced in Ionia about the year 625, the *Odyssey* somewhat later at the Court of Pisistratus. His poet does much the same work as the 'Bearbeiter' or 'Diaskeuast' of earlier scholars, only more of it.

The 'surface corruption', already ably treated of late years by such editors as Van Leeuwen and Professor Platt, is the subject of many clever and interesting conjectures in Mr. Agar's *Homerica*. Perhaps I may be allowed to urge every student who wishes either to study the language or to enjoy the music of Homer to accustom himself to 'thinking away' this destructive and often unmetrical surface-corruption. For English readers the best method is a constant reference to such texts as I have mentioned above, together with an occasional reading of Fick. The outline of this problem, as of most others affecting Homer, will be found in Father Browne's *Homeric Study* (Macmillan, 1905).

G. M.

Christ Church, Oxford,
    May 1911.

PREFACE
TO THE FIRST EDITION

THESE lectures were written in response to an invitation from Harvard University to deliver the Gardiner Lane Course for 1907. Only some half of them were actually so delivered. The subject had been so long forming itself in my mind, and I was also so anxious not to allow any mere lack of pains to prove me unworthy of the honour thus offered me, that I soon found my material completely outrunning the bounds of the proposed course. I print the whole book; but I must confess that those parts of it which were spoken at Harvard have, if it is not egotistical to say so, a special place in my affections, through their association with the constant and most considerate kindness of Mr. and Mrs. Lane and of many others who became in varying degrees my *xenoi* in America.

The book touches on some subjects where, feeling more than usually conscious of the insecurity of my own knowledge, I have not scrupled to take advantage of the learning of my friends. On several points of archaeology and primitive history I have sought counsel from Professor J. L. Myres; on points of Old French from Miss Pope of Somerville College; on Semitic matters from my colleague Professor D. S. Margoliouth, whose vast stores have stood always most generously open to me. In a more general way I am conscious of help received from Mr. J. W. Mackail and Mr. T. C. Snow, and above all from Miss J. E. Harrison, who read the Lectures in MS. and called my attention to much recent foreign literature which I should otherwise have neglected. The debt which I owe to her *Prolegomena*, also, will be visible on many of the ensuing pages.

In subjects such as these the conclusions reached by any writer can often be neither certain nor precise. Yet they may none the less be interesting and even valuable. If our evidence is incomplete, that is no reason for not using it as far as it goes. I have tried throughout the book never to think about making a debating case, or taking up the positions most easy to defend; but always to set out honestly and with much reflection what really seems to me to be most like the truth. I feel, indeed, that I ought perhaps to have stated my evidence much more fully and systematically. My excuse is that the lectures were originally written almost without books of reference, and that when I went over them to verify my statements and cite my authorities I hesitated to load the book with references which might be unnecessary, and which in any case were rather in the nature of afterthoughts.

As regards the Homeric Question, which forms in one way or another an important element in my subject, I have long felt that the recent reaction against advanced views has been largely due, not indeed to lack of knowledge, but to inadequate understanding of what the 'advanced' critics really mean. A good part of my present work has therefore lain in thinking out with rather more imaginative effort many of the common phrases and hypotheses of Homeric criticism. My own views are not, of course, identical with those of any other writer. Among English scholars I agree most closely with Dr. Leaf, and may almost say that I accept his work as a basis. For the rest, I follow generally in the main tradition of Wolf, Lachmann, Kirchhoff, Wilamowitz. But the more I read, the more conscious I am of good work being done on all sides in the investigation of Greek religion and early history, and of the astonishing advance which those subjects have made within my own memory. The advance still continues. Archaeologists are throwing shafts of light even across that Dark Age of which I speak so much in Lectures II and III. My own little book, heaven knows! indulges in no dream of making a final statement of the truth on any part of its field. It is only an attempt to puzzle out a little more of the meaning of a certain remote age of the world, whose beauty and whose power of inspiration seem to shine the more wonderful the more resolutely we set ourselves to understand it.

GILBERT MURRAY.

New College, Oxford,
Sept. 1907.

ANALYTICAL TABLE OF CONTENTS

INTRODUCTION

GREECE AND THE PROGRESS OF MAN

A. THE PEOPLE

I. THE MIGRATIONS: THE POLIS

APPENDICES

I

GREECE AND THE PROGRESS OF MAN

THESE lectures form the first part of an attempt to study the growth of Greek poetry from a particular point of view, namely, as the embodiment of a force making for the progress of the human race. By progress I understand some gradual ennobling and enriching of the content of life; or, to adopt the magnificent language of the document known in Scotland as 'the Shorter Catechism', some movement towards the attainment of that ' chief end of man ', which is 'to glorify God and enjoy him for ever'.

This conception of all the arts, even poetry, as being so many forms or parts of the service of man, may strike a hearer at first as somewhat modern and removed from ancient habits of thought. But I think the truth is just the opposite. The idea of service to the community was more deeply rooted in the Greeks than in us. And as soon as they began to reflect about literature at all—which they did very early—the main question they asked about each writer was almost always upon these lines: 'Does he help to make better men?' 'Does he make life a better thing?' We all know with what rigid and passionate Puritanism this view is asserted by Plato. But Plato can never be taken as representing the average man. There is better evidence of ordinary feeling in the *Frogs* of Aristophanes.[1] 'On what grounds should a poet be admired?' says Aeschylus, and Euripides answers—'For his skill, his good counsel, and because we make men better in their cities'. Amid all the many cross-currents of criticism illustrated in the *Frogs*, there is no protest against this judging of poetry by its fruits. The principle is accepted by all parties.

Among later writers the idea of the service of man, or the bettering of human life, has become habitual and familiar. Diodorus begins his history by a reference to the long chain of

---

[1] v. 1008, 1035, and the whole scene: cf. also Isocr. iv. § 159, and elsewhere.

B

historians who ' have aspired by their own labours to benefit our common life '.[1] Polybius speaks of history as the most obvious help towards ' the correcting of life '.

Thucydides, as we all remember, will be content if his work, whether interesting or uninteresting to an audience, is judged to be useful. Denys of Halicarnassus sums up the praises of the Athenians by saying, in the very language of an old Delphian decree, that they ' made gentle the life of the world '.

Theologians and philosophers, especially those of the more rationalist schools, carry the conception further. The traditional Gods are explained as being so many great men of past ages who have in their various ways served humanity. ' That which benefits human life is God,' said Prodicus in the fifth century B.C. ' Deus est mortali iuvare mortalem,' says Pliny from a Stoic source in the first A.D. And in later times the view is always widely current, a common meeting ground for Euhemerist, Stoic, and Epicurean. The history taught in schools largely consisted, if we may generalize from our extant Scholiasts, in lists of these benefactors of mankind :

Inventas aut qui vitam excoluere per artis,
Quique sui memores alios fecere merendo.[2]

[1] Diod. i. 1 τοῖς ἰδίοις πόνοις ὠφελῆσαι τὸν κοινὸν βίον ἐφιλοτιμήθησαν. Cf. Polyb. i. 1 (μηδεμίαν... ἑτοιμοτέραν τοῖς ἀνθρώποις διόρθωσιν) ; Thuc. i. 22 ; Dion. Hal. *de Thucyd.* p. 919 Ἀθηναῖοι ... οἱ τὸν κοινὸν βίον ἐξημερώσαντες; idem, iv. 25 (p. 701 R) on Servius Tullius. Herodotus, as one might expect, has more of the mere artist about him : he writes, ὡς μήτε τὰ γενόμενα ἐξ ἀνθρώπων τῷ χρόνῳ ἐξίτηλα γένηται, μήτε ἔργα μεγάλα τε καὶ θωμαστά, τὰ μὲν Ἕλλησι, τὰ δὲ βαρβάροισι ἀποδεχθέντα, ἀκλεᾶ γένηται (i. 1). Compare also the remarkable language of a Delphic Inscription of the second century B.C., in *Bulletin de Corr. Hellénique*, 1900, p. 96, conferring honours on certain Athenians : Ἔδοξε τοῖς Ἀμφικτύοσιν· ἐπειδὴ γεγονέναι καὶ συνειλέχθαι τεχνιτῶν σύνοδον παρ' Ἀθηναίοις συμβέβηκε πρῶτον, ὧν ὁ δῆμος ἁπάντων τῶν ἐν ἀνθρώποις ἀγαθῶν ἀρχηγὸς καταστάθεις, ἐν μὲν τοῦ θηριώδους βίου μετήγαγεν τοὺς ἀνθρώπους εἰς ἡμερότητα, παραίτιος δ' ἐγενήθη τῆς πρὸς ἀλλήλους κοινωνίας, εἰσαγαγὼν τὴν τῶν μυστηρίων παράδοσιν καὶ διὰ τούτων παραγγείλας τοῖς ἅπασιν ὅτι μέγιστον ἀγαθόν ἐστιν ἐν ἀνθρώποις ἡ πρὸς ἑαυτοὺς χρῆσίς τε καὶ πίστις, ἔτι δὲ τῶν δοθέντων ὑπὸ τῶν θεῶν περὶ τῶν ἀνθρώπων νόμων καὶ τῆς παιδείας ... ' Decreed by the Amphictyons of Delphi: Whereas it was in Athens that a union of the craftsmen of Dionysus (i.e. tragic actors and poets) first arose and was gathered together ; and whereas the People of Athens, the established leader in all human advance, first won mankind from the life of wild beasts to gentleness ; and, by introducing the Mysteries and thereby proclaiming to the world that the greatest good for mankind is a spirit of help and trust toward one another, hath been part maker of the co-operation of men with men, and of the laws given by the gods for the treatment of men and of education ...'

[2] Plin. *Hist. Nat.* ii. 7. 18. Vergil, *Aen.* vi. 663. Cf. Lucr. v, latter part. I

It is the very language and spirit of that service of humanity which lies at the heart of the practical religion of the present day. The modern artist or admirer of art is apt to be offended by it. Not, I think, justly. In a Greek society the artist was treated frankly as a friend and fellow worker. He helped to make life beautiful, which is at least one large and obvious way of making it good. In a modern society he is a distinguished alien, approached with a mixture of adulation and mistrust. We suspect that what he calls beautiful may be really wicked.

I must take for granted many fundamental theses. That man has progressed, for one thing, and that the direction in which Western civilization has moved is on the whole a good one. I think that few of us seriously deny these propositions; and those who do would not be moved by my arguments.

Now we find it generally admitted that the seeds of Western civilization are mostly to be found in Greece and not elsewhere. Yet it is curious how seldom Greek Literature is regarded from this point of view, as an embodiment of the progressive spirit, an expression of the struggle of the human soul towards freedom and ennoblement.

We have had in abundance the classical point of view. The Greeks have been the Classics, the masters in art and letters, models of a finished and more or less unapproachable perfection in form. Or rather, to put it more accurately, the Greeks round about the fifth century B. C., and the Romans of the centuries just before and after the Christian era, have been peculiarly the Classics, and other writers have been admitted to various degrees of classic dignity in proportion as they approached to the two great periods.

Now I should like, if time permitted, to trace this conception to its origin. Unreal as it sometimes sounds, it has its base in mere fact. The Greeks and Romans of those two periods did, for some reason or other, produce in most departments of thought better work than any of the generations that succeeded them for some thousand years or so; and what is more, the generations of

suspect that this view of human history was largely inspired by the great work of Dicaearchus, Βίος Ἑλλάδος. He was an immediate disciple of Aristotle; the *Life of Hellas* was a history of Greek civilization. Fragments in *F. H. G.* ii.

the decadence had the extreme good sense to see it.   As regards
literature, the point is too obvious to need illustration.   Let us
take a quite different field, the science of medicine.   If a man
wished to learn medicine in the later ages of the Roman or
Byzantine empires, and right on to the Renaissance, to whom did
he go for his knowledge ?   He went, as far as I can make out, to
various handbooks and epitomes of the works of two ancient
doctors ; of Galen, a Greek who practised in Rome in the year
160 A. D., and of Hippocrates, a Greek who practised in Cos and
Athens in the fifth century B. C.   And Galen's own work largely
takes the form of a commentary on Hippocrates.

There is an interesting MS. extant of a treatise on Dislocations
by one Apollonius of Citium in Cyprus.   The MS. was written in
Constantinople about the year 950 A. D., and it begins with a paean
of joy over the discovery of the works of this ancient surgeon,
with his accurate drawings to show how the various dislocations
should be set.   The text was written out.   The illustrations
were carefully copied.   Where the old drawings were blurred or
damaged the copies were left incomplete, lest some mistake
should be made.[1]   Why ?   Because this ancient surgeon, living
about 150 B. C., knew how to set dislocated limbs a great deal
better than people who lived a thousand years after him.   It was
a piece of good fortune to them to rediscover his work.   And
his writing, again, takes the form of a commentary on the fifth-
century Hippocrates.   Hippocrates' own writing does not look
back.   It is consciously progressive and original.

That is what the Classics once were.   I will not attempt to
trace the stages through which their empire has waned and their
power to help us dwindled away.   What they now possess is a
limited but a most interesting domain.   I will express it in this
way.   There seems to be in human effort a part that is progressive
and transient, and another which is stationary or eternal.   In some
things we find that a very third-rate person who happens to have
been born in 1860 can teach us far more than a great genius or
a great reformer who was born in 1760.   About electricity, for
instance, or steamships.   In the other sphere it is the quality of

---

[1] See Schöne's introduction to his large edition (Teubner, 1896), where
this point is proved.   See also *Greek Medicine in Rome*, by Sir Clifford
Allbutt.   1921.

the man or his work which tells.   And it tells almost unaffected
by distance : what was once beautiful is still beautiful ; what was
once great of soul is still great.   And if Shakespeare was born
nearly 400 years ago, and St. Paul 1900 and Aeschylus over 2000,
those facts do not seem to make any noteworthy difference in the
value of their work.   This distinction is, I think, implied in the
current phrase which says that the ancient Greeks are still classics
in point of style.

Now, in the narrow sense of style, any such view as this would
be almost grotesque.   No modern historian could possibly model
his style on the strange contorted language of Thucydides ; no
playwright could copy Aeschylus.   Aeschylus and Thucydides
were men of extraordinary genius who irresistibly bent the Greek
language to their will.   They are not, in any literal sense, models
of normal style.   If, however, we understand 'style' broadly
enough, so that style means the same as 'form', and 'form' includes 'spirit', then, I think, the principle is true.   The classical
books are in general the books which have possessed for mankind
such vitality of interest that they are still read and enjoyed at a
time when all the other books written within ten centuries of
them have long since been dead.   There must be something
peculiar about a book of which the world feels after two thousand
years that it has not yet had enough.   One would like to know
what it is that produces this permanent and not transient quality
of interest.   And it is partly for this purpose that we study the
Classics.   In some few ways one can know.   Form or spirit in
some sense lives longer than matter ; austerity perhaps lives
longer than sweetness ; what is simple and serious lives longer
than what is merely clever.   Much more remains unanalysable,
or can only be found by study of the books themselves.   But
there are qualities that make things live ; and that which lives
becomes classical.

Yet I think that this kernel of truth is involved in much error.
It is probable that these models of style, as they were read both
in the Middle Ages and the Renaissance, were often bad models
rather than good.   The accident was imitated, not the essence.
And the influence of the most living and original of all literatures
produced the corruptness of Classicism, a style almost certainly
very vicious, and that for two reasons.   First, because it attempted

to reproduce in an uninflected language all kinds of exquisite effects, largely connected with the order of words and the building of periods, which are only possible and natural in a highly inflected language. Secondly, because, in its appreciation of the immense imaginative value of tradition and allusion, it groped round for a tradition and found only one that was foreign and exotic and therefore could not truly serve its purpose. There is a great grandeur in the prose of Milton and Hooker; there is at least quaintness in the poetical style, largely inspired by Ovid, which ran riot during the Renaissance, a style in which people called the sun 'Phoebus' or the moon 'chaste Dian', and were proud of knowing stories of a complicated mythology which was not accessible to 'the vulgar'. There are traces of something like classicism in Greek poetry, I admit. They are the first signs of its decay. The classicist spirit is just so far related to the living spirit of Greek poetry, that it is a ranker form of the same poison by which Greek poetry died.

That sort of eighteenth-century or Renaissance classicism is perhaps dead, or no longer an active danger to the understanding of Greek. But there are other classicisms which threaten us still. Scholars in talking of the classics have allowed the object of their study to become confused with the medium through which they approach it. It is as though a man could not think of the stars except in terms of telescopes, or of mountains and sea except in terms of railway journeys and hotels. Nearly all of us approach the classics through an atmosphere of education, with its concomitants of dictionary and grammar, its unnatural calm, its extreme emphasis upon dutifulness and industry, and the subtle degradation of spirit produced by its system of examinations.

Some indeed take another path. From Winckelmann onwards there have been many critics who felt, for obvious reasons, that they could understand a Greek statue more easily than a Greek poem. Hence comes another sort of classicism, a tendency to explain the poems by the statues. A false road; partly because the immense majority of extant statues are not Classical Greek, but Graeco-Roman, and marked with the taint of the decadence: but far more because, in the essence of things, poems are made of quick words, and statues of stone, things that are not alike and never have been.

The fact seems to be that the understanding of Greek poetry needs first a good deal of hard linguistic study, and then, since every one who likes poetry must have in himself some germs of a poet, a poet's readiness of imaginative sympathy. As things are, the poetical minds are often repelled by the grammatical drudgery: and the grammarians at the end of their labours are apt to find that their little spring of poetry has dried up.

> The wise want love, and those who love want wisdom:
> And all best things are thus confused to ill.

As to all these dogmas about what is Classical, I think we should be on our guard. Classical and modern; classical and romantic; classical and Christian; there are no doubt some real differences corresponding to these phrases, but I would urge respectfully upon any student who loves poetry, that he should approach his ancient poets quite simply and take what they have to give him, not start off by expecting them to be 'classical' or 'statuesque' or 'pre-Christian' or anything else. The more you understand them, the less of these differences you will feel. And for a simple reason : that the differences lie largely in the accident of our own remoteness. We stand very far off, and have to strain our eyes. For us the comparison of ancient and modern is largely a comparison of something half-seen at a distance with something which we know intimately. We are apt to see only the bold outlines; we are apt to miss the little lights and shades, the quick vibrations of emotion that existed to a Greek in some particular word or phrase, and therefore we think they are not there. We mentally translate the words into a sort of dictionary language, never very apt indeed, but, we hope, at least dignified; removed alike from subtlety and from littleness because it is emptied of most of its meaning; serene and unemotional because we have not the knowledge or the sympathy to catch, across this gulf of years, the peculiar thrill of what was once a 'wingèd word' flying from soul to soul. It is perhaps in this department that the most pressing work of pure scholarship remains to be done.

That conception of the Greeks as Classic, then, has a basis of truth. It is only apt to be misstated, and so to darken counsel.

There is, however, a peculiar modification of it—which is almost the direct opposite of the truth ; a conception of Hellenism as representing some easy-going half-animal form of life, untroubled by conscience or ideals or duties, and the Greeks as a gay unconscious hedonistic race, possessing the somewhat superficial merits of extreme good looks and a mythically fine climate. There is no reason to suppose the ancient Greeks miraculously handsome, any more than to suppose that there is no dirty weather in the Aegean. This view has so little of the semblance of truth about it, that one wonders how it can have arisen. There are of course the causes mentioned above, the presence of the Graeco-Roman statues and the special difficulties of understanding the finer sides of the Greek language. But this particular conception of the Greeks as 'Pagans' comes, I think, largely from the mere need of an antithesis to Christianity on its ascetic side. Christian apologists, anxious to associate all the highest things in the world with their own religion, have proceeded to make the Greek a sort of type of what the natural man would be without Christianity. And they have been met half-way by the rebels of their own flock, intellectual people of an artistic, a revolutionary, or a pleasure-loving temperament, who have turned against the narrowness or conventionality of their Christian surroundings, and then accepted, as a rough embodiment of their own rebellious ideals, some imaginary Pagan Greek.

That would explain why this odd ideal of the Pagan Man should be abroad at all. But why should the Greeks be chosen as representing him? Partly for their mere eminence. They are the chief representatives of high civilization outside modern Christendom. Partly, I think, from a disproportionate attention sometimes bestowed on particular parts of Greek literature. But largely for a reason peculiar to their own case, which I believe to be very influential. We shall meet with it often during these lectures. It is that we, living in an age when certain great strides in human progress seem to be securely made and to need no more thinking about, look back upon these early pioneers of progress with some lack of historical sympathy, and attribute to the Greek spirit itself a number of primitive habits which it was not quite strong enough to conquer or else had not the leisure to grapple with.

Anthropologists have shown us what this Pagan Man really is. From the West Coast of Africa to the Pacific Isles in many varying shapes he meets us, still with the old gaiety, the old crowns of flowers, the night-long dances, the phallus-bearing processions, the untroubled vices. We feel, no doubt, a charm in his simple and instinctive life, in the quick laughter and equally quick tears, the directness of action, the unhesitating response of sympathy. We must all of us have wished from time to time that our friends were more like Polynesians; especially those of us who live in University towns. And I think, in a certain limited sense, the Greeks probably were so. But in the main, as all classical literature shows, the Greek and the Pagan are direct opposites. That instinctive Pagan has a strangely weak hold on life. He is all beset with terror and blind cruelty and helplessness. The Pagan Man is really the unregenerate human animal, and Hellenism is a collective name for the very forces which, at the time under discussion, strove for his regeneration. Yet, historically, one of the most characteristic things about Hellenism is that, though itself the opposite of savagery, it had savagery always near it. The peculiar and essential value of Greek civilization lies not so much in the great height which it ultimately attained, as in the wonderful spiritual effort by which it reached and sustained that height. The pre-Hellenic civilization of the Aegean area was in some ways very high. Minoan Crete, for example, produced larger buildings, better drainage, and in some respects a livelier art than classical Athens: it certainly controlled greater masses of concentrated capital. It does not however seem to have possessed much of the special Hellenic inspiration. And the village communities of the mainland, whether of Northern or Southern origin, cannot have been much above the level of savagery. But the rise of Greece began from something a little worse than the average level of barbaric Aegean societies. It began, as I hope to show in the second of these lectures, in the dark age which resulted when even these societies, such as they were, fell into chaos.

Allowing for indefinite differences of detail, there seems to be a certain primitive effortless level of human life, much the same all the world over, below which society would cease to be; a kind of world-wide swamp above which a few nations have built what seem like permanent and well-weathered dwellings. Others make transient refuges which sink back into the slough. *La nostalgie de la boue*—'home-sickness for the mud'—is a strong emotion in the human race. One sees it often in individual life. One can think of many instances in history: Hellenic kingdoms like that of the Seleucidae in Syria; many provinces in the decline of the Roman Empire; the west of Asia under the rule of the Turks; the rush of reaction in ancient Egypt after the religious reform of Amen-Hotep; or, again, the many efforts after higher religion in India, and the regular falling back of each reformation into the same primitive slough.

Now, as Greek civilization rose from the swampy level of the neighbouring peoples, especially the various pre-Semitic races just behind the Aegean coasts, it could not shake itself clean all at once. Remnants of savagery lingered on in obscure parts of life, expurgated as a rule and made comparatively innocent, but still bearing the mark of their origin. Such remnants, as a matter of fact, tend to receive undue attention. The Greeks themselves are puzzled at a strange practice. Herodotus says that the explanation of it is sacred, and better not mentioned. Pausanias describes it with an antiquarian's zest. Plutarch has a comforting theory of its real allegorical meaning. Our own friends the anthropologists, to whom all true Hellenists owe so much, naturally revel in such things. They search antiquity eagerly for traces of primitive man, for totems, cannibalism, human sacrifice, and the like. The traces which they discover are of the greatest value. But I think they have often mistaken the reverberation of an extinct barbarity for the actual barbarity itself.

What strikes one most in Greek society is not so much any bad things that were actually done. Of course there were bad things, and always have been in all societies. It is rather the frightful proximity of worse things still. Practices that to us seem like the scarce credible stories of a remote past were to the fifth-century Athenian possibilities and even dangers. The jungle grew thick and close all around them, and the barrier between seemed very weak, very impalpable.

You will notice in the ordinary language of ancient writers a characteristic which throws light on this aspect of Greek life.

Non-Hellenic nations are nearly always spoken of by their tribes or races—' Ethnê '—Pelasgians, Macedonians, Phoenicians; the Greeks are spoken of by their cities, or, what comes to the same thing, by their islands—Milesians, Phocaeans, Eretrians, Athenians. On the mainland it is the Polis or circuit wall that forms the essential boundary of the nation; in the case of the islands, Samos, Naxos, Aegina, it is the equivalent wall of sea. Every Greek community is like a garrison of civilization amid wide hordes of barbarians; a picked body of men, of whom each individual has in some sense to live up to a higher standard than can be expected of the common human animal. As the shield is the typical weapon of the Greek warrior, so the wall is the typical mark of Greek civilization. It is one of the facts that most need remembering in order to understand the greatnesses and the flaws of Hellenism, that it was represented everywhere by a handful of men holding an outpost, men who wrought their wonderful day's work in political and moral wisdom, in specula-tion, in beauty of outward form and inward imagining, with an ear ever open to the sternest of life's calls, and the hated spear and shield never far out of reach. No wonder that the task was too hard for them ! As a matter of fact, Greek civilization itself was never for a long enough time well policed and organized, its remoter villages were never thoroughly enough educated, to make it secure, even in its central places, against some sudden blind resurgence of the savage.

Take, for instance, the case of Human Sacrifice. The memory of a time when human beings had been deliberately slaughtered as a way of pleasing God runs through the literature of the fifth century as of something far-off, romantic, horrible. We may compare it to our own memories of the burning of heretics and witches, deeds which we know to have been done quite lately, by men very like ourselves, and yet deeds which we can scarcely conceive as psychologically possible to any sane being. In just the same way, to the earliest of the great Athenians, Aeschylus, the sacrifice of Iphigenia is something monstrous, beyond under-standing.[1] The man who did it must have been mad. To Euripides such acts are generally connected with a study of the

---

[1] Αἰσχρόμητις τάλαινα παρακοπὰ πρωτοπήμων, Aesch. *Ag.* 222. But the whole passage should be read.

worst possibilities of a savage mob, or of scheming kings led by malignant and half-insane priests. In an interesting fourth-century document, the dialogue called 'Minos', which is attributed to Plato, human sacrifice is treated as the extreme of what is 'to us unlawful', and yet, the speaker insists, it was at one time and among certain people 'the law'; and there are rumours still, he adds, of strange sacrifices in the secret places of Arcadian hills![1] It is the tone in which we might remind ourselves, for instance, that even in the last decade or so women have been tortured as witches in the Abruzzi or in Ireland. The writer himself, and the society which he addresses, feel themselves entirely remote from such practices.

And yet how close to them on all sides this abomination pressed, closer indeed than they knew! It is not only that it continued throughout all antiquity to be practised in times of great crises by all the barbarians of the Mediterranean coasts. It is not only that we find Hippônax describing the ritual execution of the *pharmakoi* at Ephesus, a grotesque and possibly a somewhat cruel business which clearly was a sort of mock human sacrifice. Hippônax was a satirist of the sixth century B. C., with a liking for horrors, and Ephesus was a partially barbarian town. But we find the thing creeping closer than that. In a well-known passage of the *Frogs* Aristophanes ends up a passage of comic abuse of certain persons much admired by his opponents by saying that, 'in the old days, people would have thought twice before using them as *pharmakoi*'—'Scarecrows,' shall we say? or 'Guy-Fawkeses'? The word means literally 'human medicines', or 'scapegoats'. Late and careless writers speak as if these *pharmakoi* were actually sacrificed. But fortunately we happen to have a fragment of an ancient third-century historian, Ister, who explains what this odd business really amounted to. Two persons, one for the men of the city, one for the women, were led out as though to execution. They

---

[1] p. 315 b. He refers also to the descendants of Athamas as practising a similar sacrifice. But there he is misinformed or, more likely, straining his point in the argument. In the Athamas ritual the victim escaped. See texts in Roscher's Lexicon. Mayer (ib. ii. p. 1509) compares a Pelops-Oenomaus ritual in Rhodes, in which the sacrificing priest pursued the victim with a spear, but was first blindfolded and had to run hand in hand with two small children.

wore necklaces, one of white figs, the other of black. They seem
to have been solemnly presented with cake and figs, and then
scourged and pelted out of the city—treated, in fact, very like
the Lion and the Unicorn. I hasten to add that the scourging
was done with little twigs and bulbs of the *skilla*, or wild squill,
and the pelting with similar ineffective objects. The victims are
said to have been volunteers, and chosen for their ugliness; and
various smaller details in the ceremony are meant to be grotesque
and absurd. At the end, the *pharmakoi* were supposed to be
dead and their ashes were thrown into the sea. The ceremony
was an 'imitation', says Ister, of a stoning to death.[1]

When did it become an imitation? When was it, as it must
originally have been, a real stoning to death? We cannot say.
The Human Medicine is the relic of a very ancient, very widespread, pre-Hellenic barbarity, which the Greeks have not swept
altogether away, but have allowed to live on with its teeth
drawn.

But the abomination creeps closer still. There is a story
about Themistocles told by Plutarch on the authority of one
Phanias of Lesbos. Phanias wrote some 200 years after the
alleged incident, and some of the other stories he tells do not
command credence: for instance, the statement that once in the
Chersonese fish came down in the rain.[2] Still the story, as he
tells it, is not incredible. And it exactly illustrates the points
which I wish to convey. 'When Themistocles as admiral was
making the chief sacrifice beside his flag-ship'—this was in the
last crisis of the Persian invasion, just before the battle of Salamis
—'there were brought up to him three prisoners, men of great
beauty, gorgeously arrayed and adorned with gold. When
Euphrantides the prophet'—there is sure to be a prophet in
such a business!—'saw them, since the holy fire at that moment
burst into a great and brilliant flame, and there was a significant
sneeze on the right, the prophet clutched Themistocles by the

---

[1] See Appendix A, on the Pharmakoi. The ritual was probably a charm
for ripening figs; see Paton in *Rev. Archéologique*, 1907, p. 51. He argues
that Adam and Eve were φάρμακοί. The word seemed in Greek to be the
masc. of φάρμακον, 'medicine'; but it was probably a foreign word. Hence
the ā in Ionic, as in Δāρεῖος and other foreign words. In Attic the a is short
by analogy from φάρμακον.
[2] I find that I was wrong to doubt Phanias's word here. There had been
a waterspout at sea.

right hand and commanded him to dedicate the young men and sacrifice them all, crying on the name of Dionȳsus Omêstes (the Raw-Devourer). "Do this," he said, "and there is deliverance and victory for Hellas." Themistocles was horrified at the prophet's strange and monstrous demand. But, as so often happens in great crises and times of suffering, the multitude, putting all their hopes in something irrational rather than in reason, shrieked to the god with one voice, dragged the prisoners to the altar, and, as the prophet commanded, compelled the whole sacrifice to take place.' It is not said that Themistocles performed the act. (Plut. *Them.* xiii.)

Now the evidence for the story is weak. Themistocles is both the shadiest and the most maligned of great Greek statesmen. The whole story may be an outrageous slander invented by his enemies after his ostracism. But that scarcely alters its historical significance. It was, apparently, a story actually told. It must have been, if not true, at least possible—not beyond the bounds of credibility to excited persons.

As a matter of fact, it is just on occasions like this that human sacrifices have most tended to occur: in a disorganized army or a rabble full of fear, egged on by some fanatical priest or prophet. There were bloody doings in Rome when the fear of Hannibal was strong, judicial murders of vestal virgins, buryings alive of 'Gallus et Galla, Graecus et Graeca' in the Forum Boarium. (Livy, xxii. 57.) There was a great burning of Jews, we may remember, after the earthquake of 1755 at Lisbon.

Perhaps the most tragic case, however, was the outbreak of human sacrifice at Jerusalem in the seventh century, inspired by the imminent terror of Assyria. Jews who had been taught to believe that Yahweh was their only refuge saw, or seemed to see, with despair that their sacrifices were availing nothing. They must give Him more: give Him anything in the world, if only He will avert the horror of an Assyrian conquest, with its pyramids of heads and its prisoners flayed alive. Looking about them, these unhappy devotees saw the human sacrifices of Tyre and Sidon, and knew that there was still one thing which they might offer. No wonder Yahweh did not hear them, when they were giving less than the heathen gave! So began the burnings of children at the *tophet* in the vale of Hinnom. Of course the

practice was denounced by the prophets, and comparatively soon
ceased. The point to observe is that in Greece, and it would
seem in Greece alone throughout classical times, we find no
parallel to this kind of thing. A desperate attempt was made
by the superstitious party to force a crime of the sort upon
Pelopidas, in the terrible moments before the battle of Leuctra.[1]
But it failed. Human sacrifice was barbaric, not Greek. If the
Themistocles story is true, that one bloody outburst of superstitious fear stands alone. There were other occasions on which
all the conditions for such a deed seem to have been present.
Think of Xenophon's Ten Thousand after Cunaxa: think of
Nicias's army after the last battle before Syracuse. All the con-
ditions for the thing are there; but not the thing. The very
idea is incongruous to one's conceptions of Nicias or Xenophon.
—That is Hellenism.

Human sacrifice, then, is one of the barbarities which Hellenism
successfully overcame. It was either abolished entirely or else,
as in the case of the *pharmakoi* at Athens, reduced to some
harmless ceremonial which satisfied religious conservatism without inflicting much harm on human beings.

But there were other strongholds of the primitive beast in man
which even Athens was not powerful enough to conquer. To
take three points: we find among the Greeks the institution of
slavery, fixed and unshaken; women in a markedly subject condition as compared with our own times, though far removed
again from the seclusion of the East; and lastly, proceeding
partly from the institution of slavery, partly from certain forms
of military organization, some startling phenomena of what we
should call unchastity in the relations of the sexes. And then
we imagine that these things are characteristically Greek! They
are just the reverse. They are the remnants of that primaeval
slime from which Hellenism was trying to make mankind clean.

The Greeks are not characteristically slave-holders. All the

---

[1] See Appendix A. The case in Philostratus, *Vit. Apol.* iv. 10, where the
thaumaturge Apollonius of Tyana, being at Ephesus during a plague,
recognized a certain deformed beggar as being a demon of pestilence, and
set the crowd to stone him to death, was a horrid act on the part of an
unauthorized mob, not a deliberate human sacrifice approved by the law.
But the Asiatic cities were terribly infected with barbarism by the time
of Nero. The incident has elements of the *pharmakos* rite in it.

world held slaves, and had always done so. The Greeks are characteristically the first human beings who felt a doubt or scruple about slavery; who were troubled in mind by it, who thought, wrote, schemed, in the face—as far as we can judge—of absolutely overmastering social needs, to be rid of it, some two thousand years before it was abolished in Christian Europe. I do not refer specially to the efforts of isolated reformers. The Cynics, we know, condemned slavery root and branch. The Stoics and certain religious organizations from the fourth century onward refused to recognize its existence, and professed to count all men free. Euripides was troubled by it, and can scarcely get the subject off his mind. The sophist Alcidamas seems to have made a preaching tour round the Peloponnese to induce all states to combine in a general emancipation; and, curiously enough, was not murdered. But the tone of the non-reforming writers is equally interesting as evidence. Homer, though of course no thought of doing without slaves ever crosses his horizon, speaks always of slaves with a half-puzzled tenderness. Slavery is to him a terrible thing that may happen to any man, and will 'take away half of his manhood'. The heroes are as courteous to the slaves, Eumaeus and Eurycleia, as to one another. Plato, bred in a far from democratic circle and generally in protest against the ideals of the great sophists of the fifth century, does not care to denounce slavery. In his ideal *Republic* he abolishes it silently by merely constructing a state without slaves. In the *Laws*, written in his old age, when the cloud of reaction had settled darkly upon his mind, he accepts it as an existing fact and makes elaborate regulations for the protection both of slave and of master.[1] The attitude of his opponents, the sentimental demo-

---

[1] See *Laws*, pp. 777–8. 'If slavery "takes away half a man's manhood" how is one to deal with slaves? Some masters utterly mistrust their slaves, treat them like wild beasts, with whips and scourges, till they make them many times worse than before. . . . No doubt the human animal is ill-tempered, and not at all easy to manage, when you introduce "the necessary distinction of servant and master". It is a bad business; the only rules perhaps are not to have slaves of the same country or the same language, and then to be scrupulously just in dealing with them, *more so than with your equals*. The only test of true justice is the way a man behaves to those whom he can wrong with impunity. "Only the unstained can sow seeds for virtue" . . . that is a rule to be remembered by every master and prince and strong man in dealing with those weaker than himself.' It will be noticed that Plato does not draw much distinction between 'servant' and 'slave'. He is

crats, can perhaps be deduced from the beginning of his dialogue, *Euthyphro, or On Piety.* The man who gives his name to that dialogue is satirized as a type of the pious and ultra-superstitious Athenian democrat. When Socrates meets him, Euthyphro is going to Athens to prosecute his own father for homicide, because the said father has caused, though not intentionally, the death of a slave who had killed another. Euthyphro has been apparently on the best of terms with his father; he admits that he had great provocation, and that the slave probably deserved to die. But he will not allow a slave to be murdered any more than another man: and, what is more, though he expects to be laughed at and thought 'mad', he is confident, if he can once get a hearing, of winning his case.[1] The father, I should remark in passing, would not be put to death.

It is unfortunate, perhaps, that our principal representative of ancient Greece upon this question should be Aristotle. Aristotle is, like Plato, somewhat anti-democratic; and, unlike Plato, devoted to common sense. It is his common sense, perhaps, that obscures his vision most. He saw that in the existing state of society slavery was a necessary institution. Its abolition would have meant anarchy, perhaps famine. And Aristotle does his best to show that the necessary institution is also just and 'according to nature'. It is the same line that was adopted by the fathers of the early Christian Church.[2] Some men are born to obey, others to rule. Put down a dozen Greeks in a bar-barous country: in a few months you will find the Greeks giving orders and the natives obeying them. But his arguments do not matter so much. The important thing is that he found it necessary to argue. Slavery could not, to a thoughtful Greek, simply rank as an accepted thing. No doubt Aristotle had a solid majority behind him: a majority composed of plain men who had no intention of seeing their business hampered by philosophers, and doubtless of those same obscurantists who

perhaps more troubled than most moderns by the existence at all of servants and masters, though far less troubled by the existence of slavery proper as a form of service.

[1] Observe how Euthyphro extracts a high moral lesson from the most revolting myths of Hesiod: 'wrong-doing must be punished, however high the offender. Zeus did not spare even his own father.'

[2] Cf. Susemihl and Hicks, Ar. *Politics*, p. 24, n. 4.

afterwards prosecuted him for impiety: not a majority of philosophers nor idealist democrats. The two most influential schools, Cynics and Stoics, stood on the other side. The popular writers of the New Comedy [1] appealed to the public with sentimental denunciations of the unnatural thing.

I do not in the least wish to deny that the slave-trade assumed enormous importance in Greece. The slave-trade in later antiquity was largely in the hands of the maritime Greek cities, just as in the seventeenth and eighteenth centuries it was in the hands of England, and for the same reason: because the slave-trade went with the general carrying trade. Polybius counts among the first necessaries of life for a large town ' cattle and slaves '.[2] Wheat is mentioned as secondary. And it stands to reason that, wherever one set of men have had absolute power over another, there must have been cases of extreme cruelty. One should remember, however, that Athens, the most Greek part of Greece, was remarkable for her gentleness to the slave population. It was part of her democratic ideal. Her friends praise her, her critics and enemies ridicule her, for making her slaves indistinguishable from free men.[3] That is something. But I think the main point which distinguishes Greece from other ancient communities, here as elsewhere, is not something actually achieved, but something seen and sought for. In Greece alone men's consciences were troubled by slavery, and right down through the centuries of the decadence, when the industrial slave-system ruled everywhere, her philosophers never entirely ceased protesting against what must have seemed an accepted and inevitable wrong.

[1] Cf. Anaxandrides, fr. 4, Philemon, fr. 94 (Kock): especially how God

$$\text{ἐλευθέρους ἐπόησε πάντας τῇ φύσει,}$$
$$\text{δούλους δὲ μετεπόησεν ἡ πλεονεξία.}$$

(' covetousness transformed them into slaves ').

[2] iv. 38 Πρὸς μὲν τὰς ἀναγκαίας τοῦ βίου χρείας τά τε θρέμματα καὶ τὸ τῶν εἰς τὰς δουλείας ἀγομένων σωμάτων πλῆθος—odious language, certainly.

[3] For instance, [Xen.] Respub. Athen. i. 10 ff. (hostile); Dem. Phil. iii. 3 (friendly); Plato, Rep. 563 B (satirical on the licence and self-confidence of slaves, male and female, in a democratic state). On the torture of slave witnesses, see Appendix B. The best recent discussion of Greek slavery is in A. E. Zimmern's Greek Commonwealth; see also his articles in the Sociological Review, Jan. and April, 1909. He distinguishes 'apprentice slavery' and 'chattel slavery'; in Greece we have chiefly the former. [See also Heitland Agricola, 1921, esp. final chapter.]

The Greeks were not characteristically subjectors of women. They are the first nation that realized and protested against the subjection of women. I speak, of course, of nations in some state of social complexity. For in primitive agricultural communities the women who worked in the fields were in most ways as free as men. On this question, again, I should not lay stress on the evidence of the isolated reformer. We all know how Plato in the *Republic* preached the complete emancipation of women from all artificial restrictions whatever. But some time before Plato other philosophers,[1] and well-known philosophers, must have advocated the same ideas, because we find all the regular ' Woman's Right' conceptions ridiculed in Aristophanes considerably before the *Republic* can have been published. And there is this to observe, unless my impressions deceive me : Aristophanes, a strong conservative writing broad comedy for the public, seems quite to understand the ideas that he is handling. He treats them as funny, as offering material for scurrilous jokes, but not in the least as things unheard of or incomprehensible. He understands his opponents better than, for instance, Mary Wollstonecraft was understood by the writers of the *Anti-Jacobin*. Before Aristophanes, again, there was Euripides, studying the woman's case with persistent insight and eloquence. Euripides was a genius too extraordinary to be useful as evidence of what his average contemporaries thought ; except, indeed, of what they must have thought after he had spoken. But consider for a moment the whole magnificent file of heroines in Greek tragedy, both for good and for evil, Clytemnestra, Antigone, Alcestis, Polyxena, Jocasta, even Phaedra and Medea : think of the amazing beauty of the Daughters of Ocean in the *Prometheus*, and of the Trojan Women in the play that bears their name. They are all of them free women, free in thought and in spirit, treated with as much respect as any of the male characters, and with far greater minuteness and sympathy. I doubt if there has

[1] I strongly suspect, Protagoras. In Diog. Laert iii. 37 and 57 a statement is quoted from Aristoxenus and Favorinus (no doubt using Aristoxenus) that 'almost the whole of the *Republic*' was taken from Protagoras's *Antilogica*. Aristoxenus is a good authority, though spiteful. If this is at all true, the *Lysistrata* (B. C. 411), and perhaps the *Ecclesiazusae* (B.C. 392 or 389?), must have been aimed at ideas of Protagoras, as the later *Gynaecocratiae* of Amphis and Alexis were aimed at those of the *Republic*. Cf. Plato, *Rep.* v. p. 457 b.

ever, in the history of the world, been a period, not even excepting the Elizabethan age and the nineteenth century, when such a gallery of heroic women has been represented in drama. And such characters cannot surely have sprung out of a society in which no free women existed.[1]

The third point is hard to discuss fully, but the explanation of it is very similar. A great deal of ancient unchastity comes directly from the institution of slavery : for female slavery was, in large part, another—and perhaps on the whole a worse—form of the custom of prostitution.   Much, again, was a mere relic from the religious ritual of pre-Hellenic peoples, and much was a survival from the times when Greece was invaded and conquered by Northern tribes inadequately provided with women. As for the myths, their immorality arises mostly from some very simple misunderstandings. Every little valley community was apt to count its descent from some local ancestress and the tribal god, a being who was often imagined in shapes not human, as an eagle, a swan, or a river-bull.   A time came when these various local gods were gradually merged in the great Achaean master-god, Zeus.   The process was a thoroughly good and progressive one ; but it had an unexpected result upon Zeus's reputation.   It

---

[1] Attic Law, in many respects primitive, is markedly so with regard to women.   A woman was always under the tutelage of the head of her family, who would as a rule be her father, or, on his death, her eldest brother.   She thus had a constant protector against any maltreatment by her husband. The guardian could annul the marriage and take her home.   She also had her own property.   On the other hand, a bad guardian could torment a woman almost as much as a bad husband can now : e.g. he could get money from the husband by threatening to annul the marriage.   The father could transfer his right of guardianship to the husband, then the wife was under her husband's 'coverture', as now.   When he died, the wife either fell under the coverture of the next head of her husband's family, or could be left by will to some person of her husband's—and in practice no doubt her own— choice.   A great deal of the Attic treatment of women strikes one as exaggeratedly romantic.   They were to be 'rulers of the hearth'.   They blushed at the sight of a strange male.   To lose his wife's esteem was the greatest blow that could befall an honourable man.   (The man in question risked losing it by being caught hiding under a bed to escape the tax-gatherer.—Dem. *Androt.* 53.)   Epicharmus the poet was actually fined, in Syracuse, for making a broad joke in the presence of his wife.   One is reminded of the Attic vases in which men are freely caricatured or treated realistically, but women nearly always idealized.   Family life must have been extremely correct, to judge by the rarity of cases or mentions of adultery in our rather plentiful law-court literature.—On this subject I can now refer to Prof. Vinogradoff's *Historical Jurisprudence* (Oxford, 1922), especially vol. 2.

provided him with a collection of human consorts, and of strange disguises, which caused much veil-drawing on the part of the religiously-minded and much open laughter among the profane.

The same sort of explanation applies to those few elements in Greek myths or ritual which strike one as cruel. They are nearly all of them little hard deposits of ancient barbarity left in the outer strata of Hellenism. Take the Marsyas story. The Greeks, when they penetrated to the town of Celaenae, deep in the heart of Further Phrygia, found a local tradition how a native god had flayed alive the native hero or king, Marsyas. The origin of the myth is not certain. Dr. Frazer takes Marsyas for one of his primitive vegetation-kings, who were slain periodically as the harvest is slain, and their skins or some similar relic some-times preserved till the next year.[1] It may, again, be a remem-brance of some Assyrian conquest; for the Assyrians when they conquered a place often expressed their satisfaction by flaying their prisoners alive. However that may be, the guides who showed the Greeks round Celaenae, wishing to call their god by some name which would be intelligible, had called him Apollo. Most barbarian gods were either Apollo or Heracles. So the hideous story takes its place on the remote outskirts of Greek myth, a thing that was perhaps never believed, and would no doubt have been forgotten had not the academic sculptors of the fourth century made use of the mythical 'flayed man' to illus-trate the distribution of the human muscles. It is the same with a dozen other cases. At Apamea, quite close to Celaenae, the Asiatic population kept up a very ancient rite of sacrificing divers beasts by burning them alive. The Syro-Greek Lucian describes the business as something curiously barbarous and uncanny.[2] These things are in no sense characteristically Greek. They are remnants of the state of things which the highest Greek civili-zation up to the end of the fifth century B. C., a small white-hot centre of spiritual life in a world of effortless barbarism, tried to transform and perished in the attempt.[3]

---

[1] *Attis, Adonis, and Osiris*, chap. v.

[2] *De Dea Syria*, 49. Something similar, however, occurred at Patrae in Achaia. Cf. Paus. vii. 18, 11.

[3] I will not discuss a third view, the Greek as a Levantine. Many very good writers make use of this conception, but I think that, if pressed, it is misleading. The much-abused modern Levantine owes his general bad name

It is then from this point of view that I wish to discuss certain parts of Greek poetry : as a manifestation of the spirit of upward striving in man, which we roughly describe as Progress. But here a further question suggests itself. I feel that many among my hearers, especially perhaps among those who care most for art and for poetry, will protest against regarding poetry from this point of view at all. Science, they will say, progresses : but poetry does not. When we call a poem immortal, we mean that it is never superseded : and that implies that poetry itself does not progress.

This doctrine, when rigidly held, is apt, I think, to neglect the very complex nature of most of the concrete works of poetry. One may gladly admit that the essential and undefinable quality that we call poetry, the quality of being poetical, is one of the eternal things in life. There is something in Homer and the Book of Job which cannot be superseded, any more than the beauty of a spring morning or the sea or a mother's love for a child can be superseded. But, after all, this essential spirit has always to clothe itself in a body of some sort, and that body is made up of elements which admit of progress and decay. All the intellectual elements of poetry are progressive. Wider fields of knowledge may constantly be thrown open to the poet. Beauty may be discovered in fresh places. There may be increased delicacy, or at least increased minuteness, of observation. There is, most important of all, a possibility of change in the emotions which form the raw material of poetry. Wordsworth was not, perhaps, so great a poet as the Post-exilian Isaiah, yet Wordsworth would not have howled for joy that 'The mountains should be molten with the blood of Edom'.

to habits which come chiefly from historical causes. He is shifty, servile, cowardly, because for centuries he has been held in subjection by somewhat ferocious and markedly unintellectual aliens. He has had to live by dodging, and has the typical qualities of a subject race. The ancient Greek was himself a ruler, and had on the whole the virtues and vices of rulers. The race elements are not the same either. The Levantine, mixed as he is, is not largely influenced by fair-haired conquering Northerners. Even the geographical conditions, though physically not much changed, are psychologically different. The Greeks are still the sailors and traders of the Levant. But what is now petty huckstering in obsolete sailing-boats was then the work of great adventurers and leaders of men. So that its moral effect on the sea-folk was different. (I should add that, as far as my personal knowledge goes, I do not agree with the ordinary wholesale condemnation of the Levantines.)

And, still more certainly, the writers of Isaiah would have been utterly incapable of taking any interest in the subjects of most of Wordsworth's poems. Poetry, in this way, can be taken both as evidence of the progress attained by a society, and as a force in its further progress. Indeed, the best poetry provides sometimes the strongest, because the most subtle and unsuspected, force; and the most delicate, because the most living and unconscious, evidence. The conscious moralist often seems rather stupid and arbitrary—he is certainly an unpopular character—and the conscious legislator perhaps worse. The poet has over both of them the immense advantage that he is not trying to say what he believes to be good for other people, or what he believes that they believe to be good for them, but is simply expressing what he himself loves most.

But what I am most concerned with now is a rather different point. I want to suggest, first, that the mere interest in human progress in general is a possible source of poetical inspiration, a source quite as real and quite as poetical as any other. And secondly, that this particular source of inspiration is rather unusually strong in Greek poetry.

Many critics speak as if for a poet to be interested in progress was a sort of disgrace or a confession of prosiness. I disagree ; I think human progress may be just as much a true inspiration to a poet as the lust of the eye or the pride of life. Of course it is not so to all poets : there is very little of it in the final stages of Homer, little in Pindar and Catullus, just as there is little in Shakespeare or Chaucer. On the other hand, it is the very breath of life to Aeschylus, Euripides, and Plato, as it is to Shelley or Tolstoy.

Let us take as an example the last work of Condorcet, written by him in hiding when condemned to the guillotine. He first intended to write an answer to his false accusers and a justification of his political career. And then, in the face of death, that discussion somehow seemed to him less important ; and he preferred to work upon the subject which he felt to be the greatest in the whole world, *Le Progrès de l'Esprit Humain*, The Progress of the Human Spirit. It is much the same subject, ultimately, as that of the enormous work projected by the late Lord Acton—a history of Human Freedom. An interest in this subject implies,

I think, at the outset an intense feeling of the value, for good and ill, of being alive. Here we are, you and I and the millions of men and animals about us, the innumerable atoms that make our bodies blown, as it were, by mysterious processes somehow together, so that there has happened just now for every one of us the wonder of wonders, a thing the like of which never has been nor shall be: we have come to life; and here we stand with our senses, our keen intellects, our infinite desires, our nerves quivering to the touch of joy and pain, beacons of brief fire, it would seem, burning between two unexplored eternities: what are we to make of the wonder while it is still ours?

There is here, first, an interest in human life as a whole, and secondly, a desire to make it a better thing than it is. That is, we shall find two main marks of this spirit: First, what is properly called realism; though the word is so constantly misused that we had better avoid it. I mean, a permanent interest in life itself, and an aversion to unreality or make-believe. (This is not inconsistent with an appreciation of the artistic value of convention. We shall have opportunities of considering that point in detail.) Secondly, a keen feeling of the values of things, that some things are good and others bad, some delightful, others horrible; and a power of appreciating, like a sensitive instrument, the various degrees of attraction and repulsion, joy and pain.

Here we run upon one of the great antitheses of life, and one which, it seems to me, is largely solved by the progressive, or I may say, by the Hellenic spirit; the antitheses between asceticism or Puritanism on the one hand, and the full artistic appreciation of life on the other. In real life and in literature these two spirits fight a good deal. But both, of course, are parts of one truth. If life is to be enriched and ennobled, you must first of all have an appreciation of life. A man who refuses to feel and enjoy life destroys it at its very heart. On the other hand, any strict Puritan can always point to an immense amount of wreckage produced by great appreciation of the joys of life, and also to a large amount of good safe living produced by the principles of avoiding pleasure, dulling the desires, and habitually pouring cold water into your own and other people's soup, 'to take the Devil out of it.' There is plenty of opportunity for dispute here in real life. In speculation there seems to me to be none. The truth simply is that in order to get at one desirable end you have to sacrifice another.   The artistic side of man insists upon the need of understanding and appreciating all good and desirable things: the ascetic side insists on the need of a power to resist, a power even to despise and ignore, every one of them, lest they should hinder the attainment of something better.

The combination of these two, the appreciation of good things and the power to refuse them, is characteristic of the spirit of progress.   I think most scholars will admit that it is also eminently characteristic of Greek civilization.   The enjoyment and appreciation of life is too deeply writ on all Greek poetry to need any illustration, though one might refer to the curious power and importance in Greek life of two words, $K\acute{a}\lambda\lambda os$ and $\Sigma o\phi\acute{\iota}a$, Beauty and Wisdom; to the intensity of feeling which makes ' $E\lambda\pi\acute{\iota}s$, Hope, or $T\acute{o}\lambda\mu a$, the Love of Daring, into powers of temptation and terror rather than joy: to the constant allegorizing and transfiguration of those two gods of passion, Dionysus and Erôs.[1]   But the principle of asceticism was at least equally strong.   Whether we look to precept or to practice, the impression is the same. In practice a respectable ancient Greek allowed himself some indulgences which a respectable modern would refuse: but for the most part his life was, by our standards, extraordinarily severe and frugal.   To take one instance.   Hippocrates, the great fifth-century physician,[2] says in one passage that many doctors object to their patients having more than one meal in the twenty-four hours: but for his own part, he thinks that, though to most healthy people it makes no difference whether they have two meals or one, still some slow digesters cannot stand more than one, while other delicate persons are positively the better for two! Our healthy persons have four; and our invalids fall not far short of a dozen.   All the great schools of philosophy, again, were in various degrees ascetic.   The general admiration felt by the ancients for every form of frugality and hardihood strikes one as altogether extreme.   The praises of Sparta show us how severity of life, coupled with courage, sufficed in the popular judgement to cover a multitude of sins.   Yet Greek asceticism is never like

---

[1] These points are excellently brought out in Cornford's *Thucydides Mythistoricus*, chap. ix, xii, xiii.

[2] *De Vet. Med.* 10=p. 593, μονοσιτέειν and ἀριστῆν are the alternatives.

Eastern asceticism. The East took its asceticism in orgies, as it were ; in horrors of self-mutilation, bodily and mental, which are as repellent in their way as the corresponding tempests of rage or of sensuality. Greek asceticism, though sometimes mystical, was never insane. It was nearly always related to some reasonable end, and sought the strengthening of body and mind, not their mortification.

One cannot but think, in this connexion, of that special virtue which the early Greeks are always praising, and failure in which is so regretfully condemned, the elusive word which we feebly translate by ' Temperance ', *Sôphrosynê*. The meaning of *sôphrosynê* can only be seen by observation of its usage—a point we cannot go into here. It is closely related to that old Greek rule of Μηδὲν ἄγαν, *Nothing too much*, which seems to us now rather commonplace, but has in its time stayed so many blind lusts and triumphant vengeances. It is something like Temperance, Gentleness, Mercy ; sometimes Innocence, never mere Caution : a tempering of dominant emotions by gentler thought. But its derivation is interesting. The adjective σώφρων or σαόφρων is the correlative of ὀλοόφρων, a word applied in early poetry to wizards and dangerous people. Ὀλοόφρων means ' with destructive thoughts ', σώφρων means ' with saving thoughts '. Plutarch,[1] writing when the force of the word was dead, actually used this paraphrase to express the same idea. There is a way of thinking which destroys and a way which saves. The man or woman who is *sôphrôn* walks among the beauties and perils of the world, feeling the love, joy, anger, and the rest ; and through all he has that in his mind which saves.—Whom does it save ? Not him only, but, as we should say, the whole situation. It saves the imminent evil from coming to be.

It is then in this light that I wish to consider certain parts of Greek poetry : as embodying the spirit of progress, that is, of both feeling the value and wonder of life and being desirous to make it a better thing : and further, with that purpose in view, as combining a spirit of intense enjoyment with a tempering wisdom, going into seas of experience steered by Sôphrosynê.

[1] *De Tranquillitate*, 470 D νοῦν σωτήρια φρονοῦντα. Ὀλοόφρων is used of Minos, Aietes, Atlas—also of a hydra, lion, and boar.

II

THE MIGRATIONS: THE POLIS

IF we regard Greece as the cradle of European civilization, we cannot help some feeling of surprise at its comparative lack of antiquity. True, we have evidence of a civilization existing in Crete and the Islands of the Aegean as far back as the end of the Stone Age. But, for one thing, our knowledge of this civilization, though based on abundant and skilfully sifted material, remains enigmatic and conjectural, inasmuch as it depends upon our interpretation of the stones, not upon literature: and, what is more important, it is emphatically not the civilization that we call Greek. I do not mean only or especially that the builders of the earliest Cretan palaces were, as far as we can judge, of different race and language from the Greeks. I mean that this civilization, so far as we know it, has few or none of the special marks that we associate with Hellenism. But of that hereafter. In any case there lies between the prehistoric palaces of Crete, Troy, or Mycenae, and the civilization which we know as Greek, a Dark Age covering at least several centuries. It is in this Dark Age that we must really look for the beginnings of Greece.

In literature and in archaeology alike we are met with the same gap. There is a far-off island of knowledge, or apparent knowledge; then darkness; then the beginnings of continuous history. At Troy there are the remains of no less than six cities one above the other. There was a great city there before 2000 B.C., the second of the series. It used red ware for its pottery, wherever the first city had used black, and it seems to have traded the newly discovered copper of the South-East against amber from the Baltic. In this second city there was discovered a fragment of white nephrite, a stone not hitherto found anywhere nearer than China, and testifying to the distances which trade could travel by slow and unconscious routes in early

times. That city was destroyed by war and fire; and others
followed.   The greatest of all was the sixth city, which we may
roughly identify with the Troy of Greek legend.   Of this city
we can see the wide circuit, the well-built stone walls, the terraces,
the gates, and the flanking towers.   We have opened the treasure
houses and tombs, and have seen the great golden ornaments
and imports from the East.   Then we see the marks of flame on
the walls: and afterwards what?   One struggling attempt at a
seventh city ; a few potsherds to mark the passage of some generations of miserable villages ; and eventually the signs of the Greek
town of New Ilion, many hundreds of years later and well within
the scope of continuous history.

It is the same in Crete. City upon city from prehistoric times
onward flourishing and destroyed ; palace upon palace, beginning
with the first building of Cnossos, in a peculiar non-Hellenic
architecture ; proceeding to those vast and intricate foundations
in which Sir Arthur Evans finds a palace, a citadel, and a royal
city round about, the growth and accumulation of many hundreds,
perhaps thousands, of years.   The ornamentation of the walls is
there, telling of the rise and decay of a whole system of decorative
art : fragments of early religion, the Bull-God or Minotaur
seated upon his throne ; the 'horns of consecration' bristling
everywhere ; the goddess Πότνια θηρῶν, Queen of Wild Beasts,
now bearing a dove upon her head, now twined with serpents ;
sometimes in human shape, sometimes a mere stone pillar erect
between her rampant lions : sometimes a monstrous fetish.
There is the Divine Battle-Axe, that Labrandeus from whose
name the fable of the labyrinth seems to have arisen[1] : a being
who has not yet reached human shape or separate existence as a
'God', but exists simply in the ancient bronze axes, scores of
which remain driven into the rock of the Dictaean cave, over-
crusted with a stalactite growth of stone, testifying to a worship
forgotten and uncomprehended.   There are porcelains reminding
one of Babylon, ornaments from Egypt, marks of a luxurious
king's court, a gaming-table inlaid with gold and coloured

---

[1] See, however, on the Labyrinth, Lecture V below, p. 138, note[2], and
especially Burrows, *The Discoveries in Crete*, pp. 107–32. He connects
λαβύρινθος with λαύρα and Λαύρειον. (So, I believe, did Wiedemann.) The
catastrophe which I am specially considering is, of course, that of 'Late
Minoan III'.

marbles, women acrobats, bull-fights, or perhaps, if we look close, something more barbaric than bull-fights—boys and girls thrown for the ' Bull of Minos' to gore : then shattered gates, flame-blackened walls and evidences of calamity, a feeble pulsing of life outside the ruined palaces, and afterwards silence. Centuries later a new Crete emerges, a Dorian island, rigid, self-centred, uninfluential, in the full light of Greek history.

It is the same with the cities of the Argive plain, Mycenae and Tiryns. They possessed less importance, and were inhabited for a less vast stretch of history, than the cities of Cnossos and Troy.[1] But the treasures yielded to the excavator, especially in Mycenae, are very great in proportion to the importance of the town, and the historical problem is simpler. We all know the Mycenaean remains : the Lion Gates, the earlier shaft graves, and the later vaulted graves ; the remains of mummified kings ; the skeletons in masks of gold, with their weapons, their drinking-bowls, and sometimes the ashes of burnt sacrifice lying beside them. And in the end, as in Troy and Cnossos, the marks of flame upon the walls, traces of a dwindling population still hovering about the old town, and quickly degenerating in the arts of civilized life ; and then a long silence.

Such is the evidence of the stones. And that of literature corresponds with it. There is an extraordinary wealth of tradition about what we may call the Heroic Age. Agamemnon king of Mycenae and Argos, Priam king of Troy, and the kings surrounding them, Achilles, Aias, Odysseus, Hector, Paris, these are all familiar household words throughout later history. They are among the best-known names of the world. But how suddenly that full tradition lapses into silence! The Epic Saga —I mean the whole body of tradition which is represented in Epic poetry—the Epic Saga can tell us about the deaths of Hector, of Paris, of Priam ; in its later forms it can give us all the details of the last destruction of Troy. Then no more ; except a few dim hints, for instance, about the descendants of Aeneas.

It is more strange in the case of Mycenae and Sparta.

[1] Under Tiryns an earlier city has recently been discovered. See W. Dörpfeld, *Athen. Mitth.* 1907.

Agamemnon goes home in the full blaze of legend : he is murdered by Aegisthus and Clytemnestra, and avenged by his son Orestes : so far we have witnesses by the score. But then ? What happened to Mycenae after the death of Aegisthus ? No one seems to know. There seems to be no Mycenae any more. What happened in Sparta after Menelaus and Helen had taken their departure to the islands of the blest ? There is no record, no memory.

In Crete there is less tradition altogether. One great name, Minos, forms the centre of all Cretan legends. Minos is never quite flesh and blood, like the Homeric heroes, Agamemnon or Achilles. He is almost like that more than shadowy personage, Creon, whose name means ' ruler ' and who appears in so many myths of the mainland whenever a mere ' ruler ', and nothing more, is wanted. We meet Minos in many different generations, in many different characters, most of them probably possessing some historical significance. He is the son of Zeus, or, still more august, not the son but the ' gossip ' or familiar friend of Zeus, a suitable position for the hereditary Priest-King, himself an incarnation of the Cretan Bull-God.[1] He is the Just Judge of the Underworld, as befits the great legislator who was the fountain of law to many islands and dependencies. Again, he is the bloody tyrant of the Theseus myth, who gives the seven youths and seven maidens to his man-slaying Bull. The reason for that is painted on the walls of his labyrinthine palace, showing —apparently—Minoan ladies looking on while the Bull is played with and maddened by skilled performers till he is let loose on his victims. Then again we have the boasting Minos of the Bacchylides poem ; the mere royal father of the lost Cretan prince, Glaucus ; the father or husband of many guilty and romantic Cretan heroines, Phaedra, Ariadnê, Pasiphaê.

After Minos, what is there ? Idomeneus in the *Iliad*, a hero of

---

[1] Διὸς μεγάλου ὀαριστής, τ 179: cf. Plato, *Minos* 319 D. See below, Lecture V, p. 136 and note there. I suspect that Minos was a name like ' Pharaoh ' or ' Caesar ', given to all Cretan kings of a certain type, and, further, that the king was held to be the personification or incarnation of the Bull-God. As to the evidence for a Minos existing at different dates, Prof. Burrows remarks that the Parian Marble puts Minos in the fifteenth century B. C. and also in the thirteenth, and that Diodorus (iv. 60) and Plutarch (*Vit. Thes.* 20) tell a similar story. See, however, Ridgeway, ' Minos the Destroyer, &c.', *Proceedings of Brit. Acad.* IV.

the second rank, a man grey on the temples, too old to run but not too old to deal terrific blows, and withal a little grim and cruel. There is also another significant feature. Nearly all the false stories told by Odysseus in the Odyssey are tales of Crete, as is also the true romance of the life of Eumaeus the swineherd. The later proverb associated Crete with 'romancing'. Was it that Crete was full of stories of a past greatness which to the ordinary forgetful world seemed merely incredible, as Juvenal afterwards sneered at 'Graecia mendax' because Herodotus had preserved more ancient history than he could believe? So near had Minoan Crete come to complete oblivion.[1]

In Thebes, as in Troy, the tradition is more intelligible because it explicitly leads up to a catastrophe. Many problems require to be cleared up about the Theban traditions, even after Bethe's work upon the subject. The prehistoric remains, as we said above, are not prominent or remarkable, chiefly, no doubt, because the place was never left for a long time deserted. It is with Thebes as with Argos, with Athens, with the many sites of towns on the coast of Asia Minor and the Italian Riviera. Continuous occupation has destroyed gradually and surely the remains of every successive period. But the Theban traditions, as preserved in literature, are particularly rich, and they lead up clearly to our Dark Age or Period of Ignorance. There is first a strange race, Cadmeans, the people of Cadmus, 'the Eastern Man,'[2] in possession of the city. The tradition is clearly not of their making, for they are credited with all the crimes and pollutions in the calendar: especially sexual crimes, which people always impute to their enemies. Three generations of the Cadmeans, Laius, Oedipus, and the sons of Oedipus, between them commit pretty well all the crimes that can be committed inside a family. Unnatural affections, child murder, father murder,

---

[1] Cf. Hdt. vii. 171. Crete had formerly been 'emptied' by an expedition of Minos to Sicily. Then 'in the third generation after the death of Minos came the Trojan wars. . . . After the return from Troy there came famine and pest slaying both man and beast, and Crete was made empty a second time. Then came the present Cretans'—i. e. the Dorian tribes—'and inhabited it, together with the survivors.'

[2] Heb. קדם *qedem*, the east. Greek tradition calls them 'Phoenicians', but it is not clear what that term exactly denotes. Ridgeway thinks they were 'red' Thracians (*Early Age*, p. 629). Cf. his 'Who were the Dorians?' in *Anthr. Essays to E. B. Tylor* (1907). See, after Beloch and Bérard, Burrows, *op. cit.*, p. 141 f.

incest, a great deal of hereditary cursing, a double fratricide, and a violation of the sanctity of dead bodies—when one reads such a list of charges brought against any tribe or people, either in ancient or in modern times, one can hardly help concluding that somebody wanted to annex their land.[1]   And this was doubtless the case.   The saga gives us full details up to the quarrel of Eteocles and Polynices and the Expedition of the Seven Greek Champions, the chariot-fighting on the plain and the assault on the Gates.   The seven were defeated: so far we hear all at length.   Then much more briefly, with much less reality, we are told that their sons made another expedition and took Thebes.   That is, the citadel of the Cadmeans eventually fell, and nothing more is said or known.

It is the same wherever we turn our eyes in the vast field of Greek legend.   The ' heroes' who fought at Thebes and Troy are known ; their sons are just known by name or perhaps a little more : Diomedes, Aias, Odysseus, Calchas, Nestor, how fully the tradition describes their doings, and how silent it becomes after their deaths !

Let us consider these destroyed cities a little closer.   We can perhaps make out the kind of civilization on which their greatness rested, and the causes of their fall.   For observe this : though we can see in some cases from the evidence of the stones that these cities came at last to a violent end, it is by no means clear that it was any definite shock of war which really destroyed the Aegean civilization.   There is no tradition at all that the realm of Minos was sacked in war [2]: no real tradition of the sack of Mycenae.   And even in the cases of Troy and

---

[1] There is also extant a simpler version, before the self-defensive slanders had been developed, in which the heroes are slain at Thebes simply μήλων ἔνεκ᾽ Οἰδιπόδαο (Hes. *Erga*, 162), in an honest cattle-raid.

[2] Mr. J. L. Myres reminds me of Plutarch's story of 'Tauros the sea-captain', who was the real lover of Pasiphae, and his sea-fight off Cnossos. This is possibly a very faint echo of a real tradition (*Vit. Thes.* xix and preceding capp.).   There would be no great siege in any case, since Cnossos and Phaestus were open unfortified cities ; their fall would follow quickly on the destruction of the Minoan fleet.   Sir A. Evans however doubts whether the sack of Cnossos and Phaestus was the work of a foreign army at all (*B. S. A.* xi. p. 14).   He suggests that both Palaces may have been destroyed by earthquake at the time of the great volcanic eruption which destroyed Santorin.

Thebes the testimony is suspicious. The Epos must say that Troy eventually was taken, but the Epos knows that Achilles did not take it, but failed and was slain. A son of Achilles, a mere replica of Achilles, has been invented to come afterwards and take it. Of course the *Iliad* as it now stands implies the future fall of the city, but it need not have done so in an earlier form. Nor need the *Odyssey*. The disastrous returns of the Greek heroes and the fall of the house of Agamemnon point rather to an unsuccessful expedition than to a great conquest. And how does it happen, one may ask, that so many Greek lays were based on the subject of 'Wraths', or quarrels between leading chiefs, between Agamemnon and Achilles, Odysseus and Agamemnon, Odysseus and Aias, Achilles and Odysseus? Does it not look— I take the suggestion from Prof. Bury—as if there was need of an excuse for some great failure? At any rate the actual tale of the Sack of Troy, though immensely influential in later literature, does not seem to be recorded in any very early form of the saga. And even incidents which have a special air of verisimilitude about them, like the stratagem of the Wooden Horse,[1] may represent only a brilliant afterthought of what ought to have been done. I lay no stress on this point, except to suggest that it is curious, if the war really ended in success, that the great national saga in its early forms should not tell of the success, but only of disastrous 'Returns', together with a quarrel, or several quarrels, between the chiefs—incidents well calculated to excuse failure.

Exactly the same thing is the case with the Theban tradition. A great expedition against Thebes is well known to the Epos, that of the Seven Chieftains, led by the far-famed Adrastus. That expedition, we are told, was defeated and all the seven slain. 'Only,' the story adds, 'Thebes did fall in the end. *Some people who came afterwards* took it.' The names of these later comers are not very certain. They are only the 'Ekgonoi' or 'Epigonoi',[2] the 'men-born-after', more shadowy even than Pyrrhus-Neopto-lemus, son of Achilles. The general result seems to me to suggest that, in the first place, the Epic tradition of the Greeks knew of

---

[1] I suggest that it may refer to a siege tower of the Assyrian type. My translation of *The Trojan Women*, p. 86.

[2] Ἔκγονοι, Eur. *Suppliants*, 1224. Ἐπίγονοι is of course the usual name.

certain heroic expeditions against Thebes and Troy, but knew also of their defeat; and secondly, this tradition had much later to be combined with the fact that in reality Troy and Cadmean Thebes had ceased to be. Can we see anything in the historical conditions which makes such a hypothesis probable?

I suggest, to put it briefly, that these great fortress-cities depended for their greatness upon industry and commerce, and that during the period of persistent barbarian invasions industry and commerce were destroyed. They resisted successfully the direct shock of war; but were gradually undermined by poverty. All of them, as a matter of fact, are situated at the junctions of important trade routes. Crete, for instance, a rough and mountainous island, credited by Strabo with ' some fruitful glens', is geographically, in Sir A. Evans's phrase (*J. H. S.* xiv), 'the stepping-stone of continents,' lying in the mid-route between west and east,[1] between south and north. The Cnossian treasury records seem to speak of a large trade in oil and silphium, as well as horses and cattle and precious metals. They had already invented, it would seem, the talent and the drachma. The lines from Phoenicia and the great Babylonian *hinterland*, from Egypt, from Libya, all tended to join at Crete on the way to the West, the Northern Aegean, or the Black Sea.[2] Some centralizing power then must have arisen in the island, and the maritime trade of such harbours as Kydonia and Hierapytna—the east of the island seems to have remained isolated—served to support the great central city of Cnossos. Thebes, again, as Strabo explains, commanded the roads between three seas, the Northern Aegean, the Southern Aegean, and the Corinthian Gulf.

But let us consider the point more in detail in two cases where it is not so easily seen.

Mycenae, as M. Victor Bérard has well explained, is what is called in Turkish a *Dervendji*; that is, a castle built at a juncture of mountain passes for the purpose of levying taxes on all traffic that goes through. There is the rich plain of Argos opening southward to the sea. At the north of it are mountains; beyond

---

[1] See also Hogarth's address to the Royal Geographical Society, 1906. A road running north and south has since been discovered.

[2] p. 400, from Ephorus. See also Bérard, *Les Phéniciens et l'Odyssée*, i. 225 f. Compare, for what follows, pp. 11 f. (Mycenae) and 79 f. (Troy).

them the plain of Corinth and Sikyon opening on the Corinthian Gulf. Among these mountains, at the north-east corner of the Argive valley, with no sea near, and no arable land anywhere about it, stands this isolated castle of Mycenae, thickly walled and armed to the teeth. It is hard to see how such a place could live, and why it needed such military preparations, until we observe that it forms the meeting-point of a very ancient system of artificial roads, cut and built of stone, and leading from the Argive plain to the Corinthian, from the southern sea to the northern. If Mycenae stood alone, she formed a sort of robber stronghold, which lived by levying blackmail on all the trade that passed. But almost certainly she did not stand alone, and M. Bérard's explanation is only a part of the truth. Agamemnon was master of a large realm, including 'all Argos and many islands', and Mycenae stood at the centre of it, able to keep open the trade routes between the northern and southern seas, and ready to strike with horse and foot in any direction where defence was needed. Paved roads, as Eduard Meyer has pointed out, are meant for the passage of chariots, not merely of caravans; and whether or no the commerce along these roads was anything considerable—a point which depends largely on unsettled questions about Corinth —Dr. Leaf is clearly right in regarding Mycenae as built more for war than for commerce.[1]

M. Bérard's explanation of Troy is even more instructive, though it also looks rather different on further consideration. It has to be modified by the observed fact that Troy does not show great affinities with the islands, and does with Thrace and its own *hinterland*. But there is more in it than that.

Six cities were built on that particular site, and six destroyed. There must have been some rare attraction about the place, and some special reason for destroying the cities built there. Greek legend, in speaking of the destruction of Troy by Agamemnon, always remembered that it had been destroyed before, though it ran all the previous expeditions into one—when old Telamon rose from his rest in Salamis, and gave himself to Heracles

---

[1] See Leaf, *Homer and History*, 220–8 : E. Meyer, *Gesch. d. Alt.* ii. 170, 180. Leaf thinks there would be very little commerce on these roads, at any rate if Corinth was not in existence in Mycenaean times, a point on which the excavations are not conclusive. (Allen, *Catalogue,* p. 64.)

For the wrecking of one land only,
Of Ilion, Ilion only,
Most hated of lands.[1]

Tradition tells us that Heracles went 'because of Laomedon's horses'[2] and M. Félix Sartiaux has pointed out in his book on the present domain of Troy that 'sa principale industrie est l'élevage de chevaux'. The Trojans in the *Iliad* have, like Hector himself, the special epithet of 'horse-taming', and have almost a monopoly of names compounded with -ιππος.[3] But horses were not the whole of Priam's wealth. Strabo (p. 680) speaks of 'gold mines in Astyra near Abydos, of which little is left now, though great slag-heaps and excavations are evidence of ancient working'. But a larger stream of riches, and a far stronger cause of unpopularity, lay well within reach of Priam's walls.

We know that in later times there was a vast body of trade passing up the Hellespont, joining Mediterranean civilization with that of the Black Sea. Obviously a city commanding this trade would grow rich: but Troy does not seem at first sight to be in the right position for commanding it. The older city, Dardania, had lain higher up on Mount Ida, the *Iliad* tells us (Υ 218), in safe retirement. But as the Trojans grew stronger, or as they discovered a more tempting source of wealth, they ventured nearer the sea. Yet even so Troy lies some miles inland on the slopes of a hill commanding only a narrow swampy plain with sea at each end of it. In modern times such a position is not of much worth. But in the conditions of ancient seafaring it was priceless.

Down the Bosphorus and the Hellespont there blows an almost incessant wind and there flows an extraordinarily strong current. If you bathe in the sultry heat down below Tenedos, near Mytilene, you may find yourself suddenly in swift and almost icy water

---

[1] Eur. *Troades*, 806 (sentiment of the whole passage, rather than any definite words): cf. 1241 Τροία τε πόλεων ἔκκριτον μισουμένη.
[2] E. 640 ἔνεχ' ἵππων Λαομέδοντος, Eur. *Tro.* 806 ff. ἀτυζόμενος πώλων.
[3] See Sartiaux, *Troie* (1915), p. 130: Prof. Grace Macurdy, *C. Q.* Jan. 1923. Ἱππόδαμοι in pl. occurs twenty-three times, always of the Trojans; their allies are Θρήικες ἱπποπόλοι, Παίονες ἱπποκορυσταί, Φρύγες ἱππομάχοι. The horse is said to have been introduced by the 'tumulus-people' (Mongol nomads) from the steppes of Asia in the third millennium B.C., when they first learnt to ride and drive horses as well as to live on the milk of mares. See Myres in *Cambridge Ancient History*, i, pp. 106 ff. On Trojan chariots see note p. 152.

sweeping straight from Russia.   This current is at its strongest just off Cape Sigeum, the promontory in front of Troy.   At the present time small steamers have some trouble in passing there, and sailing ships can be seen waiting by the score under the lee of Tenedos, till by utilizing stray puffs of favourable wind they can tack round that difficult cape, and proceed by hugging the eastern shore.   In ancient times, when boats were small and voyages short, their difficulties were much greater.   The greatest of all was the absence of galvanized iron tanks to hold drinking-water.   An ancient ship carried its water in heavy earthenware jars, and if it was weatherbound for a few days on a waterless coast the results were disastrous.

Now, M. Bérard's view was that, though it does not look so on the map, the plain of Troy is really an isthmus, or at least a formation to which he can apply his famous ' Law of the Isthmus '. Ancient cargoes were so light, and ancient ships so little accustomed to long voyages, that in numerous cases where we should make a longer voyage in order to avoid trans-shipment and 'breaking bulk' the ancients made straight for the nearest land, unpacked their bales on to the backs of mules or men, and reshipped them again at the nearest sea.   On many isthmuses they even dragged the ships overland rather than make a further round by water· Thus, M. Bérard suggested that merchants wishing to trade with the Black Sea ports disembarked their cargo at the southern end of the narrow swampy plain, carried it across on mules and re-embarked it on the further side, paying heavy taxes to Priam or Laomedon as they passed; and that this is the origin of the wealth of Troy.   In reality, however, as Dr. Leaf has shown,[1] this does not seem to have been the ancient practice.   Traffic from the south, if it wished to avoid the Etesian winds and the Black Sea currents, took to the land much earlier, at Assos.   By St. Paul's day this old track had developed into a Roman road from Troas to Assos, along which he travelled.   He was then going from north to south, so most of the party preferred to go by sea, with the current (Acts xx, 13).

The real clue to the importance of Troy in Mycenaean times is the fact that it ceased to be important as soon as there were Greek settlements up the Hellespont and on the Black Sea.

[1] Leaf, *Troy*, pp. 254-85.

When once there were friends along the coast, Greek ships passed freely up to the Euxine, and allowed no blackmailing power to grow up again at the mouth of the Hellespont or on the Black Sea. Before that time, with the currents and wind against them, and no fresh water except in the Scamander, Greek ships had not been able to pass into the Hellespont except by permission of Priam. In all probability they did not pass at all. The plain of Troy was the actual meeting-place where the trade of the Euxine touched that of the Aegean. Certainly the allies of Troy described in *Iliad B* seem to live on a network of trade routes, and in pondering on the great quantities of silver found in the Second City one cannot but remember the allies or vassals who came ' from far-off Alybê, where silver is born '.[1] Priam's misfortunes were so great that tradition is kind to him. But the perjuries and extortions of Laomedon ring loud in legend. Was it simply because the toll at the Hellespont was too oppressive to be tolerated, that all maritime Greece felt involved in the oppression, and volunteered to destroy the blackmailing citadel again and again ? Or was it, more simply still, that the position was so valuable that one band after another of northern warriors, Thracians, Dardans, Tröes, Teukri, Phrygians, Achaeans, fought for the possession ?

There are many problems still waiting solution about these fortified centres of exchange, if I may so call them. How far did they form a uniform empire or federation? Was Mycenae normally an outpost of Crete or an enemy of Crete, or when did it change from the one to the other ? What relation did either of them bear towards Troy, or towards the prevailing powers in Asia ? Of what race or races were their kings? How far was there a conscious difference between the ' Minoan ' or Island race with its sea-coast settlements and the less advanced masses of Anatolian or ' Hittite ' peoples of the hinterlands ? In any case it is, I think, perfectly clear that this Aegean civilization was not what we call Greek. Its language was, as far as we can judge, not Greek. Its art, though we can recognize in it many of the elements that went to the making of Greek Art, was in itself not Greek. As a matter of fact there were no Greeks in the world in those days, any more than there were, let us say, Englishmen before the

[1] B. 857 τηλόθεν ἐξ Ἀλύβης ὅθι τ' ἀργύρου ἐστὶ γενέθλη.

Angles came into Britain, or Frenchmen before the Franks invaded Gaul. The Greek people was a compound of which the necessary constituents had not yet come together.

We must recognize, however, that the existence of such rich and important centres, dependent entirely upon sea-borne commerce, argues both a wide trade and a considerably high and stable civilization. We must not forget that piece of white nephrite which, so archaeologists daringly assure us, came to Troy all the way from China. And we must by no means regard the masters of these cities as mere robber chieftains or levyers of blackmail. Commerce dies if it is too badly treated; and Aegean commerce lived and flourished for an extremely long time.

These empires, if we may call them by so large a name, were broken up by migrations or invasions from the north. In early times, so Thucydides tells us, all Hellas was in a state of migration.[1] We hear of all sorts of migrant tribes; of Hellenes, Achaioi, and Pelasgoi; of Carians and Leleges; of Minyae; of the sons of Deucalion, Ion, Pelops, Danaus, and the rest. Most of all we hear of the great migration of the Dorians,[2] somewhere about 1000 B.C. It is the habit of Greek tradition to remember chiefly the last of a series of events. It remembers the last migration, as it collected the last of the lyric poets, the last tragedies, the last form of the Epos. And modern research shows us that there were many successive waves of migration from the north and north-west.

If we go back to the Stone Age, it seems likely that there was

---

[1] Thuc. i. 2 φαίνεται ἡ νῦν Ἑλλὰς καλουμένη οὐ πάλαι βεβαίως οἰκουμένη, ἀλλὰ μεταναστάσεις τε οὖσαι τὰ πρότερα καὶ ῥᾳδίως ἕκαστοι τὴν ἑαυτῶν ἀπολείποντες, βιαζόμενοι ὑπό τινων ἀεὶ πλειόνων—a wonderful description.

[2] Δῶρον = 'hand', as in Hesiod's δεκάδωρος, Homer's ἑκκαιδεκάδωρος. The Lambda (λ) which served as the sign on the Spartan shields is not likely to have been originally a letter of the alphabet; perhaps it was a picture of a hand in profile pointing downwards with the thumb sticking out. Some of the pictograms for 'hand' are like that. I suspect that the Dorians were the 'Tribe of the Hand', and that δῶρον, 'gift', is a thing 'handed' or a *buona mano*, and δίδωμι the physical act of 'handing' or 'moving the hand', rather than the moral act of 'granting', a use which survives in many poetical phrases: e.g. Eur. *Her.* 1402 δίδου δέρῃ σὴν χεῖρα.—Boisacq connects Δωριεὺς with δόρυ, comparing the names Δωρίμαχος, Δωριφάνης and ἀσχέδωρος 'a wild boar' (spear-resister).

in Greece a very primitive 'Hittoid' or non-Aryan population, profoundly influenced at certain centres by the advanced material civilization of Crete.   On these conditions, probably well before 2000 B. C., came an immigration of the peoples who afterwards became the main Greek stock and who spoke a language that is the parent of Greek.   They were an Iranian people, akin to the ancient Persians : Greek and Old Persian are unique in having a Middle Voice and a dual number and in turning initial *s* into an aspirate.   They worshipped Zeus, the Aryan Sky-God.   They came, following their flocks in bullock carts, perhaps by way of the Russian steppes, down through Thrace, Macedonia and Thessaly.   They taught the inhabitants to speak Greek, and were the ancestors of those Aeolians and Ionians who were afterwards driven before the various floods of later invasion.   For later on there came waves of peoples not entirely nameless : a great movement of Thraco-Phrygian tribes with eastern linguistic affinities, saying *satem* instead of *centum* or ἑκατόν—who perhaps founded the main civilization of Troy : then the Achaeans proper, not very numerous, consisting mainly of chieftains and condottieri with their bands of followers from the North-West ; and lastly, closely akin to the Achaeans, the North-Western race of Dorians in their full mass.

The above attempt to make some statement on a subject which is extremely uncertain may be inexact in almost every detail, but it will serve as a hypothesis to work on, and is based on the views of considerable authorities, chiefly Professors Burnet [1] and J. A. K. Thomson.   By the time we approach the borders of Homeric story, we can hazard some few more definite statements about these North-Western or 'Danubian' immigrants.   They were of Aryan speech : their language, as we see in the remains of the Doric or North-Western dialects, was gradually assimilated to the Greek that was being already spoken in Middle and Southern Greece.   It is commonly said, indeed, that the Achaeans actually brought the Greek language with them and imposed both it and the Epic form upon the natives ; but apart

[1] See Burnet's articles on Pythagoras and Socrates in *E. R. E.* The augment and some points in declension could also be cited as links between Greek and Old Persian. The Achaioi perhaps spoke a 'Celtic' language. See especially *Archaeology in Greece* 1919–1921 by A. J. B. Wace in J.H.S. xli. This first mixture of Hittoid *plus* Proto-Hellenic peoples makes a 'Helladic' Age, on which supervenes a Bronze Age invasion from Crete and the south.

from other objections to this theory, the Achaeans had nothing like enough time for such an achievement. Both the language and to some extent the form of Epos must have been in Greece already. The invaders seem to have been, to a preponderant extent, tall and fair, warlike, uncivilized. Authorities differ about the shape of their heads. They too worshipped the typical Aryan patriarchal Sky-God.[1] They used, in the later streams of invasion at any rate, iron weapons, including the terrible leaf-shaped iron sword which was to cut its triumphant way through all Europe; they carried round metal shields, and fastened their cloaks with 'fibulae' or safety pins. The description of the Thracians given by Herodotus in his fifth book would probably have been true some six centuries earlier of all these invading Northerners. Professor Ridgeway, who has helped so greatly our understanding of the two elements in early Greek life, has unfortunately over-simplified his statement of the case by speaking as if there were one homogeneous invading race, and one homogeneous race of aboriginals. He operates with 'Achaeans' from the north, and aboriginal 'Pelasgians'. The terminology is convenient, but perhaps dangerously convenient since neither part of the antithesis is really simple.

First the Pelasgians. In antiquity the name Pelasgian stood broadly for pre-Hellenic. There were two main views, not always consciously distinguished. To Herodotus the Pelasgi were the aboriginal inhabitants of Greece, pre-Hellenic and therefore barbaric, though in course of time they became for the most part Hellenized. According to him the Lacedaemonians

---

Recent explorations show that Mycenae was unimportant in ' Helladic' times; then came Minoan influences and greatness; then Helladic influence re-emerged. The Lion Gate, Cyclopean Walls, and 'Treasury of Atreus' are, from this point of view, late. Cf. Wace and Thompson, *Prehistoric Thessaly*, on movements from the south; also Ridgeway, *Early Age*, p. 645 ff. (which however fails to account for the place-names).

[1] See Mr. A. B. Cook's great book on *Zeus*, Cambridge 1914. The name Zeus at any rate is Aryan, not Hittite. However, the evidence is pretty clear that there was a patriarchal Sky-god and Thunder-god in Greece before the Achaeans came. Of course every Greek god is an immense complex; it is impossible to call one Achaean and another Pelasgian. Zeus in classical times has usually dark hair, whatever that is worth as evidence (A 128); he is called 'Pelasgian' (II 233; cf. Strabo, p. 329); is identified with the Cretan Bull-god and Kouros-god, and has many strange non-Achaean attributes.

were of Hellenic race and immigrant, the Athenians were Pelasgians, who had never left their home : though he introduces this division by the statement that these two cities were 'the most powerful of the Hellenes'. Thucydides, on the other hand, seems to think of Pelasgians as part of the same general stock over which Hellên and his sons gradually acquired such power that they all adopted the name Hellenes.[1] If we attempt to reach the historical fact that lies beneath this confused language, Professor Myres would suggest that the Pelasgians were a real set of tribes, with northern rather than Aegean affinities, whom we find first in places like Dodona, the Hellespont, and Pelasgiôtis, then, as they move under pressure from above, in various parts of Greece; in Crete, in Argos, in Attica, especially and permanently in the islands of Lemnos and Imbros, where two inscriptions in a non-Greek language have been discovered, and, under the influence of Herodotus, accepted as Pelasgian. As a matter of fact it seems clear that one at least of these inscriptions is Etruscan ; it is even included in the *Corpus Inscriptionum Etruscarum*. Shall we then conclude with some of the ancients that Pelasgians and Etruscans are the same race ? Sophocles speaks of 'Tyrrhenian Pelasgi', and Herodotus remarks that the people of Plakiê and Skylakê in the Hellespont spoke the same language as those of Cortona in Etruria.[2] This seems to be a mere confusion. The strange maritime people who were called by themselves Rasna, by the Egyptian monuments Turscha, by the Greeks Tyrseni, and by the Romans Tusci or Etrusci, seem certainly to have reached Western Italy from the East of the Aegean, and may well have left several settlements on the way. The name Tyrseni is believed to be simply 'tower men' (from 'tyrsis') and was doubtless applied to any band of sea-rovers who built themselves fortified posts in Greek waters. And any strange language occurring in that area was likely without much inquiry to be called 'Pelasgian'.

---

[1] Hdt. i. 56 : Thuc. i. 3. Compare Strabo, v. p. 220 ἀρχαῖόν τι φῦλον κατὰ τὴν Ἑλλάδα πᾶσαν ἐπιπολάσαν. He regards them as βάρβαροι (σχεδὸν ἡ σύμπασα Ἑλλὰς κατοικία βαρβάρων ὑπῆρξε τὸ παλαιόν vii. p. 321), but he seems there to be thinking of degrees of civilization, not of racial affinities. I doubt if he seriously disagreed with the statement of Dionys. Halic. *Antiqq. Romm.* i. 17 ἦν καὶ τὸ τῶν Πελασγῶν γένος Ἑλληνικόν, ἐκ Πελοποννήσου τὸ ἀρχαῖον.

[2] Hdt. i. 57, reading Κρότωνα for Κρηστῶνα.

It may well be that the Pelasgi were a particular tribe specially prominent in Greece before the Hellenic period, and it may be that historians can discover some of its habitations and wanderings. But the great dispersion of the name and the apparent lack of connexion between the different peoples called by it lend great persuasiveness to a suggestion of Dr. Leaf's. He compares the name 'Welsh', which means 'march-men' and which was applied by the Teutonic tribes to all their neighbours to the west and south. Gauls, Britons, Italians, Dacians, were all 'Welsh'. The 'Walloons' of Belgium and the 'Vlachs' of the Balkan peninsula are the same. They are the strange peoples just beyond the Teutonic border. If Pelasgoi is connected with πέλας, 'near', the word would mean 'neighbour' and would denote the nearest strange people to the invading Greeks, as their shifting border moved down from the north-west.[1]

Thus it would seem on analysis that either 'Pelasgoi' is a name like 'Welsh', meaning the next people beyond the border, or else it originally denoted a particular tribe, which for some reason ended by giving its name as a general term to denote the whole population of pre-Achaean Greece.

This is a perfectly normal phenomenon in the history of race names. The tribe whose name spreads need not even be the most important: it need only be the most conspicuous as seen from over the border. Both Wessex and Mercia were bigger than the kingdom of the Angles, and England was unified under the headship of Wessex; but Europe generally called the whole country after the Angles, because the Angles were nearest to Europe. All Europeans to the Saracens used to be 'Franks'; all Greeks to the Asiatics were 'sons of Yawan'; just as in Italy they were 'Graeci' from the name of a certain Epirot tribe which was much in touch with South Italy; in Greece itself they were 'Hellenes' from the name of a dominant tribe in South Thessaly. It is safe to use Pelasgian in the two senses if we carefully avoid confusing them.

[1] See Leaf, *Troy*, chapter vii, esp. pp. 332 ff. Also Skutsch in Pauly-Wissowa on Etrusker. Soph. fr. 270 (Pearson).—On the Pelasgians as a historical tribe, see Myres in *J. H. S.* xxvii, who traces the ancient 'Pelasgian theory' to Ephorus. Pelasgians are mentioned at Dodona, Π 233 (apparently), Hes. fr. 225 (K), and Hdt.: Pelasgiotis, B 681 ff. (apparently), and later writers: Hellespont, see Myres on B 840 ff.: Hdt. i. 57, ii. 51. Lemnos in Homer (A 594, θ 294) is occupied by Hephaistos' people, the Sinties.

The little that we can make out about the race affinities of the real aborigines is based chiefly on the names of the places which they inhabited. All over Greece we find the towns, mountains, rivers, and, curiously enough, the flowers, called by non-Greek names. Names like Larisa, Corinthos, Zakynthos, Hyakinthos, Olympos, Arisbe, Narkissos, Parnassos, Halicarnassos, are no more Greek than Connecticut and Poughkeepsie or Alabama are English, or Morbihan and Landes are French. And an examination of these non-Greek place-names, as carried out with great ability by Kretschmer and Fick, leads to a result which is on general grounds satisfactory. There is a great system of place-names in a language still unknown to us, which reaches across the mainland of Greece, the islands of the Aegean, and practically the whole immense peninsula of Asia Minor: a language which is clearly not Semitic, and in the opinion of most scholars not Aryan either, and which must therefore have belonged to that pre-Semitic population of Asia Minor of which the most distinguished group is the Hittite.[1] Anthropologists and

---

[1] Especially Fick, *Vorgriechische Ortsnamen* (1905) and *Hattiden und Danubier in Griechenland* (1908), illuminating books: also Kretschmer, *Geschichte der Griechischen Sprache* (1896). Conway, however, argues that this language—quite distinct from Etruscan-Pelasgian—was Indo-European, though of course not Greek. (*B. S. A.*, viii. pp. 125 ff., x. pp. 115 ff.) He starts from the three short inscriptions found at Praesus, a town said to be 'Eteocretan', in the east of the island. They are comparatively late, saec. vi to iv, in Greek letters, but in an unknown language which bears affinities to Venetic and Osco-Umbrian. Conway takes this language as = Eteocretan and Eteocretan as = Minoan. For an historical criticism of this view see Burrows, *Crete*, pp. 151 ff.

It is rash to decide till we know more of the Hittite language, which may now soon occur. H. Winckler's excavations during 1906 and after at Boghaz-Koï in Cappadocia have resulted in: (1) a proof that Boghaz-Koï was the capital of the Hittite kingdom; (2) the discovery of the state archives, consisting of many large complete tablets and over 2,000 fragmentary ones—correspondence from Hittite vassals and from Egypt. The earliest are of the same date as the Tel-el-Amarna letters, and contain notes for the Assyro-Babylonian version of the treaty between Rameses II and the Hittite king, Chetaser. The Hittite language is written both in hieroglyphics and in cuneiform. The hieroglyphs are different from those of Egypt and have not proved easy to decipher, though they were first noticed in 1736 and a corpus of them was published in Wright's *Empire of the Hittites* in 1886. (See Campbell-Thompson, *A New Decipherment of the Hittite Hieroglyphics*, Oxford, 1913.) The cuneiform documents consist chiefly of some 20,000 tablets found by Winckler at Boghaz-Koï written in various languages, including Semitic Babylonian, Sumerian, and Hittite proper. See *Die Sprache der Hittiter* by Friedrich Hrozny, Leipzig, 1917. (Hrozny carried on Winckler's work after the latter's lamented death.) Also *Caractère Indo-Européen de la Langue Hittite*, by Carl Marstrander, Christiania, 1918, with

measurers of skulls tell us that there were in the Aegean lands
before any Northerners arrived on the scene two distinct races—
a dark long-headed Aegean race with littoral habits, never
going far from the sea; and another dark short-skulled
Armenoid race, inhabiting the highlands on both sides. How
far these races were conscious of their respective unities, how
far the ruling Minoans were racially distinct from the surrounding peoples, are questions which we need not at present face.
The Aegean world was certainly divided into many little tribes
and communities, which no doubt fought and hated one another
as gladly as so many Celtic clans. But the remains show that,
generally speaking, they were homogeneous in culture though
by no means all at the same level. And we shall, with this
apology, speak of them in future under one name as pre-Hellenic
or Aegean.[1]

And opposed to these aboriginal or quasi-aboriginal races
stand the invaders from the north, Professor Ridgeway's
'Achaeans'. The case is exactly similar. The Achaeans
formed one of the many immigrant tribes; but the name spread
beyond the bounds of the tribe and was used by the Aegean
peoples to denote the northern races in general. In Homer it
seems to include all the warriors, of whatever blood, who have
fallen under the lead of the northern chieftains. But we should
not forget that there were many branches of the invasion. From

review by Campbell-Thompson in the *Times Literary Supplement*, October 23,
1919. It appears that Hittite has (1) noun case endings, (2) possessive
pronouns, and (3) some verbal inflections of markedly Indo-European
character and indeed very like Greek. (The suffixed pronouns were: Sing.
I. -*mi*, -*mu*, -*m*; 2. -*t*; 3. -*š*. Pl. I. -*na*; 2. -*ut*; 3. -*u*. The verbs showed
an augmented past tense, e.g. *a-da-t*, 'he gave'; *a-k-t*, 'he came'. The
nouns have accus. sing. in -*n*, and, as Prof. Sayce pointed out, nom. in -*s*.
Prepositions are *ab(a)*, *ta*, *mit*, -*kan*. *Times*, Nov. 22, 1912, reporting a
lecture by Campbell-Thompson.) The vocabulary, however, is difficult to
equate with Indo-European, and Dr. Cowley and Mr. Campbell-Thompson
consider the affinity of Hittite not yet proven. See Hogarth's article
HITTITES in *Encycl. Brit.* xi; also the note in O. Weber, *Die Literatur der
Babylonier und Assyrier* (Ergänzungsband ii of *Der Alte Orient*), p. 275,
and Garstang's *Land of the Hittites* (1910); and especially A. E. Cowley,
The Hittites, 1920.

[1] The question of Semitic and Egyptian influence or settlement among
these aborigines can be left aside. There was much interplay between Egypt
and Minoan Crete, but no whole nation came in from the south or east as
there did from the north.

the forests of Central Europe, guided by the valleys and mountain passes towards Dodona and towards Thessaly, came divers
Achaeans and Hellenes; more to the east came tribes of the
same blood, afterwards called Macedonian and Thracian.[1] One
of these Thracian tribes, the Bhryges, crossed into Asia, like the
Cimmerii and the Gauls after them, and drove a wedge of
northern population into the midst of the native ' Hittoids '. If
any one is inclined to over-simplify his conception of these racial
movements, he might find a useful warning in a study of Phrygia,
or of one part of Phrygia, the Troad. If we take the various invaders of the Troad in early Greek times, we find first the
' Phryges ' or ' Bryges ': their name seems to have kept the old
Indo-Germanic *bh* which the Greeks could not pronounce. Also
the Troes or Trojans; also a branch of the Paiones, who gave
their name to a part of Northern Macedonia; further, some
northern neighbours of the Paiones, the Dardanoi, led by a royal
tribe called Aeneadae; some of their southern neighbours, the
Mygdones; a tribe which disappeared early, called Phorkyntes
or Berekyntes; some Thracians, not further specified, from the
Chersonese; and lastly the Trares. Those are the northern
invaders only. The races already settled in the land seem to
have included a main body of Leleges, a race generally known
as aboriginal further south, in Caria; some Pelasgi, who had
probably come from Thrace; Gergithes and Teucri, the latter
being perhaps a royal tribe; and, if we are to believe the *Iliad*,
important settlements of Lycians and Kilikes. And how many
other tribes may there have been, whose names are not preserved
to us? That is the sort of complex of races which existed in one
small piece of territory.

And meantime, further to the west of Greece, came the pressure of other and more barbarous peoples, called by the general
name of Illyrians, who eventually occupied the regions of Albania
and Epirus, and resisted Greek civilization till long after classical
times.

But, to get rid of these names and come closer to reality, what

[1] O. Hoffmann, *Die Makedonen, ihre Sprache und ihr Volksthum* (1906),
confirms Kretschmer's results. The language is a dialect of Greek, akin to
Thessalian, but influenced by 'non-Greek' Phrygo-Thracian and Illyrian.
The chief mark is, of course, Mac. $\beta \gamma \delta$ for Greek $\phi \chi \theta$. The eastern wing
of the Migrations seems to have been the earlier.

are we to conceive these invasions to have been like? Very different, I think, in different circumstances. It is almost a rule in history, that before any definite invasion of a new territory there is a long period of peaceful penetration. The whole process of the northern migrations must cover a period of many centuries. In the beginnings it is not an army that comes to invade. It is some adventurers or traders who come and settle: some mercenaries who are invited in. Or again, it is a few families who move a little further up a mountain, or a little on the other side of a pass, breaking up new land where it happens to be unoccupied. For a great part of the process, on the mainland at least, these may have been the normal modes of advance: on the one hand, a gradual increase of northern soldiers and northern officers in the armies of the Aegean powers; on the other, a slight change in the possession of farms and pasture grounds, in which the stronger race steadily got more and the weaker less. But violence certainly came in, and in the later stages the very extreme of violence. While there was room for both races there was perhaps little or no fighting. But a time always came when there was no room. Of that later.

One thing seems clear. While the great masses of the various northern peoples were steadily pushing downwards on the mainland, small bodies of chiefs or adventurers seem to have gone forth into the Aegean region to carve out for themselves little empires or lives of romance. They were 'invited in', as Thucydides puts it (i. 3), as allies or mercenaries or *condottieri* in the various cities. And, like other *condottieri*, they had a way of marrying native princesses and occupying vacant thrones.[1] It is just what the Normans did in their time. About the year 1035 Robert Guiscard set out from Normandy, so Gibbon tells us, as a pilgrim, with only one companion. He went south, and ended by becoming King of Calabria. 'Under his command the peasants of Calabria assumed the character and the name of Normans.' Just so Agamemnon's followers assumed the charac-

---

[1] As we shall see later, there is ground for suspecting that descent in these communities went by the female side, so that to marry the queen or princess was the normal way of becoming a king. So Xuthus = Creusa, Oedipus = Jocasta, Pelops = Hippodameia, Menelaus and Agamemnon = the daughters of the native king Tyndareus, &c. Cf. the numerous instances in Frazer, *Kingship*, chap. viii. (Also Leaf, *Homer and History*, cap. ii.)

ter and the name of Achaeans.[1] In the eleventh and twelfth centuries A. D. you could find little bands of the Northmen established at various points of the Mediterranean, as kings and nobles among an inferior population. 'The gradual association, incorporation, or alliance of the Scandinavians with the nations they came to plunder or destroy is perhaps the most decisive fact in the story of the Christian Middle Ages, and affords a basis or starting-point for every subsequent development.' So writes Professor Beazley of the mediaeval Normans.[2] And just the same might be said of these other invading Northmen in Greece in the thirteenth and fourteenth centuries before the Christian era.

The great citadel of Troy had a northern king, a Phrygian. Similarly in all the other centres of Aegean power we seem to find Northmen ruling. Minos indeed was aboriginal, and even divine: but the tradition makes him first into a 'friend', then into a son, of the Achaean Zeus[3]; and Idomeneus, the Cretan chief of the *Iliad*, is clearly counted among the Achaeans. The ships of the 'peoples of the sea' are under the Achaean Agamemnon. He is the very type and king of the Achaeans: but it is interesting to notice that his family tree is derived from Phrygia.[4] If this is right, Agamemnon belonged to those same Northmen who had come eastward by way of Thrace to occupy

---

[1] Gibbon, cap. lvi. There is a good account of these sons of Tancred in Demolins, *Comment la Route crée le Type Social*, ii. pp. 313 ff. Just so with the Dorians: Halicarnassus was founded by 'Ionians from Trozên' with Dorian leaders. It counts as Dorian. Hdt. vii. 99: Strabo, p. 653, &c. So, too, Tarentum: Τάραντα δὲ ἀπῴκισαν μὲν Λακεδαιμόνιοι (Perioikoi and Parthenioi)· οἰκιστὴς δὲ ἐγένετο Σπαρτιάτης Φάλανθος, Paus. x. 10. 3. The dialect is Achaean = Perioikian, but the colony is called 'Dorian'. So the 'Spartan' army at Thermopylae, 300 Spartans in 5,000 odd, besides Helots. Meister, *Dorer und Achäer*, p. 22 ff.

[2] *Dawn of Modern Geography*, pt. ii, chap. i.   [3] See above, p. 30.

[4] Pelops is nearly always a Phrygian (Soph. *Ajax*, 1292; Hdt. vii. 8 and 11; Bacchylides, vii. 53, &c.). Pindar says a Lydian (*Ol.* i. 24, ix. 9). Afterwards the ideas are confused, and he is merely Asiatic. (So Thuc. i. 9.) Observe that his alleged ancestor, Tantalus, was not originally a son of Zeus, but an ὀαριστής like Minos; i. e. not an Achaean, but a native prince, and Agamemnon's descent from him a fiction (Eur. *Or.* 11; Pind. *Ol.* i. 43, &c.). Tantalus also appears as the first husband of Clytemnestra, slain by Agamemnon (Eur. *Iph. Aul.* 1150). His being non-Achaean may perhaps explain why Zeus sends him to Tartaros with Sisyphus, Salmoneus, Tityos, Ixion. (See J. E. Harrison, *Prolegomena*, pp. 336 ff.) Pelops' ally and victim, the charioteer Myrtilus, bears the name of the Hittite king, Mursil, who was also a charioteer. Strange!

Troy: and when he led an army against Priam he fought in a specially close sense against his own kindred.

The later Greek imagination liked to think of Troy as an Asiatic city, and to make the Trojan War a type of the age-long struggle of West and East, Aryan and Semite. There are abundant symptoms of this tendency in the *Iliad* (e.g. Φ 88, X 48). But it seems likely that in the earliest records the Trojan chiefs were of the same race as the Achaeans. There is no difference of language. The difference of language comes in between the Trojans and their own allies, the 'Carians with barbarous tongue' and the various peoples in whom 'there was not one language nor one voice'.[1] Their mode of fighting is exactly the same as that of the Achaeans. Their gods are the same. Nay, if we examine carefully into that question the result is rather curious. According to Homer, a typical Achaean oath is by the trinity, Zeus, Apollo, and Athena.[2] And this trinity in the Homeric poems must have been originally on the side of Troy! Apollo fights openly for the Trojans. Zeus is constantly protecting them, putting off their evil day, and rebuking their enemies. Athena indeed appears in our present *Iliad* as the enemy of Troy. Yet it is to her that the Trojans especially pray. She is the patroness of their city, she the regular Achaean 'City-holder': and it is when the Palladion, or image of the protecting Athena, is stolen away, that Troy eventually can be taken. In Euripides' *Trojan Women*, one may add, the treachery of Athena in turning against her own city is one of the main notes of the drama.

[1] B 867, Δ 437.

[2] The trinity does not occur outside Homer. ('Originally a trinity of Father-Consort-Son, as usual in Aegean religion? Cf. births of Hephaistos, Erechtheus &c.' JAKT.) On Zeus see note on p. 41. Athena is on one side merely the *Athenaia korê* (see p. 97), on another, as Pallas, she is the *palladion*, or divine thunder-shield which falls from heaven; as such she is a 'daughter', almost a mere attribute, of the Thunderer. Apollo has some aboriginal characteristics, e.g. he is a stranger to the other Olympians, who fly before him, in the Homeric hymn; but as Sun-god (I have lived to see this old view, which is based on firm ancient authority, re-emerge from the depths of unfashionableness) he is closely associated with the Sky-god, Zeus. See J. E. Harrison, *Prolegomena*, p. 461 f.; Wilamowitz, 'Apollo' (Oxford, 1908); and in *Hermes*, 1903, p. 575. Also Th. Reinach, *Itanos et l'inventio scuti*, Rev. de l'histoire des religions, 1909, p. 331. The parallel between the patriarchal Zeus in Greece and Othin in Scandinavia is very striking: invading gods accepted as supreme by the native populations and imperfectly assimilated to the old system of gods. See Chadwick, *Cult of Othin*.

One great city, as we saw above, did not accept Achaean rulers. In Thebes the Cadmeans, whoever they may have been, held out to the end. The war of The Seven has a different look from the ordinary wars of one Achaean band against another. The Minyai in Orchomenos were destroyed more easily. Thebes seems to have remained like an island in the flood of Achaean invaders. She had them to the north of her in Thessaly and Phthia, to the west in Phocis and Aetolia, to the east (probably) in Euboea, to the south-west in Argos. And, if we are to believe tradition, it was from this farthest southern point that they turned, determined to tolerate no more the great fortress of the alien race.

But in the main, if we try to conceive the Aegean in, say, the thirteenth century B. C., we must think of the ancient seats of power as generally standing, but at each palace a northern chief established as king with a band of northern followers about him. Their power was based partly on sheer plunder, partly on the taxes yielded by a constantly decreasing trade. It was an unstable condition. Some northern Agamemnon might sit at Mycenae, a northern Idomeneus at Cnossos. They might have imbibed a fair amount of civilization. They were perhaps good rulers. No one could doubt their valour. But too many of their own kinsmen were prowling the adjacent world. It was only by memory that they knew the

Riches that Ilion held, the wallèd and beautiful city,
Of old in the passing of peace, ere came the sons of Achaia.

Fewer and fewer caravans of laden mules plodded up the stone ways of the Argive mountains. Fewer and fewer fleets of trading boats came to pay toll in the harbours of Southern Crete.

In this state of weak equilibrium there came further shocks from the north-west. Other tribes pressed down on the mainland, through Thessaly down to Aetolia, over from Aetolia to Boeotia, to the north of the Peloponnese, to Elis: by sea came the most dangerous of all enemies, hordes of dispossessed men, who must plunder and slay, or else die. It was possibly with some view of saving his dynasty and consolidating the various bodies of chiefs who would otherwise be troubling him that the Agamemnon of the time gathered his expedition of 'all Achaeans' against Troy, and won—if he did win it—his more than Pyrrhic victory. Troy indeed fell, but all Achaean Greece fell with it. A storm, says the tradition, scattered the returning kings over the face of the deep. Some came home to die, some were lost, some settled in strange lands. But for certain their glory was gone, their palaces shaken, and the names of their sons are blotted out from the page of history. Those old sea-rovers had among them a special title of honour, πτολίπορθος, 'Sacker of Cities'. It represented the height of romantic glory as well as the most profitable of financial *coups*. And the same idea, seen from the other side, haunted also the imagination of the civilized city-dwellers. A beleaguered city, with the men fighting in front and the women and old men watching from the wall, forms a regular subject of epic description. It is depicted, for example, on the shields of Achilles in Homer and of Heracles in Hesiod. The same theme appears on a silver vessel from Mycenae and on reliefs and mosaics from Minoan Cnossus.[1] The theme took epic shape afterwards in the tales of Thebes and Troy. It was in these ages the crowning triumph or the ultimate horror of human life.

At first when the rovers sacked a city, they could in a way rebuild it or have it rebuilt. They assimilated enough of Aegean civilization at least to live in the castles of those whom they conquered. But the same thing occurred here as in Rome afterwards. As the ruder hordes and the vaster numbers pressed down; as the pre-Achaean races had sunk in numbers and in confidence; there came at last tribes who could destroy but not build nor even keep, 'sackers-of-cities' who burned and shattered, and then could make no more of their conquest than to live huddled in war-parties among the ruins.

One must probably conceive two different processes of migration, by land and by sea respectively. By land, a whole tribe or nation tended to push on, carrying with it its women, its normal possessions, its flocks and herds. Though even on land there were many varieties in the intensity of the struggle. In Boeotia, for instance, the conquering race, pushing over from the

---

[1] Cf. *Iliad* Σ 509, *Aspis* 239 ff. Evans, *Cretan Palaces*, i. p. 314. The mosaic is Middle Minoan II.

west, seems to have settled without much massacre and without any formal enslavement of the resident population. One result of this comparative clemency was a subsequent harshness. The oligarchies in Boeotia continued through several centuries peculiarly severe and illiberal. The subject race had been admitted to something so nearly approaching equality, that it needed—in the judgement of its masters—continual thrashing. In most of Thessaly, in Argos, Corinth, Sparta, the natives were reduced to varying degrees of slavery. They became, like the Gibeonites, hewers of wood and drawers of water : like the Messenians,[1] they 'walked as asses walk, weighed down with heavy burdens'. In Attica the invaders seem to have been few and weak. They merely merged with the old population. One cannot even discern a definite ruling class. It is a fact worth noting by those who study questions of race, that among both the Greeks and the Hebrews the most prominent and characteristic part of the nation was also the part most largely mixed with the race of the despised aborigines. The tribe of Judah had the largest Canaanite element.[2] As for the Athenians, they always claim to be children of the soil, and Herodotus actually goes so far as to describe them as ' not Greek but Pelasgian '.

But what of the migrations by sea ? The centre of Greece is really not Athens nor Sparta nor any state of the mainland. The real centre is the Aegean ; and the migrations by sea are both more characteristic and for after-history, I venture to suggest, more important. When a tribe moved by land it took most of its belongings with it. When it had to cross the sea a possession must needs be very precious indeed before it could be allowed room in those small boats. Of course there are cases where a deliberate invasion is planned, as the Saxons, for instance, planned their invasion of Britain. The fighting men go first and secure a foothold ; the rest of the nation can follow when things are safe. In historical times, when the Athenians left Attica before the advance of the Persian army, they took their wives and even their herds across the narrow waters to Salamis and Aegina. When the Phocaeans deserted their city and fled to the west, they

[1] Tyrtaeus 6.

[2] See e.g. Driver on Gen. xxxviii ; Cheyne also remarks on Edomite and North Arabian elements in Judah, *Enc. Bibl.* s. v.

seem to have begun by taking their womankind at least as far as Chios, where they might hope to find a breathing-place.[1] But these were more organized or at least less helpless peoples; the movement was well thought out beforehand, and there was friendly land near. In the earlier migrations of the Dark Age a tribe, or mass of people, seldom took to the sea till driven by the fear of death. That was no time to think of taking women or herds. You might desire greatly to take your young wife—or your old wife, for that matter ; but you would scarcely dare to make such a proposal to the hungry fighters about you. You might wish to take your little boy. But would the rest of us, think you, choose to be encumbered with another consumer of bread who could never help in a fight, who might delay us in charging or flying, might cry from the pain of hunger or fatigue and betray us all ? No, leave him on the beach, and come ! Put some mark on him. Probably some one will make him a slave, and then, with good luck, you may some day knock up against him and pay his ransom.

When we are off on the sea, what is the prospect before us ? We have some provisions, though no water. Instead, we take guides who know where there are springs near the sea-shore in divers islands and unfrequented promontories. We can move by night and hide in caves during the day. The guide probably knows places where cattle may, with some risk, be raided. Better still, he knows of some villages that have been lately attacked by other pirates, where the men are still weak with their wounds. Not all their flocks have been killed. We might well take the rest. If we stay at sea, we die of thirst. If we are seen landing, we are for certain massacred by any human beings who find us. Piracy on the high seas will not keep us alive. In the good old days, when the Northmen first came, pirates could live like fighting-cocks and be buried like princes. But the business has been spoiled. There are too many men like ourselves, and too few ships with anything on them to steal. If we go back to our old home, the invaders have by this time got our women as slaves, and will either kill us or sell us in foreign countries. Is there anywhere an island to seize ? There are many little desert rocks all studded over the Aegean, where doubtless we have rested

---

[1] Hdt. i. 165. Cf. the career of Dionysius of Phocaea as a pirate, vi. 17 ; of the Samians, vi. 22 ff. And in general Thuc. I, 5.

often enough when the constrained position of sitting everlastingly at the oars has been too much for us; rested and starved, and some of us gone mad with thirst under that hot sun. A waterless rock will be no use. Can we seize some inhabited island? Alone we are too weak; but what if we combined with some other outlaws? There are some outcast Carians in like plight with ourselves in one of the desert caves near. In our normal life we would not touch a Carian. Their weapons are no gentleman's weapons. Their voices make one sick. And their hair . . . ! But what does it matter now? . . . And with them are some Leleges, who worship birds; some unknown savages from the eastern side, dark-bearded hook-nosed creatures answering to babyish names like ' Atta ' and ' Babba ' and ' Duda '; and—good omen!—some of our old enemies from near home, the tribe that we were always fighting with and had learned to hate in our cradles. A pleasure to meet them again! One can understand their speech. We swear an oath that makes us brothers. We cut one another's arms, pour the blood into a bowl and drink some all round. We swear by our gods: to make things pleasanter, we swear by one another's gods, so far as we can make out their outlandish names. And then forth to attack our island.

After due fighting it is ours. The men who held it yesterday are slain. Some few have got away in boats, and may some day come back to worry us; but not just yet, not for a good long time. There is water to drink; there is bread and curded milk and onions. There is flesh of sheep or goats. There is wine, or, at the worst, some coarser liquor of honey or grain, which will at least intoxicate. One needs that, after such a day. . . . No more thirst, no more hunger, no more of the cramped galley benches, no more terror of the changes of wind and sea. The dead men are lying all about us. We will fling them into the sea to-morrow. The women are suitably tied up and guarded. The old one who kept shrieking curses has been spiked with a lance and tossed over the cliff. The wailing and sobbing of the rest will stop in a day or two: if it torments you, you can easily move a few paces away out of the sound. If it still rings in your ears, drink two more cups and you will not mind it. The stars are above us, and the protecting sea round us, we have got water and food and roofs over our heads. And we wrought it all by our own wisdom and courage and the manifest help of Zeus and Apollo. What good men we are, and valiant and pious; and our gods—what short work they make of other men's gods!

There is no trait in the above suggestion that is not drawn from a real case. I have been imagining the case of a quite small island. More often not a whole island was at stake, but only a promontory or a foothold. Nor do we, of course, ever hear the whole complications of a conquest. It is always simplified in the tradition.

In Chios, for instance, we hear that there were first Carians, to whom a settlement of Abantes from Euboea had joined themselves. Then came an invasion of refugees from Crete—surely not of pure Cretan blood—who gradually grew and mostly drove out the Carians and Abantes. From Strabo[1] we hear, significantly enough, of a quite different founder of Chios, a man called Egertios, who brought with him 'a mixed multitude' ($\sigma\acute{u}\mu\mu\epsilon\iota\kappa\tau o\nu$ $\pi\lambda\tilde{\eta}\theta os$). It afterwards counted as one of the chief Ionian cities. In Erythrae there are Cretans, Lycians, and that mixed Graeco-barbaric race called Pamphylians, whose dialect seems to show that they spring from some settlement of old prae-Achaean vikings.[2] Later came new immigrations from all the Ionian cities. It was rather different at Colophon and Ephesus on the mainland. In both cases there was an ancient pre-Hellenic oracle or temple in the neighbourhood. In Colophon there were Greeks from Crete, from Boeotia, from the west of the Peloponnese: if we may believe the epic tradition, there were fragments of many other tribes as well. They forced a settlement somehow on the land; living perhaps, as Wilamowitz suggests, in 'Blockhuts' on the shore, fighting for a permanent foothold in the barbarian city. In Colophon they are accepted as a ruling caste, and get possession even of the oracle. In Ephesus they are weaker; they have a position rather as clients of the great temple, and 'Diana of the Ephesians' remains at heart barbaric till she can break out into confessed monstrosity in the Roman period. Round another sanctuary, the little rock of Delos, there grows up a peculiar

---

[1] xiv. p. 633. The main sources for these colonization traditions, outside the epos, are Strabo and Paus. vii.

[2] The half-barbarous Pamphylian dialect has enough points in common with Cypro-Arcadian to show this. See Thumb, *Handbuch d. Gr. Dialekte*, p. 298, and Meillet in *Rev. d. Études Grecques* for 1909, pp. 413 ff.

federation of people from divers parts of the Aegean, a league whose business it is to meet at Delos for certain festivals, to pay proper dues to the holy place and to keep it sacred. They were called 'Iawones', Iônes, and the name spread gradually to a large part of the Greek people.[1]

Nearly everywhere on the mainland and in the isles there are, as we have said, old place-names in a language not Greek, but earlier than Greek. But there are exceptions. In Cos we know of an invasion from Crete. And there all the place-names are Greek. What does that mean? Is it that in this particular island, large and fertile as it is, if the Greek invaders wanted to ask the name of a mountain or a river, there was no single native voice—not even a woman spared for a concubine—to answer them, so that they had to name all the places anew? I see no other plausible explanation. Different was the end in Lemnos. If tradition is to be believed—and, in the one large point where it can be tested, the tradition is confirmed by history—there was once done in Lemnos that act of vengeance for which one's unregenerate instinct thirsts in thinking over the bloody and relentless tale of these conquests. The men of Lemnos were duly slain. The women were duly enslaved as concubines. But they were trusted too soon: either they nursed the memory of their wrongs longer than other women, or in some way they had an opportunity denied to others. At any rate the native women rose and murdered their invaders, and the island was never completely possessed by the Greeks during all the classical period. It was a hard task for an island in that position to keep itself un-Hellenized. But somehow Pelasgians gathered there. Later on, when a part of the population showed some tincture of Greek manners and claimed descent from the Argonauts, it was expelled. When the children born of some captured Greek women began to show their Greek blood, they were murdered and their mothers with them. The 'deeds of Lemnos' ring with

---

[1] For all this paragraph see Wilamowitz's illuminating lecture *Die Ionische Wanderung* (*Sitzungsber. Berlin. Akad.* 1906, iv). As to Ephesus, the 'multimammia' form of Artemis is of course barbaric, and belongs to the regular Anatolian mother-goddess. It is most remarkable that the recent excavations at Ephesus have unearthed nearly fifty figurines of the goddess, 'ranging from the eighth to the fourth centuries B.C.,' in none of which is there 'any approximation to the "multimammia" type rendered familiar by statuettes of the Roman period'.—Hogarth, in the *Times* of Nov. 2, 1906.

an ominous sound in early Greek proverb, the extreme of horror, no other deed like them.[1]

This is the sort of picture that we can recover of the so-called Dark Age. It is just the stage of society which Professor Chadwick has shown to be in so many regions of the world the Mother of Heroic Poetry.[2] It was the climax of a long process of 'barbarian invasion', in which a young half-savage race gradually entered into the stored riches of an ancient civilization, becoming successively awe-struck visitors, servants, enemies, mercenary chieftains, adventurers, plunderers, and masters. It was a time, as Diodorus says, of 'constant war-paths and uprootings of peoples'[3]; a chaos in which an old civilization is shattered into fragments, its laws set at naught, and that intricate web of normal expectation which forms the very essence of human society torn so often and so utterly by continued disappointment that at last there ceases to be any normal expectation at all. For the fugitive settlers on the shores that were afterwards Ionia, and for parts too of Doris and Aeolis, there were no tribal gods or tribal obligations left, because there were no tribes. There were no old laws, because there was no one to administer or even to remember them : only such compulsions as the strongest power of the moment chose to enforce. Household and family life had disappeared, and all its innumerable ties with it. A man was now not living with a wife of his own race, but with a dangerous strange woman, of alien language

---

[1] Aesch. *Cho.* 631, Hdt. vi. 138. The story fits in with known historical facts ; yet perhaps it is not safe to trust it. It has too much the look of a myth built upon a religious cult of some kind. First the women of Lemnos kill the men ; then the men kill the women (and children) ; thirdly, when the Minyans of Lemnos are in prison in Sparta, their wives change clothes with them and save them (Hdt. iv. 146).

[2] *The Heroic Age*, Cambridge, 1912. Professor Chadwick discusses six societies which have produced Heroic Poetry, and decides that in five of them at least (p. 459) 'The Heroic Age can be traced back to a similar series of causes. Firstly, we find a long period of "education", in which a semi-civilized people has been profoundly affected from without by the influence of a civilized people. Then a time has come in which the semi-civilized people has attained a dominant position and possessed itself, at least to some extent, of its neighbour's property.' Such an age is a 'crowded hour of glorious life', when tribal and religious sanctions are broken down, and the individual tries his fortune with his sword and his ἀρετή, a time of 'Mars and the Muses'. See Preface, p. v.

[3] Πυκναὶ στρατεῖαι καὶ μεταναστάσεις. Cf. of course all through this discussion the 'Archaeologia' of Thucydides i. Also see Appendix C, on the List of Thalassocrats.

and alien gods, a woman whose husband or father he had perhaps murdered—or, at best, whom he had bought as a slave from the murderer. The old Aryan husbandman, as we shall see hereafter, had lived with his herds in a sort of familiar connexion. He slew ' his brother the ox ' only under special stress or for definite religious reasons, and he expected his women to shriek when the slaying was performed. But now he had left his own herds far away. They had been devoured by enemies. And he lived on the beasts of strangers whom he robbed or held in servitude. He had left the graves of his fathers, the kindly ghosts of his own blood, who took food from his hand and loved him. He was surrounded by the graves of alien dead, strange ghosts whose names he knew not and who were beyond his power to control, whom with fear and aversion he tried his best to placate. One only concrete thing existed for him to make henceforth the centre of his allegiance, to supply the place of his old family hearth, his gods, his tribal customs and sanctities. It was a circuit wall of stones, a *Polis* [1]; the wall which he and his fellows, men of diverse tongues and worships united by a tremendous need, had built up to be the one barrier between themselves and a world of enemies. Inside the wall he could take breath. He could become for a time a man again, instead of a terrified beast. The wall was built, Aristotle tells us, that men might live, but its inner cause was that men might ' live well '. It was a ship in a great sea, says a character in Sophocles (*Ant.* 191), whose straight sailing is the first condition of all faith or friendship between man and man. The old Korê or earth-maiden changes her type, and appears on coins wearing a crown made of a city-wall. The Polis had become itself the Mother-Goddess, binding together all who lived within its circuit and superseding all more personal worships. When this begins we have the germ of historical Greece.

This religion of the Polis was, I think, in the later ages of Greece, the best, and is to us the most helpful, of ancient religions. It has this in common with the others, that it implies in each

---

[1] This is the use in Homer, preserved later in the words πολίζω, πόλισμα. Of course in safer times the cities spread and far outgrew the old Polis, which was then apt to be called Acropolis—as at Athens. And some warlike tribes went on living without a wall, κατὰ κώμας, like the Spartans and the Northern invaders of Italy.

citizen the willing sacrifice of himself to something greater than himself. It has also to the full their passionate narrowness. But it differs from all the others in many things. It has its roots in knowledge and real human need, not in ignorance and terror. Its rules of conduct are based not on obedience to imaginary beings, but on serving mankind; not on observance of taboos, but on doing good.

Ἀρετὰ πολύμοχθε γένει βροτείῳ, says Aristotle in the first line of his one curious outbreak into lyrics, 'Aretê much laboured for by the race of man.' It is one of the common burdens of early Greek poetry, of Pindar, Hesiod, Phokylides, Simonides, this thirst of men for Aretê, the word that we translate ' Virtue '. It is more, of course, than our Virtue; more even than the Roman Virtus. It is ' goodness ' in all the senses in which objects can be called good, the quality of a good sword, a good horse, a good servant, or a good ruler. The religion of the Polis did essentially make men strive to be more of worth, to be ' good men '. Think for a moment of the judgements passed upon his characters by the Deuteronomic compiler of the Book of Kings. A sweeping judgement is passed for good or evil on almost every king; and on what is it based? First, on the question whether the king followed exactly the precepts and taboos ascribed to the deity worshipped by the writer; and secondly, whether he duly prevented even that deity being worshipped anywhere except at the writer's own temple. Great rulers like Jeroboam II or even like Omri, who is treated by the Assyrians as the very founder of Israel, are passed over with scarcely more than the mere statement that they ' did evil in the sight of Yahweh '.

Now the Jews who wrote under the influence of Deuteronomy represent a religion extraordinarily noble and enlightened. Compared with the immense majority of ancient religions it stands upon a mountain top. Yet contrast with these distorted judgements of the Deuteronomist those passed by Plato in the *Gorgias* on the great democratic statesmen of Athens. Plato was perhaps the most theologically-minded of the great Greek writers; he writes in the *Gorgias* with great bitterness; and I think his judgements extremely prejudiced. Yet from beginning to end he bases his indictments of the various statesmen on one question only, their service to their fellow men. Have they made Athens better and happier ?   It looks as if they had ; but he denies it.   'They have filled the city with docks and arsenals and tributes and such trash, instead of Sôphrosynê and righteousness.'

It is the difference between a soul in bondage and a free soul. But to reach that freedom the Greeks had to pass first through fire and then through a great darkness.   That is the subject which we will consider in detail in the next of these lectures.

III

CHAOS: AIDÔS AND NEMESIS

I WISH in the present lecture to consider in detail some of those sanctions of tribal custom and religion which were exposed to change or destruction in the anarchy of the great Migrations : and then, in the apparent wreck of all, to study the seed of regeneration which seems to have been left.

I do not know that we can begin better than by following a curious by-path of the decline of tribal religion, the history of 'our brother the ox'. Not that it is specially characteristic of Greece. It occurred over most of Europe and Asia. But it is one of a multitude of changes that must have befallen with some intensity and sharpness of outline in the Dark Age of Greece.

Professor Robertson Smith has shown with great skill the position of the domestic animals in the early agricultural tribes, both Aryan and Semitic. The tribe or kindred was the whole moral world to its members. Things outside the tribe were things with which no reasonable man concerned himself. So far as they forced themselves on the tribesmen's attention, they were bad, unclean, hostile. And the tribe consisted of what? Of certain human beings, certain gods—one or more—and certain flocks of animals. The thing that made them one was, according to Dr. Robertson Smith's most suggestive explanation, that sacred thing in which Life itself is, the common blood running in the veins of all. This statement is no doubt a little too explicit. The oneness of the tribe was a thing taken as obvious, not a thing reasoned about. But as far as there is any conscious analysis the blood seems to be taken as the ground of unity. It was in the flocks as much as in the men. Nay, sometimes rather more ; since the god himself was often in some sense an ox, a sheep, or a camel. If we are, say, the Sons of Moab, then our God Chemosh is the god of Moab and our cattle are the flocks of Moab.   They have shared our food and we have drunk of their milk.   The common blood runs in us all.

It would actually seem, from the evidence, that certain early agricultural folk never used their domestic animals for ordinary food.   They would not so shed the tribal blood.   They killed wild animals, or, if chance offered, the cattle of strangers.   Their own animals were not killed except for the definite purpose of sacrifice.

Now, if anything went wrong with the tribe for any unknown cause, if the harvest was bad, the cattle sick, the water scarce, the neighbouring tribes overbearing, the cause was usually sought in the attitude of mind of the god.   ' The world was against them '; in other words Chemosh was angry with his people, or had forgotten them.   His feeling for his kindred was becoming faint. It must be renewed.   And the regular and almost universal method of renewing it was to take some of the living blood of the tribe, take it especially while warm and living and full of its miraculous force, and share it between the god and the people· You went where the god lived, or you called him to come to a particular pit or stone or heap of stones—an altar—and there, after due solemnities, you shed the sacred blood for him to drink. Feeding the god caused no great difficulty.   It was easy to pour the blood into the pit or upon the altar: and that rite always remained.   There was more awkwardness, and consequently more variety of usage, about providing for the tribesmen themselves.   For men began early to shrink from consuming raw flesh and blood, and devised other ways of appropriating the virtues of the miraculous liquid.

There is only one criticism to pass on this.   It is that Robertson Smith's discovery was a little greater than he realized.   For he assumes a period in which there already exists some definite personal god with whom to share the sacrifice, and we know now that there was a previous period in which there was not yet a personal god.   There was the tribal blood there was also the live animal that bore in it the life of the tribe, set apart and consecrated, till it became full of magical vitality.   The personal god seems to have been made by abstraction and ' projection ' out of this magical *mana*, out of the ritual dances, the desires and fears of the tribe.   The bull was not holy because the god had touched him ; the god himself only existed because the bull was so charged with holiness and creative power.[1] Now, as you spared the ox in ordinary life because he was your brother and fellow labourer, so you slaughtered him on a great occasion for the same reason. Had he not been your brother, the sacrifice would have lacked half its power. If we consult the collections of anthropologists, we shall find many various ways in which this feeling of brotherhood with the domestic animal is expressed. The Todas of South India, for instance—that tribe to whom anthropologists owe so much—sacrifice a buffalo once a year only. When the victim falls, men, women, and children group themselves round its head, and fondle, caress, and kiss its face, and then give way to wailing and lamentation. In other cases you beg the animal's forgiveness before slaying it, and explain to it the dire necessity of the case, or the high honour you are really conferring upon it. Or you arrange that it shall seem to desire to die. You make an elaborate apparatus for self-decep- tion, so that the beast may seem to ask you to let it die for the tribe.[2] You even arrange that it shall kill itself. I do not think any clear distinction can be drawn here between the practices of different races. The early Aryan peoples seem to have had this conception, and therefore probably the Achaeans had it. Whereas, on the other hand, the clearest instances surviving in Greece in historical times seem to belong to the strata of more primitive peoples. The word applied to this slaughter of the domestic, the familiar and friendly, animal, is regularly φόνος, the legal word for ' murder '. And the *locus classicus* on the subject is Theophrastus'[3] description of the Athenian festival called Bouphonia, or Ox-murder, which contained an elaborate ritual for ridding the various actors in the ceremony from the guilt of the murder of their friend. The slayer flies for his life. Every one concerned in the ceremony is tried for murder. Those who drew water for the sharpening of the weapons are tried first : but they only drew the water, they did not sharpen the axe and knife. The sharpeners are next accused, and produce the men

---

[1] See note on p. 275.   [2] R. Smith, *Religion of the Semites*, p. 309.
[3] Cf. J. E. Harrison, *Prolegomena*, p. 111, note 1, and authorities there cited. There is a similar φόνος of a bear practised to-day in Saghalien. Cf. the sacral Bear-slaying in the Kalewala.

to whom they gave the weapons after they were sharpened. These produce another man, who struck the victim down with the axe : he another, who cut its throat. This last man accuses the knife, which is solemnly pronounced guilty and thrown into the sea. And besides all this, it has been arranged that the ox shall have gone up to the altar of his own free will and eaten of the sacrificial grains, thereby showing that he wished to be slain. Further still, the dead ox is quickly stuffed, set on his feet, and yoked to a plough as if he had never been killed at all ; it had all been a bad dream.

Now what, in its ultimate element of human feeling, does this mean ? When you have stripped off the hocus-pocus, the superstitious make-believe of getting rid of pollution by a number of dodges which can deceive no one, there remains at the back a seed of simple human feeling that the act of slaying your old kinsman and fellow worker is rather horrible : the feeling that any honest man has about the killing of a pet lamb for food. It was a thing, so Greek tradition tells us, that man in the golden age did not do.[1]

The Bouphonia took place in Attica, where there was, practically speaking, no violent migration, and where a large element of the old population mingled gradually and peacefully with a small element of the new. One finds traces of the same spirit in the epics of the mainland. Hesiod, in this respect representing a stationary society which had either recovered from the violence of the Migrations or had preserved throughout them much of the peaceful agricultural tradition, always speaks of the ox as a sort of kinsman and partner. 'A house, an ox, and a woman ' (*Erga*, 405) are what man needs for the facing of the world. Hesiod (*Erga*, 436 ff.) likes his ox to be nine years old : his ploughman to be forty, and not stinted of his due dinner of bread. You know one another's ways by that time, and feel comfortable together. Clearly a nine-year-old ox is not kept for eating. Notice again how Hesiod speaks of keeping the oxen indoors and well fed in the cold weather (*Erga*, 452 ; contrast

[1] R. Smith, *Religion of Semites*, p. 304, and Plat. *Laws*, 782 C 'Ορφικοί τινες βίοι. ' Plutarch' in his brilliant essays περὶ Σαρκοφαγίας takes just the opposite view : the savage can be excused for flesh-eating, the civilized man not.

559); of the east winds (*Erga*, 504) in the month of Lenaion, 'evil days, they just skin the ox, all of them'; of the cold dawn, how 'it puts yokes on many oxen' (*Erga*, 580). During the winter storms, too, you and your little girls can sit inside by the fire and keep warm, but the wind blows through the ox's hide, it cannot be kept out, and through the fell of the shaggiest goat. But not the sheep. Their wool is too thick, and they do not mind (*Erga*, 512 ff.). Do you observe the sentiment of it all? How the ox is a friend, a member of the family.

The name they kept for him tells the same story. You will remember the regular phrase in the older poetry εἰλίποδας ἕλικας βοῦς, the two epithets of rather dim and unrealized meaning that are habitually applied to cattle. Εἰλίποδες, 'rolling the feet', is an antithesis to the word applied to horses, ἀερσίποδες, 'lifting the feet'. A horse steps high, a cow's foot makes a more horizontal curve. And what of the other word ἕλικες? The Greeks understood it as 'curly-horned', the opposite of βοῶν ὀρθοκραιράων, 'straight-horned cattle'. There were the two breeds in early Greece. But one should notice this about the two adjectives: that they both belong to the class of familiar names or nicknames applied to well-known animals— names like 'puss' and 'bunny'. Hesiod, our earliest farm-yard poet, is full of such names: he has a nickname even for the ant and the snail and the octopus, 'wise-wit' (778) and 'house-carrier' and 'no-bones' respectively.—The hare is πτώξ, 'trembler,' and the goat μηκάς, 'bleater,' the hog, rather less politely, is σίαλος, 'grease.'[1] And this explains a little difficulty. Ἕλικες means 'curly', or 'crumpled'; and Dr. Leaf, in his invaluable commentary to the *Iliad*, objects that it is scarcely possible language to speak of a 'crumpled cow' when you mean a cow with crumpled horns. True, if the word were still a simple adjective with no special connotations. But it is not: it is a name, almost a pet-name. When Hesiod's forty-year-old ploughman came down as

---

[1] Unless indeed σίαλος merely meant (1) hog, (2) hog's grease. Sheep seem to have no nickname.—In general cf. 530 ff., where 'the horned and hornless wood-sleepers' in a snowstorm go with their tails between their legs, like a lame man bent over his stick. It is the same spirit. There is intimacy with animals in general, even the snake in the new fragments is 'No-hair,' ἄτριχος (*Berl. Klassikertexte*, V. 1, p. 36); a wild boar is 'spear-stopper', ἀσχέδωρος. But with the ox there is much more.

usual rather before dawn and met his nine-year-old cow, I suppose he addressed her as *Helix*; he said, 'Good morning, Crumple.'

And when for some grave reason this cow or ox had to be— what shall we say?—' murdered ' is the old Greek word—it was a solemn occasion.   Take a case where the feeling is already less keen, the sacrifice at Nestor's house at Pylos in the third book of the *Odyssey* (421–63).   Nestor is, of course, a Homeric hero, but he is now back at home, under the normal influences of home life. The occasion is a special one.   There has been a visible appearance of Pallas Athena, and it is necessary to honour her, perhaps to renew the tribal bond with her, in an extraordinary way. ' Let some one go to the field,' says Nestor, ' for a cow ; and the ox-herd is to come with him.   And bring also the goldsmith Laerkes, to put gold on the horns of the cow.   And everybody wait here.'   Then follows a solemn description of all the apparatus and the details: the goldsmith's tools and work : the purification of every person present to receive what may be called the sacrament of the kindred blood : the suitable sacrificial vessels placed so that it may not be spilt upon the ground— where it might pollute the earth or even cry for vengeance : the man appointed to strike, and the man appointed to cut the throat. Then, as the cow is struck, ' the daughters and the daughters-in-law and the august wife of Nestor all shouted aloud.'   It was not a mere cry of sorrow, it was an *ololûgê*, a special religious cry for frightening away evil influences from the stream of ' our brother's ' sacred life.[1]   One would like to know if there was originally something of that in the wail of the Todas.

[1] You uttered an *ololûgê* when any one had a fit, to frighten away the bad *kêr* which had seized him ; in the case of Jason's princess (*Medea*, 1170–7) it proves to be something much worse than a fit, and the *ololûgê* turns into a wail of horror.   For brotherly feeling toward the ox cf. Aelian, *V. H.* 5. 14 ; an old law at Athens says, ' Slay not the ox accustomed to plough or waggon, for this animal shares the labours of man.'   Also Plut. *Solon*, 21 : Solon forbade sacrifice of oxen at funerals.   (Probably for religious rather than sumptuary reasons.)   Cf. Hollis, *The Nandi*, p. 20: ' They [the Nandi tribes] love their beasts, as they say themselves, more than anything in the world : they talk to, pet, and coax them, and their grief is great when a favourite sickens and dies.'   I owe this reference to Mr. W. R. Halliday.— I know of two Papuans who committed a motiveless murder from pure rage and grief at the death of a favourite pig.   There is also a ritual in Papua in which the men kill a boar with clubs : the women wail, and then chase the slayers into a river.

Contrast with this timid, religious, almost tender slaying of the ox, the habitual sacrifices of the *Iliad*—and of those parts of the *Odyssey* where the sacrificer is not in his own land. Compared with Nestor's sacrifice, they seem like the massacres of a slaughter-house, followed by the gorging of pirates. The heroes make merry, 'Slaughtering sheep beyond number and crook-horned swing-footed oxen.' They 'sit all day long even to the setting sun feasting on measureless ox-flesh and sweet strong wine'. The sacrificial terms are there, but are somehow shortened and made brutal. The only people in the *Odyssey* who behave like that are, first, the wicked suitors, who devour Odysseus' flocks ; and secondly, Odysseus' own men when they are acting as pirates, and slaughtering the herds of the Cicones. These exceptions give us the clue. The heroes of the *Iliad* have crossed the sea, and are no longer dealing with their own kindred. The oxen they slaughter in droves are only strangers' oxen, not their own familiar herds. They kill them as light-heartedly as they would kill the strangers themselves. They think no more of the ox as a member of their tribe. The distinction of their hecatombs lies only in the general largeness and expensiveness of the whole proceeding.

It may be objected to my method here, that the difference in question is merely that between peace and war, and is not specially connected with the Migrations. My whole answer to that will come gradually. But it is at least the difference between peace and a prolonged and disorganized state of war in which ordinary wont and use has been forgotten. And that was just the state produced by the Migrations. Of course Homer's picture is in a dozen ways idealized and removed from history. Yet, in the main, the chiefs of the *Iliad*, adventurers who have forced a landing on a foreign shore and live in huts on the beach, year out, year in, supporting themselves by plunder and decimated by pestilences, never quite strong enough to capture the native city, nor weak enough to be finally driven into the sea, are exactly in the normal position of these outcasts of the Migrations. In their minds, as Achilles expresses it, ληϊστοὶ μὲν γάρ τε βόες— 'cattle can be got in raids'. But let us consider the other influences that held these men before the Migrations, and see what became of them afterwards.

First, then, their definite gods.[1]   The Achaeans at one time must have been organized in tribes, or federations of tribes, and a tribe must naturally have a tribal god.   The conception may seem somewhat abstract, because in the Greek pantheon as we know it every personal god has behind him a long and tangled history.   Each has been made up out of very many elements, of diverse origin, attached by historical processes to some one name —or perhaps two names, since so many Greek deities have at least two—and welded eventually into a sort of fictional unity by the devices of the poets.   Even Zeus, the northern patriarchal Sky-god, suffered many modifications: for example, when for purposes of theological harmony he was transformed into the long-lost son of his conquered enemy, ' Pelasgian ' Kronos.   Let us think away these historical complications, and consider what would probably happen to a pre-Hellenic migrant Achaean with regard to his tribal god.   The business of that god was, of course, to fight for and protect his tribe.   His character, and his attributes, so far as he had any, were, for the most part, simply the character and attributes of the tribe.   That is, to the tribesmen themselves he had no noticeable character: he was just what a reasonable god naturally would be.   If they used bows, so presumably did he: but they did not think the matter worth mentioning.   If they were characteristically bards, smiths, seafarers, spearmen, mine-workers, naturally their god presided over all they did. Thus to a stranger coming across the tribe the god would produce a definite impression: he would be a smith, a ruler of the sea, a spearman, a god of mines, a singer.   That is perhaps how, when a federation of tribes was made, there arose departmental gods, with special attributes and almost always special geographical homes: a Lemnian Hephaistos, an Athenian Pallas, an Argive Hera, a Cyprian or Cytherean Aphrodite.

Now, as long as the tribe remained whole, the god of course was with it.   He had his definite dwelling-places: the Pytho or Patara, the Bethel or Mamre, where he could be counted upon to appear.   Even when the tribe moved, he, in a slow and reluctant way, moved with it.   He was present wherever the

[1] Some types of pastoral and agricultural gods and divine kings might be treated here, but the same argument can easily be applied to them. See pp. 135 and 205 ff. below, Lectures V and VIII. Also above, note on p. 49.

tribe was, though on great occasions it might be safer that the chiefs should send embassies back to him, to make sacrifice at some Dodona, some Sinai, some Carmel, where he had for certain been present to their fathers.

But in these sea-migrations the tribe was never whole. The chieftains can still call on their Achaean Zeus, and he hears or rejects their call: but there is a feeling that he is not present as he once was. He has to be called by his old names, with a feeling of the distance that lies between: 'Zeus,' prays Achilles at Troy, 'Lord, thou of Dodona,'[1] thou Pelasgian, dwelling far away.' The titles—whatever 'Pelasgian' may mean—serve the purpose of showing that you really know who he is and belong to him. Our old Thessalian Zeus seated on his throne at Dodona, why should he listen to the crying of strange men in Asia? 'There be very many things between, shadowy mountains and ever-sounding sea.' But each of these words will attract his attention. It is as if Achilles said, 'Zeus, thou who art my own lord, who hast known my fathers at Dodona.'

Zeus did, in a way, move from mountain to mountain, just as the Muses did. The Muses were first at home in Pieria and Olympus, and then moved south to Helicon and Parnassus, doubtless accompanying their worshippers. Zeus was actually established on Mount Ida in front of Troy when Achilles prayed to him as Dodonaean. He had come there with his Phrygians long since. But the Zeus of Mount Ida was the god of Troy, and surely could not accept the prayer of Troy's enemies. There is a painful embarrassment. Zeus of Dodona is opposed to Zeus of Ida. The tribe is divided against itself.[2]

Even in the *Iliad*, amid all its poetical refurbishment of life, there remain these unconscious marks of the breaking up of the Achaeans. But it is clear from those cases which we considered of the various Ionian colonies that the real Greek settlements of the migration consisted of the most miscellaneous gatherings from various tribes, together, I should imagine, with a leaven of broken men, whose tribal belongings were forgotten. Now among such a σύμμεικτον πλῆθος—such a 'mixed multitude' as

---

[1] Ζεῦ ἄνα, Δωδωναῖε, Πελασγικέ, Π 233. Zenodotus, Φηγωναῖε : evidently a good and ancient variant : 'thou of the Oak Tree.'

[2] Cf. above, Lecture II, p. 49, about Zeus, Athena and Apollo.

Strabo phrases it—the influence of the definite tribal gods would be reduced almost to nothing. The common 'Wall' has to supersede them. Partly perhaps from some innate tendency of the mind, but largely also from the force of circumstances, there is a diametric opposition in this matter between Greeks and Jews. The Jews seem to have found their kinsmen in Moab worshipping a tribal god, Chemosh, according to rites practically identical with their own. They, or at least the sacerdotal party which prevailed among them, immediately regarded Chemosh as an enemy and a devil, and where they observed some small difference in the ritual they magnified it and regarded it with loathing. The ordinary Greeks would have said: 'The Moabites call Zeus Chemosh, though some say he is Heracles rather than Zeus.'

Now, when gods are fused or renamed like this, they must needs become less living and definite. For one thing, the taboos or sacred practices change. In Greece itself some people who would have died rather than eat a mouse seem to have mingled with others who felt in the same way about lizards. Their gods were both identified with Apollo.[1] When an avoider of mice found his friend eating mice freely near Apollo's temple and meeting with no condign punishment, he must naturally have been filled with religious anger. For a generation or so the anger may have remained, latent or visible. But eventually, it would seem, a time came when both parties ate what they liked, and both, on the other hand, paid an easy toll to their gods by joining in solemn sacrifices of the taboo animals on suitable days. The religion had come into conflict with the common conveniencies of life, and been beaten.

A tribal god, as we have seen, could move. As long as any fair number of his tribe could keep together, he was present among them. But other objects of worship were not movable. Among the pre-Greek populations the most prevailing and important worship was that of the dead. All Asia Minor is still strewn with the graves of innumerable worthies, whom the course of history has turned into Mahometan Walis or Christian Saints. The old races called them 'Heroes'. They were much the same

---

[1] Apollo Smintheus (A 39): cf. Isaiah lxvi. 17, and the original form of Sauroctonos. On Smintheus see Lang, *Custom and Myth*, pp. 103–20.

as the Roman Lares, ghosts of dead friends and ancestors, duly
laid in the earth and worshipped with a few simple ceremonies
and small regular offerings of food and drink.[1] Good scholars
have written of this worship as if it consisted entirely in the fear
and placation of dangerous ghosts. In later writers, like Plutarch,
there is evidence that points in this direction. But originally and
normally it is clear that this was not the spirit of ancestor-worship.
The ghost of the friend who loved you loves you still, unless you
in some way starve or injure him. The dangerous ghost is the
ghost of a strange kin. This conception certainly affected the
whole of Greece, and was one of the strongest religious bonds
regulating private life. The gigantic tombs of the great kings of
legend, alien and steeped in crime, dominated the imagination of
the mainland right on into the classical period. Both Aegean
and Northerner were bound to their tombs by a thousand
delicate and powerful ties.

But the men of the Migrations had left their fathers' graves
behind them. The ghosts whom they ought to have fed and
cared for were waiting in the old lands helpless, with parched
lips, staring through the dark earth that lay above them.[2] And
in the new lands where now they trod they were surrounded by
strange graves where lay not their own fathers, but the fathers of
the men they had wronged and slain, ghosts who hated them.
All later Greece was full of these unknown graves. They
devised many ceremonies to appease the ghosts. For one thing,
they were honestly frightened. For another, they knew that
their own dead were lying in the same condition, and they
vaguely trusted that perhaps at home also the strangers were
doing well by them. But it is a timid, uncertain honour that they
give. They may at any time be bearing some particular pollution
which specially kindles the dead man's rage. They know not

---

[1] Babrius (second century A. D.?) says definitely (fab. 63) that the gods
are the cause of good, the heroes of evil. Similarly, the still later Sallustius
says that god causes good, and the daemon evil. This becomes the normal
sense of δαίμων in post-Christian writing. But contrast Hesiod, *Erga*,
123 ff., where the Heroes are blessed guardian angels, δαίμονες ἐσθλοί. The
account in Paus. vi. 9. 8 of the mad Cleomedes of Astypalaea illustrates the
sinister kind of hero. For the whole conception compare the Choëphoroe
or the Oedipus Coloneus: the hero lies in the grave charged full of curses
and blessings. Cf. Harrison, *Prolegomena*, p. 9, pp. 326 ff.

[2] Cf., for instance, Eur. *Tro.* 1083 σὺ μὲν φθίμενος ἀλαίνεις, ἄθαπτος ἄνυδρος.

his name, and cannot call him.   He is only the Hero, one of the sainted dead, the εὔφρονες, the χρηστοί.[1]

One thing indeed they could contrive, in rare cases, by the help of their best *arêtêres*, the medicine-men and makers of charms. They could call the soul of their own dead hero from his grave and keep it following their ships to the new settlement, there to enter into an empty tomb which they had made for it.   In this way Phrixus, who had died in Colchis at the farther end of the Black Sea, was brought back to Thessaly.   In this way Melanippus was brought from his ancient grave in Thebes to Sikyon, in the hope that his presence would cause his old enemy Adrastus to move to a new grave further away.[2]   Achilles seems to have changed his grave several times, from Phthia to Skyros, from Skyros to Troy, from Troy to the happy island of Leuce. But there were difficulties in this process.   A people flying from a conquering foe could never carry it out.   And perhaps the practice itself was not very old.   It seems to have needed the help of a doctrine about the soul rather less concrete and material than that of the old Aegean races.   And one doubts whether, when all was done, the ritual always carried conviction.

Very often the tomb of the dead hero had oracular powers. His children in their perplexities could draw upon the wisdom of their great ancestor, as the Persians in Aeschylus' tragedy seek counsel from their dead Darius.[3]   Probably these oracles formed the greatest engine of divine authority in most of the pre-Hellenic tribes.   And, as far as one can make out, an oracle never moved. When a change of population took place, either it was forgotten, as happened often and often; or else it was for some reason spared or partly annexed by the new possessors of the land. Priests of the old race were often left in charge, and the old

---

[1] As to these nameless or unknown 'heroes' the clearest evidence is Diog. Laert. i. 10. 3, 'one finds even now κατὰ τοὺς δήμους τῶν Ἀθηναίων βωμοὺς ἀνωνύμους.'   Perhaps also the frequent anonymous inscriptions—Ἱκέσιος ἥρωι ἀνέθηκε, ἥρωι ὁ ὅρος, &c.   For particular cases cf. Paus. iii. 13. 7 (ἥρως τις), x. 33. 9 (δυνάστης ἀνήρ): in x. 4. 10 the unknown person has become 'either Xanthippus or Phocus'.   So i. 35. 7, 'he is not really Geryon, but only Hyllus!' vi. 6. 7 ff. he is evil, hostile, and nameless, and is at last driven out.   Cf. also i. 43. 3 (Aisymnion at Megara), i. 34. 3, v. 15. 12 (generalizing the dead).

[2] Pind. *Pyth.* iv. 159, cf. Eustath. *Odyssey*, p. 1614 on ἀνάκλησις: Melanippus, Hdt. v. 67.

[3] On Oracles, cf. my *Four Stages*, p. 51 f.

worshippers, when a time of safety came, could make pilgrimages back to it.   Nearly all the oracles of Greece were taken over on terms by the incoming Northmen.   The holy place ἐν Δελφοῖς, among the Delphians, which had once belonged in joint ownership to an Earth-Mother and an underworld serpent, typical of some departed hero, passed over, with or without battle, to the Olympian prophet, Apollo.   Apollo took the oracle of the Abantes at Abae and that of the Carian clan of the Branchidae among the barbarians in the neighbourhood of Miletus.   On the other hand, for some reason or other he left the Lebadean hero, Trophônius, in peace, and the dead man continued to give oracular dreams in the old cave according to the old rites.   But our present concern is with the men of the Migrations.   Whatever happened, they were cut off from their dead.   To those fugitive Abantes, for instance, who helped to settle Chios, it mattered little whether their deserted oracle at Abae still spoke or was silent for ever.   They at any rate had no guidance from it.

Nay : there was something worse.   At times like these of the Migrations it was best not to bury your dead, unless indeed you could be sure of defending their graves.   For you have all of you now done, and are doing, things which must make men hate you as your fathers and grandfathers were never hated in their ordinary intertribal wars.   You are taking from men everything that they live by, their land, homes, wives, cattle, gods, and the graves of their fathers.   And the beaten remnant of those you have wronged, unable to requite in due kind your many murders, are skulking round by night, as you well know, homeless and mad with rage, to do you any chance harm they can.   They may catch some wounded men, some women, or children.   They may sometimes carry off some dead from the field of battle.   At the worst they can dig up some of your fallen comrades from their graves.   And then will be repeated the well-known orgy of helpless, pitiful revenge, the lust of unhappy hate trying in a hundred ways to find its peace.   For however magnificent you may be, you conquering races, you cannot make men broken-hearted with entire impunity.

There is hardly anything in Greek antiquity which is so

surrounded with intense feeling as this matter of the mutilation or dishonouring of the dead.   Throughout all poetry, through the Epos, tragedy, and the historians, it rings, a hushed and vibrating note, telling of something scarce to be spoken, a thing which to see makes men mad.   Scholars are apt to apologize for this earnestness as a peculiarity of ancient feeling which we have a difficulty in understanding.   But I fancy that every one who has come across the reality feels much the same as a Greek did; English soldiers who find their dead comrades mutilated in wars with savages, or the combatants on both sides in the sempiternal strife in the south-east of Europe, where Christian and Moslem still are apt to dishonour infidel corpses.

There was one perfect way of saving your dead from all outrage.   You could burn them into their ultimate dust.[1]   The practice was the less painful to the feelings of the survivors, inasmuch as the Northerners, who were now influential among them, had used it in their old homes, in the forest country from which they came.   For cremation, like the other Homeric custom of roasting meat, is a practice which demands abundance of wood.   But in Greece the other system seems generally to have held its own.   Even at Mycenae, where there were Northerners in possession, the dead are buried, not burned.   And Greek language about the other life is on the whole far more affected by the conceptions dependent on burial.   The dead are always $\chi\theta\acute{o}\nu\iota\iota$, 'people of the earth'; their realm is below.   The ghosts are not thought of as so much $\kappa\nu\acute{\iota}\sigma\eta$, or vapour of burnt flesh.   And the practice of cremation might well have been forgotten entirely had not this special time of unrest revived it.   The grave was no longer safe.   And men burned their comrades

---

[1] Cf. 1 Sam. xxxi. 12, where the men of Jabesh-gilead burn the bodies of Saul and his son, to save them from further outrage by the Philistines. Burning seems to have been strongly against Israelite feeling; many commentators emend the text.   Andrew Lang suggested to me to compare Amos vi. 10 (obscure), Jeremiah xxxiv. 5 (Zedekiah: 'with the burnings of thy fathers'), 2 Chronicles xvi. 14 and xxi. 19 (Asa and Jehoram).   In Scandinavia there is some evidence to show that cremation came in with the cult of Othin.   Othin's dead were burned and their souls went off to Valhall.   In the older belief they were buried or 'howe-laid', and stayed, souls and all, in the howe, and 'exercised a beneficent influence on the fortunes of the family', or defended the grave when it was broken into.   This is curiously similar to the condition in Greece.   See Chadwick, *Cult of Othin*, p. 58.

to save them from dogs, birds, and enemies. Sometimes we find that, instead of burning, they buried them in peculiarly sacred places, or in unknown and secret graves, for the same reason:

> Lest angry men
> Should find their bones and cast them out again
> To evil.[1]

There was another form of worship which might have been expected to persist, or at least quickly to recover itself. Throughout the region that we are concerned with, from Western Greece to the heart of Asia Minor, it seems as if every little community in pre-Hellenic times had worshipped a certain almost uniform type of goddess.[2] An Earth-Mother or Mountain-Mother in the eastern and the pre-Hellenic communities, Mother of fruits and trees and of wild beasts, she is apt to be a Maiden and a Bride as well, and in Greek lands is perhaps best imagined as a *Korê* (Maiden). She is really the Earth as Woman, passing at different times through all the different normal phases of woman's life. Sometimes the intoxication of the east is strong upon her, and, like Babylonian Ishtar, she is in her own person all that woman can be. She is at once virgin, mother, sister, wife and harlot, and her virginity is ever renewed. She rears and nurses the *Kouroi*, or men-children, of the tribe. The tribe itself is her *Kouros*, her child and in the end her husband or lover. When Greek *Sôphrosynê* prevails there is an end, generally, to these dangerous confusions; Mother-Earth is distinguished from her Maiden daughter, and both protect the purity of the home.

As we meet the full-blown deities of classical Greece we find this original Earth-Korê embodied in various types. There is of course the Korê *par excellence*, daughter of Demeter, whose more terrible name Persephonê is seldom spoken. But there are many others. The 'Athenaia Korê' has been transmuted into the Virgin Pallas; her Kouros is an Odysseus or a Perseus, whom she guides towards virtue and wisdom. The Argive

---

[1] Eur. *Med.* 1380.
[2] See J. E. Harrison, *Prolegomena*, pp. 257-322, 'The making of a Goddess': W. M. Ramsay, *Cities and Bishoprics of Phrygia*, i. 87 ff.: Hastings, *Dictionary of the Bible*, extra vol., p. 135 f.: Frazer, *Attis, &c.*, chap. iii, and *Golden Bough*: and A. Evans in *J. H. S.* xxi. pp. 170-80, and *B. S. A.* ix. p. 85 f.

Korê has become Hera, the wife of Zeus: she has now no kouros, though she watches over Jason and others, and perhaps she once had Heracles to train in hard ordeals. Others are merged in virgin Artemis, with her saintly votary Hippolytus; or in the opposite figure of the Cyprian Korê, Aphrodite, with her beloved Adonis. At the back of such figures, in the dim distance, is an old tribal organization, still alive in many parts of the world, called by the general name of Initiations, or sometimes Mysteries.[1] The boys on reaching maturity are taken to the Man's House, learn their dances, pass through their ordeals or 'completions' (τελεταί), and become, by initiation into the Mysteries, full men of the tribe, fit to beget the tribe's children, to plough the tribe's earth, and to stand in war against the tribe's enemies.

The Kouros is as prominent among Greek gods as the Korê among goddesses. Apollo, Ares, Hermes are typical kouroi; in the recently discovered Cretan *Hymn of the Kourêtes* the Megistos Kouros, Greatest of Kouroi, who leads the mystic dance of initiation, is Zeus himself. And of course the same conception has left its mark on most of the heroes. Doubtless in settled conditions, where order and Themis held their own, the ordeals and the teaching that prepared for them had a great influence on character. The Australian and Red Indian evidence proves this, without drawing on the enthusiastic testimony borne by ancient writers to the moral influence of the Mysteries. But when a tribe was broken, flying or fighting for its life, the august rules of Themis must have gone by the board and the moral training become chiefly an apprenticeship in brigandage.

Now, one set of agricultural people driven over seas and taking refuge in the land of another would, as far as one can guess, generally find themselves in the midst of the worship of another Korê so close to their own that they could at once accept her. Yet one must remember, first, that the fugitives were as a rule cut off for some time from agriculture: and secondly, that every Korê was certain to have secret rites and perhaps a secret name to which the strangers would not be admitted. As a matter of fact, there is something to be deduced from the geographical

---

[1] On these *Rites de Passage* see J. E. Harrison, *Themis*, chap. I, 2: my *Four Stages*, chap. I: Webster, *Primitive Secret Societies*: Schurtz, *Altersklassen und Männerbunde.*

names which remained in vogue for the various Korai. If names like Paphia, Cypris, Cytherea, Erycina, &c. persist throughout antiquity, it clearly means that, even when a certain set of Korai were definitely merged under the name of Aphrodite, still Our Lady of Paphos was felt to be different from Our Lady of Cythêra or of Eryx. It is worth while remembering that even at the present day in Spain the people of two neighbouring villages will throw stones at one another's Madonna.[1] Frazer[2] and others have shown how much of the taboos and moral ideals of primitive communities were bound up with the Corn Maiden and her Mother. But all must have been rudely broken and destroyed for the generations of the flight by sea.

In one respect especially this antique worship of the Korê was bound up, if we may believe some of the ablest of modern investigators, with the influences of daily domestic life. We must distinguish two forms of the family in early Greece, which corresponded roughly, though not exactly, with a division of races.[3] The Northerners had, as had been abundantly proved, the regular Aryan organization of the family under the headship of the male. The women and the children were *in manu eius*, under his hand. He had accepted the duty of defending them against danger, and they correspondingly had to obey his will. Relationship was counted through the male side, and the son succeeded to his father's estate. Indeed it is remarked by Isaeus that a mother, though by nature the closest relation a man can have, is not mentioned in the list of degrees of kinship in Attic Law.[4]

---

[1] Cf. the following extract from an account of the eruption of Etna in June 1923 :

'At Piedimonti the population brought out from the church the statue of St. Anthony, their patron saint, and placed it in the central square of the village.

'At Linguaglossa on Tuesday morning the inhabitants took the pastoral staff from the statue of St. Egidius, the patron saint of Linguaglossa, and carried it in a supplicatory procession along the front of the lava. The popular belief is that on a previous occasion the staff of the saint had miraculously stayed the descent of the lava. But the population of Castiglione, when it heard of this procession, became excited and alarmed. The miracle, they thought, might have resulted in diverting the course of the lava from the direction of Linguaglossa to that of Castiglione. Therefore they marched to Linguaglossa, intending to stop the procession. A fight ensued.'

[2] Cf. especially *Psyche's Task*.

[3] Cf. the Auge (Heracles) and Aithra (Theseus) stories, and above, p. 47, note.

[4] Isaeus xi. 17 (μητρὸς ὄνομα) ὃ συγγενέστατον μὲν ἦν τῇ φύσει πάντων, ἐν δὲ ταῖς ἀγχιστείαις ὁμολογουμένως οὐκ ἔστιν.

Monogamy was the rule in Greece, though not among the Trojans.

But this patriarchal system, however defective it may seem to modern critics, and however much it was corrected by the humanity of later Greek Law, was in its day an innovation and a radical reform. Among the pre-Hellenic tribes the mother was the natural centre of the family. She stayed and ruled the household, while men fought and hunted and wandered. One family might easily have different fathers or even uncertain fathers; and when the mother wanted a male protector she turned to her brother, not to one of her mates. The children were directed by their maternal uncle. The property descended from mother to daughter. The sons, we have reason to believe, generally provided them with dowries.

It is curious to read the conflicting enthusiasms felt for and against this 'matriarchal' or 'matrilinear' system by feminists and anti-feminists at the present day. Clearly one of the two systems was suited to one type of society and one to another. But both were families.[1] Both must have possessed that power of trying the temper and training the character in which the family stands unrivalled. An institution in which life becomes unbearable unless people treat each other with pretty constant consideration, and habitually suppress their own more lunatic claims, is clearly of enormous educational value. History seems, up to the present, to have decided in favour of putting the family under the more intellectual and muscular though less sympathetic and affectionate head. And at times such as we are considering, when life was rough and hard, the weaker part of the human race very likely made a good bargain in exchanging freedom for protection. But it is important to remember, when we glibly speak of the higher conception of morals and the purer family life of the patriarchal Aryans, that after all the relation of mother to child is probably, even to our ideas, the deepest, most influential, and, if I may use such a word, the most holy of human relationships. And this relation was not

[1] See especially Tylor in *The Nineteenth Century*, July, 1896: A. B. Cook, *Classical Review*, xx. 7 ('Who was the wife of Zeus?'): Farnell, in *Archiv für Religionswissenschaft*, 1904, vii (severely critical): Frazer, *Kingship*, Lecture VIII. The subject is admirably treated in Vinogradoff's *Historical Jurisprudence*, vol. i. pt. i, *The Elements of the Family*.

only preserved by the older system, but was preserved in a clearer and more authoritative form. The influence of the patriarchate on religion is, of course, overpoweringly great. Protestant and Mahometan countries are entirely dominated by it. Yet if one tries to think for a moment of the vast volume of prayer that is steaming to heaven at any one hour from all the corners of the world, or, shall we say, of Christendom, I wonder if he will find any more intense, more human, more likely to achieve its end, than the supplication which rises from all parts of Southern and Eastern Europe to that most ancient and many-named Madonna, who has sat throned upon her rocks and been a mother of many erring children from thousands of years before the coming of Christianity. And further, if a man, who believes somehow in the reality and ultimate worth of some religion of gentleness or unselfishness, looks through the waste of nature to find support for his faith, it is probably in the phenomena of motherhood that he will find it first and most strikingly. Every living animal preys upon every other: true: yet a mother partridge will fight a dog to save her chickens, and a tigress die in defence of her cubs. The religious system connected with the matriarchal household, based on the relation of mother to child and no other, must be counted, I think, among the great civilizing and elevating influences of mankind.

And, though this point is perhaps taking us too long, ought we not also to consider the extreme beauty of those fragments or elements of the Greek saga in which the young hero is befriended and counselled by a mother or a guardian goddess? Think of Heracles and Athena, Odysseus and Athena, Perseus and Athena, Jason and Hera, Achilles and Thetis. Achilles, we are duly informed, was the son of Peleus. Peleus in himself is a great saga-figure; and it is a fine story how he caught and won his sea-goddess, how she bore his son, and how, being divine, in the end she could not dwell with him, but went back to her blue salt caverns. Yet how little, as a rule, Peleus matters to his son! When Achilles is in grief it is to his mother Thetis that he prays, his mother Thetis that helps him. And few beings even in the *Iliad* have the magic of that sea-spirit, so unearthly and yet so tender.

No. Do not let us condemn too carelessly the home of the

pre-Hellenic peoples which knew of mothers and children, but not much of husbands. Both forms of home must have acted as powerful moral influences in man's life before the time of the migrations by sea, and both equally were destroyed at that time, and their divers ties and tendernesses battered out of existence. 'As for this trouble about Briseis,' says Agamemnon to the envoys, 'tell Achilles that I will give him seven Lesbian women down, and I promise him that, when we take Troy, he can pick out twenty Trojan women—any twenty excluding Helen.' And Briseis herself has not a proper name. The word Briseis is only an adjective derived from the town of Brisa or Brêsa in Lesbos. She is 'the girl from Brêsa'.

So much for the respect for woman which forms a part of the tradition of both forms of home. And what of the father? It is interesting, though not strange, how keenly this question of the treatment of fathers is felt. It was the same in the early Aryan household, and throughout historical Greece. It is the same, I should imagine, in all societies except those in which people, like the rich at the present day, live on incomes derived from accumulated stores of wealth and are consequently far removed from the groundwork of human needs. In all poor or precarious societies there is an assumption that the children owe the parents a definite debt for their food and rearing. The parents fed and protected the child when he was helpless. Now that the old man cannot fight, the son must fight for him : when he cannot work, the son must support him. Yet when men are flying or fighting for their lives, when every weak hand or slow foot brings danger to the whole party, there must have been many old men left by their sons to save themselves as best they might. The conscience of the Greek Saga was stirred on the point. Not without purpose does it tell us how Aeneas in the very flames of Troy, when every delay might mean death, would not move without 'father Anchises', and, when Anchises' strength failed, faced all the dangers of flight amid armed enemies with the old man upon his back. That is what the saga calls 'piety'! It is the other side of Hesiod's complaint, how the men of those days, the generations that came just after the Trojan War, cursed and deserted their old parents.

For there is a passage in Hesiod which reads almost as if it

were a direct description of this period of the Migrations, the
time when all the old sanctions which guided life have been
broken by the stress of a too great trouble.   The passage comes
with an effect of interruption in the midst of the story of the Four
Ages of Man, the Golden, Silver, Bronzen, and Iron.   Four they
must of course have been : but, as the poem now stands, there
comes a curious break after the Bronzen Men.   They are
followed by the Heroes who fought at Thebes and Troy, and
they by the Iron race.   This looks as if the Heroes were a mere
interpolation, and with the Iron Men we returned to the original
story.   But the description of the Iron Men is in a style different
from that of the two earlier races.   The Iron Men are not
creatures of mere idyllic badness.   Through the dimness of the
half-childish story, through the formality of the stiffly poeticized
language, one feels something of the grit of real life.   And it is
a life very like that which we have just been analysing: the
homeless, godless struggle of the last migration.   And it is ascribed to just the same point of history, the Dark Age which
followed μετὰ τὰ Τρωικά, after the fall of Thebes, Troy, and
Mycenae (*Erga*, 156 ff.).[1]

> But when the Earth had covered away this race also, then
> Zeus son of Cronos made yet a fourth upon the land, more
> righteous and valiant: the divine generation of the Heroes,
> which are called half-gods of early times over the boundless
> world.   Bad war and awful battle slew them all ; some at
> Seven-Gated Thebes, the land of the Cadmeans, died
> battling about the flocks of the son of Oedipus : and some
> War took in ships over the great gulf of the sea to Troy-land
> for the sake of fair-haired Helen.   Where verily the end of
> death clouded them round.
>
> And father Zeus, son of Cronos, gave them a life and
> familiar places far away from men, settling them at the ends

---

[1] It is almost impossible to date the subject-matter of a given part of the
Erga.   As we have them, they represent early material, Boeotian, Phocian,
and other, in a late Ionized form.   See on this point Lectures IV and V
below.   The story of the Four Ages is probably of dateless antiquity ; the
addition of the Heroes and the re-shaping of the Iron Men may possibly have
been originally made in Ionia and afterwards taken over into the poetry
of the mainland.   But the passing of the Arnaioi, Minyai, Lapithai, fragments
of Thracians and Phrygians, &c. through Boeotia, would produce equally
well the condition here described ; and it is simplest to suppose that the
whole passage, re-shaping and all, is Boeotian or Phocian.   The Dark Age
affected the whole of Greece.

of the world, far from the immortals, and Cronos is king among them. And there they live with hearts untormented, in the Islands of the Blessed, beside deep eddying ocean, happy Heroes, and the mother of corn bears to them thrice in the year her honey-sweet harvests.

Then the Fifth Men—would that I had never been among them, but either had died before or been born after! For now is a race of iron. And never by day shall they have rest from labour and anguish, nor by night from the spoiler. The gods shall fill them with hard cares. . . . The father no more kind to his children, nor the children to their father, nor the guest true to the host that shelters him, nor comrade to comrade : the brother no more dear to his brother, as in the old days. Parents shall grow old quickly and be despised, and will turn on their children with a noise of bitter words. Woe upon them : and they hear no more the voice of their gods ! They will pay not back to their parents in old age the guerdon of their feeding in childhood. Their righteousness in their fists ! And a man shall sack his brother's walled city.

There shall no more joy be taken in the faithful man nor the righteous nor the good : they shall honour rather the doer of evils and violence. . . .There shall be a spirit of striving among miserable men, a spirit ugly-voiced, glad of evil, with hateful eyes.

A spirit of striving, I have called it : the Greek is ζῆλος, envy, competition, the struggle for life. But observe that the end is not yet ; though all normal sanctions have failed, the men of the Fifth Age have still something to lose :

Then at the last, up to Olympus from the wide-wayed earth, the beautiful faces hidden in white veils, away to the tribe of the immortals, forsaking man, shall depart *Aidôs* and *Nemesis*.[1]

How shall we attempt to translate the beautiful words ? ' Ruth

---

[1] There are interesting imitations of this passage in Eur. *Medea*, 439 ff. : βέβακε δ' ὅρκων χάρις, οὐδ' ἔτ' Αἰδὼς Ἑλλάδι τᾷ μεγάλᾳ μένει, αἰθερία δ' ἀνέπτα. Also in the new (1911) papyrus of the Cynic poet Kerkidas : Ἁμῖν δὲ Παιὰν καὶ μετ' Αἰδὼς ἀγαθὰ μελέτω· θεὸς γὰρ αὖτα καὶ Νέμεσις κατὰ γᾶν. ('Paian' here is the 'Healer' of sick humanity.)—Nemesis appears elsewhere as a form of Artemis and as the Korê of Rhamnûs, and Mr. A. B. Cook makes the very interesting suggestion that Νέμεσις is to νέμος as Λάχεσις to λάχος. Nemesis is thus like the Celtic *Nemetona*, from *nemeton*, a sacred wood, or the Latin *Diana Nemorensis*. Her statue at Rhamnûs had stags in its crown and an apple-branch in its left hand. (Paus. i. 33. 3.) See Appendix D.

and Wrath' might serve. But let that pass for the moment.
The time which the prophet feared never came. Those two
goddesses stayed with man in his loneliest and worst hour, and
provided, if I read the history aright, the most vital force in the
shaping of later Greek ethics and poetry. A full understanding
of the word *Aidôs* would take one very far towards the understanding of all the hopes and creations of the Greek poets.

Αἰδώς is usually translated 'Shame' or 'Sense of Honour',
and *Νέμεσις*, by an awkward though correct phrase, 'Righteous
Indignation.' The great characteristic of both these principles,
as of Honour generally, is that they only come into operation
when a man is free : when there is no compulsion. If you take
people such as these of the Fifth Age, who have broken away
from all their old sanctions, and select among them some strong
and turbulent chief who fears no one, you will first think that
such a man is free to do whatever enters his head. And then,
as a matter of fact, you find that amid his lawlessness there will
crop up some possible action which somehow makes him feel
uncomfortable. If he has done it, he 'rues' the deed and is
haunted by it. If he has not done it, he 'shrinks' from doing it.
And this, not because any one forces him, nor yet because any
particular result will accrue to him afterwards. But simply
because he feels aidôs. No one can tell where the exact point of
honour will arise. When Achilles fought against Eëtion's city,
'he sacked all the happy city of the Cilician men, high-gated
Thêbê, and slew Eëtion : but he spoiled him not of his armour.
He had *aidôs* in his heart for that ; but he burned him there as
he lay in his rich-wrought armour, and heaped a mound above
him. And all around him there grew elm-trees, planted by the
Mountain Spirits, daughters of Aegis-bearing Zeus.'[1] That is
aidôs pure and clean, and the latter lines ring with the peculiar
tenderness of it. Achilles had nothing to gain, nothing to lose.
Nobody would have said a word if he had taken Eëtion's richly-
wrought armour. It would have been quite the natural thing to
do. But he happened to feel aidôs about it.

Aidôs is what you feel about an act of your own : Nemesis is
what you feel for the act of another. Or, most often, it is what

[1] Z 417. The word used is σέβας, not αἰδώς : but in the connexion it comes
to the same.

you imagine that others will feel about you. If you feel disposed
to run away in battle, think of the νέμεσις ἀνθρώπων! People
will put that act to your account. When the elders of Troy look
upon Helen, ' Well,' they say, ' if men fight and die for such
a woman as that, οὐ νέμεσις: none can blame them ' (Γ 156).
Helen herself when she is expected—of course by a goddess:
no human being would be so shameless—to go to Paris and let
him make love to her immediately after he has emerged with
doubtful honour from his battle with Menelaus, refuses roundly:
' I will not go: νεμεσσητὸν δέ κεν εἴη—it would be a thing to
feel nemesis at ' (Γ 410). When Achilles is justly angered with
Agamemnon, at first none can blame him (I 523): but if he
persists after Agamemnon has sued for forgiveness, then there
will be nemesis: people will be indignant. He will know he is
doing wrong. (Observe, of course, that Nemesis does not mean
Retribution.)

Let us follow this spirit of Nemesis for a moment, and then
return afterwards to her still more interesting companion. In the
above instances the nemesis, the ' wrath ' or righteous indignation, has been that of definite witnesses or associates. There are
people who have seen your act, and know. But suppose no
one sees. The act, as you know well, remains νεμεσητόν—
a thing to feel nemesis about: only there is no one there to feel
it. Yet, if you yourself dislike what you have done and feel
aidôs for it, you inevitably are conscious that somebody or something dislikes or disapproves of you. You do not look at the
sun and the earth with peace and friendliness. Now, to an early
Greek, the earth, water, and air were full of living eyes: of theoi,
of daimones, of kêres. To Hesiod and Homer they are ' myriads,
from whom there is no escape nor hiding '. One early poet [1]
says emphatically that the air is so crowded full of them that
there is no room to put in the spike of an ear of corn without
touching one. And it is they who have seen you and are
wroth with you for the thing which you have done!

The word *Nemesis* very soon passes away from the sphere of
definite human blame. Coarser and more concrete words are

---

[1] ἀμφὶ δὲ κῆρες | εἰλεῦνται, κενεὴ δ' εἴσδυσις οὐδ' αἰθέρι, Bergk, *Fr. adesp.* 2 B,
reading ἀθέρι, as is shown to be right by the quotation in Aeneas of Gaza
(p. 399 E).—See J. E. Harrison, *Prolegomena*, p. 170, note.

used for that: ὀνείδεα, ψόγοι. Nemesis is the haunting impalpable wrath of the Earth and Sun, the Air, the Gods, the Dead. Observe, it is not the direct anger of the injured person: it is the blame of the third person who saw.

Now let us be clear about one point. You will sometimes find writers who ought to know better expressing themselves about these matters in a misleading way. They say, or imply, that when a Greek spared an enemy he did not do it from mercifulness or honour as we understand the words, but because it was a part of his religion that Zeus would have a grudge against him and punish him if he did otherwise. This may be true of a given superstitious individual. But as regards the race it is putting the effect for the cause. It was the emotion of the race that first created the religious belief. If the early Greeks believed that Zeus hated the man who wronged a suppliant, that belief was not based on any observed behaviour on the part of Zeus. It was merely that they themselves hated the man who did so, and felt that their god must hate him.

There are, then, certain actions which cause the feelings of aidôs and nemesis, of shame or ruth, when a man thinks of doing them himself, of righteous indignation when he sees them done by others. Let us notice more closely what these actions generally are. How far, for instance, do they coincide with the objects of our own, or the mediaeval, feeling of 'honour'? First and most obvious, there are the actions that imply cowardice: they bring the simplest and crudest shame : ' Aidôs, O ye Argives, will ye not stand?' 'Put in your hearts aidôs and nemesis, . . . I would not rail against one that was a weakling, for holding back in battle : but you are chieftains ! . . . I have nemesis against you in my heart' (N 95 ff.).

Secondly, actions that imply falseness : lying and perjury. I doubt if the word ever occurs in this sense in Homer, but that is because questions of false swearing never arise among Homeric heroes. The false stories told by Odysseus in the *Odyssey* are merely ruses of war. The treason of Pandaros is something which that unfortunate person might have felt shame for had he lived. The poet himself seems a little ashamed of mentioning such behaviour on the part of a hero, even a hostile hero, and arranges as usual to lay the real guilt upon a god. Homeric

heroes do not need the aidôs which prevents or 'rues' falseness.
But it is common enough in Hesiod and Theognis and in tragedy.

Thirdly, actions that imply what we may loosely term impudence or lack of reverence. The cases are few: Helen's words
above quoted are in point. So no doubt would be the boldness
of Niobê in boasting herself against the goddess Leto (Ω 602 ff.),
or the impudence of Thersites in the second book of the *Iliad*.

All these might be included as objects of any current conception of 'Honour': but there is a fourth sense, by far the most
widespread and significant, which reaches a good deal beyond
the ordinary mediaeval ideal. It is the horror of cruelty or
treachery towards the helpless. Any sympathetic reader of
early Greek poetry will have noticed the importance, or indeed
the sanctity, attached to three classes of human beings: strangers,
suppliants, and old people. What is there in common between
the three? Nothing, I think, but their helplessness. Realize
what a stranger is, in a primitive society. He is a man with no
home, no friends, no one to protect him from injury, no one to
avenge him afterwards. He has not even his own sanctuaries to
shelter him, or his own tribal god. And again, a suppliant:
a suppliant is any man or woman who formally casts away all
means of self-defence and throws himself upon your mercy.
That is the essential thing; though of course, when he could, the
helpless man tried to influence your feelings in divers other
ways. He associated himself with something that you held
sacred. He sat on the steps of an altar: he touched some sacred
object: he lay on your door-step and threatened to starve unless
you took him in; he contrived with his hand to touch your face
or your beard. But those are all accessories. The essential is
confessed helplessness. And all their literature shows what
horror the early Greeks felt at the notion of definitely and
formally rejecting a prayer made by the helpless, a horror sometimes amounting to what we should call moral weakness. They
expressed this generally in theological language. 'The stranger
and the suppliant come from Zeus.' 'Zeus is the watcher of
stranger and suppliant' (ι 270); 'The very Thunderer follows
the αἰδοῖος ἱκέτης' (η 165, 181); his own titles are Ἱκετήσιος
and Ξείνιος and even Ἀφίκτωρ.[1]

---

[1] On Ζεὺς Ἀφίκτωρ, see Lecture XI, p. 275.

And thirdly, old people. Here there enters in, no doubt, some element of the patriarchal sanctity of a father; but I think that the helplessness of age is again the main reason for an old man or woman being αἰδοῖος. That explains why they are, like beggars, strangers, suppliants, especially under the guardianship of the gods, and in particular of Zeus. It explains why the older they are the more is their claim on Aidôs: why the blind are classed with them.[1] It may be objected that, if helplessness is the criterion, children also would be αἰδοῖοι. The answer is interesting. Ordinary children are not specially αἰδοῖοι, or charged with sanctity, because they have their grown-up relations to protect them. But orphan children are.

There are some five deadly sins, says Hesiod in the *Erga*, of which you cannot say that one is worse than another. They are all beyond the pale (*Erga*, 327 ff.):

It is all as one thing—the man who does evil to a suppliant and to a stranger; the man who goeth into his brother's bed; the man who in heartlessness sins against orphan children; the man who reviles his old father on the bitter threshold of age, laying hold of him with hurting words: with that man Zeus himself is wroth.

These sins consist of four offences against the helpless and one breach of a fundamental family *taboo*. All adultery was a most grave offence. But if this particular form of it is chosen as the worst, that is the doing of Aidôs. Your brother trusts you, and is often at your mercy. That is what makes him sacred.

For apart from any question of wrong acts done to them, there are certain classes of people more αἰδοῖοι, objects of aidôs, than others. There are people in whose presence a man feels shame, self-consciousness, awe, a sense keener than usual of the importance of behaving well. And what sort of people chiefly excite this aidôs? Of course there are kings, elders and sages, princes and ambassadors: αἰδοῖοι βασιλῆες, γέροντες, and the like: all of them people for whom you naturally feel reverence, and whose good or bad opinion is important in the world. Yet,

---

[1] Cf. Soph. *O. T.* 374-7, where commentators, from not seeing this point, have altered the text. *Oed.* 'Thou art a child of unbroken night, so that neither I nor any other who sees the light would (ἂν) ever harm thee.' *Tir.* 'It is not my doom to fall by thy hand,' &c. So MSS., and cf. 448 below, where Tiresias repeats the same statement.

if you notice the language of early Greek poetry, you will find
that it is not these people, but quite others, who are most deeply
charged, as it were, with aidôs; before whom you feel still more
keenly conscious of your unworthiness, and whose good or ill
opinion weighs somehow inexplicably more in the last account.
The disinherited of the earth, the injured, the helpless, and
among them the most utterly helpless of all, the dead.[1] All
these, the dead, the stranger, the beggar, the orphan, the merely
unhappy, are from the outset αἰδοῖοι, 'charged with αἰδώς.'
Wrong them, and they become, *ipso facto* and without any word
of their own, ἀραῖοι or προστρόπαιοι, incarnate curses, things
charged with the wrath of God.[2]

The feeling seems to have been very strong. One must bring
it into connexion with the various stories of gods who were disguised as beggars, and went through the world ill or well entreated
by different men according to their different natures. It is the
counterpart of what we, in our modern and scientific prose, call
'a sense of social responsibility' or the like; the feeling roused
more or less in most people by the existence of great misery in
our wealthy societies. To the Greek poet it was not scientific,
and it was not prose. It was an emotion, the keener because it
was merely instinctive and was felt by a peculiarly sensitive people;
an emotion of shame and awe, and perhaps something like guilt,
in meeting the eyes of the oppressed of the earth; a feeling that

[1] 'Do you feel aidôs for the dead body of one that hated you?' the wise
Odysseus is asked in the *Ajax*; 'His goodness is more to me than his hate'
is the answer, an answer full of aidôs (*Ajax*, 1357). 'The stranger and the
beggar are charged with aidôs,' says Eumaeus in the *Odyssey*, and the
adjective αἰδοῖος is a regular epithet of a stranger. But mere unhappiness
is enough: 'A miserable man must needs rouse aidôs in you,' says Oedipus
(*O. C.* 247).

[2] Προστρόπαιος is not *'turning oneself towards'*, as L. and S. say: it is
the adjective from προστροπή which is the opposite of ἀποτροπή, 'aversion.'
As you can by sacrifice, &c., try to 'avert' the δαίμονας so you can 'bring
them upon' somebody. Thus an injured suppliant has a power of προστροπή:
he *brings down the gods upon* his injurer. A criminal brings them down on
himself and those who are infected by his ἄγος. These words are very often
misunderstood; e.g. the φθόγγον ἀραῖον οἴκοις of Iphigenia (*Ag.* 237) was not
a spoken curse—which would make the passage hideous—but the mere
crying of a murdered daughter, which necessarily involves an ἀρά. So when
Philoctetes charges Neoptolemus to look him in the face: τὸν προστρόπαιον,
τὸν ἱκέτην, ὦ σχέτλιε; he means: 'Me, charged with the wrath of God; me,
who kneel before thee, O hard heart' (*Phil.* 930).—I do not mean to deny
that you can say in Greek τραπέσθαι ἐπὶ or πρὸς ἑστίαν. Aesch. *Cho.* 1038,
Eum. 205.

a wrong done to these men is like no other wrong; that what these men report of you ultimately in the ear of Zeus will outweigh all the acute comments of the world and the gratifying reports of your official superiors.[1]

If you look into the history of later Greek Ethics, it is rather a surprise to find how small a place is occupied by Aidôs. Even to Plato and Aristotle it has become little more than an amiable quality, the absence of which is particularly repulsive. It has quite ceased to be the guiding force of men's moral life. These two philosophers, of course, belong to a particular school: they are aristocratic and intellectual; both perhaps too much inclined to despise those emotions which appeal to man's simplest instincts and have a touch of the animal in them. If we possessed any complete books by the more democratic and less authoritarian philosophers, by Protagoras especially and Democritus, our impression might be different. Among the philosophers of the Roman period Aidôs has quite faded away. It plays no part in Epictetus. It is barely mentioned by Sextus Empiricus. Only Kerkidas the Cynic, rejector of all organization and system and convention, falls back to primitive feelings and asks that life shall be guided by Paian—the Healer—and Aidôs. One can see the reason for this; indeed, the many reasons.

For one thing, Aidôs is a mere emotion, and therefore incalculable, arbitrary, devoid of principle. A man may happen not to feel the emotion, and then you have nothing to appeal to. Or again, if he has the emotion, there is no way of judging its strength. An emotion which is made the whole moving principle of conduct grows with what it feeds upon: it is never sated: it moves towards

---

[1] I have sometimes wondered how it happens that slaves are never spoken of as charged with *aidôs*. A particular slave may be treated with *aidôs*. He may be protected and helped because he is a stranger or a beggar. But the word is not regularly applied to a slave. I think the reason is, as Euripides says, 'Why speak of ruth where ruthlessness is the law?' The whole institution was a negation of Aidôs; a refusal to listen to the emotion in question. If you made a man your slave, that showed you did not regard him with aidôs. So the less said about it the better. As the Ocean Spirits in the *Prometheus* tell us—with a different meaning—the clank of the riveting of a prisoner's fetters frightens Aidôs away (*Prom.* 134). Of course a wrong done to a slave was hated by the gods and, one might hope, duly avenged. But that was the same with animals. Εἰσὶ καὶ κυνῶν ἐρινύες—there is vengeance in heaven for an injured dog. On the ramifications and possible origin of Αἰδώς, Δίκη, Ὅρκος, &c., see Appendix D.

the infinite. That way madness lies, as the lives of so many of the saints have shown us. Besides, behind any morality based upon emotion there is the question whether you ought or ought not in a particular case to feel the emotion : and if not, why not ? It is there that the real principle of Ethics comes in. The later philosophers wanted to understand, not merely to feel. They had to build up conduct into a consistent rational system. It would help them little if men said, ' Follow the leading of Aidôs,' ' Love your neighbour,' ' Pity humanity.' Such rules will help the conduct of men. But they do not provide an answer to a speculative problem. Perhaps the main thing which the philosophers got from Aidôs was Aristotle's doctrine of the Mean : the observation that in any emotion or any movement there is a possible best point, which you should strive to attain and shrink from passing. A great liberating doctrine, no doubt ; but one with the emotion all gone from it. That was what served Aristotle's purpose best.

Again, there is an historical reason for the decline in the importance of Aidôs. Aidôs, like Honour, is essentially the virtue of a wild and ill-governed society, where there is not much effective regulation of men's actions by the law. It is essentially the thing that is left when all other sanctions fail ; the last of the immortals to leave a distracted world. In an ordered society there are all the more concrete sanctions to appeal to—the police, the law, organized public opinion.

In a well-organized society the great majority of men are under compulsion to behave better than they naturally would, if left to themselves. It often strikes me, in certain parts of early Greek poetry, that one gets a glimpse of a society in which, by the breaking up of ordered life, men were compelled to be worse than nature intended ; where good and merciful men had to do things which they hated afterwards to remember. One may recall the character in Herodotus,[1] who wished to be the most righteous man in the world, but was not permitted by circumstances. As a rule in fiction (where motives of flattery cannot come into play) rich men are wicked. It is obviously more interesting, as well as more gratifying to the reader's feelings, to make them so. But in Homer the rich men are apt to be specially virtuous ; ἀφνειὸς ἀμύμων, 'rich and blameless' (E 9). One is reminded of the

---

[1] Herodotus, iii. 142.

naïve desire of the old poet Phokylides, first to acquire a competence and then to practise virtue. The project is amusing to us, as it was to Plato. We know so much of the result of that scheme of life. Yet think of that son of Teuthras in the *Iliad*, who 'dwelt behind the strong walls of Arisbê, rich in all livelihood, and was beloved of men. For he built his dwelling by the roadside and showed love to all who passed.'[1] One might almost think that, like Phokylides, he had made some resolution to 'practise virtue' in this way, feeding the hungry and washing the feet of strangers. But, in any case, it is easy to imagine how, in a time like that of the Migrations, a decent man who had passed through the horrid necessities of the struggle for bare life, and was at last safe and prosperous with a strong wall around him, would become just like these rich men in Homer, thankful to live at last blameless and gentle towards gods and men.

The suggestion is little more than a fancy. But it occurs to me in connexion with another. When we compare the civilization and character of Greece and of Rome, we are struck, among many other differences, with some broad general divergence. The Roman seems to have all the faults and the virtues of successful men. He is severe, strong, well-disciplined, trustworthy, self-confident, self-righteous, unimaginative, a heavy feeder, a lover of gladiatorial games. The Greek, less gregarious, less to be relied upon, more swept by impulse; now dying heroically for lost causes; now, at the very edge of heroism, swept by panic and escaping with disgrace; capable of bitter hatreds and massacres in hot blood, of passionate desires and occasional orgies; but instinctively hating cruelty, revolting from the Roman shows, frugal, simple and hardy to a degree which we can with difficulty realize: above all, possessed of an unusual power of seeing beyond himself and of understanding his enemies; caring for intellect, imagination, freedom, beauty, more than for force and organization, crying aloud for orderliness and symmetry, in part from mere artistic sense, in part because he knew his own needs and dangers; much as Plato prayed to be delivered from poetry because poetry was to him a seducing fire. The causes of such a difference are innumerable. There may have been a greater proportion of pre-Aryan elements in Greek civilization.

[1] Z 15.

There were important geographical differences. But one cause, I think, is the early experience of the Greek race during the great sea-migrations. The Romans had an almost steady history of stern discipline, of conquest and well-earned success: the Greeks at the beginning of their history passed through the very fires of hell. They knew, what Rome as a whole did not know, the inward meaning and the reverse side of glory. They knew the bitterness of lost battles, the sting of the master's lash; they knew self-judgement and self-contempt, amazement and despair. They had their triumphs and conquests. They must, I suppose, be counted, even politically, among the most successful races of mankind. But in their highest successes, in the times both of Pericles and of Alexander, there is always something daring and precarious. Their armies are always fighting against odds; their little cities trying by sheer energy and intellect to stem the strength of great military empires. It is a wondrous fabric held together for an hour by some splendid grasp of human genius, not one based on strong material foundations by the gregarious and half-conscious efforts of average men. They began their life as a people, it would seem, in a world where palaces and temples were shattered, armies overthrown, laws and familiar gods brought to oblivion. Perforce they questioned and they wondered. It is not for nothing that Greece produced Heraclitus and Plato, thinking that all things pass like a stream and that the idea is the only abiding reality. Thus, like the prophet in Callimachus' great poem, they saw early the world that is behind the ordinary world of human strivings, more real and more intangible; and throughout their history somehow this ideal haunted the race, a vision perturbing their sight, unfitting them for continued empire, yet shedding strangely over their defeat a splendour denied to their conquerors.[1]

---

[1] Call. *Lavacra Palladis* 87 τέκνον ἄλαστε, | εἶδες Ἀθαναίας στάθεα καὶ λαγόνας, | ἀλλ' οὐκ ἀέλιον πάλιν ὄψεαι.

IV

AN ANCIENT TRADITIONAL BOOK

So far we have been considering the people: I wish now to turn to the literature. For one of the clearest facts that we know about these driven fragments of society who form the soil from which Hellenism sprang is that they must have had a literature. The vast store of prehistoric tradition preserved in the Greek heroic saga is evidence enough. The Northerners can scarcely have known the art of writing before some few of them learned it in Greece. But it is quite conceivable that in very early times they possessed epic lays, and that these lays were in dactylic verse. So much we can conclude from various formulae imbedded in the Homeric language. On the other side, the Cretan script, coming on the top of other evidence which was already sufficient, shows that long before the Migrations there were scribes and 'wise men' in the Aegean who had the power of writing.

I am not proposing to discuss the Homeric Question, but rather to put forward some general considerations preliminary to the Homeric Question. If the men of the Migrations possessed a literature, that literature was not in the least what we mean by ' Homer ', viz. the *Iliad* and the *Odyssey*. It was not even what the Greeks of the sixth and early fifth centuries meant by ' Homer ', viz. the whole body of heroic tradition as embodied in hexameter verse.[1] It must really have been something far more primitive and less differentiated, of which the didactic epos, the lists of ancestors, the Stesichorean lyrics, the local chronicles, the theological, magical, and philosophical writings, as well as the heroic poems, are so many specialized developments. It has long been clear to students of early Greece that the *Iliad* and *Odyssey* are not primitive poems. Not only their art and construction, but

---

[1] See Wilamowitz, *Homerische Untersuchungen*, pp. 329–80.

their whole outlook on the world and the gods is far removed
from that of the most primitive Greeks known to us. Both
poems, indeed, contain a great deal of extremely ancient matter:
but both, as they stand, are the products of a civilized age and a
long process of development. It is the beginnings of literature
that we are now considering.

Let us begin by trying to imagine the position and practice in
an early society, say in Ionia before Thales, or on the mainland
before Solon, of what the Greeks generally described as a λόγιος
ἀνήρ, or 'man of words'.[1] I say 'words' because I despair of
an adequate translation of *Logoi*. The conception *Logos*, 'word'
or 'speech', had, as we all know, a peculiarly distinguished
history among the Greeks. It was the word spoken: it was the
power of language; it was the word which implies reason,
persuasion, interpretation, and which settles differences instead
of the armed hand; it was thus the word which mediates between
the soul of man and man, or, in theological language, between
man and God; to the philosopher it was the silent but eternal
word upon the lips of Nature, the speech by which the Cosmos
expressed its inborn reason. But for our present purpose it is
another aspect of the Logos that comes into play. The *Logios
Anêr*, or Man of Words, was the man who possessed the Things
Said, or traditions, which made up the main sum of man's
knowledge. He knew what Logoi really existed, and what were
mere inventions or mistakes. He could say λόγος ἐστίν,[2] much
as a Hebrew could say 'It is written'. This implies, what is of
course the case, that Greek saga was mainly preserved by oral
tradition.[3] Yet it would be rash to assume that there were no
writings. The extant Cretan records are far earlier than any
possible Homer. The ancients themselves tell stories of the
'books' of the early minstrels. The use of MSS. by the
composers of our *Iliad* and *Odyssey* seems almost as certain as

[1] See also Prof. Butcher's Lecture on 'The Written and the Spoken Word'
in *Some Aspects of the Greek Genius*.
[2] Ar. *Frogs*, 1052: 'What I said about Phaedra, was it not an ὦν λόγος?'
[3] I see that Drerup has mistaken my meaning, *Omero*, p. 68, note. I
discuss the books because they are there to discuss; the oral tradition in each
case was more important, as I explain, but it has vanished. The MSS. of
the *Roland* still exist, but no one living can hear 'Thorold' or Taillefer
improvising. See the excellent remarks of F. Bölte on *Rhapsodische Vor-
tragskunst* in *Neue Jahrbücher*, 1907, I. Abt. xix. 8.

such things can be, and, though those composers themselves belong to a much later date, the fragments of minute and, we may add, uninteresting history preserved in the epic suggest the use of some surer and more positive method than mere oral tradition. The Man of Words, we may assume, would in many cases not trust entirely to his memory, but would make a permanent Logos of his own in the shape of a book.[1]

A book in those days was not what it is now. It was not a thing to be given to the public, not a thing to be read for pleasure.[2] One can find parallels in the East or in the Middle Ages. There was the great book of Michael Scott, the magician, which was read by no man but one, and was buried in its master's grave. There was the book of Thoth, carried off by Nefrekepta; the Book of Catyllus, reported by the Spanish Mandeville.[3] There is the great list of Arabic chronicles, the rule of which is that each chronicle was the property of the author or of his heir, and could not be read by others without his permission. There are the innumerable and

---

[1] Mr. Lang suggested to me the comparison of the Gaelic 'sennachie': 'sean' = old; 'seanachas' = story, tradition; 'seanachaidh' (pronounced 'shen-ach-ay') = a man of tales, historian. It seems quite clear that the sennachies could not read or write.

[2] All through antiquity a book remained a thing to be recited from, or to be read aloud to an audience by a skilled person. It is partly due to facts like this that the oral repetition of stories continued so extremely late in human history to be the normal way of keeping alive the records of the past, even if the past was vitally important. In the case of the Gospels, for instance, where a modern would have considered it of absolutely overwhelming importance to have a written record as soon as possible of the exact deeds and sayings of the Master, we find, as a matter of fact, that it was left for a considerable time to oral tradition. Compare the well-known phrase of Papias (died c. A. D. 135), deliberately preferring a third-hand oral report to the written word:—

'Whenever any person came my way, who had been a follower of the Elders, I would inquire about the discourses of those elders, what was said by Andrew or by Peter or by Philip or by Thomas or James, or by John or Matthew or any other of the Lord's disciples, or what Aristion and the Elder John, disciples of the Lord, said. For I did not think I could get so much profit from the contents of books as from the utterings of a living and abiding voice.' (I cite from Estlin Carpenter's *First Three Gospels*, p. 4.)

In the time of Papias there were libraries with books by the hundred thousand, yet a book is still to him a dead and troublesome mode of communication. He is said to have been rather a stupid man, πάνυ σμικρὸς τὸν νοῦν. But a thousand years earlier than Papias this attitude of mind was the normal one.

[3] Griffith's *Stories of the High Priests of Memphis*; Spanish Mandeville, fol. 1376. (I owe this reference to Mr. W. R. Halliday.)

constantly varying MSS. of stories like the *Arabian Nights*, each copy originally meant to be the private stock-in-trade of a professional story-teller. In all these cases the man lived by his book. It must be kept from the public; above all, it must be kept from the eyes of professional rivals. It can be given or bequeathed to a son or a favourite disciple, as in the Greek story one of Homer's scrolls, the 'Cypria', served as his daughter's dowry, another, the 'Taking of Oechalia', was left to his heir, Creophylus.[1] For the ancient Man of Words was not exactly a story-teller, not exactly a chronicler, not exactly a magician. He was all three, and something more also. His Logos contained, with no distinction of subject, all that he specially wanted not to forget, or, at least, all that was worth the immense trouble of writing down, letter by letter.

There was an ancient Greek tradition, superseded in general by the Cadmus story, which somehow connected the invention of writing with Orpheus and the Muses. Orpheus' voice seems to have recorded itself in books in some mysterious way.[2] And the Greek bards always owe, not only what we should call their inspiration, but their actual knowledge of facts to the Muses. The Muses 'are present and know all things'. They are, to Hesiod at least, 'the daughters of Memory.'[3] Hesiod professes, roughly speaking, to be able to sing about everything; but he always explains that he is dependent on the Muses for his knowledge. Other sources of knowledge are indeed recognized. When giving the names of all the rivers in the world, Hesiod stops at a certain point and says that for the names of the rest you had better consult the people who live on their banks, and they will be able to tell you (*Theog.* 370). But most often he consults the Muses (*Theog.* 1 ff., 105 ff., 966, 1022, Catalogues). So does Homer for such subjects as the Catalogue of the Greek army (cf. α 7, B 486, 761, cf. M 176). One suspects that that consultation was often

---

[1] Cf. the case of Jendeus de Brie, author of the *Bataille Loquifer*, cent. xii: he 'wrote the poem, kept it carefully, taught it to no man, and made much gain out of it in Sicily where he sojourned, and left it to his son when he died'. Similar statements are made about Huon de Villeneuve, who would not part from his poem for horses or furs or for any price, and about other poets.—Gautier's *Épopées Françaises*, vol. i, p. 215, note 1, cited in Lang, *Homer and his Age*.

[2] Θρήσσαις ἐν σανίσιν, τὰς | Ὀρφεία κατέγραψεν | γῆρυς, Eur. *Alc.* 967-9.

[3] *Theogony*, 54, 916: for subjects, 100–15.

carried out by the bard retiring to some lonely place, or maybe barricading the door of his hut, bringing forth a precious roll, and laboriously spelling out the difficult letter-marks. Γράμματα, the Greeks called them, or 'scratches'. And right on in mid-classical and later times the name for a scholar was 'grammatikos'. He was a 'man of *grammata*',[1] one who could deal with these strange 'scratches' and read them aloud, knowing where one word ended and another began, and when to make big pauses and little pauses. For things like that were not indicated in the *grammata*.

You will have noticed that a wise man in antiquity—and the same is true of the Middle Ages—generally has a boy or disciple attached to him. And the first thing which that disciple learns when he begins to be 'wise' himself is to read in his master's book. Not in any book, mark you. They did not learn reading in that way. You were not expected to understand the *grammata* unless they were first read aloud to you. The case is clearest with Semitic books, where the vowels are not written at all, and in some cases the meaning cannot possibly be made out for certain without help from the writer of the book. But it was the same in the Middle Ages: with Michael Scott's book, for instance. It was the same with various of the old Sanskrit books, the meaning of which has in some places been absolutely lost because there was a breach in the series of disciples to whom the meaning was orally explained by the master. The thing that most tangibly constituted a disciple was the power to handle, or to read in, his master's book. Of course a very clever man would, if you gave him time, be able eventually to make out other books too. But that would be a special undertaking.

This limitation, if you think of it, is inevitable. In the first place there will probably be no other books in the neighbourhood on which to practise. Then further, it must be remembered that, as the man's book is a private thing, so also is his method of making signs. Handwritings always differ; and the handwriting of a man who practically never saw any other person's handwriting and who used his own merely to make notes for his own private use, not to be read by others, would be sure—even apart from

---

[1] See Rutherford's *Scholia Aristophanica* vol. iii. chap. i, and my *Religio Grammatici*.

the writer's own conscious wish for secrecy—to grow in a hundred little ways specialized and abnormal. I have seen an Arabic book which professes to give the special alphabets[1] used by the ancient sages, Cleomenes, Plato, Pythagoras, Scalinus, Socrates, and Aristotle, all of them different, 'in order that none should know them but the sons of wisdom.'

Consider, then, the position of a man who possesses such a book, and also can make *grammata* himself. Suppose he hears news of strange events which he would like to record accurately. Suppose he is lucky enough to hear another wise man expounding new lore, or giving details on a subject where his own book is vague. Suppose he finds, or borrows, or inherits from a wise relation—wisdom runs in families—another book containing valuable information. In all these cases he will want to make additions and changes in his own book. Let us consider how he is likely to set about it.

It is a difficult process to conflate two or more accounts of a transaction into one, difficult even for a modern writer, with all the battery of modern appliances at his command; clear print, numbered pages, indices to show you just where and how often a subject is mentioned, paragraphs and chapters, divisions of words and sentences, and abundance of cheap paper for making notes and rough copies. Our ancient sage had his book written on very expensive material, usually the skins of beasts carefully prepared. He could not lightly throw away a scroll and write it again. He had no facilities for finding references; no index, no pages, no chapters, no stops between sentences, no divisions of any sort between one word and another; only one long un-divided mass of *grammata*, not by their nature well calculated to be legible. On the other hand, he probably knew his own book by heart. It was an advantage which sometimes betrayed him.

What he generally did was to add the new matter crudely at the end of the old. He could write on the margin or between the

---

[1] *Ancient Alphabets*, by Ahmad bin Abubekr bin Wahshih, translated by Joseph Hammer, London, 1806. 'Every one of these kings invented, according to his own genius and understanding, a particular alphabet in order that none should know them but the sons of wisdom' (p. 14). Are the 'sons of wisdom' the disciples of the wise? The book is said to have been written An. Heg. 241. It is concerned with alchemy.

lines. At a pinch, he might cut the hide with a knife and sew in a new strip at a particular place. He had only to make the roll intelligible to himself. And any one who has had experience of the difference between a MS. fit to be sent to the printer and a MS. that will do to lecture from will appreciate what that means.

No book has come down to us from antiquity exactly in this state. All the books that we possess have at some time been published, and therefore prepared in some sense to be intelligible to the reader. But many Greek books retain clear marks of the time when they were not meant to be read by strangers, but only to serve the professional needs of the writer. The later Homeric hymns, containing merely a number of suitable openings and closes for recitations, point pretty clearly to the handbook of the professional reciter. The voluminous writings of the Peripatetic school which come to us under the name of Aristotle bear innumerable traces of their composition for private use in the school. So do the remains of Hesiod; so do, as far as I know them, most of the late magical writings. In oriental literatures the instances are, I believe, even clearer.[1]

In imagining the proceedings of this old sage we have taken one particular crisis, as it were, in the history of his book. But all the ancient traditional books which have come down to us have, without exception, passed through many such crises. The book which contained the whole Logos of the wise man was apt to be long-lived. It was precious; it had been very difficult to write; it was made of expensive and durable materials. It

---

[1] Peculiarly instructive is the record of the first writing down of the text of the Koran. Islam, being historically a late religion, has its origins exceptionally well attested. Zaid Ibn Thabit was entrusted by Abu-Bakr, the first Caliph, with the task of collecting the Prophet's revelations—Surahs— preserved in part only in the breasts of the faithful. He made one official copy for the Caliph, being guided by his general knowledge of the credibility of his witnesses. As the informants naturally varied in dialect, a question arose as to the genuine dialect in which the revelations came; this was determined to be Korashite. The third Caliph made a public edition, thus really establishing the Koran. Unofficial copies proved to be in existence. These were all destroyed, and official copies sent out to the chief towns. The same editor was employed for this work of publishing, perhaps because only he could read the first edition with any certainty. The official copies were, after all, not much more than *memoriae technicae*. One who had read the text with a teacher could afterwards recall what he had read thereby; one who saw the text for the first time would be confronted by an enigma.— I take this from Prof. Margoliouth's *Mohammedanism*, chap. ii.

became an heirloom: and with each successive owner, with each successive great event in the history of the tribe or the community, the book was changed, expanded, and expurgated. For the most jealously guarded book had, of course, its relation to the public. It was not meant to read; it was meant to recite from. The Logos only came into full existence when spoken to an audience, and obviously it had to suit that audience. It was the source of stories and lays which must needs be interesting; of oracles and charms and moral injunctions which must not seem ridiculous or immoral; of statements in history and geography which had better not be demonstrably false. The Logos must needs grow as its people grew. As it became a part of the people's tradition, a thing handed down from antiquity and half sacred, it had a great normal claim on each new generation of hearers. They were ready to accept it with admiration, with reverence, with enjoyment, provided only that it continued to make some sort of tolerable terms with their tastes, under which general head we must include their consciences and their common sense.

I am tempted to take instances from our own times to illustrate what I mean by a traditional book. The most obvious of our traditional books are collections of mere information like *Whitaker's Almanack* and the *Statesman's Yearbook*, or those strange prophetic Almanacs and magic Herbals which continue, I suppose, to enjoy a flourishing though subterranean existence in all European nations. Or we might take the various Guides to Navigation published by various countries. The Pilot series, issued by the British Admiralty, seems now to hold the field; but M. Victor Bérard[1] has traced its origin step by step from a remote past, through French, Italian, Dutch, Spanish, Latin, Greek, and perhaps Phoenician sources. An historical lawyer, again, could show the same process of traditional growth in various legal codes. Such literature reminds one much of the Catalogues of Hesiod.

But the best modern instance of a traditional λόγος is provided by stage plays. A play which lives beyond a century or so regularly consists of (1) a slowly changing book to guarantee its potential existence and (2) a series of frequently changing

---

[1] *Les Phéniciens et l'Odyssée,* i. p. 52.

performances before an audience to bring it to fullness of life. The best parallels to an ancient lay, of course, would be those plays which are not printed, but exist only in the prompt-books and the actors' memories.   Unfortunately, under modern conditions, it is almost impossible for a successful play to live long without getting printed.   And the printed book with its hundreds or thousands of identical copies produces a terrible fixity of text. The traditional Mummers' Play, having had no authoritative text, has almost perished of degradation.   But one would like to have records of the variations of *George Barnwell* or *The Stranger* between their first production and the times when Thackeray saw them; or even of plays like *East Lynne* and *The Private Secretary*, which are acted all over the English-speaking world at the present day.   But let us take at once the most august example.

Hamlet, as every one knows, long before it was an English play was an ancient Scandinavian story, not invented by any one, but just living, and, doubtless, from time to time growing and decaying, in oral tradition.   The first mention of it is in a song composed about the year 980; the first complete version is in Books III and IV of *Saxo Grammaticus* about the year 1185. There is a later form in the Icelandic 'Ambales Saga', and, of course, there are innumerable variants in all parts of the world.[1]

There was a play called *Hamlet* extant in England about the year 1587, apparently not by Shakespeare and doubtfully attributed to Kyd.   Many difficulties and peculiarities in Shakespeare's *Hamlet* are presumably due to the unconscious discord between the old matter which he took from Kyd and the new matter which he invented.[2]   The first version of Shakespeare's *Hamlet* is in the Quarto of 1603 (perhaps really printed in 1602), a version widely different from that which we generally read. It has only 2,143 verses as against 3,891 in the Globe, the order of the scenes is occasionally different, the names of the characters are not all the same: for Polonius we have Corambis, and for

---

[1] See *Corpus Hamleticum*, by Professor Josef Schick, Munich, vol. i, 1912.
[2] See especially *Hamlet, an Historical and Comparative Study*, by Prof. Elgar Stoll, Univ. of Minnesota, 1919: *The Genesis of Hamlet*, by Prof. Lewis of Yale (Holt, 1907): *Hamlet Once More*, by the Rt. Hon. J. M. Robertson, 1923.

Reynaldo, Montano; the Queen, too, is definitely innocent of her husband's murder.

The Second Quarto is dated 1604 and describes itself as 'enlarged to almoste as much againe as it was, according to the true and perfecte coppie'. The First Folio was published after Shakespeare's death in 1623. It omits a good deal that was in the Second Quarto and contains some passages which are not in the Second Quarto but were in the First. In nearly all cases, however, it has rewritten and altered them. There are many critical questions about these three versions which we can here pass by, but surely one thing is clear to any one who uses his imagination. The three versions which happened to be printed cannot possibly represent all the variations of the play which were spoken on the stage. Shakespeare took an old play and rewrote it. He rewrote his own play again and again for many years. He added a great deal to it, but he sometimes cast out again his own additions. Who can tell what additions or what cuts were made at various performances where Shakespeare himself was producing; what additions or what cuts by other producers, when Shakespeare was not there? And after his death, though as far as we know strange hands did not make further additions to the play, as they certainly did to the Homeric poems and to some Greek tragedies, there are great variations of text all through the eighteenth and nineteenth centuries.

There is a very instructive book in twenty-five volumes called *The British Theatre*, by Mrs. Inchbald, published at the beginning of the nineteenth century. It consists of a collection of the plays acted at Drury Lane, Covent Garden, and the Haymarket, *printed from the prompt-books then in use* under the authority of the managers. One can there see what shape *Richard III* had assumed after Colley Cibber and other distinguished people had produced it. One can see Restoration comedies expurgated in accordance with later eighteenth-century taste; Congreve making references to the Coronation of George IV; and some old wine in Farquhar's 'Beaux' Stratagem' altering its date from 1706 to 1792. The process is normal, inevitable, and, to my judgement, entirely right, if the plays are to live and hold an audience. It differs from the similar process in antiquity chiefly because the ancients in pre-classical times had no sense of obligation to the authentic words of an author, and, in any case, were not, like the adapters of the eighteenth century, chained by the leg to a printed text.   The eighteenth-century producers could not treat *Hamlet* as Hamlet himself proposed to treat *The Murder of Gonzago* : ' Set down and insert in't ' on the spur of the moment ' a new speech of some dozen or sixteen lines.'   They left out more than they added ; in particular, they expurgated profanities.   They said ' For Heaven's love ' instead of ' For God's love ' and the like.   They expurgated what seemed grotesque or violent, or what the Alexandrians would have called ἀπρεπές, ' unseemly '.   They did not let Marcellus hit at the ghost with his partisan (Act I, Sc. ii).   They cut out all the ' Old mole ' and ' Truepenny ' business in Act I, Sc. v.   They removed the indecencies of Hamlet's conversation with Ophelia ; and, while they left in the whole of ' To be or not to be ' without a word changed, they cut out the whole of ' O, what a rogue and peasant slave am I ! '   And this, roughly speaking, was the form in which *Hamlet* gradually conquered the world throughout the eighteenth and early nineteenth centuries.   At least, it was a form very much nearer to this than to either of the texts that appeared in Shakespeare's life.   It is instructive to imagine how much greater the changes would have been if, with the same amount of enthusiasm for Shakespeare and the same skill and creative power in dramatic composition which existed in the eighteenth century, there had been no printed books for the public to read, while Dryden and Pope and Garrick and Johnson had had a fairly free hand in retouching the prompt-copies !

But having realized from *Hamlet* what might have happened, let us notice what actually did happen in the full light of the eighteenth century, in the midst of printed text and professional critics, to two of the most famous plays of Shakespeare.   I quote from the fascinating book of Prof. George Odell, *Shakespeare from Betterton to Irving* (Scribner's, 1920) :

> In 1681 Nahum Tate's *King Lear* was shown at Dorset Garden.   Tate's dedication to his ' esteem'd Friend, Thomas Boteler, Esq.' says that in Shakespeare's *Lear* he had found ' a Heap of Jewels unstrung and unpolish'd ; yet so dazzling

in their disorder that I soon perceiv'd I had seiz'd a Treasure.'
The three most striking alterations were (1) an 'Expedient
to rectify what was wanting in the Regularity and Probability of the Tale', by making Edgar and Cordelia (who
never meet in the original play) lovers from the start; (2)
the omission of the Fool; and (3) 'making the Tale conclude
in a Success to the innocent distrest Persons', Lear restored
to his throne, the wicked sisters dying of poison, and Edgar
and Cordelia married. 'Yet,' says Tate, 'was I wrack'd
with no small fear for so bold a change, till I found it was
well receiv'd by my Audience.'

The first change was due to a desire for love-interest of
the stilted 'heroic' kind then popular on the stage. It
involved doing away with Cordelia's suitor, the King of
France, and an implication that her cold answer to Lear
was due to hatred of Burgundy and love for Edgar; it
necessitated keeping her in England and compelling her to
wander about on the heath in the fearful storm, accompanied by an interpolated confidant, Arante, useful for
sending on errands. Cordelia comes to beg Gloster to help
her father in the storm; Edmund's passion is excited by her
beauty, and he sends two villains to the heath to capture her
and carry her to him. She fortunately and fortuitously stops
in front of the cave of Edgar, who drives off the rogues and has
an opportunity to behold his long-lost love at every lightning
flash. The well-known portrait of Mrs. Cibber as Cordelia
gives a picture of this interpolated scene. The omission of
the Fool removed from the play one of the most fascinating,
unearthly characters in Shakespeare; he was not restored
to the English stage till 1838. The third alteration took
from the sufferings of Lear all their bleak, elemental tragedy,
and reduced the play to melodramatic limits. Finally,
the Edmund-Goneril-Regan episode was unpleasantly am-
plified.

Tate's mangling persisted for a century and a half;
Shakespeare's *Lear* was never once acted in all that time.

Again:

We have seen how great was the vogue of Tate's *King
Lear*; another play to live on even longer in equally
mangled form was Colley Cibber's *Richard III*, played
first by the author at Drury Lane, in 1700. This version
has really never been driven from the stage; it is probably
a more effective acting vehicle than Shakespeare's. It
simply strings together bits of *Henry VI*, *Part III*, *Richard
II* and *Richard III*, interpolating even much of the best
part of the first scene from *Henry IV*, *Part II*, where North-

umberland learns of the death of Hotspur.   Many lines of this are given to King Henry in his first scene, where he is informed of the death of his son.   *Henry V* also contributes. Into Richard's soliloquy on the eve of battle, fourteen lines are interpolated from the fourth chorus of *Henry V*; lines more out of character it would be hard to imagine.   A few other lines are included from *Henry V*, about the host of ' mounted scarecrows ', over which the greedy crows fly, ' impatient for their lean inheritance.'   This play, then, is a thing of shreds and patches.   It omits many passages of Shakespeare's *Richard III*, Clarence's dream and Margaret's curse, for instance, and it interpolates one by Cibber himself, that in which Richard informs his wife—Lady Anne—that he is weary of her, and means to marry her successor.   The pathetic scene of Elizabeth's farewell to her sons is also Cibber's; it contains but little Shakespearian material.   The aim is to make the leading character, as Hazlitt says, more villanous and disgusting; hence, the play opens with several scenes from the end of *Henry VI, Part III*, showing the murder of the King by Gloster.   It has always been a thriller, and, as Shakespeare's play is not among his best, perhaps no great harm is done.

Few people know that the line so much admired by critics, the fearfully succinct line assigned to the tyrant,

Off with his head ; so much for Buckingham !

is Cibber's; also the frequently-quoted ' Richard's himself again !' [1]

These instances show how, even in modern times, and even among the greatest works of imaginative art, this process of traditional reshaping to suit the needs of new generations has gone on under the nose of critics who deny its possibility or regard it as a wicked outrage on poetry.   In antiquity the process was both more habitual and more drastic, but of course the evidence is far less full.

Perhaps the most curious instance in Greek literature is the work which comes to us under the name of *Callisthenes' Life of Alexander*.   It is the source of all the mediaeval romances of Alexander, and old translations of it are extant in Latin—one made in the fourth century and one in the tenth—Syriac, Armenian, Coptic, Ethiopic, Persian, Turkish, Malay, Siamese,

[1] Odell, vol. i. pp. 53 ff. and 75 ff.

and doubtless other languages. The basis in each case is a word-for-word translation, but in every language the substance varies; for it was told in each country by *jongleurs* and story-tellers who added, omitted, and altered with a view to their audience. For instance, Alexander is usually—in accordance with mediaeval taste—made the child of a secret amour between his mother, Olympias, and the exiled wizard king of . . . Of what? Of whatever country is most likely to please the audience. The earliest version was written by an Egyptian Greek. Consequently Alexander begins as a son of Nectanebos, king of Egypt. Then he is a Persian, and so on. One version, in Ethiopic, leaves him the son of his proper father, Philip, but makes Philip a Christian martyr, who committed suicide on hearing from a prophet that some day the Creator of the world would be crucified.

But it is not only the different translations that vary. Every copy of the book differs from every other. As one editor, Meusel, puts it : 'Like the MSS. of the *Nibelungenlied*, every MS. represents a different recension.' 'The writers,' says Karl Müller, 'combined the offices of scribe and author.' That exactly expresses it. Each scribe who earned his living by it made it as good, as edifying, as entertaining a history as he could. The book became a thing of tradition, and grew with the ages.[1]

The oldest version seems to have been written in Greek, in Egypt, in the time of the Ptolemies. So much can be made out. It professes to be the work of the philosopher Callisthenes, a real person, who accompanied Alexander on his campaigns, and whose real works have perished.[2] We can also trace with some probability an earlier stage of the same story : viz. a series of imaginary letters, between Alexander and his friends, composed by some sophist in Egypt not long after Alexander's death.

I will not speak of the mediaeval epics, the *Nibelungenlied*, the Arthur Legends, or the great French epics centring in the *Chanson de Roland*. Each one of these subjects has its own peculiarities and special difficulties ; but each one would illustrate our main thesis equally well. Let me merely quote some words of Gaston Paris to illustrate the nature of a traditional book.

---

[1] See Appendix E. The Pseudo-Callisthenes.

[2] An interesting fragment of Callisthenes has lately been discovered, cited by Didymus on Demosthenes. (Teubner, 1907. A papyrus.)

He is speaking of the controversy whether ' the author of the *Song of Roland*' had ever seen the valley of Roncesvaux, where the scene of his battle is placed. The great savant answers :—

> *The Song of Roland* is not a work composed in one effort at a given moment. It comprises in itself elements of very different date and origin. Some go back to the immediate impression of the event which it celebrates ; others have been introduced in the course of centuries by professional poets, who invented wholesale episodes calculated to increase the interest of the poem and develop its power of heroic and national inspiration. . . . The name of the author of the *Song of Roland* is Legion. And among those who, from the seventh to the eleventh century, would have the right to rise and answer any appeal addressed to that author, it would be very rash to affirm that not one had ever passed by Roncesvaux, at a period when so many people used that road.

How many controversies about Homer might be answered in similar words ! [1]

The most instructive example of the growth and change of a traditional book under ancient conditions is to be found, I think, in the Hebrew scriptures. I often wonder that the comparison has not been more widely used by Greek scholars. The scientific study of the Old Testament has been carried out with remarkable candour and ability by many Semitic scholars of the last two generations. The results of their researches are easily accessible ; the main results may be said, in a sense, to be practically certain. You cannot, indeed, often say with certainty in any particular place of difficulty, ' This is what happened '; but you can very often say with certainty, ' This is the sort of thing that must have happened.'

The subject is one of great interest. I fear, however, that interest largely depends on details ; and I am compelled here to content myself with the merest outline of the main facts about the growth of the Pentateuch.

The central voice and the informing spirit of the Old Testament is the Book of Deuteronomy. We all know its main characteristics : an insistence on a rigid and highly spiritual

---

[1] Gaston Paris, *Légendes du Moyen Age*, p. 46 ff. See also Appendix F on the *Roland* and the *Vie de St. Alexis*.

monotheism, and an avoidance of all remains of idolatry: a great system of law, governing in a theocratic spirit all the details of life, and resulting in an ideal too strict, and in some ways too high, to have ever been carried out in practice: lastly, for the sake of this purity of religion and morals, which was associated with the conception of the Jews as Yahweh's peculiar people, and the Temple at Jerusalem as the one seat of correct ritual and doctrine, an intolerant condemnation of all other places of worship, however sacred, and a ferocious dread of all foreign elements which might corrupt the orthodoxy of the chosen race.

Deuteronomy was found in the Temple by certain sacred persons—we are not told who had put it there—in the eighteenth year of King Josiah (B.C. 621: 2 Kings xxii. 8 ff.). It was accepted at once as the standard of a great religious reformation. Josiah supported the Deuteronomists, and the reformation was successfully carried through. Now among the other tasks which the reformers had before them was the re-editing of the ancient traditional books of the people. They needed reform in count-less ways. Both of them, indeed, must have been originally pagan and polytheistic. I say ' both ' rather than ' all ', because in the main we can distinguish two great documents, which have been welded by the Deuteronomists into the narrative of the Pentateuch. One of the most obvious differences between them is that in one God is called ' Elohim '—the word translated ' God ' in our version, though it is really a plural; in the other he is called Yahweh, or Jehovah, the special unspeakable name of the Hebrew God, translated in our version ' The Lord '. The documents are called ' Jahvist ' and ' Elohist ', or J and E respectively.

J seems to have been composed—that is, put together out of more ancient material—in Judah in the ninth century; E in Israel in the eighth. They were very similar in general contents. Each was an almost undifferentiated tribal Logos, a sort of history of the world and all the things in it that were worth writing down.

A copy of J or E before the Deuteronomists altered it would be, for Semitic historians, the most valuable book in the world. The strange thing is that the reformers were able to carry their project through. It was necessary for them not only to alter

their own versions at Jerusalem, but to suppress all old copies
that differed from their own. Had the kingdom of Israel still
been standing, the task would scarcely have been possible.
There must have been, one would imagine, copies of the old
books unexpurgated in the sanctuaries [1] of the Northern Kingdom.
But Israel was now in captivity, and most of the extant copies of
his old half-pagan books had doubtless gone with him. There
was little danger of their idolatrous voices being heard from
Halah and Habor and the river of Gozan and the cities of the
Medes. Yet even so there were difficulties in Judah itself.
There seems to have been a regular military expedition against
the remnants of Paganism, a formal destruction of the old High
Places, and a massacre of the priests at Bethel. At last Jerusalem
stood alone as the only sanctuary, and the reformers had
undisturbed control of the Book. One is reminded of Greek
stories about the interpolation of Homer, how Solon or
Pisistratus or another bolstered his city's claim to the island of
Salamis by citing a passage in the *Iliad*, which the opponents of
Athens thought spurious but were not, apparently, able to convict
by producing an authoritative text with different wording.

So far, then, we have found in the Pentateuch a document
compiled from three sources, the earliest written in the ninth
century, the latest about the year 621. But that is to leave out
of account, at any rate as regards Genesis, the greatest, or at
least the most formative and omnipresent, of all the sources.
The whole book was revised again, increased by large stretches
of narrative, and, roughly speaking, brought into its present
shape after the return from exile, between the years 440 and 400
B. C. This reviser, known to critics as P, was a member of the
priestly caste. He wrote, among other things, nearly the whole
of Leviticus. That is to say, in an average chapter of Genesis
we may read a verse written in the ninth century followed by one
written in the fifth, a gap of four hundred years. And sometimes the gap will occur in the middle of a verse. Sometimes
other sources, of unknown date, will intervene.[2]

---

[1] 'But was there any connexion in Ancient Israel between the priestly
caste and literature? The later *Sôphêr* was the literate man.' D. S. M.

[2] e. g. Gen. ii. 4 is partly J and partly P. (See Driver's Commentary.) So
is xiii. 11, while xiv is from an unknown source. (Abraham, Lot, and
Amraphel.)

Of course, even apart from the wholesale excision of paganism from the most ancient books, the peculiar qualities of these versions must have been much clearer when the books existed as separate wholes. We know them only in fragments : and those fragments have all passed under the hands both of revisers and of religious reformers, who must both consciously and unconsciously have modified the more striking discrepancies of style or statement between their various sources. Still, the differences are even now pretty clear : I take a few points from Canon Driver's *Introduction to Genesis*.[1]

J, or the Jahvist document, is a *Logos* of the most broadly human interest. It is full of poetry and drama. It delights in explaining the origin of human institutions—why men wear clothes, why snakes crawl, why child-birth is painful : who invented agriculture, pastoral life, music, metallurgy, the drinking of wine : how men came to have different languages : why Moabites, Ammonites, Canaanites, Edomites, are what they are, the cause being generally some significant first action, or some oracle spoken by a patriarch.

The writer is full of interest in the sacred sites of Palestine, the altars, pillars, trees, and high places, and the reasons why each one of them is sacred. He has no idea of condemning any of them. They had not yet come into competition with the Temple at Jerusalem. He calls God by the name ' Yahweh ' from the beginning, and supposes that the true religion naturally belonged to the primaeval patriarchs. In this, of course, the other prophetic book, E, differs from him. In E the ancestors of Israel ' beyond the river ' were idolaters (Joshua xxiv. 2, 14, 15), and the name Yahweh is not revealed to man till Exod. iii. 14. Again the Yahweh of J is frankly and naïvely anthropomorphic. He not only feels human emotions, but he performs sensible acts ; he *moulds* man out of earth, he *plants* a tree, he *shuts up* Noah in the ark, he *smells* burnt meat, *wrestles* with Jacob, and *takes off* the wheels of the Egyptian chariots.

Now let us contrast with this the work of the latest writer of all. P takes no interest in the origin of human institutions, only in ritual : no interest in sacred sites, only in the Temple at Jerusalem ; his God is, practically speaking, never anthropo-

[1] Differences of J, E, P.

morphic. His history of the world has been mapped out in a scheme of genealogies and dates, and especially of covenants between Yahweh and his chosen people, Israel. There are three stages of history marked by a gradually diminishing length of human life, and by the revelation of God under three distinct names: *Elohim*, *El Shaddai*—the obscure name revealed to Abraham in Gen. xvii—and finally *Yahweh*. The Patriarchs raise no altars, perform no sacrifices. ' No act of worship seems to be thought of till the appropriate place has been constructed and the right persons appointed for its performance. The first sacrifice recorded is that of Aaron and his sons in Lev. vii.' The promises of God are strictly limited to Israel itself, and the abiding presence of Yahweh with his people is dependent on the directions for the exact construction of the tabernacle (Exod. xxix). It is all sacerdotal through and through.

Thus there is a period of four hundred years between the earliest and latest of the large integral documents constituting the Book of Genesis. But the period of growth was much longer than that. In the case of Genesis the argument does not come out quite so clearly ; we can take our illustration more easily from the Books of Samuel. As the earliest source in Samuel we have the so-called ' Court narrative ' of David, attributed to the tenth century B. C. At the other end there are considerable slices of narrative which are found in the ordinary Hebrew text, but not in the Septuagint translation, which was made about the year 200 B. C. Of this fact two explanations are possible. Either, and this seems the simpler hypothesis, the narratives in question were not in the Hebrew text from which the Septuagint was translated ; or else they were in the Hebrew text, and were deliberately left out by the translators. On either hypothesis it is clear that the authorized text was not definitely established. A traditional book of which large parts can be left out or put in at discretion is still in the stage of growth. The Book of Samuel, then, was in process of growth for considerably more than seven hundred years. And that is without reckoning the small corruptions or verbal changes which seem to have occurred much later. In some books, for instance, there are changes directed against the claims of Christianity.

But, returning to the Pentateuch : when J or E was first composed, it was not composed out of nothing. Each of them was really put together in the same way as the whole composite Pentateuch of the Priest, by taking an older existing book, copying it out, adding, omitting, and sometimes altering. Many of these earlier sources are quoted by name, as the *Iliad* quotes the older Argonautica. There is the Book of Jasher. From it come the standing still of the Sun and Moon (Joshua x. 12), David's lament over Saul and Jonathan (2 Sam. i. 17), and perhaps some verses spoken by Solomon when the Ark was brought to the Temple (1 Kings viii. 12). The song in Num. xxi. 14, again, ' is it not written in the Book of the Wars of the Lord ? ' In these cases the name of the older book is explicitly given. Much more often it is omitted. Sometimes a quotation betrays itself by being in verse, like the Sword-Song of Lamech, and the oracles spoken over their respective children by Noah, Isaac, and Jacob. But an insertion from a prose work would be hard to detect : and even the verse was apt to be worked back into prose (see commentators on 1 Kings viii. 12).

Among other sources would be the mere tribal traditions, such as we have in the Book of Judges. Sometimes they are full and clear, and seem to depend on written documents. Sometimes a tradition consists merely of a name and a burial-place. ' After him Elon the Zebulonite judged Israel : and he judged Israel ten years. And Elon the Zebulonite died and was buried in Aijalon in the land of Zebulon.' Aijalon is probably the same word as Elon. The chronology will not work. And the story seems merely to mean that there was at Elon or Aijalon an unknown grave which was regarded with reverence.

There was more detailed tradition at the various ancient sanctu-aries, Hebron, Bethel, Gilgal, and the like, a source particularly prominent in J and E, but discountenanced by the priestly editors. There were fragments of history or learning adopted by hearsay or otherwise from more advanced nations. This is a regular process in primitive races, and is admirably illustrated in Professor Margoliouth's short *Life of Mohammed*.[1] That prophet was constantly picking up scraps of Christian and Jewish lore, and incorporating them, with inevitable mistakes, in his Koran. In

---

[1] Especially pp. 106 ff. Mohammed got Goliath's name as Galut ; the name of Saul, David's other enemy, he had forgotten, so he made him Talut.

the Hebrew scriptures there seems to be an especially large debt
to Babylon, such as the stories of the Creation and the Flood;
certain fragments about Abraham, who perhaps had the honour
of meeting the great law-giver Hammurabi or Amraphel; and
many elements in the Hebrew laws themselves.

Now I realize that all this description must remain rather
ineffective when unaccompanied by detailed illustrations. But
the detailed illustrations would clearly take us quite beyond the
limits of our present subject. And it is, of course, not any part
of my business to prove the truth of the analysis of the Pentateuch.
I merely take the results reached by a consensus of the best
Semitic scholars, in order to show the sort of process which was
normal in the formation of one type of ancient Traditional Book,
and the qualities which naturally resulted therefrom. To produce
such a composite work as one of these books in its later stages
without inconsistencies and awkward joints would be difficult, as
we said above, even for a modern editor with all his mechanical
accessories and his opportunities of revision. To the ancient
editor the difficulties were insuperable. And, as a matter of fact,
most ancient compilations betray themselves. I will not dwell on
the various doublets and inconsistencies which careful reading
discovers in the Pentateuch; the two divergent accounts of the
Creation, and of the Flood, with traces of a third in which there
was no Flood; the inaccuracies of the chronology so laboriously
inserted by the Priestly writer—ancient numbers, when at all
complicated, seldom come out quite right; much less on the
many small confusions, like that of the two wives of Esau who
are mentioned three times, each time with different names; nor
yet on such curious formal points as the case of the Twelve Tribes
of Israel, which are mentioned again and again as twelve, yet
always add up as thirteen. Such weaknesses as these are normal
things among primitive historians. If they serve to illustrate the
writer's lack of critical control over his complex material, they
also are often evidence of his good faith.[1]

---

[1] The Jahvist, very simple and anthropomorphic, narrated how Yahweh
'moulded' a clay man and breathed life into him, and planted a garden and
put the man to keep it. Then as the man was lonely, Yahweh made all
sorts of beasts as companions for him, but none was quite satisfactory till he
made a woman out of one of the man's ribs, and then the man was content.
The Priestly Document, more advanced and scientific, gives the other story

I hope that by now I have succeeded in illustrating two points about these ancient authorless books; first, the immense periods of time during which they remain fluid and growing ; and second, the difficulties which they have in combining their multiplex sources. The object which I have in view is, of course, Homer. And I wish now to notice briefly some two or three more of the phenomena characteristic of this kind of writing, in order that we may know their faces again when they meet us in the *Iliad*.

First, there are the various disturbing influences that are apt to affect the primitive historian. I will not lay stress on mythology and folk-lore, such as we find in the story of Samson, the Sun-man,[1] or in the Babylonish part of the Creation : nor on what I may call Romance, or the story-teller's instinct, such as we find in the narratives of David and of Joseph. These factors are enormously powerful in Greek legend; Semitic scholars differ as to their influence in Hebrew. I will not lay stress on the tribal spirit, with its ramifications of patriotic devotion, party

of the six days of creation, with a gradual process of development, as it were, from the lowest forms of life up to the highest, culminating eventually in man. We cannot be sure about the account of the Israelitish Elohist; for the Reviser, while combining the other two, omitted it altogether. Similarly in the Flood, the Jahvist tells how Noah took seven of each clean animal and two of each unclean ; how the flood lasted some ninety-four days; and how Noah came out at the end of the time and offered sacrifice. The Priest tells how Noah took two of every animal, with no distinction of clean or unclean ; that distinction, he apparently argues, cannot have been known to Noah, because it was first revealed to Moses in Lev. xi and Deut. xiv. He tells how the flood lasted a year and ten days, and how at the end God made a covenant with Noah and set his bow in the heavens for a sign thereof. There seems also to be a trace of a version in which the first Man was not called Adam, but Enosh—the other Hebrew word for man. As to the chronology so carefully introduced by the Priestly writer, Canon Driver shows that Judah 'marries, has three children, and after the third of them has grown up becomes a father again, and through the child thus born becomes a grandfather, all in the space of 22 years'. (Thirty-five would seem to be about the minimum possible.) The age of Ishmael at the time of his casting out varies between babyhood and adolescence. So does Benjamin's. The wives of Esau are given in Gen. xxvi as Judith, daughter of Beeri, and Bashemath d. Elon : but in Gen. xxxvi they are Adah d. Elon and Bashemath d. Ishmael. And in chapter xxviii the daughter of Ishmael is Mahalath. One can see what sort of process this implies. The compiler of the two, or the three, narratives did not keep constantly looking forward and backward. He had no index to show him all the places where he had mentioned Esau's wives, and help him to reduce them to order. In the case of the more important matters his memory no doubt served him, and he arranged his story consistently. But in smaller things, which were not of real gravity to him, he copied his authorities faithfully without noticing the occasional contradictions.

[1] שִׁמְשׁוֹן from שֶׁמֶשׁ 'Sun'.

feeling, and *odium theologicum*, forces at times responsible for the wildest misreadings and misrenderings of history. We must remember that as a rule an ancient writer only recorded what he wished to have remembered: that his book was only read within his own tribe or circle, and that his only business with his tribe's enemies was to injure them. He thought tribally. He used his book as he would use his sword. But consider, as one significant point, the helplessness of language which generally dogs these early writers as soon as they have anything complicated to express. The writer of Gen. x. 15, for instance, wishing to express the relation of the Canaanites of the interior to the Phoenician city of Sidon, can only say: 'And Canaan begat Zidon his first-born.' The relation of the Canaanites to the Hittites, a great foreign nation which seems to have had some settlers in Canaan, was certainly different. But it is expressed in the same way: 'Canaan begat Heth.' The tribe, the alien city, the foreign nation, are all treated as individuals, and their complicated relations reduced to that of father and son.[1] Similarly Bethuel is mentioned as a person, the father of Rebekah, but his brothers Huz and Buz are tribes. Machir in Gen. l. 23 is a person: in Num. xxxii. 40 he is a clan: in Num. xxvi. 29 he 'begets' Gilead, which is a district. That district again 'begets' the judge Jephthah—perhaps rather a special case, since Jephthah had no legitimate father.

The disturbing influences hitherto considered are all, in the main, unconscious. Let us consider for a few moments two conscious influences. Then we can make an end of these Semitic analogies and return to Greece. In the first place, is there in such a book as Genesis, for example, any conscious archaism? The answer is clear. The latest of all the writers of the Pentateuch, P, is the one who is most particular to give an archaic and primaeval colour to his narrative. He has used his historical imagination, and constructed a remarkable picture of the age of the patriarchs, quite unlike his own age or even that of his immediate authorities. According to him, the Patriarchs knew not the name of Yahweh, knew no altars, no

---

[1] The statement in x. 6, 'Ham begat Canaan', is different. It is definitely untrue, and comes from tribal animosity. It suited the Israelites' self-respect to think as ill as possible of their not very distant kinsmen, the Canaanites. Consequently these undoubtedly Semitic tribes are assigned to Ham, the accursed.

sacrifices, no difference between clean and unclean meats. All these things were specially revealed to them at later and definitely mentioned periods. The earlier writers, J and E, are much less particular. Their writing was centuries older, but the picture which they draw is actually more modern. They allow Abram to come to 'Bethel', or pursue his enemies to 'Dan', without being troubled by the reflection that those names were only the later representatives of 'Luz' and 'Laish'. The Jahvist tells us that in Seth's time 'men began to call upon the name of Yahweh', without thinking it necessary to revise his earlier narrative in which both the name and the person of Yahweh seem to be known to all. Probably, if we only knew it, they also archaized after their fashion, but, if they did, it was nothing to the archaizing of the Priest. It so happens that the Hebrew priestly writers were not interested in such things as the comparative antiquity of bronze and iron or the date of the Dorian migration. But, if they had been, you may be sure that they would never have allowed a mention of iron nor a hint of the existence of Dorians to defile their pages. These things are of importance for Homer.

The practice of archaism is closely related to something far deeper and more wide-reaching, the practice of expurgation. In the case of these ancient and traditional books, which carry on the *Logos* of one age to grow into the *Logos* of the next, there must always emerge points of belief or feeling or conduct where the new age differs from the old. In advanced states of society, where the books exist in large numbers and the text cannot be tampered with, the usual resort is allegory. All that is objectionable is interpreted as meaning something else. But while the books are still growing, two courses are open to each new set of revisers. The simplest is tacitly to alter the document and cut out from the venerable book all that seems unworthy of it. This is expurgation. The other, more complex and more dependent on an advanced historical sense, is to recognize the difference in manners, and to try even in the new writings to maintain the colour of the older age. That is archaism. One may say that on the whole archaism is the normal practice, in style, in vocabulary, and in the selection of facts to relate. But when the writer is brought face to face with something which he honestly hates or disapproves, then his archaism breaks down and he resorts to expurgation.

Now the whole of the Pentateuch is permeated by a conscious didactic purpose, and therefore by the spirit of expurgation. For one of the processes which have formed the Pentateuch is the gradual conversion of the sagas of primitive Semitic pagans into the great book of Jewish monotheism. At what date the early sources ceased to be pagan is open to doubt; but that they were once pagan is practically certain; and probably the work of the Deuteronomists and the Priests consisted almost as largely in their unseen excisions of objectionable matter as in the composition of their great codes, Deuteronomy and Leviticus, and the innumerable small additions by which we now trace them. Of course, as a rule, we have no means of knowing what expurgations or omissions have been made. The thing is cut out, and there is an end to it. But sometimes the excision has not been complete, or has in some way left traces. Let us take some instances.

There is the curious set of cases in which the word *Bosheth*, 'Shame' or 'Shameful Thing', has taken the place, or distorted the form, of some genuine but objectionable word. For instance, the title *Melekh*, King, was applied to Yahweh as to other deities: and at one time in the seventh century human sacrifices were offered to him under that name. This was an abomination to the purer Jewish feeling. Wherever the word *Melekh* occurred in descriptions of these rites, the practice in the Synagogue was to avoid pronouncing it and say instead *Bosheth*. To indicate this, though the consonants of MLKH were not altered in the text, the vowels of Bosheth were written under them. Hence arose an imaginary word 'Molekh'—afterwards corrupted to 'Moloch'—which was then taken for the name of some unknown god of the Gentiles.

Again, the word 'Ba'al': this word, meaning Lord, or Master, was originally a perfectly innocent title, applied to Yahweh as well as to the gods of Canaan. Consequently many Hebrew names in early times were formed from Ba'al. But to a later age they sounded idolatrous, and they have nearly all been altered. Saul's son Ishba'al ('Man of the Lord') is turned into Ishbosheth, 'man of shame.' Jonathan's son Meriba'al becomes Mephibosheth.

In the case of Jerubba'al or Gideon a different line was taken. The name must really have meant ' Ba'al founds or strengthens '; but it is carefully interpreted as a sort of *calembour* or play on the sound of the words, so as to mean ' Let Ba'al plead '. This explanation then gives rise to one of the usual stories of the confounding of the false God. Gideon defies Ba'al, and Ba'al cannot plead, but remains dumb[1] (Judges vi. 32).

To take a different kind of expurgation, there seems to be some omission in the story of Cain's sacrifice (Gen. iv. 5). No reason is given for its rejection. Probably the point of the story lay in the ritual which Cain followed. There must have been—so at least many authorities believe—some description of the two rituals. Cain performed his sacrifice in some way that was considered unholy or savouring of the gentiles. The older story mentioned Cain's ritual in order to condemn it, the later editors declined to speak of it at all. There is almost certainly a great omission just before the story of the Flood, in the passage (Gen. vi. 1 ff.) which tells how ' the sons of God saw the daughters of men that they were fair, and took them wives of all that they chose '. The next two verses are confused and unintelligible, and the subject is promptly changed.

These instances, few as they are, will perhaps suffice to establish the mere fact that expurgations have occurred. They may also incidentally show how vitally the study of the expurgations in an ancient book helps towards the understanding of its whole spirit. The expurgations and the interpolations; all that a man rejects from his traditional teaching and all that he puts in its place; a knowledge of those two together will surely contain the main secrets of all that is most alive in the man's own character. And the same is true of an age. The interpolations and expurgations, if we followed the subject up, would

---

[1] Exactly the same process has given rise to the mysterious 'Abomination of Desolation' set up by Antiochus Epiphanes, in the well-known passages of Daniel (ix. 27, xii. 11). The word for abomination, Heb. שִׁקּוּץ, is used exactly like בֹּשֶׁת to supply the place of the unmentionable name Ba'al. What Antiochus really 'set up' was *Ba'al Shamâim*, the Lord of Heaven; an altar, that is, to Zeus Ouranios. In place of *Ba'al* we say *Shiqquç*, abomination: and in place of *Shamâim*, heaven, which is here equally unclean, inasmuch as it is part of the name of a heathen god, we put the almost identical word *Shomêm*, from a word meaning to destroy or lay waste. *Ba'al Shamâim* becomes *shiqquç Shomêm*; the Lord of Heaven becomes the 'pollution' of 'desolation'.

teach us much about the age of the Deuteronomists and the later age of the Priests.[1] And I wish now to apply this method, at least in one of its aspects, to Homer. I shall not attempt to face the question of interpolation. It is too complicated a subject. But the traces of expurgation in Homer have been very little studied, and seem capable of yielding some interesting results. We will consider them in the next lecture.

---

[1] I have not attempted to analyse the expurgations of the Deuteronomists (D), or to find out what sort of thing they most objected to. The above cases are nearly all expurgations of idolatry or paganism, and that is evidently and by far the greatest preoccupation of the revisers. There are also some expurgations of immorality. As regards cruelty, they were much less particular than Homer, provided that the cruelty was directed against suitable objects. They approve of the ferocity of Samuel (1 Sam. xv) and the *Herem* generally: i.e. the extermination of all living things, beast and human alike, in heathen countries. (See BAN in *Enc. Bibl.*, and compare the Scandinavian custom of dedicating hostile armies to Othin by throwing a spear over them.) They allow even such a sympathetic hero as Gideon to 'thresh' the elders of Succoth 'with thorns of the wilderness', without comment; the same may be said of David and others. In this particular one may note that the very late book, Chronicles, expurgates its sources: e.g. 2 Sam. viii. 2: 'And he smote Moab (and measured them with the line, making them to lie down on the ground: and he measured two lines to put to death, and one full line to keep alive). And the Moabites became servants to David and brought gifts.' This is repeated in 1 Chron. xviii. 2, except that the Chronicler *omits the words in brackets*.

Similarly the account of the taking of Rabbah, where David 'brought forth the people that were therein and put them under saws and under harrows of iron and under axes of iron, and he made them pass through the brick-kiln' (2 Sam. xii. 31), is omitted altogether in Chronicles. (Driver and others, however, think that torture is not intended here, but only slavery.) On the other hand, when religious motives come in, the latest writers can be very savage. See 1 Kings xiii. 2 and 2 Kings xxiii. 20, where Josiah's wholesale sacrifice of the priests of Baal is described with exultation. (The end of chap. xxiii is ascribed to a very late source, but the tone is really much the same in the rest of the chapter, which is by J.)

Not perhaps actual expurgation, but something very similar, seems to have been at work in those cases where we find that certain very old parts of our extant composite narrative were not included in the Deuteronomic revision. For instance, in the Book of Judges, D is not responsible for chap. ix (Abimelech: a story possessing historical interest, but no religious value), nor for xvi-xxi. He ended Samson at xv. 20, after the jaw-bone victory, at the words: 'And he judged Israel in the days of the Philistines twenty years.' The part omitted consisted of Dalilah and the end of Samson; the stories of Micah, the Danites, the sin of the Benjamites, &c.—all somewhat unedifying. Similarly in Samuel, D has no hand in 1 Sam. xxviii. 3 to end (Witch of Endor), which breaks the continuity of his narrative; nor in 2 Sam. ix-xx, which contains all the intimate Court stories, Bath-sheba, Rabbah, Tamar, &c. D ended his narrative of David with the *résumé* in 2 Sam. viii. 15 ff., 'And David reigned over all Israel, &c.' These stories are not later inventions. They come from the oldest material, and must have lain before D, who deliberately rejected them. They were, however, preserved and eventually inserted into the composite narrative which we now possess in an age which was more open than that of D to historical, antiquarian, or merely human interests.

THE ILIAD AS A TRADITIONAL BOOK

I. THE EXPURGATIONS: THE HOMERIC SPIRIT

'As for these passages and all others of the sort, we will beg Homer and the other poets not to be angry if we draw our pen through them.'—PLATO, *Rep.* iii. 387 b.

IN considering the subject of Homeric expurgations I will take my instances chiefly from the *Iliad*, because I believe the *Iliad* to be, in the ancient phrase, 'more Homeric' than the *Odyssey*, that is, both to have more of the definite Homeric spirit, and to have undergone a more thorough process of revision and expurgation.

But before studying what things the poets reject we should be clear what sort of world they wish to represent. And we can. They are with conscious art depicting a past age, but an idealized past; a past, as Grote says, which never was a present. It is the normal method of high romance; the method of Scott in depicting the ages of chivalry; of Tennyson or Morris in writing about the knights of King Arthur. There is a conscious use of tradition and of what may almost be called archaeology; a genuine attempt to be true to the manners of a simpler society. Yet, with all its simplicity, it must be an age of chivalry, of heroism. Nausicaa, the king's daughter, may go out with the dirty clothes in a mule-cart to wash them by the sea shore: so simple was life in those days! But her beauty and stature, and her language, and the language of others in speaking to her, have a majesty and a graciousness which, I suspect, the poet did not find or expect to find among contemporary young women. Those were the days when a hero was really a hero and a princess a princess!

The picture of the past is constructed with wonderful consistency. Where there is a slip or a doubtful point we find that it has nearly always been observed and discussed by the Alexandrian scholars. Greek taste, at the time when our text was finally fixed, was extremely careful about anachronisms. Thus it is likely that a text of the time of Pisistratus or earlier, if we could find one, would have many more anachronisms than our present text, which was punctiliously watched and re-edited by generations of ancient scholars. But from quite early times the Homeric poets must have been imaginatively interested in the Heroic Age, and have tried to represent it vividly. Though all the higher Greek poetry is about the same ideal past, no other poems treat it with quite such scrupulous tenderness as the *Iliad* and *Odyssey*. No other poems have been so fully studied and commented and re-edited.

Attempts have been made, and are still far too common, to suggest that the Homeric picture of the Heroic Age is actually the work of a naïve and primitive poet who lived in it, and simply described his own surroundings. But, apart from other difficulties in this theory, it is definitely disproved by a curious difference between the narrative itself and the poet's comments upon it. In the narrative we have the complete heroic world. The heroes of the *Iliad* consume only heroic food, consisting chiefly of 'unspeakable flesh and sweet strong wine'. They eat enormous slices of roast ox or sheep or boar, and that three times a day. They do not condescend to boiled meat, much less to fish, fowl or vegetable, milk or cheese. When the companions of Odysseus are twice reduced to fish and wild-fowl, it is a case of extreme need (μ 331 ff, δ 368). In the similes, however, there is quite a lot about fishing, alike with rod and net and spear ; about diving for oysters and the advantages of a sea rich in fish. There are similes taken from the catching of larks and pigeons, and perhaps from hawking. There is much about milk and cheese, and one mention of boiled pork. That is the poet's own work-a-day world, where people had at most two meals a day and meat was a scarcity, not the world of the great Zeus-born heroes.

Similarly in metaphors we hear of the trumpet (Σ 219, Φ 388), which, as the ancient scholars had observed, is unknown in the narrative. So riding is mentioned twice in similes (O 679, ϵ 371), but in the body of the narrative $i\pi\pi\hat{\eta}\epsilon s$ are charioteers. (The

riding in *K* is, of course, exceptional.) Crowns and garlands
were a commonplace of Greek social life in classical times, and
are referred to in metaphors freely (*N* 736 and Schol., *E* 739,
Δ 36, *O* 153, *Σ* 485, *κ* 195); but the ancients have noted that
they are never used by the Heroes. It is very significant, as
will be seen further on, that, though the Heroes habitually fight
with bronze, when the poet wants a hard metal for a metaphor
he mostly speaks of iron.[1]

Thus it is certain that the poet is representing with conscious
art a past age of heroism and chivalry. Naturally, therefore,
he excludes from it not only what is low and modern, but also
a good deal that was really ancient, but indicated the squalor
and brutality of the past, rather than its chivalry.

But first a word as to method. If only we had still two or
three versions of the *Iliad* belonging to different times, such as
we have of the *Roland*, the *Alexis*, or the *Nibelungenlied*, our
task would be plain. If we had any remnant of a pre-Attic
text, or even if one of our fragmentary pre-Aristarchean MSS.

---

[1] See Drerup I, chap. iv; and cf. the following passages :—Fish : Π 747
πολλοὺς ἂν κορέσειεν ἀνὴρ ὅδε τήθεα διφῶν, see note below. δ 368 αἰεὶ γὰρ περὶ
νῆσον ἀλώμενοι ἰχθυάασκον γναμπτοῖς ἀγκίστροισιν, ἔτειρε δὲ γαστέρα λιμός. Π 406
ὡς ὅτε τις φὼς . . . ἱερὸν ἰχθὺν ἐκ πόντοιο θύραζε λίνῳ καὶ ἤνοπι χαλκῷ (ἕλκει).
μ 251 ὡς δ᾽ ὅτ᾽ ἐπὶ προβόλῳ ἁλιεὺς περιμήκεϊ ῥάβδῳ ἰχθύσι τοῖς ὀλίγοισι δόλον κατὰ
εἴδατα βάλλων . . . Nets E 487 μή πως, ὡς ἀψῖσι λίνοι᾽ ἁλόντε πανάγρου . . . Ω 80
Iris plunges into the sea μολυβδαίνῃ ἰκέλη ἐς βυσσὸν ὄρουσεν ἥ τε . . . ἔρχεται
ὠμηστῇσιν ἐπ᾽ ἰχθύσι κῆρα φέρουσα. χ 384 the dead suitors lying in a heap ὥς
τ᾽ ἰχθύας οὕς θ᾽ ἁλιῆες . . . δικτύῳ ἐξέρυσαν πολυωπῷ. Spearing : κ 124 ἰχθῦς δ᾽ ὡς
πείροντες ἀτερπέα δαῖτα φέροντο. Good fish as an economic asset is among the
blessings of the good king, τ 113 τίκτῃ δ᾽ ἔμπεδα μῆλα, θάλασσα δὲ παρέχῃ ἰχθῦς.
Perhaps also I 360 Ἑλλήσποντον ἐπ᾽ ἰχθυόεντα.
    Birds caught in a net : χ 468 ὡς δ᾽ ὅτ᾽ ἂν ἢ κίχλαι τανυσίπτεροι ἠὲ πέλειαι ἕρκει
ἐνιπλήξωσι, τό θ᾽ ἑστήκῃ ἐνὶ θάμνῳ . . . Hawking : χ 302 οἱ δ᾽ ὡς αἰγύπιοι . . . ἐπ᾽
ὀρνίθεσσι θόρωσι . . . χαίρουσι δέ τ᾽ ἀνέρες ἄγρῃ.
    Milk and cheese : B 471 Ἠΰτε μυιάων ἀδινάων ἔθνεα πολλά, αἵ τε κατὰ σταθμὸν
ποιμνήϊον . . . ὅτε τε γλάγος ἄγγεα δεύει. Cf. Π 643. Δ 433 ὥς τ᾽ ὄϊες . . . μυρίαι
ἑστήκασιν ἀμελγόμεναι γάλα λευκόν. E 902 ὡς δ᾽ ὅτ᾽ ὀπὸς γάλα λευκὸν ἐπειγόμενος
συνέπηξεν . . . (rennet curdling milk). Boiled pork : Φ 362 ὡς δὲ λέβης ζεῖ ἔνδον
ἐπειγόμενος πυρὶ πολλῷ, κνίσην μελδόμενος ἁπαλοτρεφέος σιάλοιο. On which
Schol. T observes 'The poet himself knows the use of boiled meat, but does
not represent the heroes using it'. So on the oyster-diver in Π 747 the
Schol. T says 'This does not agree with the general life of the heroic age.
Not even the luxurious Phaeacians or the Suitors are represented as using
such things (as shellfish). . . . He represents them using neither fish nor
birds, tho' Odysseus' companions do try them under stress of need (δ 368).
In general he avoids such usage because of its meanness (τὸ μικροπρεπές) and
makes them use roast flesh, so that he can say of Achilles 'Automedon held
the flesh and Achilles cut'; imagine what the effect would be of making the
Son of Thetis clean a fish or boil soup !'

vere complete! As it is we are forced for the most part to
search in our present text for small things that look suspicious
and lead us to probabilities, not facts. Yet there is some
positive and definite evidence also. Our knowledge of the text
of the *Iliad* does, after all, just reach back to the time when
it was not yet absolutely fixed, when it was still possible for
a reader who greatly disliked something in his MS. of the *Iliad*
to 'obelize' it or cut it out as unworthy of Homer. If we study
the passages deleted or condemned by the earliest critics known
to us, it is impossible not to see that, though the text was by
then almost fixed, the process of expurgation was still active.
Passage after passage is condemned or criticized as ἀπρεπές,
'unseemly'. The only cases that are perfectly demonstrable,
of course, are those in which two versions are preserved; where
either our text contains lines which some other authority con-
demns, or some other authority preserves lines which have been
dropped out of our text.

For instance, there are four lines in the Phoenix story (I, 458–
61) describing that hero's wish to murder his father, of which
Plutarch tells us that Aristarchus cut them out 'in fear', because
of their bad morals. There is a line just above (453) where
Phoenix, speaking of his mother's infamous suggestion, says
'*Her I obeyed and did*' (τῇ πιθόμην καὶ ἔρεξα): certain ancient
critics read the line, '*Her I disobeyed and did not*' (τῇ οὐ
πιθόμην οὐδ' ἔρξα). In the Story of Ares and Aphrodite in the
Odyssey, the scholia tell us of ten lines (θ 333–43) which were
absent from some copies 'because of the unseemly suggestion',
while we know that some ancient critics rejected the whole
episode. There is an interesting deletion on quite other grounds
in *H* 195–9. Aias is going forth to single combat with Hector,
and bids his companions to pray to Zeus '*silently within your-
selves, so that the Trojans at any rate may not hear*'—and
so use counter-prayers. A little mean, that, especially for Aias; a
little like mere witchcraft, such as the Norse heroes so vehemently
denounce and repudiate. It is followed by a healing line: 'Or
pray openly if you will; I am not afraid.' But the best critics,
Zenodotus, Aristophanes, Aristarchus, all unite in rejecting the
whole passage. It was safest away.

It is instructive to look through the whole list of passages

rejected from the *Iliad* by the great critics. Our testimony i
miserably deficient, especially for Zenodotus, who matters mos
of the critics because he was the earliest and the most drasti
But there is enough to show that they rejected a great quantit;
of lines on pure grounds of expurgation :[1] passages where th
Gods misbehave more grossly than usual, passages whicl
attribute to the heroes coarse language or unworthy motives
above all, passages where the suspicious eye of a moralist sav
traces of the work of those infamous persons who misinterpreted
the relations of Achilles and Patroclus.[2]

---

[1] Whether they had or had not MS. authority for their deletions does no
affect the argument. If they had, then the pre-Alexandrian confusion wa
even greater than our existing evidence proves. And we should then have t
assume (1) that the attempt to expurgate these passages had been mad
before Zenodotus (which is pretty certain); (2) that in the turmoil of text
the critics were largely decided by expurgatory motives. I append a rougl
list of some typical 'unseemly' passages which were condemned by ancien
critics :

Unseemliness in the Gods : A 396–406 (gods frightened by Briareôs)
B 111–18 (Agamemnon's blame of Zeus); B 157–68 (Hera to Athena)
Γ 396–418 and 423–6 (Helen and Aphrodite); Θ 35–40 (violent speech of Zeu;
followed by apology); Θ 385–7 (Athena puts on her father's tunic); Θ 420–٤
(Iris repeats message and adds insults of her own); Λ 78–83 (Gods angrу
with Zeus; perhaps other reasons for excision); Ξ 317–27 (the Leporello-
catalogue of Zeus's amours); O 5 a (decidedly ἀπρεπές, and dropped from ou
texts); O 18–31 (threats of Zeus to Hera); O 212–17 (threats of Poseidon)
Π 432–58 and 666–83 (discussion of gods about Sarpedon and its sequel;
probably some religious objection at work to reinforce critical reasons);
Σ 356–67 (Zeus to Hera); Φ 471, 475–7 (Artemis reviling Apollo); Ω 20 f.
(Apollo and the dead Hector; religious expurgation); Ω 23–30 and 71–3
(proposal that Hermes should steal the corpse, and statement that he could
not); 423 (cf. 20 f.).

Unseemliness in Heroes : A 225–33 ('Drunkard with the eyes of a dog,'
&c.); B 193–7 (treachery imputed to Agamemnon); Θ 164–6 (abusive
language?); Θ 284 ('reared you in his own house, bastard as you were');
I 458–61 (Phoenix and his father); Λ 794 f. (suggestion of cowardice in
Achilles); Π 89–90 (mean motive in Achilles); T 77 (Agamemnon not rising :
ἀπρεπές); Υ 180–6, 195–8, 205–9, 251–5 (all in the discourteous scene between
Achilles and Aeneas); Ψ 804–6, 810, 824 f. (the barbaric gladiatorial
combat); Ω 556–7 and 594 f. (unworthy motives). One may add Θ 189
(giving horses wine; barbaric); and the abusive language of Thersites in
B 227 f. and 231–4.

[2] The primitive character of these practices is proved by the archaic
inscriptions of Thera and convincingly explained by Bethe in *Rhein. Mus.*
N.F. lxii. 438–75. By this rite the full warrior adopted the squire and
imparted his *mana* to him. Cf. Preuss in *Archiv für Relig.* 1910. That the
'silence of Homer' is intentional is proved by E 266 and Υ 231 f. (on Gany-
medes). The clearest text about expurgation is Schol. T on Π 97 : παντελῶς
ἐκβλητέον τοὺς δ᾽ στίχους, says Aristarchus with unusual emphasis ; 'Zenodotus
was right in suspecting that they were inserted ὑπὸ τῶν ἀρσενικοὺς ἔρωτας εἶναι
λεγόντων παρ᾽ Ὁμήρῳ καὶ ὑπονοούντων παιδικὰ εἶναι Ἀχιλλέα Πατρόκλου.'

This is the only part of the subject which is difficult to discuss.
t is too important to omit altogether. The evidence is clear
hat there existed in early times, among both Aryans and
Semites, and notably among the Dorians, who are generally
eckoned among the more primitive races of Greece, certain
orms of sexual irregularity which were in the end totally con-
lemned by the Jewish and the Athenian law, but were tolerated
n various parts of the Aegean and even in such well-conducted
ommunities as Crete. Sodom and Gomorrah, according to the
radition, were consumed by fire from heaven. The tribe of
Benjamin was almost blotted out. Laius, king of Thebes, was
nvolved in a fearful curse, together with his whole race. But
early Greek traditions testify both to the existence and the
oleration of these practices. Now Homer has swept this whole
business, root and branch, out of his conception of life. Exactly
he same spirit is seen at work when we compare the rude
thyphallic Hermae of ancient Greek cults with the idealized
messenger of the Gods in the *Odyssey*. But that is merely one
nstance : for this kind of expurgation really pervades the whole
of our Homer.

Closely akin to this is the spirit in which our present text of
he *Odyssey* treats the marriage of Alcinoüs and Arêtê, the king
and queen of the Phaeacians. 'Her name was Arêtê, and she
was born of the self-same parents that begat king Alcinoüs'
(η 54 ff.). Exactly; Hesiod too, the scholia tell us, made the
royal pair brother and sister. There are abundant instances of
that sort of marriage in the houses of the ancient divine kings.
The royal blood was too superhuman to make it desirable for
the king to wed any one lower than his own sister. Hera herself was sister and spouse of Zeus. The Pharaohs and the
Ptolemies after them made a practice of having their sisters for
queens. In the first of Griffith's *Stories of the Priests of
Memphis* the doctrine that the only fit bride for Nefrekepta is
his sister is explained and insisted upon. Hesione was sister
and wife to Prometheus, though Aeschylus, gently expurgating,

Schol. A agrees. They ought also, while they were about it, to have
expurgated the word περ in Ω 130. The passage of Aesch. *Myrmidones*,
fr. 135, Nauck, has been grossly misinterpreted by Athenaeus. Blass
has pointed out that the words are addressed to Ares; his 'kisses' are the
wounds.

makes her only half-sister by the father (*Prom.* 559). Such a queen was doubly august. Arêtê, we are told, 'was honoured as no mortal woman is honoured in these days, of all who hold their houses under a husband's rule.' She was hailed like a god when she went abroad (η 66 ff.). This is the genuine language of the Saga, and we know how to understand it. But in classical Greece there had arisen a spirit to which such a union was 'unholy', *incestum*. And as we read on in the *Odyssey* we find a genealogy inserted which in somewhat confused language explains that when the Saga said 'parents' (τοκήων) it only meant 'ancestors', and when it said that Alcinoüs' brother Rhexenor, died 'childless' (ἄκουρον) it only meant 'without male child'! Arêtê was really the daughter of the said brother It was only a marriage between uncle and niece.

Next, there has been a very careful expurgation of divers cruel or barbarous practices, especially, I think, of those which seemed characteristic of inferior races. The *Iliad* is full of battles, and of battles fought with extraordinary fire. Yet the spirit of them is not savage. It is chivalrous. No enemy is ever tortured No prisoners—with one exception to be noticed later—are ever maltreated. Let us take two special cases where signs of ex-purgation are visible.

We know that the dead body of Hector was dragged by Achilles round the walls of Troy. That seems bad enough It seemed so to the poet: and the repentance of Achilles is the main theme of the last two books of the *Iliad*. But a far worse story was really handed down by the tradition. There are fragments of the rude unexpurgated saga still extant, according to which Hector was still alive when his enemy tied him to the chariot rail and proceeded to drag him to death. Sophocles, always archaic in such matters, explicitly follows this legend (*Ajax*, 1031). So does Euripides (*Androm.* 399). Even so late a writer as Vergil seems to adopt it.[1] In fact, it may be said on the whole to dominate the tradition. But Homer will have none of it (X 361-95). Hector was dead—we are told so not only in explicit language, but with rather peculiar repetition

---

[1] *Aeneid* ii. 273 'perque pedes traiectus lora *tumentis*.' Vergil was probably copying the *Iliu Persis* in this passage.

—before Achilles began the ἀεικέα ἔργα, 'the shameful deeds.' 'And a dust cloud rose about him as he was dragged, and the long dark hair spread wide, and all the head lay in the dust, which before was beautiful; but now Zeus gave him up to them that hated him, to be foully wronged in his own fatherland.'

Again, there is, as we have said, no torture in the *Iliad*. But there is a passage where a particularly dreadful wound is described with, possibly, a certain gusto. The writhing man is compared to a bull struggling in a net, and his pain is dwelt upon. So far, perhaps, some older poet. But immediately a saving line is added—a line of the sort that is technically called 'inorganic', that is, which can be added or left out with no effect upon the grammar or continuity. It runs, 'So he struggled *quite a little while, not at all long*' (μίνυνθά περ, οὔ τι μάλα δήν, N 573). Now in the *Odyssey*, which, as I have said, is less rigorously cleaned up than the *Iliad*, there is one scene of torture. It is where the treacherous handmaids and the goatherd are to be killed. It has been decreed that the handmaids shall not 'die by a clean death'. They are then hung up in a row with nooses round their necks, 'so that they should die in grievous pain'. So far, I think, the older poet. There follows instantly the same saving verse: 'Their feet struggled for quite a little while, not at all long!' (χ 473). The torture of women was unpleasant even to an audience which approved the cruelty to the goatherd.

Take another case, equally clear. The ordinary practice of Homeric war allowed a warrior to take his dead enemy's armour. This has, I suppose, been the case in all ages. But there was a way of stripping the slain which added a sting of outrage to the spoiling. The victor tore the dead man's tunic and left him naked. This practice has been for the most part expurgated out of the poems. Heroes are allowed to speak of it as a possibility, or even to threaten it.[1] But they are not allowed actually to practise it. There are two instructive passages. In N 439 Idomeneus has pierced a man through the breast, and then 'rends his tunic about him'. That is not pleasant: so the line is added, 'even the tunic of bronze, which aforetime pro-

---

[1] B 416, Π 841, just as they speak of αἰκία to the dead as a possibility, Π 545, 559, and often.

tected his body from death.' The tunic becomes a tunic of
bronze. It was only the man's breastplate that Idomeneus
'rent'! In another passage, too (Δ 100), there are signs of a
confused effort to escape from this barbarity. Agamemnon has
slain some men and taken their armour; then he leaves them
'with their breasts gleaming, when he had stripped off their
tunics'. So it must originally have run. But in our present
texts, instead of 'tore' or 'stripped', there is a word (περίδυσε)
which occurs nowhere else in Homer, but which must by all
analogy mean 'drew round' or 'put on'. Agamemnon has
decently drawn the dead men's tunics over them![1] There are
many struggles on the part of commentators. There is a variant
reading which settles the matter by saying nothing about tunics
at all. Perhaps the most curious thing, linguistically, is that the
force of the context was too strong for the natural meaning of
the word περιδύω, and in later Greek it was normally taken, on
the strength of this passage, as meaning 'to strip'. Of course,
this sort of thing breeds confusion, and the corrector is no doubt
prepared to face it. The audience may be puzzled for a second.
But that will pass. If you told them that Agamemnon, their
great king, did on the battle-field one of those revolting things
that barbarians delight in and all decent Greeks utterly abjure,
the awkwardness would not pass so easily.

Another very interesting instance has been pointed out to
me by Professor J. A. K. Thomson. All through the poem
the heroes threaten at times to cut off one another's heads, and
sometimes in hot blood actually do so (e. g. Δ 147, N 202 ff.).
In P 39 Euphorbus threatens to carry off the 'armour and head'
of Menelaus; at 125 Hector is dragging Patroclus in order to
'cut the head off his shoulders with sharp bronze'. In Σ 177
Hector's heart urges him to cut off Patroclus' head and fix it up
on a post, like an African chief. And in the same book, 334,
Achilles, addressing the dead Patroclus, says, 'I will not bury

---

[1] στήθεσι παμφαίνοντας, ἐπεὶ περίδυσε χιτῶνας, Λ 100. See various interpre-
tations and strange constructions in Ameis, Anhang. Povelsen, the first of
modern scholars to point out the proper meaning of περιδύω, actually thought
that Agamemnon put on the shirts himself. Van Leeuwen and others call
the lines spurious or corrupt. The ancient v. l. referred to is ἐπεὶ κλυτὰ τεύχε'
ἀπηύρα. Aristarchus himself made παμφαίνοντας agree with χιτῶνας, an
obvious makeshift.

thee till I bring to thee here Hector's armour and head.' Compare X 348.

'Now I think,' writes Mr. Thomson, 'that in the original story Achilles carried out his threat. Look at the passage where Achilles' dealings with the body of Hector are described, Ψ 24 ff. "So spake he, and devised upon godlike Hector hideous deeds (ἀεικέα ἔργα): having stretched him prone by the bier of Patroclus . . ." He did what? Presumably deeds that deserved to be called 'hideous', but all that follows is: "in the dust; and the Myrmidons began to put off their armour and loosed their steeds." I cannot get away from the impression that something objectionable has been left out after τανύσσας, and the threat beforehand enables us to guess what that something was.'

It is interesting in this connexion to remember the story in Herodotus ix. 78, how Lampon, son of Pytheas, proposed to King Pausanias, after the battle of Plataea, that he should cut off the Persian Mardonios' head and fix it up on a pole, and the rage with which Pausanias rejected such barbarity; or the horror with which Aeschylus speaks of 'lands where men's heads are cut off and their eyes put out by process of law, boys castrated as eunuchs and men mutilated, stoned and impaled' (*Eum.* 186). Such deeds belonged to the "Beastly Devices of the Heathen," and were not likely to be tolerated in Homer.

Again, there is the matter of poisoned arrows. There is no doubt whatever that the primitive inhabitants of Greece poisoned their arrow-heads. The very word for poison,[1] τοξικόν, means 'belonging to an arrow'. And many myths tell of the incurable and burning pains caused by arrows. The arrows of Heracles in Hesiod (*Aspis*, 132) 'had death on the front of them and trickled with drops' (cf. Scholia). Think of the hydra-dipped shafts of Philoctetes. Think of the arrows of Apollo, bringing pestilence. Think also of the peculiar word, so often applied to arrows and arrow wounds, ἄφυκτος, 'from which there is no escape'. Does it not mean 'incurable' much more than

---

[1] This has been questioned, but cf. Strabo, p. 165 d Ἰβηρικὸν δὲ καὶ τὸ ἐν ἔθει παρατίθεσθαι τοξικόν, ὃ συντιθέασιν ἐκ βοτάνης σελίνῳ προσομοίας. Also Dioscorides, vi. 20 τοξικόν, ἐκ τοῦ τὰ τόξα τῶν βαρβάρων ὑπ' αὐτοῦ χρίεσθαι. This puts the point exactly: poison was barbarous. Cf. also Luc. *Nigrin.* 37 and Paul. Aegin. 5. 53, where τοξικόν is a special poison.

'unerring'?   The same thought explains why Erôs is generally
armed with arrows, not with a great spear.   He makes a wound
which looks slight, which perhaps hardly shows: but there is
in it a burning poison from which the stricken man does not
escape.

Now in the *Iliad* this poison has been completely cleaned
off from the arrow-heads.   Poison is treacherous, ungentle-
manly; a weapon for low barbarians, not for heroes.   Yet you
can see from a number of lines what the arrows originally were.
Old phrases have been left unchanged: when Pandaros shoots
Diomêdês in the shoulder he shouts in triumph that he cannot long
'support the strong arrow', that is, that he cannot long survive
(*E* 104).   In *Δ* 139 the arrow only just grazed Menelaus's skin;
but Agamemnon immediately thought he would die.[1]   In v. 218
Machaon the leech attends to this wound, and the first thing he
does is to suck out the blood.   Why, unless it was poisoned?
In *E* 394 the story is told how Heracles once wounded Hera with
an arrow, and 'the incurable pain laid hold of her'.   Archers in
Homer chose out an arrow 'unshot before', whose poison had
not been rubbed off (*Δ* 117, &c.).   An arrow is habitually
described by epithets which gain point as soon as we remember
that arrows once were poisoned.   They are 'bitter', 'charged
with groans', 'a foundation of black anguish'.[2]   The *Odyssey*,
as before, being less expurgated, is more explicit.   In *α* 261 we
are told how Odysseus once went to Ephyra, to Ilos, son
of Mermeros—an ominous name—to seek a man-slaying drug
to anoint his arrows withal.   But Ilos would not give it him.
He feared the *nemesis* of the eternal gods.   'But my father,' the
speaker continues, 'gave him some.   For he loved him greatly.'
The Odysseus of the earliest legends must of course have used
poison.[3]

We come next to a more complicated subject.   With one exception, to be considered later, both *Iliad* and *Odyssey* are completely expurgated of the abomination of Human Sacrifice.

---

[1] Of course, in the present course of the story, Agamemnon is reassured by
finding the wound slight.

[2] πικρὸς ὄϊστός, βέλεα στονόεντα, μελαινέων ἔρμ' ὀδυνάων (whatever ἔρμα may
mean).

[3] Cf. *Laws of Manu*, vii. 90.   'In war no poisoned weapons are to be
used, and no insults are to be addressed to a fallen enemy.'   I take this note
from Mr. Romaine Paterson's eloquent book, *The Nemesis of Nations.*

The Homeric spirit would have no dealings with such things. It had too much humanity : it had too little intensity of superstition. It did not denounce human sacrifice as Jeremiah, for instance, denounced the rites of the Tophet outside Jerusalem.[1] It is not Homer's way to denounce a thing that he objects to. He merely sweeps it out of existence.

The early Greek myths are full of human sacrifices. One can think at once of Menoikeus, Athamas, Phrixus and Hellê, the children of Heracles, Macaria, Iphigenia, Polyxena, and the numerous virgin-martyrs of tragedy. If these stories were mere fiction, it would be possible—though still difficult—to hold that they were unknown to 'Homer': that they were the horrid inventions of later poets, trying to outbid their predecessors. But they are not fiction. Nearly all of them come straight from some ancient and disused religious rite, or some relic of very primitive tradition. Iphigenia, for instance, is a form of an ancient anthropoctonous goddess, identified with Artemis.[2] Polyxena is a queen of the Underworld, 'Poly-xeina,' 'She of the many Guests,' the wife of 'Polydector' or 'Polydegmon'. Some of these bloody traditions are doubtless Phoenician, and therefore later.[3] But others are pre-Hellenic. And even those due to Phoenician influence were more than early enough for those middle and later generations of the Homeric poets which were mainly responsible for the work of expurgation. In the case of Iphigenia, indeed, one can almost see the marks of the excision.[4] Now Homer has cut out these stories for their revoltingness, just as he cuts out the cannibalism of Lycaon and Pelops, or the mutilations of the Hesiodic gods. That is a sufficient reason,

---

[1] Jer. vii. 31, xix. 5 ff., xxxii. 35; Ezek. xvi. 20 f., 36, xx. 26, 31, xxiii. 37, 39. Cf. Mic. vi. 6–8, &c., and laws in Deut. xii. 31, xviii. 10, &c.

[2] Artemis-Iphigenia worshipped in Hermione, Paus. ii. 35. 1. Cf. Hesych. Ἰφιγένεια· ἡ Ἄρτεμις (Farnell, *Cults of Greek States*, vol. ii, chap. xiii, note 34), and βωμὸς θεᾶς μοι μνῆμα τῆς Διὸς κόρης (Eur. *I. A.* 1444), i. e. Artemis's altar was Iphigenia's tomb !

[3] On the date of the main period of Phoenician influence in Greece see Myres in *C. R.* x. pp. 350 ff., and my article 'Odysseus' in the *Quarterly Review* for April, 1905.

[4] (B 303–29; cf. Aesch. *Ag.* 115 ff., and the *Cypria*.) In Aeschylus and the *Cypria*, when the bad omen occurs, Calchas declares that Artemis is wroth with Agamemnon and demands the sacrifice of Iphigenia. In B, when the δεινὰ πέλωρα invade the hecatombs and the Greeks are silent with horror, Calchas rises and declares—merely that they will take Troy in the tenth year ! One cannot but suspect that originally there was a price demanded for that victory.

and, as regards the *Odyssey*, it may be the only one that operates. But if we look closer into the old stories of human sacrifice we shall see that the subject has ramifications, and that there were other causes contributing to this cleansing of the Homeric atmosphere. With most of them we shall sympathize, with one possibly not.

To take the latter first. The stories of human sacrifice that have come down to us in myth are nearly all, for some reason or other, sacrifices of virgins. One cannot be quite sure whether this is due to history or to romance. The stories generally occur in the climax of a tragedy or some similar place, where they are intended to produce an effect of romantic horror. So that naturally young virgins are chosen as the victims, rather than, let us say, middle-aged merchants. Yet, on the other hand, it is likely enough that when such deeds were done it was more the practice to slay a young girl than a man. The girl was more likely to be ceremonially perfect: she was of less value to the tribe; she would be, at the best, more ready to die willingly, and, at the worst, easier to kill.

Now the *Odyssey* stands on a different footing; but I suspect that these stories would have been rejected from the *Iliad*, not only because human sacrifice was a barbarity, but also because the stories involved too intense an interest in women.

The Achaioi of the *Iliad* are habitually described by a rather curious phrase, κάρη κομόωντες, not so much 'long-haired' as 'letting the hair on the head grow long'. We may remember the long hair of the Spartans at Thermopylae, and the Δωριέες τριχ-άϊκες. As to the original meaning of this phrase, I cannot help suspecting that we may follow up a hint thrown out long since by Robertson Smith. It means that the men were votaries.[1] They had made a vow – ὑπόσχεσις is the Homeric word[2]—to take Troy, and this implied a vow not to do certain specified things until they had taken Troy. Like the warriors of the Old Testament, they were consecrated.[3] In modern language they

---

[1] Analogous cases in *Religion of the Semites*, p. 333, and Additional Note 1, Taboos incident to Pilgrimages and Vows.

[2] B 286 ff. ὑπόσχεσις of the Greeks. In B 349 it is Διὸς ὑπόσχεσις; in B 339 it is ὅρκια. In Υ 84 Aeneas ὑπέσχετο (had made a vow) to fight Achilles. The Franks had similar practices.

[3] Cf. 2 Sam. xi. 11 (Uriah), 1 Sam. xxi. 4 f., and WAR in *Enc. Bibl.* Cf. also Paus. i. 37. 3, viii. 41. 3 (hair kept for river worship).

were *taboo* while on the war-path, and the duty of never cutting,
combing, or washing the hair was the visible sign of various
other abstinences.   The most important among these was
abstinence from sexual relations with women.   I think that the
Iliad is quite consistent throughout in the recognition of this
taboo, a somewhat surprising fact.   For the Poems seldom care
to be consistent about anything that does not occupy the front
plane of a hearer's attention.   The nearest approach to a breach
of it is perhaps the situation in *A*.   It seems odd that men under
a vow of this sort should quarrel about women-captives.   But it
only seems odd because we think of the siege of Troy as a long
period.   The Greeks had some hopes of taking Troy that very
day (*B* 29, 66, 413), and then the vow would be ' off '.   Agamemnon's language is strictly correct (vv. 31, 113).   He always
associates his love of Chryseis with ' home ' and ' returning to
Argos '.   True, Achilles and Patroclus do not observe the taboo
in *I*, but that is because they have definitely renounced it, as they
have renounced their part in the war (*I* 665 ff.).[1]   Agamemnon
seems to have observed it (*I* 133, 275).   Nestor is too old to be
bound by it, and is waited upon by a handmaid, Hecamêdê
(*Λ* 624).   I suspect that the peculiar woman-ignoring atmosphere of the *Iliad* may have been due originally to this ancient
taboo of warriors on the war-path;   and that later, when the
actual religious ground had been forgotten, there remained
a womanless atmosphere and a feeling that any female interest
was out of place in a high story of war.   That is why there is no
Brunhild or Guinevere among the motive forces of the *Iliad*:
only a Patroclus.   Love for a friend and fellow soldier is the only
love austere enough for this strife of heroes.

The exceptions to this ignoring of women are to be found
among the women of Troy, chiefly Helen and Andromache.

---

[1] Cf. Ψ 144, where Achilles renounces, for specific reasons, the vow not to
cut his hair.   This perhaps explains the breach of the taboo in Ω 676.
There seems to be a dim recognition of some such custom as I suggest in
Schol. AD on B 11, explaining the words κάρη κομόωντες.   ' The Greeks of old
used to let their hair grow long ἀρετῆς καὶ ἀνδρείας χάριν.'   Where was the
' courage and virtue' unless it was in some vow of the war-path?—Of course
it is not suggested that everybody who was not keeping his vow had his hair
short; e. g. Hector in X 402, Euphorbos, P 51 f., and of course Paris, whose
motives are obvious.   There may be a reference to this custom in the
complaint of Ajax's sailors, ἐρώτων δ' ἐρώτων ἀπέπαυσεν οἴμοι (ὁ πόλεμος), Soph.
Aj. 1205.

The Trojans were not under any such vow as the Achaeans. They would have been only too glad for the war to stop any day. They were not growing their hair long.   In a Trojan atmosphere women can be described and made interesting.   It is in a Trojan atmosphere, in the close neighbourhood of the great parting of Hector and Andromache, that we have the one mention in the *Iliad* of tragic or guilty love, the story of Anteia's passion for Bellerophon.   And how sternly it is cut down to a bare *résumé* of facts !   That whole subject, which has formed the most fruitful spring of modern drama and romance, occupies in the whole *Iliad* six lines out of some fifteen thousand ! (*Z* 160–5).   These Trojan princesses in the *Iliad* and many beautiful passages in the *Odyssey* show how the Homeric poets could write about women if they would.   But in the case of the Trojan women themselves we may notice two points.   In the first place, splendid as their pictures are, there is no love interest about them.   The whole of that subject is steadily ignored.   Secondly, the great passages all occur in what are generally considered as late parts of the *Iliad* : and, as we shall often have occasion to notice, the later parts of Homer show in many ways a growth of the spirit of drama or tragedy.   To the mind of a poet who had begun to move toward that great conception, the position of the women in a besieged and doomed city must have been in itself a subject of such compelling interest that he might well venture to the very verge of his traditional field in order to treat of it.   Andromache, the loving and noble wife of the great enemy, is a being made for tragedy.

But outside these two or perhaps, if we add Hecuba, three Trojan women there is a steady suppression of female interest in the *Iliad*.   There is no sacrifice of Iphigenia ; no sacrifice of Polyxena.[1]   The Amazons, firmly seated as they are in early Epic legend, are only mentioned in late and so-called spurious passages (*Γ* 189, *Z* 186).   The crimes of the great wicked heroines, Clytemnestra, Epicaste, Eriphyle, Procne, Althaia, Skylla, and the like, are kept carefully away from the *Iliad*, and

---

[1] Cf. Paus. i. 22. 6 of Polyxena: 'Homer did well to omit so savage a deed ; and he did well, I think, to represent Skyros as captured by Achilles, therein differing from those who say that Achilles lived in the company of the maidens at Skyros.'   The case of Clytemnestra in the *Odyssey* is peculiar, and needs separate treatment.

allowed only a scanty mention in the *Odyssey*. There is nothing about Creusa, Aeneas's wife, though she was an important character in saga and received worship as a goddess. There is nothing about the prophetess Cassandra. The prophesying of Troy is done by a man, Helenus. Through nearly all the *Iliad* there reigns that austere and unsympathetic spirit which breathes in the words attributed to Pericles, 'that a woman's fame is to be as seldom as possible mentioned by men, either for praise or blame' (Thuc. ii. 45). This Thucydidean spirit is curiously different from that of Aeschylus and Euripides. It is quite different even from that of the *Odyssey*. It is a spirit so monstrously arrogant that we are apt to overlook a certain grandeur which it possesses. When one thinks of the part sometimes played by women in history—for instance, in French history— one must feel, to put it at the lowest, a certain perverted spiritual dignity in the fact remarked upon by Wilamowitz, that in the whole political history of Athens there is only one woman, but she pervades everything: the mail-clad Virgin of the Acropolis.

The victims, then, in these stories of human sacrifice are in most cases virgins. But they have another characteristic. They are all, without exception, persons of royal blood. That is to say, they all owe their original creation to that dark and wide-reaching tract of early religion which has lately been illuminated to us by the work of Dr. Frazer. At the back of them stands that to us almost incomprehensible being, which somehow commended itself to the mind of primitive man, the divine king who embodies the life of his tribe, and who must be born anew at fixed periods lest that life should grow weak. He is generally called a vegetation spirit, since the welfare of the trees and crops is the first need of an agricultural tribe. But he affects not only the fruits of the soil, but also the flocks and the human beings. So it is better to consider him as embodying the life, or the vital force, of the community. As such he is the seed and origin of the tribal god. If the tribal god is a beast or totem, as he may be, it is because at a pre-theistic stage such a beast was the chosen vehicle of the tribal life.

I will not spend more words in explaining this worship of the divine king; is it not written in the *Golden Bough*, in the *History of the Early Kingship*, and the lectures on *Attis, Adonis, and*

Osiris? In their origin the slaughtered king, the god-king, and the beast-king belong to the same region.[1] They were largely identical beings. In Greek mythology as we know it, these beings, like other barbarisms, have been in divers ways transformed; but we can see their traces.

In Phthiotis, in Thebes, and in Athens we meet well-known stories of the usual type: the city is doomed to destruction unless one of the royal blood shall die for the people. In Athens the last king, Codrus, sacrifices himself. In Thebes the one remaining male of the royal line, Menoikeus, sheds his life-blood into the dragon's den. In Phthiotis the stories are more confused. Phrixus and Hellê fly away, though Hellê ultimately dies; the king Athamas is condemned to die, but always escapes at the last moment. In some cases, it would seem, the divine king was ἐννέωρος. He was allowed to live for 'nine seasons',[2] and then was removed before the sacred force had time to abate.

[1] On the original Greek βασιλεύς or θεός as medicine-man, and the κράτος καὶ βία, or *mana*, that filled him, see *Anthropology and the Classics*, p. 75 f. The history of this divine *mana* would well repay a monograph. It is always, I think, associated with the power of the thunder. In Hesiod, *Nikê, Kratos* and *Biê* are always at the hand of Zeus; in Call. *H. Jov.* 67 it is they who made him king; in the *Prometheus*, of course, they are his ministers. The divine kings of the Ptolemaic period regularly possess νίκην καὶ κράτος εἰς τὸν ἅπαντα χρόνον, implied in their βασιλεία (Dittenb. *Orient. Gr.* 90, 35, and note 102); or κράτος alone, or σωτηρία καὶ κράτος, or σωτηρία καὶ νίκη, or the like. The same with Roman emperors: Ditt. *Or. Gr.* 614 init.; 625, 5; 678 init. Id. *Sylloge* 757. 932, 5. Our own liturgy has familiarized us with a development of this, ἡ βασιλεία καὶ ἡ δύναμις καὶ ἡ δόξα εἰς τοὺς αἰῶνας. In earlier times Tyrtaeus (4) says it is right that the Kings, honoured of God, should lead (ἄρχειν), δήμου δὲ πλήθει νίκην καὶ κάρτος ἕπεσθαι, the real divine power should belong to the demos! Solon (5) claims that he has given the κράτος to the Demos, 'as much as is sufficient.'

[2] As to ἐννέωρος, the first thing to notice is that the word means 'of nine seasons', and leaves us to find out what the 'season' is. And as a matter of fact it varied in successive ages. First, in the time of the primitive Moon Calendar it was a month or a quarter (Eustath. κ 390); at another stage it was a half-year, a summer or a winter, a mode of reckoning which has left its traces even in Thucydides. Last, when the Solar Year was well established, it was a year. We shall find traces of all three uses; for the present the second is the most important. What, then, is the meaning and the special relevance of *nine half-years*? In the first place, let us realize that when the Greeks said 'every nine half-years' they did not mean 'every four-and-a-half years' as we should; they meant every four years. Just as, when reckoning in whole years, they called the same period a *Penteteris*, 'a five-yearly period.' Ἐννέωρος means the same as 'penteteric'. The special importance of the four-year period is, of course, that by a little adjustment, and giving the Olympiad 50 and 49 months alternately, it enabled the Solar and Lunar years to coincide. Hence the great four-yearly games and festivals. Minos, we learn, ἐννέωρος βασίλευε, Διὸς μεγάλου ὀαριστής (τ 179). I cannot

Nine seasons comprised the life of the two vegetation-heroes, the Sons of the Threshing-floor, Otus and Ephialtes, who tried to scale heaven and were slain (λ 311). Nine seasons also, strangely enough, formed the limit of each incarnation of the divine Minos, the perpetual king of Crete (τ 179). Mr. A. B.

help suspecting that Minos was a divine king, periodically subjected to some ordeal or deposed or murdered; i. e. the Bull-King was regularly every nine *horai* driven into the Bull-God's cave and there, really or ostensibly, sacrificed. Compare a coin of Magnesia, a great centre of Bull-worship, in which the Bull is kneeling at the entrance to a cave, which it seems about to enter. It kneels, of course, as a sign of willingness. (*Brit. Mus., Ionia,* xix. 9; I owe this reference to Miss Harrison.)

The evidence is: (1) He ruled for nine *horai*, therefore presumably he somehow ceased to rule at the end of that period. (2) We have the definite tradition that he went up into the Cave 'every nine years' to converse with Zeus, to receive new commandments (προστάγματα or νόμους) and give an account of his stewardship (Plato, *Minos*, 319 d, *Laws*, 624 b, 630 d, 632 d; Strabo, pp. 476, 482, 762, citing Ephorus and Plato). 'Zeus' is merely the Greek way of naming the Cretan Bull-God. The word 'years' has crept in with the change of custom in reckoning. (3) This going into the cave of the Bull-God can hardly be separated from going into the Labyrinth to be slain by Mino-tauros. And the bloody tribute of seven youths and maidens was, according to Plutarch, sent to the Minotaur 'every nine years' (*Vit. Theseus*, xv). Did they conceivably at some stage die with the king or for him? It is noteworthy that the said divine Bull was originally 'made angry' (ἐξηγριώθη) against Minos by the special wrath of Poseidon (*Apld.* iii. 1. 1, 3), which looks as if originally it was Minos himself who was supposed to be killed by it. (4) It bears out these suspicions that we have no saga-tradition of Minos's death. (The first is Hdt. vii. 170, how a Minos was killed in Sicily and his tomb worshipped.) That is, perhaps, he did not die, or his death was a secret. He went into the holy cave and came out rejuvenated after his converse with God.—There is, or was a few years ago, an ordeal in Lower Nigeria, by which people go up a sacred road to the cave of the 'Long Juju', and, if condemned, never come out again. Minos's mother, Europa, who, as a young girl (I cannot find if she was nine years old), was carried off by the Bull-Zeus, was also the wife of Asterios, which was the name of the Minotaur. Minos himself pursued Dictynna-Britomartis 'for nine months'; at the end of which time she threw herself into the sea (Schol., Eur. *Hip.* 1130). Has the proverbial 'nine-year-old ox' of Hesiod (*Erga*, 436) any bearing on this subject? Aristotle, *Hist. An.* 575 b, says that an ox is at his prime when πεντέτης or ἐννέωρος: 'which is the same thing'. In view of the connexions between Crete and Sparta, it is interesting to find that the Ephors 'every nine years' watched for falling stars and then sent to Delphi to ask if the kings should continue to reign or not (Plut. *Agis*, 11). Cf. also *Aetia Graeca*, 12 (Charila sacrifice), and Paus. viii. 2. 6 (the were-wolves resume human shape after nine years). Also Pind. ap. Pl. *Meno* 81 b (p. 133 Chr.) ἐνάτῳ ἔτεϊ ἀνδιδοῖ ψυχὰς πάλιν. The way in which these rituals stuck to the letter of nine *horai* while freely varying the meaning of *horê* is instructive to a student of human nature.

I subjoin the other passages where the word ἐννέωρος occurs in Homer: in κ 19 the mystic bag given by the King of the Winds is ἀσκὸς βοὸς ἐννεώροιο: *ib.* 390, Kirkê's enchanted victims are σιάλοισιν ἐοικότες ἐννεώροισιν: cf. Eustath. *ad loc.*: in Σ 351 Patroclus' wounds are filled ἀλείφατος ἐννέωροιο, which had some magic power, ὡς φαρμακώδη τὴν δύναμιν ἔχοντος says Schol. A.

Cook has shown how Minos was a bull-god as well as a king,[1] and established his connexion with other periodic kings, such as the Olympian victors. It is pretty clear from various evidence—the Minotaur itself would be enough—that Minos on certain occasions wore the bull-mask which asserted his divine nature. It was the same with that other perpetual king, Pharaoh. At the periodical feast of the royal marriage Pharaoh was masked as Osiris and Pharaoh's wife as Isis, the deities whose incarnation they were. I will not multiply instances from the daemonic masks of tragedy, the apotropaic masks of comedy, the totem masks of Red Indian tribes, the bull-headed and snake-headed maidens and youths in the Mithras ritual. I will not dwell upon βοῶπις πότνια "Ηρη and the γλαυκώπιδα κούρην. There can be no doubt that these names reach back ultimately to a cow-goddess and an owl-goddess.[2] And we shall see in a later lecture how real is the historical connexion between such saga-figures as Agamemnon, Diomedes, Achilles, and these part-human, part-animal, part-divine tribal kings. But it is just this sort of barbaric bestial haziness that Homer will least of all things tolerate. For Homer there are no cow-goddesses nor yet cow-headed goddesses, no owl-goddesses nor yet owl-headed goddesses; only a goddess in supremely beautiful form who takes a blameless interest in cows or is attended by a faithful owl.

And in just the same spirit Homer has drawn sharp and clear the dividing line between men and gods. There are no persons

---

[1] See Mr. Cook's remarkable articles in *Class. Rev.*, 1903, and *Zeus* vol. i. pp. 491 f. (Minotaur the Cretan crown prince masquerading on a Bull), 662 n, 527 n. See also Bethe on Minos as the Bull-god of the Kefti (Egyptian for 'Cretans') in *Rh. Mus.* N.F. lxv. The saga reflects the fights of the Kefti in Attica.

[2] See also Cook on 'Animal Worship in the Mycenaean Age,' *J.H.S.*, 1894. 'The custom of wearing a mask of the deity worshipped is common in the religions of animal worship, in Egypt, Mexico, the South Seas, and elsewhere. Lang, *Myth, Ritual, and Religion*, ii. 284; ib. 130. Cf. also Moret, *Caractère religieux de la Monarchie égyptienne*; Dieterich, *Mithrasliturgie*. The main Greek text for Pharaoh is Diod. i. 62. The fabled metamorphoses of Proteus into various animals or a tree or fire are explained by the priests: ἐν ἔθει γὰρ εἶναι τοῖς κατ' Αἴγυπτον δυνάσταις περιτίθεσθαι περὶ τὴν κεφαλὴν λεόντων καὶ ταύρων καὶ δρακόντων προτομάς, σημεῖα τῆς ἀρχῆς· καὶ ποτὲ μὲν δένδρα ποτὲ δὲ πῦρ, ἔστι δ' ὅτε καὶ θυμιαμάτων εὐώδων ἔχειν ἐπὶ τῆς κεφαλῆς οὐκ ὀλίγα, καὶ διὰ τούτων ἅμα μὲν ἑαυτοὺς εἰς εὐπρέπειαν κοσμεῖν, ἅμα δὲ τοὺς ἄλλους εἰς κατάπληξιν ἄγειν καὶ δεισιδαίμονα διάθεσιν. The trees and the fire are perhaps invented for the sake of the Proteus story in the Odyssey, but the rest of the account seems to be true.

in the *Iliad* or *Odyssey*, as there are in the rest of Greek tradition, who appear now as one and now as the other. There is a definite avoidance of the makeshift bridge which satisfied Hesiod : ' the divine race of heroes, who are called demi-gods.' (See Leaf on M 23, and Schol. BL, *ibid*.) Kings may be descended from gods, and specially favoured by particular gods. But that is all. The peasants of the Peloponnese continued long after Homer's time to worship at the altars of a being called Zeus-Agamemnon.[1] They may have been far from clear as to the distinction between the God Cronos and his son Pelops at Olympia.[2] But in the *Iliad* Zeus, son of Cronos, is quite definitely a king of gods ; Agamemnon, son of Pelops, definitely a king of men. There is no shade of confusion between them.

It was a remarkable achievement of the Hellenic intellect, this clear realization that a man was not a god, and that it was no use calling him so. It needed such clearness of sight, such daring, such humanity.[3] We can see how hard the step was when we reflect how small a part of the human race rose to the height of following it. Think of the divine honours paid ages after this to the Roman emperors. Think of the senate agreeing to Caligula's claim of such honours for himself and his horse.[4] No doubt there were mitigating circumstances in Caesar-worship. The divine horse was an admitted eccentricity. Sensible men

---

[1] I see that Dr. Farnell doubts this ; in deference to so high an authority I cite my grounds for the statement at greater length : Lycophron, 1123 ff. (where Cassandra prophesies ἐμὸς δ' ἀκοίτης Ζεὺς ... Σπαρτιάταις ... κληθήσεται), also 335, 1359 ff., and Scholia. Also Clem. Al. *Protrept*. pp. 11, 18, cites Staphylus for the worship of Ἀγαμέμνονά τινα Δία ἐν Σπάρτῃ. Usener has pointed out what looks like an early trace of the same worship in Aesch. *Choeph*. 255 καὶ τοῦ θυτῆρος καί σε τιμῶντος μέγα (cf. also ibid. 358, πρόπολός τε τῶν μεγίστων | χθονίων ἐκεῖ τυράννων). This may be a case of the well-known sort, where two gods clash until one is made the priest or πρόπολος or κληδοῦχος of the other, as e. g. Iphigenia was κληδοῦχος of Artemis. Agamemnon was King of Sparta (Stesich. 39, Simon. 20), and died at Amyclae (Pind. *P*. xi. 32), where Pausanias saw his tomb.

[2] See Mayer in *Roscher's Lexicon*, 'Kronos': especially ii. 1507 ff. Observe that Pelops *is* Kronios, and that he also *conquered* Kronios. Paus. vi. 21. 11.

[3] Of course the making of the god in the first instance may have involved a confusion of thought; the god may be only a projection of the 'mana' of the medicine-king or the medicine-beast, or even simply 'le désir collectif personnifié'. See below, p. 275, note. But the advance remarked in the text was nevertheless enormous.

[4] Caligula also was an ὀαριστής of Jupiter Capitolinus, exactly like Minos. Suet. *Calig*. 22.

were conscious that the worship was in some sense metaphorical. Politicians found it useful for testing and impressing the loyalty of a distant oriental population. But the fundamental fact of the matter is that such deification of kings did not seem to educated Romans a thing unfamiliar or absurd. The old Roman kings themselves, as Dr. Frazer has shown, had been in their time personifications of gods. The various kings whom they had conquered were all gods, the kings of Egypt, of Syria, of Parthia. The old Hellenic spirit was not then alive to testify. The half-Greek Alexander and his generals had walked up and down in barbaric places, where the old unpurified swamp was still lying in the sun, and had caught the contagion of savage ideas. *La nostalgie de la boue* laid hold upon them. Alexander, who destroyed classical Greece, insisted that he was a god, and the son of a divine snake. Demetrius received a semblance of divine honour even in Athens. That is just the atmosphere which Homer and the spirit of early Hellenism had cleared away—one might have hoped, for ever.

Like other morbid growths of the primitive human mind, these deifications of living kings have had some particular developments that were beneficent and even splendid. But the verdict of sane thought is against them. It is not only that their history is written in blood. It is that they are in their very essence degrading to humanity. And their abolition during the few centuries in which the Hellenic power stood unbroken might of itself be taken as a fair measure of the importance of Greece to human progress.

So far, then, the cases which we have taken are instances of successful expurgation. The reforming Hellenic spirit has ultimately, with what difficulties and against what opposition we know not, executed its will. Let us now consider a place where it was baffled. Such passages were sure to occur in a traditional book. For the first business of all these ancient poets was to record history: and at times it happened that objectionable facts were clearly and ineradicably fixed in the history. The panegyrist of David who compiled our Book of Samuel could not ignore David's treatment of Uriah. The poet of Achilles cannot ignore the savagery of his hero's triumph.

The origin of the Uriah story in the midst of a tradition so greatly modified for the glorification of David is in many ways difficult to explain.[1] But in the case of Achilles we may take it as certain that in some early form of the saga, and even of the poem, the ferocity of his revenge was part of his glory. Hector did, it is true, by miserable treachery, contrive to kill Achilles' dearest friend. But what a revenge our great Achilles took! He tied Hector by the heels to his chariot, and dragged him to death : all his friends looked on and dared not interfere. Then he had fun with the body in all sorts of ingenious ways day by day, till there was nothing left of it. Much the Trojans could do to stop him! And as for Patroclus, a round dozen of Trojan nobles were slaughtered over his grave. That was how Achilles treated his enemies. That kept the dogs in their place.

Now what was to be done with such an incident as this? To Homer—if we may use that name to denote the authors of the prevailing tone of the *Iliad*—it was all odious and ugly. But it was too firmly fixed in the tradition to be denied. A part of the story, indeed, could be modified. Hector was saved from torture. As we saw earlier, he was killed first, and dragged behind the chariot afterwards. But what of the sacrifice of the twelve Trojans ? Any sacrifice was an important and lengthy act. The ordinary sacrifice of a bull in the *Iliad* has five lines allotted to it, or ten, if we count in the roasting operations (A 458-67, B 421-30). You would expect this sacrifice to have at the very least twenty. As a matter of fact it is crowded into a shamefaced line and a half! (Ψ 175). And that line and a half is merely part of another sentence : it has not a whole verb to itself. And it is followed by what certainly looks like one of the extremely rare phrases of moral condemnation in the Poems : 'Yea, his heart devised evil deeds.' You could scarcely have a clearer case of a poet recording a fact against his will. It is in a very different tone that the Book of Kings records the human sacrifices of the pious Josiah, when 'he slew all the priests of the High Places that were there, upon the altars, and burned men's bones upon them' (2 Kings xxiii. 20 ; cf. 1 Kings xiii. 2, where the word used is ' sacrifice ').

Even so, however, the fact stands recorded, and so does the

[1] Though see note at end of Lecture IV. The Deuteronomists did omit it.

maltreating of Hector's corpse.   No other corpse is so treated in the *Iliad*.   It is a difficulty like this that brings out the real greatness of Homer.   The whole of the last two books of the *Iliad* is occupied with the psychological tragedy of this foul action of Achilles.

In the first place there is not the faintest doubt as to the general sympathy of the narrative.   The gods, the reader, the poet, are all at one.   There is no exultation in the barbarity : there is only shame and regret.   I will go further.   Of all the thousands of ferocious young soldiers, Greek, Roman, mediaeval, and modern, who in their various days have read the *Iliad* and been ordered by their teachers to admire it, it is hard to imagine a single one rising from these last two books with a feeling that it was a fine feat to do as Achilles did, and mutilate your dead enemies.   But the wonderful thing that Homer does is to make you understand Achilles' state of mind.   The cruelties which he practises are those of a man mad with grief, a man starving and sleepless, who, when he yields at last, yields in a burst of helpless tears.   And it makes some difference, also, that Achilles is deliberately giving up his own life.   He has the special supernatural know-ledge that his revenge will be followed immediately by his death. He heaps all that he has, as it were, upon the pyre of the friend whom his own petulance and pride have caused to die.[1]

Homer, with his vibrating sympathy, his amazing language, and that fiery splendour of narrative which seems almost to have died out of the world when the *Iliad* was complete, can carry off these deeds of horror, and leave Achilles a hero.   Yet, even so, Achilles as a subject for poetry, like the actual Achilles of legend, paid for these savageries with an early death.   It is curious how little the Greek poets cared for him.   He was the uncontested hero of their greatest epic ; yet Greek literature as a whole tends to pass him by.   There is one lost Achillean trilogy by Aeschylus, of which it would be rash to speak : there is one

---

[1] Starving and sleepless for twelve days, Ω 31 ; tears, Ω 510 ff.   His own death, Σ 96 ff. ; cf. his wonderful words to Lycaon, Φ 106–13 : 'Nay, friend, die like another! What wouldst thou vainly weeping? Patroclus died, who was far better than thou.   Look upon me! Am I not beautiful and tall, and sprung of a good father, and a goddess the mother that bare me? Yet, lo, Death is over me and the mighty hand of Doom.   There cometh a dawn of day, a noon or an evening, and a hand that I know not shall lay me dead,' &c.

poignant and clever study of Achilles in Euripides' *Iphigenia in Aulis*. Late philosophers and pedagogues idealized or allegorized him at their pleasure. But he inspired little great poetry, and roused little imaginative interest compared with lowlier heroes. He was associated with some of the faults that Greece most hated, and he had not enough depth and variety of character to make him fascinating in spite of them. Even the man of many wiles, whose record in so many ways was far from stainless—for instance, in that little matter of the arrows—speaks much more in accordance with normal Greek feeling. When his great victory is accomplished and his wife and house delivered from outrage, and the old Nurse is about to shriek for joy, he bids her keep her joy in her heart, and refrain and make no cry:

Unholy is the voice
Of loud thanksgiving over slaughtered men (χ 412).

One cannot help remembering in this connexion that the *Iliad* in the fifth century occupied a central place in Greek education. All well-born youths were trained upon it. And later Attic writers speak with enthusiasm of the moral superiority of Homer —and when they say 'Homer' they chiefly mean the *Iliad*— over the other ancient poets. Such is the common way of human idealism. You first imagine ideal heroes and reshape your old traditions till they yield the patterns that you desire: then, forgetting they are your own creation, you contemplate them as real historical beings and are kindled into a burning desire to be like them. Whether this educational use of the *Iliad* began in Ionia as early as the seventh century, which is likely enough, or whether it only began in Attica in the sixth and fifth, we can hardly help supposing that it had some share in these processes of purification with which we have been dealing. The hand of the schoolmaster certainly seems to have been at work—though of course by different methods—in the case of another poet much used in education, Theognis. Such parts of his poetry as are obviously unedifying are relegated to a sort of appendix at the end of the book, and in many MSS. are omitted altogether.[1] But our evidence fails us. The use of the *Iliad* and *Odyssey* in

---

[1] Edifying passages from the old Ionic hortatory writers seem to have been introduced into Homer. See Mülder, as cited below, Lecture VII, p. 186. Also Bréal, *Pour mieux connaître Homère*, pp. 14 f.

education in classical times is a known fact, and a fact which must have operated in the way required. It is a *vera causa*. Yet it is quite likely that the educational use itself is also a result of some original moral superiority in the traditions of the conquering Northmen.[1]

Further consideration of this subject would lead us too far afield. I am content for the present moment if I have shown the mere fact that there was in the formation of the *Iliad*, and to a less extent in that of the *Odyssey*, a strong element of reform and expurgation. The tradition of early Greece, vast and tangled in its wealth of varied beauty and ugliness as some South American forest, was left by the Homeric poets a much cleaner and colder thing than they found it. In this result two influences chiefly were at work. First, a general humanizing of the imagination, the progress of a spirit which, as it loved beauty, hated cruelty and uncleanness. Secondly, the remnants of a race prejudice. The relations of the Northern and the aboriginal elements in the Homeric poems are involved, when you come to details, in inextricable unity. But in its origin the 'Homeric' convention seems to represent some far-off idealized image of the Achaean or northern spirit: the spirit of those scattered strong men who in their various settlements were leading and shaping the Aegean world. The special myths, beliefs, and rites that were characteristic of the conquered races are pruned away or ignored, the hero-worship, the oracles, the magic and witchcraft, the hocus-pocus of purification: all that savours of 'the monstrous regiment of women', the uncanny powers of dead men, and the baleful confusion between man and god.

Yet race prejudice is not quite the word. It is a race ideal, and more than a race ideal. For it finds its main impulse not in any maintenance of actual Northern tribes, past or existing, but in the building up of something yet unborn. The earlier bards had perhaps no name for this thing; it was only a quality which one felt in true Achaioi, Danaoi, or Argeioi. The later poets knew it as Hellenism. True, the great division between Hellenes and *barbaroi* is never in so many words expressed in the conventional language of the Epos. The words are, no doubt, too

---

[1] See note on p. 263 f.

modern. They would break the convention, and are deliberately excluded. But the feeling is there so strongly that eventually the name cannot be kept out, and it enters, when it does enter, in a strengthened and more un-epic form: 'Pan-Hellenes' or, rather more disguised, 'Pan-Achaioi'.[1]

Hellenism, as has often been remarked, denotes really not a unity of race, but a unity of culture. Through all antiquity the sons of Hellên were reckoned according to the spirit, not the flesh. And the word 'Pan-Hellenes' expresses just this. It implies a readiness to extend the great name to all who are willing to bear its burden, all who will live as Hellenes and take sides with Hellas.

Students of early Greek tradition are constantly brought up against a certain broad contrast, between what is Homeric and what is local. The local religion, the local legend, the local feuds between Greek and Greek—these are things for which Homer has in general no place. The Pan-Hellenism of Homer strikes a reader even at first sight: but it strikes him much more keenly when he reflects in what a network of feuds and fears and mutual abhorrences the life of primitive communities is involved. 'Thou shalt not abhor an Edomite; thou shalt not abhor an Egyptian,' says the Deuteronomist, breaking down the wall of hatred at particular points by definite injunctions. The Homeric bards issue no such commands. They strike unnoticed at the root of the whole system. They draw into the great orbit of the Epos the ancestral heroes of all the Achaioi, Argeioi, Danaoi· They show 'all Greeks' labouring together, all of them suitably idealized, all good men and true. They ignore everything that is really tribal and exclusive, all the peculiar local rites, the taboo tombs and secret names, which formed the very core of each little village worship. They will deal only with such gods as can stand publicly in the eyes of all Greece. It was a great attempt, and it involved a considerable imaginative sacrifice. But meantime the new nation came into being. It worshipped Zeus Hellanios, it attended the great Pan-Hellenic festivals, and there in the four-yearly Homeric recitations Hellas found its book.[2]

---

[1] Πανέλληνες B 530, Παναχαιοί at least 12 times.
[2] For an instance of the extension of this spirit to the 'Homeric' Hymns see Appendix G.

VI

THE ILIAD AS A TRADITIONAL BOOK

II. EVIDENCES

BUT let us turn to a question of evidence. I have been arguing on general grounds that what we should expect to find in the Homeric poems is some form of Traditional Book, which, like the *Song of Roland*, or the *Nibelungenlied*, or the Pentateuch, or even *Hamlet* or the Covent Garden text of *Richard III*, has reached its present form by a process of gradual growth and constant rehandling. That is what we should expect. And our study of the expurgations confirms our expectation. But is there in the poems themselves definite evidence to show that this is actually what happened? There is: and I will ask you to spend some time in considering it. At this point, unfortunately, the air begins to thicken with controversy, and controversy generally obscures understanding. I propose to argue as little as possible, but merely to make a re-statement of some of the evidence already observed by various Homeric critics. My case will be by no means complete. The evidence of language, for instance, to my mind the most fundamental of all, is not suitable for discussion in these lectures. But my object all through is illustration rather than argument.

What we require for our purpose will be a series of cases in which we already have reason to believe that a change of custom took place between the Mycenaean and the Classical ages, that is, roughly speaking, between the thirteenth century B.C. and the sixth. If the *Iliad* is, as we have argued, a traditional book, modified by succeeding generations, we shall expect to discover some traces of this process. Probably we shall find, roughly speaking, that on the surface the poem complies with the later customs, while deeper down there are marks of the older. For it is, by our hypothesis, an ancient poem worked over from time

to time to suit various new generations, or—to put the same thing
in another form—a comparatively later poem using masses of
ancient material. Let me say at once that we shall find nothing
amounting to demonstration. There is no possibility of demonstration in the case. We shall only find a number of comparatively
small and inconspicuous phenomena which are quite simple and
normal if the *Iliad* is a traditional book, and extremely puzzling
if it is not.

Perhaps the clearest case is the change of armour. The Greek
of Classical times was a conspicuous figure in his Ionian panoply.
He was clad in solid metal from head to foot : helmet, breastplate,
and backplate, small round shield, and greaves, all of metal.
When Psammetichus, king of Egypt, was driven from his throne,
he was told by the oracle at Buto to find *bronzen men* who
would restore him. He found them in the shape of Ionian and
Carian mercenaries (Hdt. ii. 152).[1]

---

[1] Hdt. I. 171 (οἱ Κᾶρες) . . . καὶ ὄχανα ἀσπίσι οὗτοί εἰσι οἱ ποιησάμενοι
πρῶτοι· τέως δὲ ἄνευ ὀχάνων ἐφόρεον τὰς ἀσπίδας πάντες οἵπερ εἰώθεσαν ἀσπίσι
χρᾶσθαι, τελαμῶσι σκυτίνοισι οἰηκίζοντες, περὶ τοῖσι αὐχέσι καὶ τοῖσι ἀριστεροῖσι
ὤμοισι περικείμενοι. Hdt. II. 152 ὡς τίσις ἥξει ἀπὸ θαλάσσης χαλκέων ἀνδρῶν
ἐπιφανέντων.... Ἴωνάς τε καὶ Κᾶρας. (*Circa* 650 B.C.) In view of criticism, let
me correct some false impressions. It is not part of my case to deny that
there were round shields and may have been breastplates in Crete or Egypt
in Minoan times: the evidence is doubtful; it depends on the Zakro seals,
which are difficult to interpret. The seal (*B.S.A.* xii. 241) selected by
Mr. Lang (p. 73) as most conclusive seems to me to represent a person
of uncertain sex carrying, not wearing, a ritual cope like that worn by the
leader of the Harvest Procession on the well-known steatite vase from Hagia
Triada. At any rate it covers the arms, and therefore can hardly be a
breastplate. But in any case Minoan is not Homeric, οὐδὲ ἐγγύς; it is
pre-Mycenaean, and Mycenaean is pre-Homeric.—My case is that we know
of a big-leather-shield-and-no-breastplate period both from the remains
and the definite statements of Herodotus ; and we know of a classical period
with small round shields and complete metal body-armour. And both these
periods can be traced in Homer. So far the argument is archaeological ;
then comes the philological confirmation, the fact that wherever the *thôrêx*
occurs in the poems it is always 'inorganic' and generally troublesome.
G. Lippold (*Münchener archaeologische Studien*, 1909, pp. 400–504) ably
argues that 'Mycenaean' is a misnomer. The big hanging leather shield of
Homer is the Dipylon shield, which he separates from the Mycenaean
and connects with the Boeotian. Dipylon shield-bearers often appear on
chariots, Mycenaean shield-bearers never.
    Mr. Lang, besides his valuable argument about the date of the Homeric
breastplate, raises interesting questions about the chiton, and why Homer
does not mention the κύπασσις or archaic bathing-drawers. I will not
attempt to deal with that question now, but I welcome it, as also the question
he raises about women's dress. The general result of such inquiries will be,

Now the warrior of an earlier generation—we will call him for convenience 'Mycenaean'; but the type lasted much later; it is assumed in parts of Tyrtaeus, and Herodotus conceives it as still normal about 650 B.C.—went to battle in a very different state. He was not in the least a 'bronzen man'. He had a leather helmet, sometimes perhaps adorned with bits of metal. He may have had sometimes a thick waistcoat or jerkin of linen to serve for a breastplate, and soft leather leggings in place of greaves. But normally he wore only a loin-cloth[1] and a linen tunic, while instead of any corselet or body-armour he used the loose skins of beasts, treated in one of two main ways. The common man got the best beast-skin he could, the fell of a wolf, a goat, a pard, or, if he could afford it, an ox; he tied this skin by the paws round his neck and let it hang. Then in battle he caught the lower flapping edge with his left hand and held the skin tight in front of him. It would keep off stones and arrows and perhaps sword cuts, and would give him at least one extra chance of dodging the cast of a spear. For he could whisk the skin aside as the spear pierced it.

The chieftain or rich man improved upon this simple defence. He had his ox-hide dried and made stiff and held in position by cross staves of wood. As to the shape, the hide might be left roughly in its natural condition, a sort of oblong; a shield, as Homer says, 'like a tower.' Such a shield covered the man admirably from head to foot. But unfortunately it was a little weak. It could be pierced by a spear-thrust. To meet that difficulty you could of course increase the thickness. You could have two, three, or four hides instead of one. But that increased the weight very seriously. Aias is said to have had a shield 'like a tower' consisting of seven ox-hides and a layer of metal. If so, it must have weighed rather more than twenty stone; we need not be surprised that it was famous, nor yet that no one else would have anything to do with it. But you could strengthen the shield without adding to the weight by another device.[2] It

in my judgement, that our *Iliad*, on the surface at least, is merely classical— it represents the normal expectations of an audience in Athens in the fifth century. To them, as to us, a hero dressed in bathing-drawers or a Helen in archaic flounces would be ἀπρεπές. (See on Cretan armour Prof. Burrows, *Crete*, pp. 37, 207.)

[1] See also Mackenzie in *B.S.A.* xii (1905-6).

[2] This remark I owe to Prof. J. L. Myres, who also suggests that the

can easily be practised on a half-sheet of note-paper. Take a piece of the rim of the ox-hide about the middle on both sides, a piece about a foot long, pinch the ends of each piece together and at the same time draw both pieces inwards. That will make the shield bulge out, both vertically and horizontally, till it projects into a boss or point in the centre. It will so be stronger in itself; it can easily be coated in the centre with a piece of metal; and, thirdly, weapons will glance off from it. The price you pay for these advantages is, of course, that you make your shield narrow in the middle. This is one reason, says Prof. Myres, why so many people in Homer get wounded in the thigh or flank.

Now this shield was not regularly held on the arm by a strap and handle like the later small shields. Its only strap was a long one which passed over the left shoulder and under the right arm. In the stress of battle a man's shield-strap 'sweated about his breast' (B 388), so that evidently there was no breastplate. The cross-staves perhaps formed a kind of handle by which you could move it to and fro at need—*steer your dry cow*, as Hector expresses it.[1] But you could, if necessary, let the shield simply swing, and advance on your enemy holding a great spear in both hands, or two smaller spears, one in each hand. The shield was so heavy that the warrior usually went in a chariot to the place

shields on the 'warrior Vase' are very likely Mycenaean shields with the staves taken out, folded up for carrying on the march. They do not fold flat, of course, hence the concave line at the bottom. The Dipylon shield is so badly drawn that it is hard to be sure about it, but it is Mycenaean in general character—large, leathern, suspended by a *telamôn*. The large leathern shield has left a great mark on poetic tradition. Protesilaos in the legend was buried in his shield; it was therefore Mycenaean. Similarly Astyanax in the *Troades* is buried in Hector's shield. Amphiaraus when he drove down to Hades was flying from the battle, and had his Mycenaean shield hung on his back; a vase-painter of the fifth century (*Wiener Vorlegeblätter*, 1889, xi. 8), not understanding this, makes him—very awkwardly—hold a small round metal shield behind his back (see Reichel, *Waffen*, p. 64). The shield in Eur. *Electra*, 430–80, shows Mycenaean tradition. In Tyrtaeus I think one can show a clash or blending, much as in Homer; this is natural enough. In fr. 11 the young Spartan is to stand ἐν προμάχοις . . . μηρούς τε κνήμας τε κάτω καὶ στέρνα καὶ ὤμους | ἀσπίδος εὐρείης γαστρὶ καλυψάμενος . . . ὑμεῖς δ', ὦ γυμνῆτες, ὑπ' ἀσπίδος ἄλλοθεν ἄλλος | πτώσσοντες μεγάλοις βάλλετε χερμαδίοις: a very 'Mycenaean' picture. In 12, 26, however, there is a θώρηξ and the men fight in lines (φάλαγγες 21). See Wilamowitz, *Die Textgeschichte der gr. Lyriker*, in *Abh. der Göttinger Gesellschaft der Wiss., philol.-hist. Klasse*, N.F. iv. 3 (1900).

[1] νωμῆσαι βῶν | ἀζαλέην, H 238. Herodotus uses the metaphor more strongly of the pre-Carian, i. e. Dipylon or Mycenaean, shield: τελαμῶσι σκυτίνοισι οἰηκίζοντες (i. 171).

where he wished to fight.   Arrived there, he dismounted, and stood with the shield 'like a tower' in front of him, or 'edged himself step by step forward' (ὑπασπίδια προποδίζων) into striking distance, being careful to keep always under cover.   Dangerous moments were those of getting down from the chariot, or getting up again, or turning to retreat.   There was also some danger of tripping, both when you turned and when you moved forward. For your shield-rim was close upon the ground, and you could not safely look so far over the top as to see the earth close in front of you.   When once you were in position, however, the cover was excellent, and there ensued what Homer calls a *stadiê husminê*, a 'standing battle'.   If no vital part of your enemy showed round the edge anywhere, you entered into conversation with him.   A happily directed insult might make him start, lift his head too high, or expose a piece of his flank.   Then you speared him.   If you were a very strong man, you could try to drive your spear clean through all his layers of ox-hide and reach his unarmed body.   Or you could even, as Hector and Aias some-times did, by a blow with a huge stone, knock his shield right back upon him and send him flat on the ground beneath it.

Peculiar and special tactics, as any one can see; and quite different from those of men armed with a small shield and a breastplate.   But now let us observe one particular piece of what I may call the normal defensive drill.   Suppose an enemy threw his spear with all his force against your shield, the proper plan, since you could not move the heavy 'cow' swiftly about, was to edge it as best you could in one direction and yourself twist rapidly in the other.   Then even if the spear came right through your shield, it probably missed you or only grazed your side.

Now what sort of armour, and what sort of tactics, do the Homeric poems describe?   It ought to be quite easy to say, considering how much close description of fighting they contain. As a matter of fact, if you consult Dr. Reichel, the discoverer of this whole series of facts, he will tell you that the Homeric heroes all fight in Mycenaean armour with the large shield and no breastplate, except for some few late interpolated passages. If you turn to Dr. Ridgeway, he will explain that the heroes all have metal breastplates and round shields, except some few individuals with 'Pelasgian' antecedents. Neither of these admirable writers has, I think, faced the fact of the gradual growth of the poems.[1] Each tries to make the poems square with one style of fighting or the other, and, when they refuse to do so, proceeds to casuistry or violence. That is not a fair way to behave. We must take the poems as they stand. And, as they stand, the main impression is pretty clear. The surface speaks of the Ionian or Athenian style of fighting, the heart of the narrative is something different and more primitive.

By 'the surface' of the poems I mean such parts as the formulae of introduction and transition, the general descriptive phrases, the inorganic lines and some of the perpetual epithets: all these are full of the Men of Bronze. We hear countless times of the 'greavèd Greeks',[2] of 'the bronze-clad Greeks', of 'the clash of men in bronzen breastplates' (Δ 448 = Θ 62), of 'the whole plain blazing with bronze' (Υ 156), of how 'men's eyes were blinded by the glitter of bronze from blazing helms and breastplates, new-burnished and gleaming shields' (N 341), of a warrior whose 'whole body shone with bronze, like the lightning of aegis-bearing Zeus' (Λ 66), or who 'gleams with the bronze wherein his body is clad' (M 463, cf. N 191, X 32, 134, &c., &c.). It is the Men of Bronze everywhere. The gods who watch the battle look down upon the 'flashing of bronze, men slaying and men slain' (Λ 83). And not only is it 'men of bronze' that we find in this sort of passage, but it is the tactics of 'men of bronze', the movement of ordered regiments of infantry in line, obeying their officers and making concerted movements, like the classical Greek *hoplitae*. 'The Trojans came on, like lines of waves on the sea, line behind line, flashing in bronze, to-

---

[1] See Robert, *Studien zur Ilias*, who makes this same criticism on Reichel (chap. i). Also Lippold, l. c.

[2] εὐκνήμιδες, only once χαλκοκνήμιδες, so that Reichel says the word only means 'with good gaiters'. But gaiters, even when not hidden behind a big shield, are not conspicuous or exciting objects, whereas the bronze greaves of a line of men marching would be both, as the legs moved and the bronze glittered. An epithet of this sort must be taken from something striking. I am informed by the Hon. Oliver Howard that among the Suras, a tribe against which he fought in Northern Nigeria in 1907, the cavalry wore permanent iron greaves fastened on by a blacksmith so that they could never be taken off, and fitted with a blunt spur on the inside of the calf. They wore nothing else, except perhaps a loin-cloth. I know of nothing like this in antiquity, however.

gether with their commanders' (*N* 801). The Greeks 'advanced in silence and in order, fearing their commanders, their hearts set upon supporting one another' (*Γ* 1–9, *Δ* 427–32). That is the way in which Nestor from time to time exhorts the Greeks to fight, 'so that clan shall support clan, and tribe tribe' (*B* 362 f.). It is the way which, we are told, the god Ares, as a professional, especially commended; that men should advance in *phalanxes*, or lines, in close array, shield touching shield, an impenetrable wall (*N* 126, 130 ff., 145). It is in this way that people are said to be going to fight before each great battle begins. But strangely enough it is not at all in this way that they really fight when the battle is fairly joined, in the heart of the poem. In the heart of the poem, when the real fighting comes, it is as a rule purely Mycenaean. It is essentially a battle of *promachoi*, or champions. Usually each champion drives forward on his chariot, dismounts and stands forth alone behind his big shield, to engage in a series of duels. At most two or three occasionally form together in a small group to check a rout or an advance.[1] At certain rare moments they drive their chariots into the thick of a yielding foe (*Θ* 88 f., 348).

We have illustrated enough already the tactics of these Mycenaean *promachoi* or 'champions in the forefront'. But the background of the Mycenaean battle deserves a word in passing. Behind the great shielded champions there seem to have lurked, in the real Mycenaean battle—first, individual

---

[1] This is perhaps the movement indicated on the small vase from Hagia Triada, described by Burrows (p. 38) from Paribeni in Rendiconti, *Acc. Linc.* xii. 324. See A. Mosso, *Escursione nel Mediterraneo*, Figs. 33, 34. In any case the chariots present some difficulties; see Cauer, *Grundfragen*, P, p. 268 f. Why is the chief epithet of the chief hero 'swift-of-foot'? Why, after the elaborate chariot-scene at his going forth in *T* 392 ff., does he never use the chariot in pursuing the Trojans all through the next three books? It is only once mentioned, and then in repeated lines in a simile (*Y* 499–503 = *Λ* 534–7 and 169). The only real chariot-battle, in the full sense, is in the 'horseman' Nestor's reminiscence, *Δ* 711–61; cf. his advice about chariot-tactics in *Λ* 297–309, advice which seems never to be followed in the *Iliad*. Diomedes also uses his chariot to charge Ares and Aphrodite in *E*.—I suspect that we have a combination of sources; for instance, tradition always gives chariots to the heroes of the Thebais, Adrastus, Amphiaraus, Tydeus, &c., which might account for Diomedes (Mülder, *Quellen*, p. 72). Again, why do 27 Trojans have chariots, and only 9 Greeks? For historical reasons, because the Trojans are at home on their horse-breeding plain (see p. 36, n. 3), while the Greeks have crossed the sea? Or for merely romantic reasons, as Drerup thinks, because it is glorious to fight on foot against chariots? (Drerup, I. p. 152).

distinguished archers, sometimes crouching behind the shield of
a *promachos* in the very front, sometimes taking cover wherever
it offered; and secondly, an almost unarmed rabble, shooting
arrows and little darts and stones from the sling or the bare hand,
making as terrible a noise as they could, and defending themselves with their flapping *laiseïa*. Now the distinguished archers
are of course present in the *Iliad*,[1] but on the whole the bow is
somewhat fallen in repute, and, as one might expect, little is said
of the rabble. We can discern its existence clearly enough. We
hear how the Trojans in one place come on like flocks of birds,
screeching as they come (Γ 2). We have a good many mentions
of the stones and arrows coming from no specified hand.[2] But
in the main those undignified adjuncts of the ancient battle have
tended to be forgotten or omitted. The later poets were full of
the pride of Bronzen Men and the tough hand-to-hand death-
shock of spear and shield, as we hear of it in classical Greek
history.

Let us stay a moment at this point. 'What', it may be
objected, 'is this going to prove? Why should you expect
a mixed army, collected from all parts of Greece, to be uniform
in its accoutrement? The army of Xerxes contained Persian,
Median, and Assyrian soldiers, with the best weapons that the
century could produce, together with Ethiopians clad in lion
and leopard skins, and armed with stone-pointed arrows, and
Sagartians who carried daggers and lassos. The Chinese army
in the late war against Japan contained some soldiers armed with
the newest rifles, and some with bows and arrows. Early vases
combine Boeotian shields with round shields.'

Let us distinguish. Of course, the varieties in the armour
would not prove much. The poet often comments on the
peculiarities of different races in battle. We hear in Π 419 that
the Lycians wore no *mitrae* to their tunics; in N 712 f. that the
Locrians 'had no bronze helmets nor round shields nor ashen

---

[1] Paris, Pandaros, Teucer, for example. See Lang, *Homer and his Age*,
136 ff.

[2] Arrows, Γ 79, Λ 191, Φ 113, O 313, &c.; stones, M 154, Π 774: but in
general scarcely a χερμάδιον is mentioned in the *Iliad* but has its definite
thrower. I suspect that every big stone lying on the plain of Troy had
its legend. It was thrown there by Aias or Hector or Aeneas or Diomedes,
as similar stones in Cornwall have generally been thrown by St. Paul, or
by the Devil.

spears; they came with bows, you know (ἄρα), and cords of sheep-gut!' So we hear that the Dardanoi were ἀγχιμαχηταί, which seems to mean 'fighters in dense formation', like the ἀγχεμάχοι Abantes, who advanced μεμαῶτες ὀρεκτῇσιν μελίῃσι, 'straining forward with long ash-spears stretched out.' Professor Macurdy[1] shows that the same formation was practised by the Macedonians with the long *sarissa*, by the Dardani in Livy, and by the Germans in Tacitus.

There is nothing here to cause difficulty, or to suggest confusion of dates or places. What makes the difficulty and suggests the confusion is that the poets themselves seem not to be conscious of the mixture of Mycenaean and 'Bronzen' fighting, or at least not to mean that the audience shall be conscious. The men are, so to speak, advertised as being about to fight in one way, and then, without a word of apology, they proceed to fight in another. The fact is that, in all parts of the poem, it is understood that, unless otherwise stated, each hero is clad in the normal armour of the best style of Greek warrior. But in the old lays that normal style was Mycenaean, or at least pre-Carian; in the editorial parts it was the style of the sixth or fifth century.

In one or two places an actual correction of the text has been made. There must have come a time—after Mr. Lang's arguments we must not put it earlier than the age of Pisistratus, and for myself I should now put it later—when the whole conception of high warfare was wrapped up in these hand-to-hand battles of Bronzen Men in full armour. Probably some reciter or editor of the *Iliad* found among his sources lays describing both kinds of fighting, and had to blend them together. Of course some slight editing was necessary; many omissions of lines no doubt, a few simple and rather mechanical additions. For one thing, the heroes, nearly all, find themselves summarily provided with corslets, θώρηκες. The notion gives one something of a shock; it is so hard, in the atmosphere of modern print, to understand the simple artifices of a Traditional Poem. Yet the fact is there. If we knew nothing of archaeology, if we could suggest no explanation at all of such a proceeding, we should have to suspect that the *thôrêx* had been put into the poem by a later hand. For, often as it occurs, it is almost always in what is

---

[1] *Troy and Paeonia*, chap. 3.

called an 'inorganic' line. That is, the phrasing is such that it can be dropped straight out without any injury to grammar, sense, or metre. This is too extraordinary a state of things to be the result of mere coincidence.[1]

To illustrate what is meant by 'inorganic', let us take a fairly innocent example. There is a passage twice repeated describing the first clash of battle:—

> Together they dashed their ox-hides, together spears and
>   rages of men
> [Clad in bronzen corslets, and bossy shields]
> Came one against another, and a great turmoil arose.
>   Δ 447 ff. = Θ 61 ff.

The line in brackets is inorganic. It does no great harm, except that one does not quite see the difference between the 'ox-hides' and the 'shields'. But drop it out, and sense, grammar, and metre are as complete as before. There are many such lines scattered about the poems, now here, now there, and the fragments of papyri which have come down to us from the second and third centuries B.C. often show such lines in places where our texts omit them, and sometimes omit them where our texts have them.

Sometimes the inorganic breastplate-line does actual harm. There are two identical passages where a man performs the sleight mentioned above.[2] An enemy's spear comes through his shield, but, standing well back from the shield, he twists aside and the weapon grazes past him. I translate line by line:—

> Right through the shining shield the strong spear came
> [*And drove heavily* [3] *through the richly-wrought corslet*]
> And straight on beside his flank it cut through his tunic,
> That spear did: but he twisted aside and escaped black death.

---

[1] A curious obstacle in the way of further analysis is the fact that we do not know the derivative or original meaning of the words θώρηξ, θωρήσσεσθαι. The verb is fairly common in the poems and was taken in classical times to mean 'to put on a corslet', though that is hardly its original meaning, and there are many passages it does not suit (B 526, 587, 818; Π 218, cf. 133, &c.; see exx. in Ebeling). Reichel thought θώρηξ was a general word meaning 'protection, clothing', afterwards specialized to a particular kind of protection. Another suggestion is that the verb means 'to make oneself bold', and so 'to prepare for battle'; this suits most of the Homeric passages, and accounts for the slang fifth-century meaning, 'to get drunk'.

[2] Γ 358, Paris; H 252, Hector: cf. Λ 436, Sôkos; and Δ 136, Menelaus.

[3] ἠρήρειστο, 'was pressed,' or 'driven with weight', τὸ βίαιον τῆς πληγῆς παραδηλοῖ τῷ τραχεῖ τοῦ ῥήματος, Schol. BL.

Without the bracketed line the sense is clear. But with it? Does not every reader feel some difficulty? You can twist aside from a spear that is coming through your shield, but not from one that has 'driven heavily' through your breastplate. Doubtless the audience understood it as a pluperfect: 'he had twisted aside.' That is quite possible Greek. He had twisted just before the spear struck, so the spear struck the very edge of his corslet and, strange to say, instead of glancing off 'drove' through. Sit down with a good will and you can imagine ways in which, with exactly the right kind of corslet, such a thing might conceivably happen: for of course the poets who recited the *Iliad* would never leave a stark naked impossibility. Only the thôrêx can never be the real metal breastplate of ἀνδρῶν χαλκεοθωρήκων. But how much simpler it would be with that thorex-line away! It occurs thus four times, making always the same kind of difficulty.

There is an arrow in Δ 134 ff. whose performances are described at great length, and very puzzling they are. Pandarus had shot at Menelaus, and Athena was protecting him. She brushed the arrow aside

And *herself directed it* where the clasps of his girdle
All-golden joined and a double protection met it.
Down dropped the bitter arrow on the fixed girdle,
And on through the cunning girdle it flew,
[*And it drove heavily through the richly-wrought corslet*]
And through the *mitrê* which he wore to protect his flesh,
    a fence against darts,
Which was his greatest defence ; right on through that it went,
And just grazed the man's flesh, &c.

Read this without the bracketed line and it is fairly clear. We may at worst be a little puzzled by the exact relation between the *mitrê*, or waistbelt, and the *zôstêr* or girdle. Later on (185 ff.) Menelaus is reassuring his brother about the wound :—

The keen bolt did not fix in a vital spot ; the flashing girdle warded it off, and lower down the loin-cloth and *mitrê* wrought by smiths.

He makes no mention of any breastplate, but says it was the girdle that saved him ; he is able to say this because he has just (v. 151) *looked*—apparently by pushing back the belt—*and seen* that the string and barbs of the arrow are outside his flesh. All is reasonably clear.

But now read the passage with the thorex-line in, and all is confusion. The arrow went right through his breastplate. What did the clasps of the girdle matter if there was a solid metal corslet there? How could Menelaus see the wound? Why is there so much talk about the piercing of the girdle, and 'the *mitrê* which was his greatest defence', and not a word about the much more remarkable piercing of the breastplate?[1] Other awkwardnesses occur as one studies the passage: and they all disappear with the removal of one inorganic line.

These superpositions of armour upon armour are not infrequent in our MSS. of early Greek poetry, though we must always remember that, if a bard liked to have two versions of a description or a metaphor in his private book, it does not follow that he used both when he was reciting. One small case was noticed by the Alexandrians. We are told of the archer Paris in Γ 17 that he 'fought in front, with a pardskin on his shoulders and a bending bow', the natural accoutrement for an archer, who needs both his hands. Then follow the lines (18–19)

And sword: and brandishing two spears tipped with bronze
He was challenging all the Argives to battle.

Zenodotus, and perhaps Aristarchus too, deleted these lines. No doubt rightly. The two spears destroy the picture and

---

[1] Mr. Lang bravely tackles the difficulties of this passage, and offers the explanation that the arrow went, not through the *thôrêx*, but between the two parts of the thorex in the narrow open space in front. Athena had, in fact, by mistake, directed it to the one dangerous spot! (*World of Homer*, p. 76.) I cannot help suspecting that the μίτρη also is interpolated here, or rather, that there has been a contamination of two sources, in one of which it was the μίτρη, in the other the double thickness of the girdle that saved him. It is worth observing that the θώρηξ-line makes a slight grammatical awkwardness wherever it occurs: it brings in a καί clause between μέν and δέ. Possible language: but odd that it should occur always! Apart from the above passages the making of the *thôrêx* plays a curiously small part in the Armour-Making, Σ 478–613; 133 lines are given to the shield, one to the *thôrêx*, one to the greaves, two to the helmet. That is, the shield was originally all that mattered much. And in Υ 259 f. Achilles does seem rather to forget that he has a breastplate. Again, in the great passage describing Patroclus' death, Π 801 ff., Apollo, by a blow with the flat of his hand, makes Patroclus stagger, so that his helmet falls off and he drops his shield. That originally left him unarmed; but the bard who armed him with a breastplate has had to add the disastrous line 804: 'And the Lord, the son of Zeus, Apollo, also unbuckled his breastplate!' (λῦσε δέ οἱ θώρηκα ἄναξ Διὸς υἱὸς Ἀπόλλων).

would prevent Paris from using his bow.   It is interesting, too, to
see what happens later when Paris has to fight a duel in full
armour with Menelaus.   He borrows the necessary breastplate
from Lycaon (Γ 330-8) and 'takes' a sword and a spear.   The
lines are, as usual, carefully arranged so as to avoid a direct contradiction with the previous passage.   But it is worth observing
two facts: a Papyrus (Hibeh 19) of the third century B. C. has
three additional lines here, describing armour, while Zenodotus
on the other hand deleted two of these in our text.   We do not
know his reasons: possibly he only meant to delete the sword
and spear in one place or the other.   But we see his method,
and can make out from it how an ancient bard or editor avoided
contradictions.

A very clear superposition can be seen in Hesiod's Shield of
Heracles (*Aspis*, 139-320).   The shield gives its name to the
poem, and has 180 lines of description, the rest of the accoutrement sixteen.   But this is not all.   Apparently in the groundwork
of the poem the hero had a Mycenaean shield for practically his
whole defence.   Then, as in Achilles' case (see note, p. 157),
other armour is added.   But Heracles in tradition was represented
not only as a hoplite ; he was also an archer, also a *korunêtês* or
club-bearer.   Consequently in Hesiod, as the text now stands
(*Aspis*, 122-38), he wears, all at the same time, greaves, breastplate, and helmet ; an iron club ; a quiver and arrows ; a spear,
and a Mycenaean shield !   The explanation in its general lines
would seem to be that bards had varying forms in which they
used to recite the battle of Herakles and Kyknos.   In one
Herakles had a club and arrows, in another a Mycenaean shield
and spear, in another a full panoply.   Some person in his ' book '
had notes of the alternatives, but when the book was published
the alternatives were added together.[1]

Before leaving this subject, there are two points we should
notice for the sake of their historical significance.   In the first
place, while the breastplate and shield have been inserted almost
all through the *Iliad*, there is no clear trace of them in the
Doloneia (*K*) nor yet in the *Odyssey*.   *K*, we have reason to
believe, was a separate poem and not inserted in the *Iliad* till
a late date ; how late we shall discuss in Chapter XI.   The breast-

---

[1] Cf. Deiters *de Her. Scuti Descriptione*, pp. 59, 399.

plate-inserter would seem to have done his work before K was incorporated. In the *Odyssey* there was of course less reason to revise the armour, as the military interest is much slighter than in the *Iliad*. But this absence of the breastplate is another instance of the fact we have noticed before, that the *Odyssey* seems to have been altogether less worked over, expurgated, and elaborated than what many books still persist in calling without qualification ' the older poem '.

The second point is an observation on the epic style. The introduction of the breastplate, on almost any conceivable theory, makes, not indeed an absurdity, but at least some awkwardness, some blurring of the presentation. The confusion of two styles of fighting does the same. What we have to realize is that, like most ancient poetry, the *Iliad* produces its effect not by accuracy of detail but by a broad emotional sweep. It does not stimulate our powers of close attention as do, for instance, the battle-scenes of Tolstoy : it rather hypnotizes them by its rush and splendour and stately music. We shall dwell on this characteristic more in detail in Chapter IX ; for the present we may note one further instance of it. A mark of the epic style is, as we all know, the conventional epithet. All objects of interest have descriptive adjectives habitually attached to them, and among such objects are, of course, shields. Now you would expect, if the poet wished to give a clear conception of what he was describing, that the epithets would show at once whether a particular shield was conceived as the great Mycenaean tower of ox-hide or the small round metal targe of later Greece. But in fact it is not so. When indeed a shield is called χάλκεον, ' bronzen,' there is a strong presumption that it is of the later type : when it is ἀμφιβρότη or ποδηνεκής, ' man-enveloping ' or ' reaching to the feet ', it is of the earlier. But as regards the greater part of the epithets scholars differ. Reichel and Leaf try to make as many as possible suit the Mycenaean shield. Ridgeway does the opposite. What is clear is that shields which must from the tactics have been Mycenaean, which are, for instance, large enough to cover a man from head to foot, are called ' round ' or ' even in every direction ' or ' orbed ' or ' bossy '—words which at first sight seem to apply much more naturally to the later shield.[1]

[1] Εὔκυκλος, κυκλοτερής, πάντοσ᾽ ἐΐση, ὀμφαλόεσσα.

It is just the same with the geography. Almost every traveller who examines the plain of Troy or the isle of Ithaca identifies the various landmarks to his own satisfaction, but the identifications are all different. Let any reader study, for instance, the discussions by Leaf and Robert about the position of the Scamander. Both are quite first-rate investigators. They differ completely as to the lie of the river, and only agree that the one definite statement into which the poems are betrayed, that the Simois and Scamander join their streams (E 774), is a mistake and an interpolation.

A result like this cannot be attained by accident. It is a matter of deliberate skill, this subtle avoidance of detail so as to concentrate interest on the central impression. In that respect it is closely parallel to the use of types instead of portraits in classical art ; but the artistic method may well have grown through historical causes. A simplification of issues, a sweeping rejection of the sort of detailed fact which is easily forgotten or which may suit one reciter but give trouble to the next, a determined loyalty to the broad poetic convention, undismayed by research and untainted by personal idiosyncrasies : these are principles which naturally suit the work of the ' Homeridae ' in carrying on by corporate efforts a long-lived poetical tradition.

Let us briefly run through some other cases where the changing customs of different ages have left their marks upon the poems. There is the change from bronze to iron. The excavations have produced no iron at Mycenae, and only two little lumps at Troy. No weapons of iron have been found in the pre-Hellenic remains anywhere. And on this subject the epic tradition is very clear and vigorous. Bronze is the conventional metal of war : Ares himself is χάλκεος, ' bronzen,' and ' the bronze ' proverbially means ' the sword '. Iron is known as a rare and very hard material, difficult to work, but suitable for ploughshares, for clubs, for arrow-heads, for axes.[1] It is only now and then by accident that a poet drops into using ' iron ' for a sword or spear, as we should use ' steel '. Antilochos is afraid lest Achilles should 'cut his throat with the iron ' (Σ 34). Slaughtered oxen 'writhe about

[1] Hesiod also thinks of iron in connexion with work rather than fighting. *Erga* 150 χαλκῷ δ' ἐργάζοντο, μέλας δ' οὐκ ἔσκε σίδηρος. On the antiquity of iron see Montelius in *Praehistorische Zeitung*, 1915, esp. pp. 304 f. (Egypt 1300–1200, Troad c. 1100, Central Europe 1000–875 B.C.).

the iron' (Ψ 30). So far we might be dealing with a 'transitional' age in which iron was just coming into use as a new metal; but then comes twice over the proverbial phrase, 'iron itself draws a man on'—a weapon is a temptation (π 294, τ 13). Such a saying would only be current in an age to which iron weapons had been long familiar. Of course, though these mentions of iron show clearly that the writers knew of iron weapons, the general use of 'bronze' and 'bronzen' is no sign that the writers still used bronze weapons. The memory of a bronze age happens to have stamped itself on the language of poetry. That is all. All Greek poetry was archaistic in language because it was permeated by a sense of style. It felt that modern words and phrases were out of tone with the heroic past. Swords are spoken of as 'bronze' down to the latest times of the Greek epic, when such a thing as a bronze sword had perhaps not been seen for centuries.

More complex is the treatment of funeral rites. Burial was at all times the usual Greek custom, but the flaming pyres of the great Northmen of the Migrations lived in tradition, so the Homeric heroes are burned. Yet both story and language are pervaded by faint memories of a still earlier splendour, when Mycenae buried and embalmed her kings.[1] Hector was not burned till the twenty-second day after his death. Achilles himself was not burned till the eighteenth (Ω 31, 413, 665, 785: ω 65). Surely those touches come from a time when embalming was practised. The actual word which meant 'preserve' or 'embalm' ($\tau\alpha\rho\chi\acute{\upsilon}\epsilon\iota\nu$) is used in Homer to denote the ordinary burying of burned ashes. This is a clear case of survival, though sometimes, from its very inappositeness to mere burial, the word gathered to itself a metaphorical suggestion of 'preserving' the dead man's memory. 'His brethren and kindred will preserve him with a mound and a pillar: for that is the honour of the dead' (Π 456, 674). The honey once used for embalming is

---

[1] On the gradual change from bronze to iron and burial to burning in Crete see Burrows, pp. 100 f. Even in classical times kings who died abroad were embalmed: e.g. Alexander, Agesipolis, Agesilaus. It is interesting to note that in Scandinavia the general testimony of early writers put burning before burial—the reverse of the truth. See above, p. 74, note. Dörpfeld believes in a combination of the two, *Comptes rendus du Congrès Archéol. à Athènes*, 1905, p. 161. But see Drerup, I, p. 160.

still vaguely associated with the last rites, though its meaning has
been forgotten.   When Patroclus was burned upon a pyre they
set leaning against the bier two great jars of honey and unguents
(Ψ 170).   And Achilles himself was burned 'in raiment of the
gods and plenteous unguents and sweet honey' (ω 67).   The
honey and unguents were useless: but man was reluctant to stint
his beloved dead of any honour that he had once given him.

There is a very interesting development in the forms of worship.   The oldest Greek worship, like the Semitic, seems to
have had no temples and no graven images.   You did not make
a god, at least not consciously.   You found him: found him
dwelling in some strange rock, some ancient tree, in the water
that came from unknown depths and made the earth fertile.
You found him in the pillar that supported your dwelling, but
might fall, if angered; in the battle-axe that fought for you so
bravely, but might at any moment wilfully break or miss its aim
or turn in your hand and betray you.[1]   And where you found
him you worshipped, and gave him sacrifice.   Hence come the
'pillars and high places', the Hebrew *bâmôth* and Greek *bômoí*.
At later stages you marked off a little space around the divine
object as specially sacred or haunted: this was a *Temenos*, a
Precinct.   Later still, as the faithful proceeded to make offerings
to the god at this precinct, you must needs have a resident priest
to act as caretaker; and eventually, since, in spite of all the most
appalling curses on sacrilege which society could devise, the
offerings, hung on the tree or set in the crannies of the rock,
became too great a temptation to passers-by, it was best in the
end to build a properly walled house for the god and his belongings to dwell in.   How the images of the god arose it is not
clear.   Dr. Reichel[2] believed that in general thrones came before
images.   You found on some rock or high place some sign of
the god's habitation, a place where he sat or stepped or the like.
You improved the seat for him; in your temple you made a still
better seat, and eventually you put an image of the god himself to

---

[1] See especially Evans, *Mycenaean Tree and Pillar Cult*, in *J. H. S.* xxi;
R. Smith, *Religion of Semites*, pp. 97, 135, &c.; W. M. Ramsay on Anatolian
Religion in *Dict. Bibl.*, extra volume.   Of course the combination of 'ani-
conic' and 'iconic' forms is common in later Greek religion: *Prolegomena*,
pp. 18 ff., and ASHERAH in *Encyc. Bibl.*
[2] *Vorhellenische Götterculte.*

sit there. The image would always serve an important purpose. For the very simplest way of getting a god to do something was to have an image of him and make the image do it. The chief difficulty lies perhaps in the transition from the real fetish to the mere imitation or image. I find it difficult to see how a purely artificial image can originally have been worshipped except as an imitation of something already known or supposed to exist. Our early Greeks, driven out and cut off from their natural holy places, would be reduced to making with their own hands imitations of the god whom they had left behind.

Now it is clear that during the greater part of the *Iliad* and *Odyssey* worship is carried on at High Places or altars in the open air. 'We were gathered round a spring by the holy altars, under a beautiful plane-tree, where bright water ran': so says the *Iliad* of the sacrifice at Aulis, where appeared the wonder of the birds and the snake (*B* 305, cf. Θ 238 f.). So in the *Odyssey* (ζ 162) the sight of Nausicaa reminds Odysseus of the young palm-tree which he saw 'growing beside Apollo's altar' at Delos. It did not grow indoors. You hear normally, not of the Temple of any god, but of the 'very beautiful oak of aegis-bearing Zeus' (*E* 693, *H* 60, ξ 328, τ 297): of 'Athene's grove beside the way, all of poplars; and spring water runs through it, and meadow-land is all around' (ζ 291): of a grove of Poseidon, a grove and altars of the Nymphs (*B* 506, ι 200, ρ 210: cf. υ 278).

Then occasionally we hear of a *temenos*, a precinct fenced off from common life. We hear twice of the 'marble threshold of the Archer Apollo in rocky Pytho' (*I* 404, θ 80): and lastly, some seven times in all, we hear of definite temples. In Z there is a full description not only of a temple and the worship therein, but of a definite seated statue of the goddess Athena, on whose knees a robe is to be laid, exactly as was done at the feast of the Panathenaea, at which the poem itself was being recited. Is not that a ritual centuries later, one asks, than the sacrifice by the spring at Aulis? And observe a curious point. Chryses, in the first book of the *Iliad*, is a very antique figure, not exactly a priest, but rather a professional 'cursing man', or *arêtêr*, like Balaam, son of Beor, in the Book of Numbers. And naturally, when he performs his sacrifice, he does so (*A* 446 ff.) at an altar in the open air. Yet in the introductory prologue he is made to cry to his Mouse-God with the appeal, 'If ever I roofed for thee a gracious temple' (*A* 39). It is the same phenomenon which we noticed in the case of the armour. The writer of that line did not observe, or did not choose to observe, that in his original there had been no temple, only an altar. To him and his audience an altar implied a temple, so he took the temple for granted.

It is the same with another social change, affecting marriage customs. In the primitive ages of Greece, as Aristotle has remarked (*Pol.* 1268 b), 'men carried weapons and bought their women from one another.' That is, the suitor paid a price, normally calculated in oxen, to the father of the bride, who thus became her husband's property. In classical Greece the custom was just the opposite. The father gave a sum of money with his daughter to induce the suitor to marry her. Speaking very broadly, this means that in the early times there were not enough women for the marriage market, in the later times too many. It would seem that the first custom arose in an age when, owing to dire poverty and continual wars, men hesitated a good deal about rearing their children at all, and especially were reluctant to burden themselves with daughters. There is something touching in the frequency with which during the heroic times you find names of women compounded from *bous*, an ox. Oxen were the gold currency of the time, and these names seem perhaps to express the excuse which the parents made to themselves for venturing to rear the useless female child.[1] The real reason was simply that they could not bear to kill it. But they would never allege that. It is not the way with the human race to avow such motives. We are much too shy. No doubt their neighbours and the less agreeable of their elder relatives considered it extravagant of them, foolishly sentimental or ostentatious. Well, maybe it was: but after all perhaps the girl would bring in a good price some day: so they called her Alphesiboia, *winner of kine*, Phereboia, *bringer-in-of-kine*, Polyboia, *worth many kine*, or Stheneboia, Periboia, Eëriboia, Meliboia, and the rest of the names.

---

[1] Cf. Letter in Witkowski *Epistulae Privatae* (58 = Pap. Ox. 744) from a man to his wife: 'if it is a boy, rear it; if a female, destroy.' Apollod. *Bib.* 3, 9, 2 (Ἀταλάντης) ὁ πατὴρ ἀρρένων παιδῶν ἐπιθυμῶν ἐξέθηκεν αὐτήν.

Now the poems as a rule maintain this older conception of the marriage bargain. Hector bore his bride 'out from the halls of Eëtion, when he had paid countless bride-gifts' (X 472). Iphidamas was slain before he brought home his bride, and 'had no joy of her, though he gave a great price' (Λ 243). Othryoneus, the suitor of Cassandra, gave his services in the war instead of a bride-gift (N 366: cf. λ 289). Hephaistos in the *Odyssey*, when Aphrodite is false to him, vows that he will keep her in prison till her father returns all the bride-gifts, 'yea, all that I put in his hand for the sake of his dog-faced maiden' (θ 319). There are special exceptions which perhaps merely prove the rule. Old Altes gave a great dower to his daughter Laothoë when she married Priam (X 51). Agamemnon, among the gifts with which he vainly sues Achilles, offers to give him one of his daughters, not only without exacting a bride-gift, but giving her a dowry as well (I 146 ff.). There is also an intermediate stage in which the gifts are paid, not to the bride's father, but to the bride herself.[1] They seem not so much a real gift as a proof of the suitor's power to maintain a wife.

Now, so far, the evidence might be interpreted in either of two ways. It might denote a long progress of time during which customs changed, or it might point merely to an age in which the custom varied according to circumstances. Two passages in a late part of the *Odyssey* decide the question (β 194, α 278). 'Let Telemachus bid his mother go back to her father's house. And the folk there shall make a marriage-feast and furnish *eëdna* in plenty, such as are meet to go with a dear daughter.' A dowry is meant; but the word used is ἔεδνα, 'bride-gift.' The writer of the lines was accustomed to the later practice of φερνή or προίξ, 'dowry,' and mistook the meaning of ἔεδνα because his generation had forgotten the custom (cf. also β 53).

It is the same with the question of the Homeric house. One reason for the divergent theories of scholars about that elusive object has been that they tried to work with only one form of house, and there are really at least three. The house of Odysseus at the end in the Battle with the Suitors stands by itself. It is a

[1] ζ 159: cf. Schol. Π 178: also cf. Aesch. *Prom.* 559 ἔδνοις ἄγαγες Ἡσιόναν πειθών. The code of Hammurabi has marks of an intermediate stage, practically equivalent to this. The suitor paid a bride-price to the father, and the father also gave a dowry which normally included the return of the bride-price, but did not always do so. See Ham. 160, 163, 164.

Mycenaean palace, not unlike Tiryns, as Prof. Myres has shown.[1] But the normal house of both the *Iliad* and *Odyssey* is quite different. There seem to have been two types of house in the Aegean in early times, the Cretan or Southern palace and the Hellenic or Northern one-roomed 'Megaron'. The Cretan palace consists of countless rooms leading one out of the other, and a whole structure so complicated that it has perhaps given rise to the story of the labyrinth. Its main rooms tended to have the entrance door or doors on the long wall of the room so that the southern sun came in through the broad opening. Consequently they had no fireplace.[2] The Hellenic house was like a modern shed or a Greek temple *in antis*, an oblong building with a door at the narrow end, a porch in front, and a fireplace in the centre of the big hall, which was called *megaron* or *thalamos*. In the palaces of Greece proper, Mycenae, Tiryns, and Arne in Lake Copais, this northern megaron has been combined with the 'labyrinthine' scheme of the Cretan palaces. But in the *Iliad* and *Odyssey* the houses are normally one-room halls. The master and mistress live in the megaron in the daytime and sleep there at night; strangers are invariably given a bed in the porch just outside the front door. That is where Telemachus is put when staying with Nestor and with Menelaus (γ 395–406, δ 296–307); Odysseus with Alcinoüs (η 228–347), and when he is a stranger in his own house (υ 1); Priam with Achilles (Ω 643–50). Grown-up sons and daughters have separate 'halls' or *thalamoi* built for them close by (γ 413, β 2–5). When Hector goes to find Paris in his *thalamos* (Z 321 ff.), he finds Paris cleaning his armour, and Helen with her handmaids spinning, all in the same room; and the room is certainly the place where Helen and Paris slept. When the gods are summoned to Hephaestus' house, they stand in the porch and see from there his bed with chains like spider-webs drawn round it (θ 304, 325). And Alcinous speaks of the night being long; 'it is not yet time to sleep in the hall' (λ 373).

That is the normal Homeric practice. But there are other passages where the master and mistress have a separate bedroom away from the hall; Penelope, in particular, and certain young

[1] *J. H. S.*, vol. xx, and Monro's *Odyssey*, Appendix VI.
[2] There is a central hearth in the second city at Troy—perhaps owing to the climate, perhaps to some exceedingly early influx of Northerners.

girls dwell in 'well-wrought upper-chambers'. And here, as before, the poet who brings in the later use does not notice that he is contradicting an earlier use. So Helen and Menelaus go to rest in the usual way 'in the inward part of the lofty hall'; but in the morning Helen comes out of her 'fragrant high-roofed bower' (δ 304, 310, 121). In the case where Achilles puts the aged Priam to sleep in the porch, the later poet seems to be troubled at such apparent lack of hospitality, and invents a reason, which no commentator has ever succeeded in understanding, for not asking him to sleep properly inside (Ω 643-76). Apparently he did not understand the custom which he found implied in his source.

Other evidence could be added to this:[1] evidence from the treatment of the gods, a most curious subject; from the law about guardianship of a widow; from land tenure, government, and, most important of all, from the changes and misunderstandings of linguistic forms. All are involved in a network of small but ever-thickening difficulties as long as we try to regard the poems as the work of one man or one age. All begin to clear and become intelligible as soon as we recognize what the Poems really are. They represent, not the independent invention of one man, like some modern books, but the ever-moving tradition of many generations of men, like almost all ancient books. They are wholes built up out of a great mass of legendary poetry, re-treated and re-created by successive poets in successive ages, unities which have not perfectly assimilated the sources from which they draw.

[1] Cases of conscious avoidance by Homer of 'modern' subjects are given by Bréal, *Pour mieux connaître Homère*, pp. 7-11: e. g. writing, statues, paintings, money. Cf. also Drerup, I, chap. iv.

NOTE.—My discussion of the armour is based chiefly on Reichel, *Homerische Waffen*, Leaf's Appendices to his edition of the *Iliad*, and Robert's *Studien zur Ilias*; Lippold's valuable article (see p. 147 note) only came to me while the second edition was in the press. The passages about funeral customs, bronze and iron, temples and dowries, are taken chiefly from P. Cauer's admirable *Grundfragen der Homerkritik* (third edition, 1921, 1923). Some remarks also are due to Finsler's *Homer*, and of course Helbig (*Homerische Epos aus den Denkmälern erklärt*) and Tsountas and Manatt. From the 'unitarian' side the best discussion of the armour is that of Andrew Lang in *The World of Homer* and *Homer and his Age*. On houses I would specially refer to Noack, *Homerische Paläste* and *Ovalhaus und Palast in Kreta*, and the four articles by Mackenzie on *Cretan Palaces* in the Annual of the B. S. A., xi-xiv. Cf. also Ridgeway in the *Athenaeum* for

Nov. 21, 1908. (The gable and pediment are northern; the flat roof and frieze Mycenaean.)

Miss Lorimer of Somerville College, in an unpublished paper, has pointed out that the typical Mycenaean weapons (figure-eight shields, inlaid sword-blades, long rapiers) seem to have disappeared from the mainland of Greece before 1400 B.C.; that is, some 250 years before the Siege of Troy. Homer does not mention these specific objects, but he uses freely the big ‘Mycenaean’ shield, and he describes inlaid metal work in the Shield of Achilles (and Euripides in a sword-blade, *El.* 476), elaborate palaces with bath-rooms (ἀσάμυνθος, a pre-Greek word), as well as objects like Nestor's cup, Λ 633 f., and the helmet with boar's tusks in K 261–265, all of which are attested before 1400 but not after. Miss Lorimer considers that this points to the existence in Homer of pre-Homeric and even pre-Trojan-War poetry, a conclusion not at all improbable. However, tradition *plus* relics will explain all but the shield, and the big shield did continue, as Herodotus tells us, at any rate in Asia, till about 650 B.C. Mr. Hall has published in *J. H. S.* xxxi. p. 123 a relief representing Sennacherib (705–680 B.C.) receiving a deputation of Carians or Ionians with crested helmets and big tower-shields. And on the mainland, in spite of the silence of the monuments, the language of Tyrtaeus (p. 149 n.) seems to imply the use of the big shield. See p. 196 n.

In the realm of language two general results seem to me to emerge with increasing clearness: (1) the mixture of old and new is proved to the hilt; (2) the task of separating the strata is shown to be much more difficult than the last generation of scholars imagined; you cannot simply cut out ‘late parts’ and leave the rest uniform (see above, Preface to the Second Edition, p. x).

Fr. Bechtel, *Die Vocalcontraction bei Homer*, supports the general results of criticism, especially those of Robert, and is usefully criticized by K. Meister, *Die Homerische Kunstsprache*, 1921. Particularly valuable are Wackernagel's *Sprachliche Untersuchungen zu Homer*, 1916. Dr. Hentze, in several articles (*Beitr. zur Kunde der IG. Sprache*, xxix, p. 280 ff., *Philologus*, N. F., xix. 2, p. 161 ff., *Zeitschr. f. vergleich. Sprachforschung*, N. F., xli, p. 356 ff.), has treated the different stages in Homeric syntax, especially in conditional and final sentences. Signor Della Seta, in the *Rendiconti della R. Accad. dei Lincei* (*Classe di sc. morali, etc.*), serie v, vol. xvi, pp. 134–210, shows interesting results about the comparative age of the words Ἀχαιοί, Ἀργεῖοι, Δαναοί; Ἀθήνη, Ἀθηναίη, and Ἴλιον, Τροίη. The age comes out in the above order. The late and perhaps Attic form Ἀθηναίη occurs oftenest in the Converse of Hector and Andromache, Z (10 Ἀθηναίη, 4 Ἀθήνη), a significant suggestion. Prof. J. A. Scott of Illinois, in *Classical Philology* (Chicago), iv. 3, v. 1, and *Classical Review*, xxiv. 1, has ably argued that some of the commonly received differences of language between the *Iliad* and the *Odyssey*, as wholes, are fallacious, but has carried his own methods, I fear, to still more fallacious conclusions in *The Unity of Homer*, University of California, 1921. See G. M. Bolling in *Class. Phil.* xiv. 4 (1919) on Abstract Words in Homer, and *ib.* xvi. 4 (1921) on Infs. in -εμεν. Miss Stawell (*Homer and the Iliad*, Dent, 1910, a finely written book) has attempted a new division of the poems into parts written by Homer and parts added later. (See Mr. Shewan in *C. Q.*, April and October, 1910.) The problem of the mixture of dialects in Homer receives much light from Thumb's admirable *Handbuch der griechischen Dialekte* (Heidelberg, 1909).

In the domain of metre, the enormous importance of which for Homeric Language was demonstrated in Schulze's *Quaestiones Epicae*, an article by Mr. J. A. J. Drewitt on *Scansion in Homeric Verse* (*C. Q.*, April, 1908) is remarkable, both for its fine observation and its curious results. Solmsen's *Untersuchungen zur Gr. Laut- und Verslehre* (1901) have had much influence, but to me remain unconvincing; cf. Danielsson, *Zur Lehre vom Hom. Digamma*, Ind. Forsch. xxv. 264–284, and especially Witte in Pauly-Wissowa on *Homeros, Sprache und Metrik*.

VII

THE ILIAD AS A TRADITIONAL BOOK

III. PECULIARITIES

WHILE I was trying in my fourth lecture to draw a general comparison between the Hebrew traditional history and the Greek epic as regards their manner of growth, an objection may have occurred to some of my hearers. The objects compared are too unlike. The Book of Genesis or of Judges is essentially a chronicle, a prose record of traditional history, narrated as far as possible in order of time, year after year, generation after generation. The *Iliad* is a definite poem, composed with great artistic elaboration for an artistic end, beginning in the middle of the action, and leading up to a skilfully prepared climax. Its methods are the methods not of conscientious pillar-to-post chronicle, but of artistic fiction. The time of its main action amounts to some four days.[1]

This is true; and before going further we should try to realize how the difference has come about. Both books, I believe, are made from much the same raw material, but they have developed it in different ways. In the simplest form of the saga there were probably elements of both prose and poetry—poetry where you happened to find it, in lyrics or ballads, and prose to fill in the facts. We find that style of composition in the Book of Judges and some Icelandic sagas. But Hebrew poetry, as it developed afterwards, is too impatient and emotional to narrate history. In a book like Judges, on the contrary, poetry has been conquered by prose. The saga has been developed, to the best of the writer's power, into a systematic prose history, chronologically arranged and edited with a view to religious instruction. In the Greek saga it looks as if poetry had things its own way. Greek poetry developed special forms for telling continuously

---

[1] More exactly, four days of fighting followed by twenty-two of funeral.

the deeds of the past. And it told them as it pleased. The versified chronicle became more and more of a poem and less of a history. It meant no harm; but it had in it from the first a dangerous and unprincipled element, the poet's sense of beauty, which in that particular soil grew, and overpowered in number-less elusive ways the honest spirit of chronicle.

The early French epics were mostly known by the name of *Chansons de Geste*, that is, apparently, Songs of *Gesta* or *Deeds*. This plural *Gesta* was often used in the title of historical books, like *Gesta Francorum*, which was interpreted to mean *History of the Franks*, as though 'Gesta' as a feminine singular was equivalent to 'History'. The Epics were Songs of History. The poet found his material sometimes in traditions and popular songs, sometimes in the direct prompting of monks who read or showed him their chronicles.[1] Possibly some similar origin should be assumed for most of our Greek epic remains; but, here as elsewhere, the difficulty is that our record begins so late. We have none of the raw materials left; we have only finished poems or fragments of finished poems. We have no Aeolian epos; no Ionian; we have not even the text as recited at the Panathenaea when it first came from Ionia. We have only, so to speak, a text edited 'from the prompt-books of the best theatres' at some time later than the death of Aristotle. Still it may be instructive to spend a few minutes in trying to think out something of the processes by which poems could be made out of saga.

Suppose, for instance, that some early editor of the Book of Judges had been not a scribe or priest, but a Homeric bard or rhapsode, how might he have treated his material?[2] Our Book of Judges consists mainly of the exploits of four Judges or Heroes who delivered Israel from oppression: Ehud of Benjamin, who slew Eglon, King of Moab; Barak, of the northern tribe of Naphtali, who defeated Sisera, the general of Jabin, King of Hazor, and whose story contains the splendid song of Deborah;

[1] See *Les Légendes épiques, Recherches sur la formation des Chansons de Geste*, par J. Bédier. Paris, 1908. Also *La Naissance de la Chanson de Geste*, by J. Flach, *Journal des Savants*, vii (1909).—Did the phrase 'rerum gestarum scriptor' = 'writer of chronicles' help in the change of meaning of 'gestes'?

[2] If I remember rightly, the old scholar Joshua Barnes did actually make a Latin epic out of the Book of Judges.

Gideon of Abiezer in Manasseh, who overthrew the Midianites;
and Jephthah of Gilead, who smote Ammon and sacrificed his
daughter. There is added to these an account of Samson, who
did not exactly deliver his people, and was rather a 'strong
man' of folk-lore than a judge; and an appendix on the sins
and destruction of the tribe of Benjamin. There are also brief
mentions of seven other Judges who are little more than names.
This raw material is worked up into an appearance of continuous
history with fixed, though fictitious, dates and a special religious
moral.

Now what would a Homeric bard have done with it? He
would, we may suppose, select a hero and a centre for his poem.
The choice would lie between three heroes: Gideon, who has
three chapters devoted to him, besides a long account of the
doings of his son; Jephthah, who has two chapters and a fine
tragic story; and Samson, who has four chapters. Now my
instinct tells me that he would not choose Samson: and to
choose Jephthah would lead at once to a human sacrifice in the
front plane of the story. It follows that he would probably
choose Gideon. Then he would consider how to draw into
his poem as much as possible of the rest of the book. He
certainly must not lose the Song of Deborah, for instance.
Looking through the record, he would find that at a certain
point (vi. 34 f.) 'Gideon blew a trumpet and Abiezer was
gathered together after him. And he sent messengers throughout all Manasseh . . . and unto Asher and unto Zebulun and unto
Naphtali; and they came up to meet him.' There is an opening.
When the herald went to Naphtali, we should be told, he spoke
to the men of Naphtali, and the men of Naphtali wavered, and
did not wish to join the war. They feasted and bade their
minstrel sing to them. And an old minstrel—in Greek saga he
would be a blind minstrel—came and smote his harp and sang
the Song of Deborah, how Jabin the Syrian had oppressed
Israel; how Barak awoke and led his captivity captive; how
Deborah arose, a mother in Israel; how the river Kishon swept
them away, the ancient river, the river Kishon. So the princes
of Naphtali were reminded of the great deeds of their forefathers
and came in their strength to fight for Gideon. All the Song of
Deborah will come straight in.

The story of Ehud, again; it is easy to get that told by some Benjamite. Then the great story of Jephthah must not be omitted. It only needs a little boldness. When the embassy comes to the men of Gilead, we shall be told, their aged chieftain, Jephthah, is bowed with grief and cannot join Gideon himself, because he is not yet purified from the slaying of his daughter. He or another Gileadite tells the story, and he sends his followers with a blessing. The only real difficulty lies in the dates. Very unfortunately, Jephthah seems to have been later than Gideon. If the chronology is firmly established, our bard will have to bring in a prophet who can foretell Jephthah's story. But if the chronology is not beyond dispute, or if our poet feels that, be the facts as they may, the poem will be much the better for the change, he will ignore the dates and let the Muse have her way.

And Samson? Well, one of two things must be done. Either we will leave Samson entirely aside, to be celebrated in separate lays of his own, or, if we must cover that piece of history too, we may have some character like Nestor in the *Cypria* and *Iliad*, like Menelaus in the *Odyssey*, who can make a digression and tell the whole story. Gideon's father, Joash, might do, or his armour-bearer, Purah. Joash can regret that men are not now as they once were, when he was young and was entertained at Zorah by Samson: Samson, son of Manoah, who . . . Or he can warn some young man to be prudent, lest he should fall like Samson, who . . .

And for the rest of the Judges, I believe that a Greek bard, such as the authors of the *Cypria*, would have got them all in. The wise Joash would denounce the weakness of the present race of men, how unlike to Shamgar, the son of Anath, who smote with an ox-goad six hundred Philistines! Or Gideon, in a great speech refusing to bow down to Baal, would explain that nothing would induce him to do so, not all the riches of Jair the Gileadite, who gave to his thirty sons thirty cities and set them to ride upon thirty asses: not all the still vaster wealth of Abdon the son of Hillel. And so on.

As a characteristic of the Hellenic races, in contrast with the Hebrew, there is great significance in this tendency to work up tradition into an artistic and poetical form. And it does add one more to the already numerous forces which turn all legendary history away from the path of truth.[1] If you take up the *Iliad* as a record of history, you will soon put it down as so much mere poetry. But if you read it as fiction you will at every page be pulled up by the feeling that it is not free fiction. The poet does not invent whatever he likes. He believes himself to be dealing with real events and real people, to be recording and explaining things that have value, primarily, because they are supposed to be true. And again, when you come to the passages that do not represent real tradition but merely serve to join or to introduce parts that originally did not belong together, you will inevitably be struck by the extreme reluctance of the Homeric poets to trust long to their own invention. It is one of the things that sometimes irritates an ordinary modern reader in the analysis of the *Iliad* or *Odyssey* to be forced to observe how the later poets or editors, those responsible for α or Θ, for example, will go to any lengths in patching up centos of old lines, taken from the most varying places, rather than invent new lines. Perhaps their command of the epic style was not confidently perfect. But after all it was not the business of a bard to invent. It was his business to know, by information from the Muses or elsewhere, the history of the past, and to tell it to his new audience accurately, word for word, as the Muses had told it to him. Even in the case of new songs, which naturally had their attraction, the poet's praise is that he knows them and tells them accurately. 'Accurately?' Well, σαφῶς ἕκαστα; each detail vividly and clearly, so that you feel it must come straight from the Muses. The imagination which he puts into it is merely one of his best means of persuading people that it is true.

I suspect that the element of conscious fiction comes in first of all in the formulae of transition and introduction. The writer of Z, for instance, makes Glaucus tell to Diomêdês during a battle the whole story of Bellerophon. That is merely his way of getting the history of Bellerophon told. He does mean that the story is true; but he does not in the least mean to assert that Glaucus actually told it on such an occasion.[2] It would probably

[1] Cf. note on p. 193 below.
[2] We happen to know that some ancient critics transferred the whole incident to another place; presumably they were following their MSS. Schol. Z 119.

be a very complicated business to unravel in the *Iliad* what the reader is meant to take as history, and what is merely the device of the poet for convenience in narrative or for dramatic effect. And I fancy that the instinct of most readers will generally lead them right without any rules. The important thing is that there are real masses of supposed historical truth, somehow connected together, and beautified, as they pass, by the processes of fiction. The main basis is not fiction, but traditional history. A clear proof of this lies, I think, in the general agreement as to statements of important fact between all our different sources of tradition; the wide range of epic or quasi-epic poems ascribed to Homer, Hesiod, Stesichorus, and others, and even, where we can get them, the local legends attached to temples and oracles. The differences between these various sources are of course large and numerous; but the underlying consensus of statement quite unmistakable. And its significance can only be minimized by adopting a theory which was universally prevalent a few decades ago, but which in our present knowledge can only be described as desperately improbable. According to this theory, there is really in Greece no traditional history at all: the *Iliad* and *Odyssey* are two primaeval works of fiction, preserved as it were by miracle from pre-historic times; and all the other epic tradition is made up out of these two books by the deductions, imitations, and inventions of ingenious commentators.

In some cases this process has no doubt occurred. In others it may have occurred. For instance, there existed in the sixth century a tradition of a marriage between Telemachus and the youngest daughter of Nestor, Polycastê. Now, in the *Odyssey*, when Telemachus goes to Nestor's house, Polycastê is put in charge of him and, after the custom of the age, gives him a bath. Did the poet of the *Odyssey* know the tradition? Did he perhaps know people who claimed descent from Telemachus and Polycastê? Or, on the other hand, did the poet of the *Odyssey* mean nothing at all when he mentioned this one daughter by name and put Telemachus in her charge, and is the supposed tradition a mere embroidery worked up from that accidental mention? In that case I hesitate to decide. But in the great mass of cases one cannot hesitate. The existence of a real saga behind any particular treatment of it forces itself upon the mind of the reader. As a matter of fact, the *Iliad* and *Odyssey* not only refer to other legends as already existing and treated by other poets; that every one admits;[1] but they often in their digressions tell stories in a form which clearly suggests recapitulation or allusion. They imply the existence elsewhere of a completer poetical treatment of the same subject. Take, for instance, the story of Bellerophon in *Iliad Z*. The queen, Anteia, her love being rejected, falsely accuses Bellerophon to her husband. (Z 165.)

> So she spoke, and fury seized the king for the thing he heard. Slay him he would not: he had aidôs of that in his heart. But he would send him to Lycia, and gave to him grisly signs, which he wrote inside a folded tablet, many and murderous, and bade him show them to his wife's father, that he might perish. And he went to Lycia *under the blameless guiding of the gods*. And when he came to Lycia and the flowing Xanthus the king of broad Lycia honoured him with open heart: for nine days he feasted him, and nine oxen he slew. But when the tenth rosy-fingered dawn appeared, then he questioned him and asked to see the sign that he brought with him from Proitos his son-in-law. Then, when he had received the evil sign, first he bade Bellerophon slay the raging Chimaera (She-goat). Now she was of birth divine, and not of men: in front a lion, behind a serpent, and in the midst a She-goat, breathing out a fearful force of burning fire. *And her he slew, following the signs of the gods.*

So on and so on. Bellerophon surmounts all his trials; the king of Lycia repents and gives him his daughter in marriage. He seems to be on the point of living happily ever after.

> *But when he also was hated of all the gods*, then verily along the Plain of Wandering alone he wandered, eating his own heart, avoiding the footfall of man.

What does it all mean? Is that the way to tell a new story unknown to your hearers? One wants more explanation all through. What 'blameless guiding of the gods' led Bellerophon to Lycia? What 'signs of the gods' showed him how to slay the Chimaera?[2] Above all, how did he become 'hated of all the

---

[1] Monro, *Odyssey*, Appendix, p. 294.
[2] Pegasus is omitted by Homer as a monster: he occurs Hes. *Theog.* 325

gods ', and go wandering? And why the phrase ' when he *also* '?
Is it not plain that the poet of Z is in the first place referring to
an existing legend, and secondly, one may almost say, quoting
from an existing poem? And what can that poem have been?
Bellerophon was a Corinthian hero. So that when we find that
there did exist an ancient mass of poetry vaguely called ' Corinthiaca ', and attributed to one Eumêlus of Corinth, which is on
general grounds the obvious source for any Corinthian traditions,
we naturally conjecture that some early form of the ' Corinthiaca '
is probably the source of our particular digression.

Let us follow this conjecture further. Shortly before this
Bellerophon passage there comes in the *Iliad* (Z 130 ff.) another
digression, telling how Lycurgus, King of Thrace, came to an
evil end because he ' fought with the gods ' in resisting Dionysus,
and the gods hated him. The passage troubles commentators
because Homer usually ignores Dionysus. As Dr. Leaf says,
' Dionysus is an absolute stranger to the Homeric pantheon.' If
we look into the scholia we find that the story of Lycurgus
resisting the god Dionysus was told by Eumêlus of Corinth in
the ' Europia '. The Europia, or ' Verses about Europa ', are
presumably the parts of the *Corinthiaca* or general Corinthian
traditions which dealt with Europa. The same source which we
suspected for Bellerophon! Evidently Homer—if we may so
name the poet of Z—since he was using the Europia for the
story of Bellerophon, took the Dionysus-Lycurgus story from
them at the same time. And he speaks, you remember, of
Bellerophon *also* being hated of all the gods. That *also* has no
meaning where it stands in the *Iliad*. Apparently in the original
Bellerophon came in a list of such people, following upon
Lycurgus. Lycurgus was hated of the gods and went blind:
' Bellerophon also ' was hated of the gods, and went mad. It is
all clear. If anything were needed to make it clearer still, it
would be that the Verses of Eumêlus are quoted as the earliest
known authority for the story of the Argo and Medea [1], and the

---

τὴν μὲν Πήγασος εἷλε καὶ ἐσθλὸς Βελλεροφόντης, and is mythologically very
ancient. (The Chimaera, a savage monster in remote lands, is obviously
less incredible than the tame Pegasus in a stable in Corinth.)

[1] e. g. by Schol. Pind. *Ol.* xiii. 74 ; Schol. Ap. Rhod. iii. 1372 (six lines
directly borrowed from Eumelus); Paus. ii. 3. 10. That is, the most authoritative form of the Medea-Argo epic, in Alexandrian times and later, was the

composer of our *Odyssey* speaks of the Argo as a subject of which ' all minds are full '.

There has been an extraordinary reluctance among scholars to look facts like these in the face, or even to understand the possibility of their occurring.   This comes from two causes. First, criticism is still beset by the unfortunate phrase ' Cyclic poets ', and all the false ideas it connotes.   When the *Iliad* and *Odyssey* had become canonical some scholar unknown made a complete ' cycle ' of epic history based primarily upon these two poems and, where they failed, on the remains of the various old traditional epics.[1]   To call the poets themselves ' Cyclic ' because others made up a ' cycle ' out of their remains is as unfair as to call an insect ' microscopic ' because persons over whom it has no control choose to look at it through a microscope.   It suggests, what is quite contrary to the evidence, that it was the original poets themselves who made this ' cycle ', deliberately completing the *Iliad* and *Odyssey*.   And secondly, Greek scholarship is not yet familiar, as Hebrew is, with the idea of a traditional book. The truth, as we have already seen, is that all these poems or masses of tradition in verse form were growing up side by side for centuries.   Either could quote or be quoted by the other as easily as the Book of Judges could refer to Samuel or Samuel to Judges.   Both these books, if we are to believe the most careful Biblical scholars, had begun to exist by 900 B.C.; but Judges was only finished a little before 200 B.C., and Samuel not quite finished then.   Or, to take a much stronger concrete instance, to show how complicated this process of mutual quotation may be.

Corinthian epic of ' Eumelus '.   It is the habit of the Grammatici to quote the earliest authority they can find.   ' Eumelus ' is, so to speak, the ' Homer ' of the Corinthian-argonautic traditions.   So far as we can guess at the date of any personal ' Eumelus ' he would seem to be a Homer according to Nitzsch, not a Homer according to Hermann—i.e. not the original inventor but the late perfector of a floating epic tradition.   The Corinthiaca had a most interesting history and well deserve a new monograph.   One can trace in them (1) old mythical material; (2) the fables generated by the earliest exploring voyages to the NE.; (3) a gathering-up and development of these legends in Corinth as a centre; (4) late re-editing and abridgement, such as occurred to the poems that were made into an ' epic cycle '.   Clement of Alexandria (*Strom.* vi. 267, Sylb.) thinks of Eumelus as the man who made the prose epitome then extant of certain epic traditions.   See Appendix H.

[1] Περατοῦται ὁ ἐπικὸς κύκλος, ἐκ διαφόρων ποιητῶν συμπληρούμενος μέχρι τῆς ἀποβάσεως Ὀδυσσέως τῆς εἰς Ἰθάκην, ἐν ᾗ καὶ ὑπὸ τοῦ παιδὸς Τηλεμάχου ἀγνοοῦντος κτείνεται, Proclus *apud* Phot. Bibl. 319 A.   See Appendix H, ' The Epic Cycle.'

Isaiah, chap. xxxvi–xxxix, is quite full of quotations, sometimes complete, sometimes abridged, from the Second Book of Kings. (Driver, *L. O. T.*, p. 227.)   On the other hand, the Second Book of Kings quotes not merely Isaiah but the much later writer, Jeremiah; and quotes him not directly but by way of Deuteronomy.   That is, it takes from Deuteronomy passages which Deuteronomy has already taken from Jeremiah.   (Ib. p. 203.) All the great books were growing up together, and passages could be repeated from any one to any other.

These facts should guard us against two possible misconceptions.   They show that the *Iliad,* though in one sense it may be called an independent work of fiction, is also a Traditional Book, dependent on a living saga or tradition.   It was meant to be history, or what then stood for history.   And secondly, that it is not alone among such books, a great original copied by a few late and obscure imitators, but one among a great number, each embodying the traditions specially prominent in their own circles of influence, and all of them freely overlapping and intercommunicating as the enterprise of a bard or the interest of his audience suggested.

I have jotted in the margin of my *Iliad* notes of the probable sources of the various bits of legend which seem foreign to the main story of the *Iliad* or alien to their immediate context. Many of them have been in ancient times or modern marked as 'spurious' or as 'interpolated'—a phrase which seems often merely to mean that the critic wishes a line were not there when it plainly is.   One finds in the first few books of the *Iliad*: first, the Catalogue of Ships, belonging originally to some Boeotian source, the school of genealogies and catalogues. This was known even in antiquity.   The ancient title of the whole passage was 'Boeotia', and it is omitted in many MSS.[1] But we can see that there was an intermediate source before the Catalogue came into the *Iliad*.   Various points of language show that the heroes are described, not as they were in the tenth year of the war, nor even as already disembarked at Troy, but as in the act of assembling at Aulis.   For example

---

[1] In *D, T, U,* and pap. B, among the best ones (Leaf).   Mr. Allen, in his great collation, cites an even longer list.   The similes introducing the Catalogue, however, are not omitted.

695–710, 716–717.   We have in 716 ff. a description of the men of Methone, 'whose leader was Philoctetes the skilful bowman, and in each ship were fifty rowers skilled to fight with the bow.' So far all is according to the usual formula, and all is correct— as a description of the fleet assembling at Aulis.   But by the time of the beginning of the *Iliad* Philoctetes had long been marooned on Lemnos ; so, without any alteration in the original version, eight lines are mechanically added to explain that Philoctetes was not there.   Similarly in 695–710 Protesilaus is described as leader of the contingent from Phylakê, and then a correction is added to explain that he was now dead.   Most conclusive of all, the tenses of the verbs are imperfect : ' He proceeded to draw up his ships ' or ' his ships moved into line.' (ἄγε νῆας, νέες ἐστιχόωντο.)   Now we happen, by the luck of a quotation, to know that there was an old poem, the Cyprian Verses, which narrated at length the assembling of the Greeks at Aulis and also contained a Catalogue.   True, our authority only speaks of a ' Catalogue of the Trojans ', such as forms the second part of our Catalogue in B.   But to any one who has grasped at all what literature was in the days before the book trade and the reading public it will seem a strained hypothesis to suggest that a Greek bard, reciting to Greeks, would give a catalogue of the enemy and leave out his own people.[1]   We

---

[1] See Wilamowitz, *Hom. Unt.*, p. 374.   On the later Catalogues (Apollodorus' *Epitome* ; Hyginus ; Dictys Cretensis, Dares Phrygius) see Allen, *Catalogue*, pp. 22–31.   In general they put the scene at Aulis ; their numbers are variable, but often less grandiose than those in B ; Hyginus, in the manner of his time, tries to give more details, while Dictys and Dares add some names.   They are all dependent on B, or at least on the same source as B and Euripides.   See also Appendix J.   The curious Catalogue inserted in Eur. *Iph. Aul.* 164–302 is, of course, abbreviated from some older source, and that source seems to be the *Cypria* rather than B.   First, the ships are there described at Aulis ; Protesilaus is alive and so is Palamedes (195–9) ; there is a reference to the Judgement of Paris (181) ; all these points would come straight from the *Cypria*, they would imply conscious change if the source was B.   Also, it is very interesting that the problem how to harmonize the positions of Adrastus and Agamemnon—one being, as Mülder puts it (p. 60 ff.), the great king of Argos in the *Thebais*, the other in the *Iliad* or *Achilleis*—is solved in a different way from that followed by B.   In B Agamemnon leads his forces from Mycenae and ' *Sikyon where formerly Adrastus was king* ' (B 570) ; in *Iph. Aul.* 269 Agamemnon leads the ships of Mycenae, ' *and with him was Adrastus, as a friend with a friend.*' The emendation ἀδελφός is a wilful refusal of light.)   The question we cannot answer is how far the MSS. of the Catalogue may have varied in Euripides' day, but, as they both stand, it seems that the Catalogue in the *Iph. Aul.* is in many points nearer to the source than that in B.

may fairly suppose that our Catalogue, wherever its origin, stood at one time in the *Cypria*.

In any case the Catalogue provides us with an instructive example of method.[1] Whatever the source from which the Catalogue comes, the poet of the *Iliad*, in taking it over, has taken over not only the facts but the actual words, even when they did not quite suit their new context. The imperfect tenses, for example, are certainly not natural as they stand. They are left standing because the bard did not think it worth while—or perhaps did not think it right—to re-write the lines. It is exactly like that ' *also* ' in the Bellerophon passage.

It is of course hard to get clear instances of this process of verbal borrowing because the poems which served as sources are not extant. But sometimes we get a glimpse of one. For instance, in the fifth book (*E* 385 ff.) there is a list of the injuries done to gods by men, especially by Heracles, which seems to be taken from the *Heracleia* (cf. especially 403 f., with Leaf's note). We happen to have a quotation from the *Heracleia*, as composed and re-formed in the sixth century by Panyassis, the uncle of Herodotus, and the quotation has a startling verbal and rhythmical similarity with this passage in *E*. If the passage in *E* could be original there, then Panyassis might have been merely imitating *E*; but the passage evidently is not original in *E*. Presumably Panyassis and the author of *E* are both adapting the same passage in an older form of the *Heracleia*.[2]

Another interesting reference to the *Heracleia* is in The Tricking of Zeus (*Ξ* 249-69), where Sleep mentions how Hera once before, in the matter of Heracles, bribed him to put his

---

[1] Two remarkable books have appeared on the Catalogue since my second edition : Leaf's *Homer and History* (Macmillan, 1915) and T. W. Allen's *Homeric Catalogue of Ships* (Oxford, 1921). Both regard the Catalogue as coming from an alien source, but beyond that they differ. See below, p. 202.

[2] The lines are, in the *Iliad*, 385, 392, 395 :

τλῆ μὲν Ἄρης, ὅτε μιν Ὦτος κρατερός τ' Ἐφιάλτης . . .
τλῆ δ' Ἥρη, ὅτε μιν κρατερὸς πᾶϊς Ἀμφιτρύωνος . . .
τλῆ δ' Ἀΐδης ἐν τοῖσι πελώριος ὠκὺν ὀϊστόν,
εὖτέ μιν ωὑτὸς ἀνὴρ κτλ.

In Panyassis, fr. 16 :

τλῆ μὲν Δημήτηρ, τλῆ δὲ κλυτὸς ἀμφιγυήεις,
τλῆ δὲ Ποσειδάων, τλῆ δ' ἀργυρότοξος Ἀπόλλων,
ἀνδρὶ παρὰ θνητῷ θητευέμεν εἰς ἐνιαυτόν.
τλῆ δὲ καὶ ὀβριμόθυμος Ἄρης ὑπὸ πατρὸς ἀνάγκῃ.

spell upon Zeus and how he suffered for it; another, very clear, in T 95-136 tells how, by a plot of Hera's, Heracles was born a servant to Eurystheus. There seem to be other fragments of *Heracleia* in some of the stories about Pylos. Other passages, again, seemed to be derived from those poems or groups of saga stuff which were eventually handed down under the names of the *Cypria*, the *Little Iliad*, the *Sack of Ilion*, the *Aethiopis*, the *Argonautica*, the *Battle of Gods and Titans*, and the *Naupactia* or Aetolian verses.[1]

But the whole problem of Homer's sources has been brought brilliantly into the foreground of interest since the first appearance of this book by Dietrich Mülder's *Die Ilias und ihre Quellen* (1909). Mülder conceives the main idea of the *Iliad* to be a great united war of all the Greeks against an arrogant barbarian city, and that the poet builds up this idea partly by pure invention, partly by free use of existing poems. The Meleager story, the *Thebais*, and a judicious fictional use of Nestor account for the greater part of the *Iliad*. The Meleager poem quoted at length in the Embassy to Achilles (I 527-599) contains a μῆνις with all the motives of the Achilles μῆνις as told in the *Iliad*. It is, of course, earlier than the book which quotes it. It also seems more original and better grounded. When Meleager abstained from battle because of his mother's curse, he stayed perforce in his θάλαμος in the besieged city, whereas Achilles might easily have gone away from Troy. And several peculiarities of the Embassy Story in I would be natural enough in an embassy to Meleager. This poem, then, provides the motive of the 'wrath', which is for fictional purposes highly convenient. The poet can have his chief hero either present or absent from the war, and thus make room for the deeds of all the other heroes of legend whom he wished to draw into his great story. Then comes the *Thebais*. There was, according to Mülder, no detailed record of any siege of Troy, only a tradition of the Aeolic colonization and the actual remains of more than one burnt city. But there did exist one great epic describing the expedition against Thebes of a federation led by Adrastus, King of Argos. This provided a mass of fighting by mixed Greek champions in a plain against a city

---

[1] See Leaf on E 392. Also below, pp. 219 ff.

on a hill, an ancient motive of art which we find already extant in Middle Minoan frescoes and in a silver vase from
Mycenae.[1] This explains why Homer's Greeks are called
Ἀργεῖοι and Δαναοί equally with Ἀχαιοί, which is the proper
name for Achilles' men. It also explains the presence of Greek
chariots in the *Iliad*. The charioteers of the *Thebais* are famous;
witness Adrastus, Amphiaraus, and Tydeus; while it is not
likely that an early Greek army would have been capable of
transporting horses and chariots in an expedition overseas to
Troy. The actual heroes of the *Thebais* are not brought over
to Troy. That would have been counter to tradition. But
Diomedes, the son of Tydeus, is there, and brings with him
a tremendous ἀριστεία embodying the only real chariot charges
in the *Iliad*, and perhaps taken straight from his father. The
place of Adrastus is taken by Agamemnon. He is the leader of
all Greece, and we are told that he has succeeded Adrastus as
King of Argos, though in most aspects he and his brother
king look remarkably like two normal kings of Sparta, and
it is in Sparta, or the neighbourhood, that, outside Homer,
they have their graves and their worship and most of their
roots.[2] It somewhat confirms these arguments when we find
that Hector, the defender of Troy, has quite independently been
shown by Dümmler and Bethe to have intimate Theban connexions and to have been worshipped in Thebes as a local hero.
This bold theory needs more careful consideration than it has
received. Probably Mülder errs in underrating the amount of
genuine saga material about Troy which is embodied in the
Iliad; but I think he has shown that there is in it much more
conscious fiction than the present writer, at any rate, was
formerly inclined to believe; and, further, that the *Thebais* is
probably one of the poet's most important sources.

On the other hand there are books, and very fine books,
which seem to be pure original fiction. The most brilliant of
all are perhaps Z and Ω. Then there is I, embodying, besides
the Meleager story, the realistic and perhaps genuine history
of Phoinix. There is also K, describing a midnight raid by
Odysseus and Diomêdês, in which they catch a Trojan spy with

[1] Evans, *Palace of Minos*, I, pp. 302, 314.
[2] See below, pp. 210 f.

a fictitious name—Dolon, *Crafty*—and through him succeed in killing Rhêsus, chief of the Thracians. This looks like a piece of fiction made up out of two separate traditional sources: a tradition of the slaying of Rhêsus by Diomêdês, presumably in Thrace,[1] and another about the midnight expedition of Odysseus and Diomêdês into Troy to carry off the Palladium.[2] Of course that is only conjecture. But it serves to illustrate the kind of material with which we are dealing in the *Iliad*.

In its actual working up, however, our *Iliad* has reached a further stage of development than the ordinary run of poetic chronicles, if I may use the term. The imaginary epicizing of the Book of Judges which we discussed some time ago would land us, not in a poem like the *Iliad*, but in one like the *Cypria* or the *Corinthiaca*, in one of those authorless chronicle-poems of which we hear so much in Greek literature, and know, at first hand, so little. It was their fate, first, to be superseded by the *Iliad* and *Odyssey*, and then, in a later age, to be strung together in what was called an 'Epic Cycle' by some scholar or historian. Here again the *Odyssey* shows itself a stage nearer to the raw material. And, curiously enough, there is one quite late poet who, partly by conscious love of the archaic and partly from the peculiar nature of his genius, has returned to a type of epic chronicle earlier than either the *Iliad* or the *Odyssey*. I mean the Alexandrian poet of the Argonaut legend, Apollonius Rhodius.

Let us consider this point more closely. What is the meaning of the name *Iliad*, in Greek ἡ 'Ιλιὰς πόησις? *Ilias* is an adjective meaning 'about Ilion'. *Poêsis* means 'verse-writing': that is, first, it denotes the process of 'making' verses, and secondly, the result of the process, a mass of verse-writing. Not, you will observe, a thing quite so definite as a *Poêma*. It is 'poetry', not a 'poem'. The name 'Ιλιὰς πόησις, then, means 'the poetry about Troy'. That is the traditional name,

---

[1] See below, Lecture VIII, pp. 215 ff.
[2] K of course occupies a peculiar position. The Townley Scholia have a very ancient note: 'They say that this rhapsody was "drawn up by itself" (ἰδίᾳ τετάχθαι) by Homer, and is not part of the *Iliad*, but was put into the poem by Pisistratus.' The language of K is also in many ways divergent from that of the rest of the *Iliad*. See Leaf's Introductory note to K, and Monro, *H. G.*, p. 234. (See, however, Shewan's *Lay of Dolon*, which tries to rebut this observation.) It is a brilliantly written book.

and it is generally felt to be pretty satisfactory. But how does the *Iliad* itself begin? Does it begin, for instance,

> I sing of Ilion and Dardania of the swift horses, for whose sake the Danaans, servants of Ares, suffered many things?[1]

That would be the natural sort of beginning for an *Ilias Poêsis*. And the lines did, as a matter of fact, form the beginning of one of the old chronicle epics: the poem which afterwards supported a mutilated and obscure existence under the name of the *Little Iliad*.

Our *Iliad* begins with quite a different appeal:—

> Sing of the Wrath, O Goddess, of Pêleus' son, the wrath accursed which laid many pains upon the Achaeans.

That is, it professes to tell the story of a fatal quarrel between Achilles and Agamemnon, which took place in the tenth year of the war and lasted for a very few days. Nay, it does not tell even the whole of the Wrath quite exhaustively. It might have included the capture of the two causes of it, the maidens of Bresa and of Chryse. The poet appeals to the Muse to 'sing of the Wrath, *beginning there where first there was strife and sundering* between Agamemnon, King of men, and divine Achilles'.

Now, we can understand this language. It implies the existence of a plentiful and well-known poetical tradition. It is the phrase of a bard selecting for purposes of recitation some special episode out of a longer history. It is the same in the opening of the *Odyssey*: '*From somewhere amid those tales*, O Muse, speak to us also.' It is the same with the bards who are spoken of in the *Odyssey*.

> And Demodocus called upon the god and made minstrelsy, *beginning where the Greeks had gone upon their benchèd ships*, and were sailing the sea, but Odysseus and his comrades lay hidden in the market of the Trojans (θ 500).

That is how the Phaeacian bard is described; and his lay seems to have lasted for a few hundred lines at most. That is as much

---

[1] Ps. Hdt. *Vita Homeri*, § 16:

> Ἴλιον ἀείδω καὶ Δαρδανίην εὔπωλον
> ἧς πέρι πολλὰ πάθον Δαναοί, θεράποντες Ἄρηος.

as people will usually endure to listen to. The poet proposes to select out of a mass of legend the particular episode of the Wrath, an episode just large enough to make a good 'Lay'.

The incidents of the Wrath are these: Agamemnon, provoked by the free-speaking of Achilles, puts a dishonour upon him. Achilles withdraws from the war. Agamemnon fights without him and is defeated by the Trojans. The Greek ships are in danger. Achilles is implored to save them. He still will not fight himself, but sends his bosom friend, Patroclus. Patroclus is killed by Hector. Achilles, furious with remorse, joins in the battle himself, slays Hector, and gives Patroclus a splendid funeral. The subject, as here announced, is not Ilion as a whole, not even the last war of Ilion; it is merely a four-days' incident in the tenth year of the war. And yet the poem is called 'Ιλιὰς ποίησις, the 'poetry about Ilion'.

And not unsuitably. For no sooner has the poet explained in the first book the origin of the Wrath than he leaves that subject and, roughly speaking, does not return to it until the eleventh book. He goes back in the second to a catalogue of all the Greek host, describing the fleet, not as it was in Troy after nine years of fighting, but as it was in Aulis before it started for Troy. After the catalogue come various battles, including a duel or ordeal by combat between the two principals in the international quarrel, Paris and Menelaus: battles which are rather curious as they now stand, but fall into place at once if you realize that they properly belong to the very beginning of the war. The ordeal by battle was tried first: owing to some Trojan's treachery it failed, and the two nations sat down to a ten years' conflict. Then follow further battles; in Δ an obscure duel between two other heroes:[1] in E a whole brilliant poem about Diomêdês,[2] which not only runs the risk of upsetting the balance of the *Iliad* by dwarfing the exploits of Achilles, but also shows in itself a definite connexion with another context. Next, a fine stretch of poetry in Z, which tells of Troy from the inside and treats Hector as a sympathetic hero, not a hated enemy. Every line of it is noble: but how is it introduced?

---

[1] Very possibly pointing, as Bethe suggests, to a form of the legend in which Aias was the chief hero. There seem to be traces of such a form.

[2] See note on p. 179. Cf. Mülder, *Quellen der Ilias*, 1910.

How is Hector brought into Troy? In the thick of a desperate battle, when Diomêdês is slaughtering the Trojans and Hector is the only man at all capable of resisting him, Hector leaves the field to take a message, not in the least of a confidential nature, to his mother, and to converse with his wife!

I am touching on all these points very lightly. The proof of each one depends for its validity on detailed and accurate examination of the words of the poem. I am using them merely to indicate the sort of process by which the short Lay of the Wrath of Achilles has been made into the great 'Poetry about Troy': or, to put the case from a different point of view, how the most diverse traditions of heroic fighting have been joined together and made fairly consistent by this ingenious device of the 'Wrath'. I cannot think that the Wrath was mere fiction. It was an old traditional motive. But it was chosen, I suspect, for its fictional convenience. One chieftain after another can be the greatest of the Greeks while Achilles is away from the field.[1] If another is expressly asserted to be the best, or swiftest, or handsomest, of all warriors, even that statement can be retained by the addition of an inorganic line, like

$$τῶν ἄλλων Δαναῶν μετ' ἀμύμονα Πηλεΐωνα,$$

or

$$ὄφρ' Ἀχιλεὺς μήνιεν· ὁ γὰρ πολὺ φέρτατος ἦεν:$$

'of all the Greeks, else, after the blameless son of Peleus', or 'while Achilles was in wrath. For he was the strongest far'. The composer, as a matter of fact, has reached out on every side and collected the most diverse masses of heroic tradition to insert between the joints of his Wrath-Lay.

The result of this process is that the *Iliad* is really a Lay which has utterly outgrown its natural boundaries. It professes to be a Lay, but is so no longer. There are other instances of this kind of growth in Greek literature. The Homeric Hymns give themselves out to be Προοίμια, 'Preludes'; that is, mere addresses to a god, preparatory to beginning a real poem: the

---

[1] See Mülder, *Homer und die altionische Elegie*, pp. 19 ff. Also Wecklein, *Studien zur Ilias*. Cf. N 321 ff., B 673 f., 768 f., H 111 ff., 226 ff., contrasted with B 530, Γ 227, 229; Z 98 ff.; H 289. These last are perhaps the only passages where a superlative is applied to another hero without the addition of some qualifying clause about Achilles. Mülder's arguments are attacked by Rothe (*Ilias als Dichtung*, pp. 31–8), but not, I think, successfully.

sort of prelude that Demodocus used when he 'began from a god'. But these preludes have grown in interest and beauty and length, till now the first five of them run to some hundreds of lines apiece. They have become, not Preludes to a Lay, but complete Lays in themselves. Again, the victory songs performed by Pindar's choruses generally contain less than fifty lines; but one of them has over four hundred lines, bursting all its natural bounds. That particular lyric, the *Fourth Pythian*, was composed to be a great gift and peace-offering laid at the feet of the King of Cyrene by an exiled noble. It was to be a gift such as no other noble had ever given, no king ever received.

But now comes a difficulty. Every work of art that was ever created was intended in some way to be used. No picture was painted for blind men; no ship built where there was no water. What was to be the use of the *Iliad*? What audience would listen to the recitation of such a poem? It contains over fifteen thousand verses. It would occupy twenty to twenty-four hours of steady declamation. No audience could endure it, no bard could perform it, in one stretch. And it is specially constructed so as not to fall apart in lengths. From Lachmann onward innumerable scholars have tried to break it up into separate recitations, and have all failed. It is all one—at least, as far as its composers could make it so. A single lay could be recited at one sitting. A chronicle poem, falling easily apart into separate stories, could be recited evening after evening in several sittings. The *Cypria*, from what we know of them, would fall apart excellently into separate episodes; so would a good deal of the *Odyssey*. It has the 'plots of many tragedies in it', as Aristotle has observed, and as we have noticed before. But the *Iliad* has been deliberately elaborated on a plan which puts it out of use for ordinary purposes of recitation. Yet recited it must certainly have been.[1]

The late F. A. Paley was so much impressed by this difficulty that he actually came to the conclusion that the *Iliad* was a poem composed for reading, not for recitation, and that con-

---

[1] Cf. Bréal, l. c., pp. 43 ff., who lays stress on the influence of Public Games on the *Iliad*. His general conclusion agrees almost exactly with mine.

sequently it was not an early epic at all, but a learned poem composed in Athens at some time between Euripides and Plato, when there existed a reading public. This view, as it stands, is opposed to much that we regard as certain about early Greek literature; but Paley's arguments have never been answered, and the difficulty is a real one.[1]

Now here, as it happens, the very first fact certainly known about the *Iliad* and *Odyssey* comes to our aid. They were performed at the Panathenaea at Athens, just as tragedies were performed at the Dionysia. They were recited, not by one bard, but by relays of bards in competition. The order was fixed, the next bard having to begin where the last left off. These festivals meant much more in ancient life than any similar ceremony at the present day. In drama and epos, as in other things, the ancients were accustomed to rarer and more prolonged indulgences than we, their weaker descendants. After waiting four years for a full-dress epic recitation they expected something ἄμεμπτον, which no one could call insufficient. The Panathenaea was the greatest of all Athenian festivals, recurring once in four years and lasting several days. Established in the sixth century, it formed the occasion for the gathering of all the Ionians from their diverse settlements under the wing of the great 'Metropolis' or mother-city, who was their champion and leader against the barbarian. The Panathenaean recitation exactly explains what without it would be inexplicable in the form and size of the *Iliad* and *Odyssey*.

The fact may suggest to us a question. What, after all, is the meaning of the name 'Panathenaea'? Who are the 'All-Athenaioi' for whom the feast is made? Not the Athenians themselves; that would give no meaning to the 'Pan'. The answer occurs immediately. Who can the 'All-Athenians' be

---

[1] There is some answer to Paley in Geddes, *Problem of the Homeric Poems*, Appendix A. My own view will come out in Chapter XII. Roughly speaking, I think Paley erred because he still operated with a single poet, who created the whole *Iliad* about 415 B.C. If he had grasped the conception of a Traditional Book, and argued that work was still being done upon the *Iliad*, that it was being edited with a view to readers, instead of audiences, as late as 415 and even later, I think he would have proved his case. See Paley, *Remarks on Prof. Mahaffy's account of the rise and progress of Epic Poetry* (Bell, 1881), *Post-Epic or imitative words in Homer* (Norgate), *Homeri quae nunc exstant an reliquis Cycli carminibus antiquiora jure habita sint* (Norgate). Also Sayce's Appendix to vol. i of Mahaffy's *Classical Greek Literature.*

but the very people whom Athens was then shepherding, and whose universal character was that they were 'all sprung from Athens'? Twelve cities in especial called themselves Ionian, and had their great meeting at the feast of the Panionia at Cape Mycale. But they were not more Ionian than many other cities, says Herodotus: 'In reality all are Ionians who are sprung from Athens and keep the Apaturia'—an Athenian festival (i. 147). Only, he observes, many of them, and especially the Athenians (143), avoid the name, and do not wish to be called 'Ionians'. Exactly; the name 'Athenaioi' was more honourable; it was also wider in range. For it included those various cities that did not belong to the Ionian Twelve, but admitted that they were 'sprung from Athens'.[1] The informal league of which Athens was chief, at a time when 'the Ionian race was of lowest account, and had no city of weight, except only Athens' (Hdt. i. 143), could have chosen no better name than 'All-Athenians' when it gathered for its great festival every fourth year, exactly at the same time when the great Dorian gatherings met for the Pythian games at Delphi.

And, to return to the *Iliad*, what after all is its essential story? Is it not the story of the battle of All-Greeks against the barbarians of Asia? 'All-Greeks': the wonderful word rings out again and again in the poems—what though it comes chiefly in later parts, and against the tradition of the epic style? It is a modern formation, markedly out of tone; forcing itself in just because it so exactly expresses the meaning for which the older language had no word. 'Panachaioi', you will say, or 'Panhellênes'; not 'Paniônes'. True, Homer uses generally the older and more dignified term, 'Achaioi', to denote the whole race whom the Italians called 'Graeci', the Asiatics 'Iâones', the Greeks themselves in later days 'Hellenes'. The Ionians knew this, and even claimed themselves to be not only 'Iones' and 'Athenaioi', but also 'Achaioi'. To justify the claim they brought their founders from Achaia. In later times, at any rate, they had the legend that, while coming ultimately from Athens, their ancestors had

---

[1] The theory that the Ionians were all sprung from Athens may not, of course, have had much historical foundation. That difficult problem does not here concern us.

gone quite out of their way and stayed for a time in the little district of the Peloponnese which was called by that name (Hdt. i. 145).[1]   Paniones, Panhellenes, Panachaioi, and at last Pan-athenaioi; there is the same conception behind all these names, only some minor differences of time or of local centre.   It is a union of men of Hellenic civilization against the multitudes of eastern barbarism.

In many ways the Pisistratean festival of 'All-Athenians' forms exactly the occasion for which our *Iliad* might have been composed.   The poem is not Athenian in the special sense, but 'All-Athenian' in the sense just explained is exactly what it is.   It is Pan-Achaean; from the point of view of Ionia it is Pan-Hellenic.   If it breathes the spirit of any single city it is that mother-city which was claiming to be the champion and the centre of all who stood as Greeks against the barbarians of Asia.   We know of no city except Athens which could have fostered a Hellenism so broad, so utterly un-parochial.   Besides this, if we are to believe some recent researchers, the ordinary armour of the poems, the ordinary men's dress, the women's dress, the conception of the appearance of the gods and much of the actual religion of the two poems, seem to tally exactly with Athens of the sixth or fifth century, and do not suit any earlier period of which we have historical knowledge.   These broad facts are so strong and far-reaching that we need not lay stress on the so-called Athenian interpolations—on the statement that the almost unknown Athenian, Menestheus, was the greatest 'marshaller of men and horse' (B 554) in the army, that Orestes came home 'from Athens' (γ 307) and not from Phocis, or that Athena, when seeking her natural abode, went into the 'House of Erechtheus on the Athenian acropolis' (η 81): we need not debate whether the fact that Nestor's son in the *Odyssey* (γ, δ, o) bears the fictional name 'Pisistratus' is based upon a compliment, or whether the verse '*Multitude of masters is no good thing; let there be one master*' (B 204) is a manifesto, undetected and unexpurgated, in favour of the mild Tyrant of Athens.   Beyond all doubt the influence of the Panathenaic recitation upon our poems was immense.   Yet, though it in-fluenced it cannot have created.   The language was there

---

[1] On this point cf. Wilamowitz, *Die Ionische Wanderung* and *Panionion*.

before, pre-Attic and pre-Ionic, already established as the correct vehicle for epic. As to the Attic forms, apart from mere errors of copyists, they do seem to prove the existence of Attic poets, composing in good epic style, but occasionally, in spite of all skill and care, slipping into their own dialect. It may well be that the first emergence of a written Iliad which we could recognize as such took place in Athens in the sixth century; but, if so, it was a re-composing of old themes out of old words and verses and formulae.[1]

Behind the recorded Panathenaic recitation there must lie long years of unrecorded recitation at various great Ionian gatherings. Pisistratus, or whoever he was, must have taken over to Athens an institution already existing in Ionia. One thinks first of the Panionia, the great gathering feast of the Twelve Cities at Cape Mycale. That is the obvious correlative to the Panathenaea. And there is some confirmatory evidence. It has been remarked long since that, among the Homeric gods, there stand out three who are never jeered at or made ridiculous; two of them really grand figures, Poseidon and Apollo; the third, at least a very faithful and formidable partisan of the Greek cause, Pallas Athena, who is especially prominent in the very latest additions to the *Odyssey*. Athena was the patroness of Athens in general, and in particular the visible champion of Pisistratus. Poseidon and Apollo were the two patron gods of the Panionia at Cape Mycale.

Or one might think of the great four-yearly festival at Delos, at which the Homeric hymn to Apollo was sung by 'the blind minstrel of craggy Chios' to a gathering of all the 'long-robed Ionians'. The gods would suit almost equally well. About this festival there is a curious passage in Thucydides (iii. 104). In narrating how the Athenians in 426 B.C. 'purified' the island of Delos, he mentions that Pisistratus had purified it before, though not completely. He had moved only those pollutions that were in sight of Apollo's temple. He continues his narrative of the doings of 426 :—

And the Four-yearly festival was then celebrated by the Athenians for the first time since (or, after) the purifica-

---

[1] Wackernagel, *Sprachliche Untersuchungen zu Homer*, 1916. Cauer, pp. 99–136.

tion. There used to be in quite ancient days a gathering of the Ionians and the neighbouring islanders to Delos. They came to the games with their wives and children, as the Ionians still go to the festival at Ephesus. There was a gymnastic contest and a contest of minstrels, and the various cities sent dances to the gods.

This seems to say that the Athenians in 426 celebrated the feast for the first time since the cleansing of the island by Pisistratus. If so, much would become clear. We could suppose that, when Pisistratus cleansed the island and made the old fair or gathering-place sacred and 'untreadable' (ἄβατον), the Delia naturally came to an end, and the contest of minstrels was transferred to Athens, as the federal treasure was transferred afterwards.

We sometimes find Homeric critics, misled by mediaeval analogies, discussing whether the Homeric poems are 'Court poetry' or 'popular poetry', and generally deciding in favour of the former. But the parallel does not hold. The poems do not show consistently the marks of either style. There is high and prolonged artistic tension, there is no buffoonery or vulgarity, there is an implication of dignity and culture in the audience as well as the poet. So far we are reminded of court poetry. On the other hand, they contain no flattery towards any patron, no glorification of any special royal house, no hinted demands for bakshish, no affectation of language. They go into neither pigeon-hole. And very naturally so. For we know from history that they were recited to an audience and on an occasion completely different. They were recited at a Panegyris, one of those solemn Pan-Hellenic gatherings which formed the centre of so much of the higher life of Greece.[1]

There is the conventional mixed dialect, the conventional generalized religion, best explained by the mixed and pan-hellenic atmosphere of the whole occasion. There is a sacred truce between all Greek cities. No Greek is an enemy; no race or tribe of Greeks is maligned or satirized. There is war

---

[1] The French Epic, *Le Pèlerinage de Charlemagne*, was composed for the Fair at St. Denys known as L'Endit. Bédier, op. cit., thinks that recitation at the mixed gatherings of the great pilgrim centres explains the conventional mixed dialect of the Chansons de Geste.

in the air, but it is not a war of neighbour against neighbour
in the common way of the mainland, it is a war of All-Hellenes
against the Barbarian, yet a war in which the Dorian nobles,
the martial aristocracy of Greece, are strangely ignored.[1]   There
is the religious *euphemia* or avoidance of evil words, which is
known to have been incumbent at these festivals and which
probably explains not only much of Homer's expurgation of
ancient legends, but his deliberate abstinence from all those
notes of horror and ghastliness which are common in the rest
of early epic tradition as well as in Attic tragedy.   Apollo was
more insistent on euphemia than Dionysos.

What a difference, after all, there is between the Greek and
the Hebrew traditional book!   The general process at work was
much the same in both, but a great divergence must have begun
early.   The Hebrew reviser, except where religious motives
came into play, tampered so little with his wording.   He took his
raw material just as it was, and copied it out, merely inserting his
introductory and connecting formulae, smoothing out contradictions, and correcting the orthodoxy of his authorities where they
needed it.   A Homeric scholar cannot but be surprised at the
extreme ease with which interpolations in the Hebrew writings
often betray themselves.   They are made quite undisguisedly,
with no artifice and sometimes no regard for grammar.[2]   No
Greek editor ever dreamed of doing his business like that.   For
every Son of Homer was himself a poet, and kept modifying
and working up into poetry everything that he touched.

Consider the ultimate purpose to which the literature was
destined in either case, and most of the differences in form and
spirit will follow.   The Hebrew scriptures became, to use the
rather strange technical term, 'books that defile the hands'.
That is, they were holy: after touching them you must wash

---

[1] One might compare, allowing for differences of date and circumstance,
the exhortations of Lysias and of Isocrates at Olympia, delivered to an
audience representing the whole of Greece.

[2] For instance, the older phrase 'the Ark' was expanded by later editors
into 'the Ark of the Covenant', or 'the Ark of the Covenant of Yahweh'.
Now an elementary rule of Hebrew grammar is that a noun in the construct
case (i.e., in our terminology, followed by another noun in the genitive) cannot
have the definite article.   Yet these pious correctors did not venture to delete
the article before 'Ark'.   They preferred to leave the utterly ungrammatical
phrase הָאָרוֹן הַבְּרִית (Josh. iii. 14) or (*ib.* 17) : הָאָרוֹן בְּרִית יְהֹוָה.

your hands before touching any mundane thing. They were kept sacred and apart. Their purpose was to be read aloud accurately letter by letter in the synagogue for the instruction of the people. If a member of the audience was not interested, more shame to him. No one dreamed of imputing any blame to the writings.

But the Greek traditions from the very outset were made into Lays to be recited by bards for the delectation of the company. If men were not interested, it was the fault of the bard and his poems. And in the very earliest times of Greece we meet with that characteristic and only half praiseworthy Greek institution, the public competitive recitation. The poems became, in the Greek phrase, ἐπιδεικτικά, things of display. The bards who knew the traditions came to recite at the great games and gatherings. Each recited his own poems—i. e. those that he 'possessed', not necessarily those that he had composed—and tried to make them more attractive than other people's. He was bound, of course, not to violate history too grossly; not to be ψευδής, or 'false-speaking', above all, not to be ignorant. But he might, by the help of the Muses, tell his audience a great deal more about the heroes than by any human means he was likely to know. He might transfer incidents from one legend to another, he might alter names or disregard times and places, provided the change really made his poem better and did not stir his hearers to contradiction. He could work up the known incidents till they became more and more moving, more edifying, or more pleasing. An element was thus admitted which leavened the whole lump, an element which, in the hands of a less wonderfully gifted people, must, one would think, have led to bombast and vulgarity, but which was somehow stopped when it had done its maximum of good and was only just started on its career of evil; I mean that strange mixed passion known to all artists, which consists, at its higher end, in the pure love of beautiful or noble creation, and, at its lower end, in conscious strain for the admiration of an audience.

VIII

THE HISTORICAL CONTENT OF THE ILIAD

ONE of the last letters which I received from Andrew Lang before his death contained the words ' The next thing Homeric critics will go mad about is historicity'. Far be it from me to say that the prophecy has been fulfilled, but a fashion has set in somewhat violently in favour of accepting the poems as historically valid. This makes a new cross-division among Homeric scholars. Some of the strictest ' Unitarians', naturally enough, take the sceptic side and treat the poems as mere fiction, and some of the most radical analysers talk cheerfully of pre-Homeric ' documents' and ' archives', which it would be a sin to doubt.

Euhemerus, as we all know, started a great movement in ancient theology by the hypothesis that the Greek gods were all real men, and the myths about them real facts embroidered and exaggerated, and some of the champions of historicity apply his method with the same impartiality to the whole Greek tradition. They are prepared to believe in the reality of Dionysus, Asclepius and even Hippolytus, and think that very likely Cadmus did follow a cow and build a city where it lay down: why should not he? I cannot generally agree with these scholars, but I think it likely that their method when critically applied may sometimes yield historical results. They profit, for example, by a comparison of the Egyptian and Assyrian records and the researches of anthropologists.[1] It is at least possible that the mythical Amazons represent some real race of nomads who seemed to be female because they were beardless; that the Golden Fleece may well come from real fleeces which were used to collect gold dust in the rivers of Phasis; that the King of

[1] See particularly Myres and Frost, *Historical Background of the Trojan War*, in *Klio*, xiv (1915).

Troy may have had a real golden candlestick with seven branches, which he obtained from the Assyrians or Hittites; or even that the Flight of Danaos with his fifty daughters to escape the sons of Aigyptos may have been connected with the defeat of the Danauna by the Egyptians about 1200 B.C.[1]   But this general problem lies outside our special task.   We have to face a more particular one. Some learned and distinguished writers, such as Dr. Leaf and Professor Chadwick, take the view that, while the Greek myths as a whole are more or less futile and negligible, the Homeric narrative is largely historical and correct.   It is argued that it fairly represents the central thread of Greek tradition; that it is in the main reasonable and in accordance with possibility; that it is not violently contradicted by itself or by known facts outside it; and, lastly, that in most myths, amid all the nebula of exaggeration, fancy, and mere muddle, there is apt to be an historical nucleus without which the nebula could not have formed.

To take these points in order, in what sense do the Poems form the main or central thread of Greek tradition?   We know that from about the sixth century onwards Homer formed the staple of Greek education.   Every one knew Homer, and all parts of Greece accepted him.   Consequently, any local tradition which conflicted with Homer tended to die out, or else to be trimmed and fitted into consistency with him.   So much will be agreed.   Now, the Poems formed the dominant Greek tradition, not in the least because historical research showed them to be true, but because they were such good and successful poems. They constituted the *fable convenue*, and surely, if ever we have to choose between the *fable convenue* and some stubborn fragment of inconsistent local tradition which for some reason continued to maintain itself in the teeth of the prevailing fashion, at first blush an historian's preference should be for the latter. I do not, of course, suggest that it is necessarily true.   Hecataeus

---

[1] Problems arise about the definitely Minoan objects which occur in Homeric and Attic poetry: e.g. sword inlaid with racing horses, Eur. *El.* 476; dog-and-fawn buckle, τ 228 ff.; Skylla (dog-headed sea-monster), μ 86 ff.; man clinging under ram's belly, ι 432 ff.; snake and eagle, Soph. *Ant.* 126; cf. Evans, *Palace*, i, pp. 274, 666, 698, 715.   The explanation is probably κειμήλια in families or temples *plus* popular tradition.   I see no trace of Minoan 'documents'.   See above, p. 168.

found the traditions of the Greeks 'many and ridiculous', but those of them which answer the above test deserve more respect than most, and at least compare favourably with 'the lies of the poets'. But almost more dangerous than the lies of the poets are, I think, the devices of the harmonizers. For example, if Homer says that Hector was buried in Troy, and the Thebans in historical times are found worshipping his tomb in Thebes, we shall not, if we are prudent, try to get out of the difficulty by accepting the explanation that Hector was, of course, really buried as Homer said, but that later no doubt,—though no ancient writer happens to mention it,—in obedience to an oracle the Thebans sent to Troy to dig up his bones. Or again, if the Homeric Catalogue makes the Boeotians the central force of Agamemnon's army, occupying the whole of Boeotia, while the rest of Homer almost ignores their existence and Thucydides says that they were first driven from Thessaly into Boeotia sixty years after the Trojan War, we shall not solve that contradiction by accepting the suggestions of old historians that perhaps a small section (ἀποδασμός) were already in Boeotia before the Trojan War, or that perhaps they all came in before the War and were all unexpectedly driven out and returned again. Such hypotheses are generally figments invented to explain a difficulty, and, after all, do not explain it.

But then, it will be said, the Homeric narrative is in the main so reasonable and possible, and the Homeric characters make such an impression of reality! 'Contrast the *Iliad*', says Dr. Leaf, 'with the *Argonautica* with its shadowy characters and its abundantly miraculous incidents.' But surely to argue thus is to put oneself at the mercy of the story-teller. By such canons *Pendennis* and *Resurrection* would be historical, and the *Song of Roland* not. As a matter of fact, the *Argonautica* contains, as no doubt Dr. Leaf would admit, a great deal of historical deposit: the passage of the Bosphorus, the exploration of the Euxine, the discovery of strange tribes and perhaps of gold dust in rivers. But it is composed in the romantic and miraculous style, while the *Iliad* is full of σωφροσύνη and verisimilitude. Thus Professor Chadwick shows by examples that the carrying off of a princess was in the Homeric Age a quite possible cause of war, and invites us therefore to believe in an historic

Rape of Helen.   Dr. Leaf has made a careful reconstruction of the walls of Troy and shows that the chase of Hector round them was nowise impossible.   But the critics who doubted the truth of these stories never, as far as I know, doubted their possibility.   It is not likely that a Homeric poet engaged in fiction would, with all the world before him, deliberately choose a fiction that was incredible.   It is a matter of style and of artistic competence.

'But at least the Homeric story is seldom or never contradicted by known facts.'   Here again, as I have already ventured to suggest, critics have been misled by a point of style; I mean the deliberate care with which the Homeric poets, and indeed most poets in the classical tradition, avoid committing themselves to details. We have noticed it in the matter of the shields and the armour. Scholars and poets innumerable have read the descriptions of the Homeric battles, and in their mind's eye have clad the heroes in the most diverse styles of armour without ever coming on a flat contradiction.   That could never happen to readers of *Marmion* or *The Lady of the Lake*.   It is much the same with the topography.   The rivers of Troy, Scamander and Simois, are vividly presented to our imaginations.   But no hint whatever is given of where they lie, and all geographers agree that the one definite topographical statement which the poems have been rash enough to make about them cannot be true.   They cannot have run into one another (*E* 774).   Such slips are exceedingly rare.   As a rule, all descriptions are merely generical.   Think of the innumerable ships that are mentioned in the *Odyssey*.   Most of them have their suitable epithets.   They are 'hollow', 'black', 'even', 'rowed on both sides', 'swift', and sometimes 'red-cheeked'.   Yet not one, if I remember rightly, has any single definite quality to separate it from any of the others.   It is much the same with rivers, plains, mountains, harbours, and all else that goes to make up that beautiful and heroic, but strangely standardized, world.   There are indeed some topographical details in Ithaca, and a vast deal of trouble they have given. There is far less detail about the Plain of Troy.   Dr. Leaf appeals with much apparent force to the success with which his topographical reconstructions can be built up without contradicting Homer.   He thinks it is due to Homer's geography being exact and true, and would have us believe in the location even of the

Ford and the Wild Fig Tree.   His work is so beautifully done
that it is with real regret that I find myself reflecting that other
travellers have made quite different reconstructions with almost
equal success, at any rate, in avoiding any contradiction by the
text of Homer.

The theory of the historical nucleus surrounded by a nebula
of fanciful or mythical additions seems at first sight attractive.
An Indian god, Nikal Seyn, has grown up with mythical appurte-
nances round the solid figure of John Nicholson.   Another has
grown round Sir Courtenay Ilbert, or rather, since the name of
the god appears to be Illabuttabil rather than Illabutta, round
the famous Bill associated with his name.   We are told in the
mediaeval life of Alexander the Great how Iskander Khan once
flew on an eagle with the Prophet Elijah to obtain the water of
life.   And so, it is argued, there is a *prima facie* case for
believing in the reality of Achilles, Agamemnon, Helen, and the
rest.   But, in the first place, what kind of ' historicity ' would this
be ?   What single true fact should we know of Alexander, Ilbert,
or Nicholson, from the stories cited ?   Names and nothing more.
Nay, not even the names, for, after all, it was not Ilbert but the
Ilbert Bill that has taken divine form in the myth, and Iskander
Khan is not quite the same name as Alexandros.   But further,
what is nucleus and what is nebula ?   The historic Alexander is
not the nucleus which has attracted the Eagle story : that story is
the nucleus which has attracted one famous name after another.
It was told of Gilgamesh, the Babylonian, long before Alexander
was heard of, and of a Sumerian, Etanna, before the days of
Gilgamesh.   That is a very important fact in large masses of
stories.   Even if an historical name does occur, the nucleus is not
history but fancy.   If Hamlet was the name of a real Danish
prince, the story of Hamlet was considerably older than his day.
Most of us know nothing of St. George except that he killed the
dragon.   Gibbon, indeed, identified him with a fraudulent army
contractor who supplied bacon to certain forces in Cappadocia,
but Gibbon, it seems, was merely yielding to the seductions of
' historicity '.   The truth about St. George is said to be quite
different.   There was a very ancient bas-relief at Lydda representing a hero slaying a gigantic monster.   The Christians
called him George, but the Greeks before that called him Perseus,

while the Babylonians were confident that he was their favourite Gilgamesh killing Tiamat. There is a canon of Pope Gelasius establishing the canonization of St. George which prudently refers to him as one of those ' whose names are justly revered among men, but whose acts are known only to God '. If that is historicity, we need not grudge it to Agamemnon. And, further, when once the goddess of fiction has really set to work, surely the quality of the original peg or nucleus shows very little in the finished product. There is a character in *Kenilworth* called Weyland Smith. He was originally the Norse god, Wielant, Icelandic Volündr, but in *Kenilworth* he has just as solid flesh and blood as Tony Foster or Amy Robsart, whose bodies now lie in Cumnor Church. When Attila the Hun or Guthhere the Burgundian is drawn into the Saga of the Volsungs and Nibelungs there is no visible quality to show which of those gigantic cloudy figures were originally made of mist and which of bone and muscle. Nay, even where a real person is taken over to fiction and in the fiction remains vividly real and palpable, what guarantee have we that the fiction, because life-like, is true to life? Sir John Oldcastle, the Lollard, was a man of eminent piety and high character. The report of his trial for heresy is still extant.[1] Yet when he became a favourite character on the Elizabethan stage (where in Shakespeare's later work his name was eventually changed to Falstaff) he was an extraordinary and shining type of all the most un-Lollardish failings, while innocent as a babe of the crime of heresy.

Modern instances have largely to be taken from fiction. We do not in modern times find faded gods turning into heroes, except in odd cases like Weyland Smith. That is merely because we have no mythological gods. But the Greeks had numbers of them, and their mythology, as soon as literature begins, appears as the commonest source for poetical composition and the ordinary food for popular imagination. In modern India, under our eyes, as the great gods and goddesses of the plain conquer new territory, the local gods whom they supersede are very apt to become their human votaries or door-keepers. There is certainly no ground in general literature for denying that gods may become men.

[1] In Pollard, *Reprints of Fifteenth Century Verse and Prose.*

Bearing these cautions in mind we may proceed to our problem. In most traditional poems there are three fairly distinct elements. There are masses of mere fiction—that is, stories and personages deliberately invented by the poet out of his head. There are, secondly, the shapes of myth and saga, which the poet narrates in good faith, as he received them, with at least a modicum of belief in their reality. And, thirdly, there are fragments of definite history. Take the *Nibelungenlied*, for instance. There the whole web of the story is woven on lines of romantic fiction. But many of the characters, the Niblungs and Odin and apparently Sigurd himself, belong to the region of myth. Again, we have historical persons in Atli, who is the Hunnish King Attila, and Dietrich of Berne, who is the real Theodoric.

In Homer we may make the same sort of division. There is, in the first place, much deliberate fiction. The whole framework into which the incidents are fitted, the wanderings of Telemachus in the *Odyssey*, the Embassy to Achilles in *Iliad I*, are evidently mere inventions of the poets. On the other hand, such beings as Zeus, Hephaestus, Bellerophon, Typhoeus, the Chimaera, clearly belong to the realm of myth. And, thirdly, the excavations have proved the historical reality of the great towns of Troy and Mycenae. As to the persons, it is a different matter. Professor Chadwick persuasively argues that Heroic Ages are rich in striking and picturesque personalities, who find a place in poetry not because of their historical importance but because of some purely romantic or adventurous interest. If so, they will obviously become almost indistinguishable from the heroes of fiction. If there are any Attilas and Theodorics hidden among the various gods and tribal heroes, there is unfortunately no independent historical document by which to identify them.

Now, as to the fictional parts of Homer, I do not wish to dwell upon the value of fiction as indirect history. One might point out that fiction, to adopt a phrase of Aristotle's, if it does not tell you what did take place on a given occasion, constantly shows you what might well take place. And even where the main subject of the fiction is romantic or marvellous the background or setting in which it is placed is very likely to be drawn from normal life. The Cyclops, for instance, is a fictitious monster; but his processes of dairy-farming are real and historical. And that kind of information is sometimes what helps us most toward the understanding of a far-off state of society. If the *Iliad* and *Odyssey* were all fiction we should still learn from them a great deal about early Greek customs, about practices of war and of government, about marriage, land-tenure, worship, farming, commerce, and, above all, the methods of seafaring. Let any one read thoughtfully the story which Eumaeus the swineherd tells of his life in *Odyssey o,* and then consider how much history of the life of the Aegean, about the seventh century B. C., he has learnt from three pages of poetical fiction. In the same way, even if the main story of the *Iliad* is fiction, it is significant that the social world in which it is placed is curiously like the real world of an ' Heroic Age '. Figures like Diomedes, Ajax, and Odysseus, as they appear in the *Iliad*, wandering chieftains with a band of followers and some ships instead of a kingdom or even a fatherland, are typical; and Achilles and Agamemnon hardly less so. We have here the greatest of the general differences between the Catalogue in *B* and the rest of the *Iliad*. For the Catalogue starts with a conception of Greece as a settled country divided into clans and kingdoms, and has fastened each Homeric chieftain down to a fixed geographical district.

The historical value of the Catalogue has been recently discussed in two striking books.[1] It is by general agreement an alien document, written by some non-Homeric author or authors for a non-Homeric context, and afterwards, with omissions and additions, incorporated in the *Iliad*. Mr. Allen, like an advocate fighting for a client's life, endeavours with great learning to show that there is no flat contradiction in terms between the Catalogue and the rest of the *Iliad*, and no statement which is demonstrably untrue of an age before our records begin. It is pretty certainly of Boeotian origin and connected with the school of Hesiod ; and there is reason to suspect that it had been used in the *Cypria* before it was put into the *Iliad*.[2] But here arises an interesting question of principle. When it differs from the rest of the *Iliad*, which is more likely to be historically true ? The dull list of names and figures, with not much apparent reason for existence

---

[1] Leaf, *Homer and History*, 1915 ; T. W. Allen, *The Homeric Catalogue of Ships*, 1921. Also Leaf, *Troy*, 1912, on the Catalogue of Trojan Allies.
[2] See p. 179 and cf. Appendix J, note.

except as a record of fact, or the brilliant and moving narrative, exposed to all the temptations of fiction? One would say the Catalogue; and probably this in some sense holds good. It probably does represent some genuine belief, based on tradition and perhaps helped out by guesswork, held by a school of bards in Boeotia about the condition of Greece at the time of the Trojan War. Certainly it is not a deduction from the *Iliad*. It is a deduction from other sources and, as such, an early historical document of great interest.

Dr. Leaf has shown, in my judgement beyond the possibility of refutation, that the whole point of view of the Catalogue is very different from that of the *Iliad*. The prominence of Boeotia, the gathering of the fleet at Aulis, the strange Corinthian kingdom which is all that is left to Agamemnon after Argo shas been taken away and given to Diomedes, the large navies provided by the Arcadians and other inland peoples who never appear again in the *Iliad*, are all ' un-Homeric '. Also, we may be sure that the document was not put into the *Iliad* early. It was put in late. The fitting-in is mechanical and shows the joints: it has not been either re-created by a poet or frequently worked over by skilled rhapsodes. Of course, to be ' un-Homeric ', or even to be ' late ', is not necessarily to be untrue. Yet on most of the points of difference the Catalogue version does seem improbable.

Truth must have been lost in the course of the Catalogue's history in at least three ways. The original Boeotian authors doubtless tended to exaggerate the importance of Boeotia; the Athenian reciters, who had the poem in their hands from the time of the Panathenaic recitation onwards, are shown both by external and internal evidence to have affected the text a good deal, more perhaps by omission than by interpolation. Twelve passages in the Catalogue are known to have been marked as spurious by ancient critics, most of them for reasons in some way connected with Athens. Modern critics have detected others. Again, if one looks for the important places which are ' suppressed ' or belittled in the Catalogue they form a list which is hard to understand until we ask what places a tactful reciter would be likely to suppress when competing for a prize before an Athenian audience; then it is intelligible: Aegina, Megara,

Thebes, Delphi, and to some extent Salamis and Corinth.   Then, again, the adaptation of the Catalogue to its place in the *Iliad* must have involved some changes of statement, made in the interest of harmony and not of truth.

And, even when the document was intact, before any of these perversions had begun, what was it ?   The other catalogues give lists of goddesses who had human children, of heroines who had divine lovers, of ancestresses of various tribes, of rivers, of Nereids, of lucky and unlucky days.   The Catalogue of Ships, and even that of the Trojan Allies, so brilliantly expounded by Dr. Leaf, was perhaps based on less speculative foundations, but can hardly claim an impeccable authority.[1]

I do not think that we have in the Homeric Poems any 'document' or 'archive' which can claim on its own authority a right to be accepted as true.   But I wish at present to deal with a different question, viz. the origins, historical or otherwise, of some typical characters or incidents in the Poems.   First, let us take a character of pure fiction.[2]   Many might be cited : the herald Ἠπυτίδης, the bard Φήμιος Τερπιάδης, many of the Phaeacians in θ 11 ff. and the Nereids in Σ 39 ff., with their transparent names.   The most striking, perhaps, is Briseïs, the maiden who is taken by Agamemnon from Achilles and thus becomes the passive heroine of the Wrath.   She has no father or mother : no history apart from the one incident for which she is invented and which is presumably an invented incident; as before mentioned, she has not even a real name.   For *Kourê Briseïs* only means ' Maiden of Brisa ',[3] the Aeolic form of Brêsa, a town in Lesbos, taken by Achilles in the course of the war. It is worth noticing, indeed, that, like other characters in good fiction, Briseïs eventually acquired independent legendary life and even rose to some importance in Chaucer and Shakespeare, under the name of Cressida.   (Cressida is the accusative ' Bri- seïda ' slightly corrupted, and confused with the name of the other maiden, Chryseïs.)

---

[1] The Trojan Allies lie along an ancient trade route; Leaf, *l.c.*
[2] For the following, cf. E. Bethe, *Homer und die Heldensage*, from *Neue Jahrbücher f. d. klass. Alt.*, 1902; F. Dümmler, *Hektor*, Anhang ii to Studniczka's *Kyrene*, 1890.   Also Bethe's *Märchen, Mythus und Sage*, and Radermacher, *Die Erzählungen der Odyssee* (Vienna, 1915).
[3] Wilamowitz, *Hom. Unt.*, p. 409 ; Tümpel, *Lesbiaka*, p. 106.

But in the *Iliad* Briseïs is a shadow, a figment of the poet. Contrast her, for instance, with a real saga-heroine, Helen. Helen appears in the Troy legend, but was certainly not created for it. She dominates other legends as well. We know her parents and her home. She was an important goddess, a marriage-Korê, in Sparta. Her temple at Therapnae has been excavated; she and her husband Menelaus were worshipped there together, ' not as heroes but as gods ', and she had sacred trees and wells in many places.[1] In most of her functions she resembles the other Korai who preside over the affairs of women, but Helen has certain special characteristics. She is a Swan-child:[2] her mother may be Leda or may be Nemesis, her father Zeus or Tyndareus, but she is always the daughter of a white swan. Her brothers, the Dioscori, Castor and Polydeuces, are twins and also stars. She and they appear to sailors in time of storm as those balls of the fire that is called ' St Elmo's '. It used once to be ' St Helen's '. The chief point in her saga is quite clear: she is always being carried off by a ravisher. And, I venture to suggest, the origin of this trait is so clear that one can hardly understand its having so long escaped notice. A Spartan bride-goddess was bound to be carried off, since in Spartan marriages the carrying off of the bride was part of the ritual. The same set of ideas explains two other peculiarities of Helen, why she is always brought back from her ravishment and why she is so much associated with an *Eidôlon* or Image,[3] which is like Helen but is not the real Helen. In the ritual the Image of the goddess would probably be carried off, but would have to be secretly restored afterwards to its place in the temple. We have no detailed information about the rite at Sparta, but in Samos, where Hera was the marriage-goddess, her Image was regularly carried off in the Feast called Tonaia, and then secretly recovered and brought back.

---

[1] Isocr. x. 72 ; Paus. iii. 19, 9; Theocr. xviii. 43 ff. &c.

[2] Euripides revels in this white-swan atmosphere. Helen is ὄμμα κυκνόπτερον καλλοσύνας, *Or.* 1386. Cf. *I.A.* 793; *Hel.* 214.

[3] The εἴδωλον occurs first in Hesiod: then in Stesichorus, Euripides, Herodotus, Plato, &c., and plays a great part in the later Greek literature: see reff. in Bergk, *P.L.G.*, under the *Palinodia* of Stesichorus. The old view that the Eidôlon story was a fiction of Stesichorus is clearly untenable. It is cited from Hesiod and has all the marks of genuine myth. (πρῶτος Ἡσίοδος Ἑλένης τὸ εἴδωλον παρήγαγε. Schol. to Lycophron 822.)

A third characteristic of Helen has also a marked ritual or sacral appearance. When she is restored, she is always restored by Twins or something very like Twins. She was carried off to Egypt by Hermes, to Sidon or else to Troy by Alexander-Paris, to Deceleia by Theseus or the Apharetidae; but always recovered either by the so-called 'Twin' Atreidae or the genuinely Twin Dioscori. She was also carried off to Mount Parnon by a robber, and we do not happen to hear who brought her back. But I should be much surprised if the rescuers were not Spartans and Twins.

Passing from the rich saga-figure of Helen, let us turn to the comparative barrenness of Achilles. Apart from the fine psychological treatment of his character in the later books of the *Iliad*, Achilles in saga is little more than a typical heroic Kouros, as Hermes and Apollo are divine Kouroi. Like all the Kouroi he is young, swift, tall, and beautiful; like Balder, Hyakinthos, Hippolytus, Adonis, Linos, and many others, he is cut short in his youth and ritually lamented: in the saga by a choir of Nereids, in actual life by choruses of women. The odd story of his dressing in girl's clothes has pretty obviously a ritual origin. Even his many 'wraths' or 'strifes',[1] which might look at first sight like the real memories left by a hot-tempered soldier, seem only to be derived from the regular 'strife' of the Kouros with his enemy, the Summer with the coming Winter, the New Year with the Old. The real history that we can legitimately extract from Achilles is, I venture to think, what we may call tribal history. Only we must remember that it was not exactly a tribe that Achilles led at Troy; it was a *comitatus*, a mixed band of clansmen and strangers who followed the chief's fortunes. But we know from Greek history that these mixed bands, when they founded cities, generally formed themselves into fictitious tribes and adopted common ancestors. The men who counted Achilles as their chief, Hellenes of Achaia Phthiotis, and the strangers who joined with them, did all that Achilles did. They left their home on the mainland: they stayed first at Skyros, till they

---

[1] Wraths with Agamemnon, one about Briseïs, one because of a late invitation to dinner; with Diomedes; with Odysseus; with Thersites. All seem to have some oracular significance, as when Achilles strove with Odysseus and Agamemnon 'rejoiced in heart because the bravest of Achaioi were at strife'—remembering an oracle. (θ 78.)

were grown strong: they conquered and occupied Lesbos. They fought on the Thracian coast. They eventually went through the Hellespont and Bosphorus up to the Black Sea, and made settlements which bore the name of Achilles in later ages. But there is something to be learned from studying the various places where Achilles was worshipped. The worship in Thessaly was, we are told, ordered from Dodona (Philostr. *Heroicus*, p. 741, quoting an interesting hymn to Thetis). This agrees well with Achilles' prayer to Zeus of Dodona (*Π* 233). It is natural enough, too, that he should be worshipped at Sigeum, at Skyros, at Mytilene, in the island of Leuce, and that inscriptions should be found at Olbia and Odessos calling him *Pontarchês*, 'Lord of the Pontus.' But he had worship in other parts of Greece too. He was worshipped in Laconia, says the scholiast to Apollonius (iv. 815), citing Anaxagoras. Pausanias saw a great Achilleion, or shrine to Achilles, on the road from Sparta to Arcadia. There was worship at Brasiae; in Elis; in the island of Astypalaea; probably in Cos, since the Aeacidae in general had a shrine there. And in Tarentum there were shrines both to the Aeacidae in general and to Achilles. What does this mean? Does it not destroy our conception of Achilles as a special tribal hero? No: it only serves to illustrate a point of cardinal importance for the understanding of prehistoric Greece, the extreme mobility and the frequent scattering of the various tribes. It is the natural result of that time when all Hellas was ἀνάστατος, 'driven from its home'; the time of the 'constant war-paths and uprootings of peoples'. There were fragments of tribes cast away in the most diverse parts, and where they were strong enough they carried their tribal gods with them. The Achaioi, who settled in the Peloponnese and migrated again beyond it, naturally took with them the worship of Achilles.

If any one would have a conception of the way in which tribes and races can be scattered, when in a mobile condition of life, I recommend him to look at some map of the linguistic stocks of the North American Indians.[1] If the Iroquoian or Siouan or,

---

[1] e. g. Élisée Reclus, *Géogr. Univ., Amérique*, ii. 40 f. Or, to take a less remote parallel, the Germanic tribe called Eruli 'are first mentioned in the third century A. D., at which time they appear almost simultaneously on the Black Sea and the frontier of Gaul'. Chadwick, *Othin*, p. 33.

still more, if the Athapascan-speaking races had been in the habit of building shrines to their tribal heroes, in what extraordinarily diverse parts of the vast continent we should find the *heroa*! And the Iroquoians would have made the Algonquins worship him too. The result would completely dwarf any strangeness which we may at first feel in the scattering of the shrines of Achilles from Tarentum to Odessos. He remains the hero or *kouros* of the people who followed him from Thessaly, of whom we can only say in Homer's words that 'Myrmidones were they called and Hellênes and Achaioi'.

The figure of Agamemnon presents unsolved problems. Famous as he is, there are comparatively few legends about him, and most of these belong to well-known mythical types. Yet the existence of some great federated Achaian expedition against Troy seems almost as certain as the destruction of Troy itself, and it presumably had some chief leader. The position of Agamemnon, in the *Iliad*, as a 'king' with authority over all the other 'kings', based not on law or hereditary position, but on an *ad hoc* oath which they have all sworn, to serve him till Troy is taken, seems to correspond exactly with what we should, with our present knowledge, expect to be true of the Heroic Age. The *Anax Andrôn* looks like real history, whatever his name may have been. He would be a 'Lord of Ships', leading the Akhaiusha and the 'peoples of the sea' or some offshoot of them. It is likely enough that his predecessors, with or without their *comitatus*, at some period had settled in Phrygia, which would explain why Agamemnon's family are Pelopidae, sons of Pelops the Phrygian.

He was a King of Kings. As such he steps into the inheritance of the regular King myths. Especially the old sequence of Ouranos-Gaia-Kronos, Kronos-Rhea-Zeus, is repeated in Agamemnon-Clytemnestra-Aigisthos. The Old King is slain by the Young King, who is helped by the Queen and then wedded to her: the Old Year slain by the Young Year, while the same Earth-Mother is wedded to all of them.[1] An old beam or trunk of wood worshipped at Chaeronea becomes Agamemnon's sceptre (Paus. ix. 40, 11), which even in the *Iliad* is a thing

---

[1] See my Shakespeare Lecture to the British Academy: *Hamlet and Orestes*.

of tradition (A 234 ff.). As King of Kings, also, he inevitably becomes involved in the Human Sacrifice of his daughter, Iphigeneia. It is regularly the King's daughter who has to be sacrificed. Naturally, too, he is specially associated with Zeus, the greater King of Kings : his attendant and sacrificer (Aesch. Cho. 255, 358 ff.) and in various ways his special charge. Nay, we find a worship of Zeus-Agamemnon at Sparta, like that of Zeus-Lakedaimon (Hdt. vi. 56) or Zeus-Pelops.

The peculiar manner of his death seems to ask for explanation. The legend tells that he was killed with an axe, in his bath, after being wrapt round and round in an enormous or 'endless' robe. Now the word for bath, δροίτη, also denoted the stone sarcophagi in which great potentates in pre- and post-classical times were wont to be buried. Can it be that in the Dark Age or later, when some of the royal graves at Mycenae were opened by peasants or robbers, a royal figure was found, its skull perhaps broken from a wound in battle, wrapped in a rich and royal winding-sheet and lying in a δροίτη? The finders would weave a story round it, as they did about the Tomb of Midas or the bas-reliefs of Sisyphus and Tantalus.[1]

One is not surprised, if the historical King of Kings was a chief of the ships of the Akhaiusha, to find some difficulty in locating Agamemnon's home. The Greek tradition wanted naturally to give him an empire on land. In the *Iliad* he generally refers to his home as Argos; once or twice it is Mycenae rich in gold; but his empire is over 'many islands and all Argos'. True, in the Catalogue Argos proper is taken away from him in order to provide for Diomedes; that may well be a mere mistake by the Catalogue-maker, as Dr. Leaf argues. But the word Argos itself seems to mean 'a watered plain', and in Homer it appears to have at least three meanings. It is the Argos of Thessaly, the Argos of the Peloponnese, and it is also a general name for Greece, especially when combined with Hellas—ἀν' Ἑλλάδα καὶ μέσον Ἄργος. The point has been worked out by Cauer,[2] who thinks that Agamemnon was originally Thessalian. Outside Homer, however, the local habita-

---

[1] See Salomon Reinach, 'Sisyphe aux Enfers et quelques autres Damnés', *Cultes, Mythes, et Religions*, vol. ii, pp. 159–205.
[2] *Grundfragen*[3], pp. 284 ff.

tion of Agamemnon admits of little doubt.   He and Menelaus are, quite simply, joint kings of Sparta; the dual monarchy of Sparta exactly suits them.   The Spartan Syagrus, when it was pro- posed that Sparta should yield up the leadership of Greece to Gelo of Syracuse, answered by a hexameter line, pre- sumably Homeric, though it does not occur in our texts: 'Bitterly would Pelops' son Agamemnon groan' if any but Spartans led the host (Hdt. vii. 159).   His tomb was shown at Amyclae near Sparta among the other ancient Spartan kings. Pindar mentions that he died at Amyclae; Stesichorus and Simonides both refer to him simply as King of Sparta.[1]   And, curiously enough, there is a passage in the *Odyssey* which points in the same direction.   It is apparently a quotation from the Nostoi, or Homecomings, and describes Agamemnon's voyage home in language that is unintelligible if he is bound for Mycenae or Argos or Corinth.   When he 'was nearing Cape Malea' he was driven to sea by a storm; but why did he ever approach that dangerous cape if he only wanted to make Argos or My- cenae?   If he was bound for Sparta it was his natural way. And the poet, though he has suppressed the mention of Sparta because the *Odyssey* in general put Agamemnon in Argos, seems to let out his secret when he makes Telemachus ask about Agamemnon's death: 'Where was Menelaus?   Why did he not help his brother?'   That certainly suggests that both kings are expected to be together.   Probably, therefore, the Nostoi, like Pindar, Stesichorus, Simonides, and most of the non-Homeric tradition, had located the King of Kings of the Sea-People in the natural position for any supreme commander-in-chief of the Greek forces; they made him the senior of the two Spartan kings.   Why the Attic-Homeric tradition removed him from there we can only conjecture, but it is not difficult to see possible reasons.

Odysseus, though now prominent in the *Iliad*, seems as a saga figure to have had little or nothing to do with Troy.   In the *Odyssey* he is mostly a folk-lore hero with folk-lore adventures, though, of course, one can never be sure that these adventures have not been attached to a historic name.   Some of them, at any rate, were actually told in the Middle Ages of Iskander Khan,

[1] Pind. *Pyth.* xi. 32, *Nem.* xi. 34: Schol. Eur. *Or.* 46.

But myth has been at work also, and myth of a pronounced and curious kind. The point has not yet been noticed and needs a fairly full statement. It is a matter of the solar and lunar calendar.

Time has been generally measured by the ' eniautoi ', or repeated circuits, of the moon and the sun, i. e. by the month and the year. The object of a scientific calendar has always been to find a period in which the two circuits should correspond; the New Moon should coincide with the winter solstice, and Sun and Moon begin their life together. (As a matter of fact, the two circuits are incommensurable, but that is a recent discovery.) The lunar month is twenty-nine days plus a fraction; twelve months make 354 days plus some hours; a solar year equals 364 days and a little over. Various cycles were tried with poor results. The simplest was a Trietêris, or double year; next a Pentetêris or period of four years, such as regulated the Olympian and Pythian Festivals. This period had fifty and forty-nine months alternately, and came fairly right every second time, in what was called the Ennaetêris. This ought to have come out at eight lunar years of 354 days each *plus* three intercalary months of thirty days, that is 2,922 days; the same figure as is given by eight solar years of $365\frac{1}{4}$ days; unfortunately the fractions were wrong, and there was an error of about a day and a half in eight years.

Hence came the greatest effort of ancient calendar-making, Meton's Eikosietêris, as it was called, or Grand Eniautos of Nineteen Years. On the last day of the nineteenth year, which was also by Greek reckoning the first of the twentieth, the New Moon would coincide with the New Sun of the Winter Solstice; this was called the 'Meeting of Sun and Moon' (Σύνοδος Ἡλίου καὶ Σελήνης)—a thing which had not happened for nineteen full years before and would not happen again for another nineteen.

Now when did Odysseus return to Penelope? The date is given with a precision most unusual in epic poetry. He returned to Ithaca 'just at the rising of that brightest star which heralds the light of the Daughter of Dawn' (ν 93). He rejoined his wife ' on the twentieth year '; i.e. he came as soon as the twentieth year came, as soon as the nineteenth was complete (ψ 102, 170; o 327, β 175). He came at the New Moon, on the day which the

Athenians called ' Old-and-New ', ' when one month is waning
and the next rising up' (τ 307, ξ 162). This New Moon was
also the day of the Apollo Feast, or Solstice festival of the Sun
(υ 156, ϕ 258), and the time was winter.[1] The Σύνοδος 'Οδυσσέως
καὶ Πηνελόπης exactly coincides with the Σύνοδος of the Sun
and Moon.

There was an ancient Wise Man, Cleobûlus, who showed his
wisdom by making conundrums. One, recorded by Diogenes
Laertius, runs thus : ' One father, twelve children ; each of them
with thirty children, partly black and partly white ; and though
immortal they all die.' The answer is ' The Year ', or rather the
Eniautos, with its 360 day-and-night periods, which all pass.
Can we be surprised to learn (ξ 20) that Odysseus had just 360
boars, and that one of them died every day ? Or can we any
longer neglect the other solar characteristics that seem to cling
about Odysseus: that the Sun is his rival and enemy ; that he
goes under the world in the West, visits the realm of the dead
and comes up in the extreme East, ' where the Daughter of
Dawn has her dwellings and her dancing-floors and the Sun his
uprising' (μ 3) ; that he is brought back home asleep, in a magic
boat, like the Sun in Mimnermus,[2] by Phaiâkes ('Dark Ones?'
who do even the furthest journeys in twenty-four hours (η 326)
that he lives in an island in the sea, ' low-lying, apart from others
furthest of all towards the sunset' (ι 25 f.), a description that can
not be twisted so as to suit Ithaca ; that he is a Far-darter of
arrows ; that his death comes to him out of the sea ; and that
like most Year-kings, he is doomed to be slain by his son ?

To turn to another type, let us consider one of Achilles' parti
cular enemies ; to wit, Thersîtes. Every reader of the *Iliad*
remembers his brief and inglorious appearance in *B*, where he
rails at Agamemnon with unseemly words, and is thrashed with

---

[1] ξ 457 νὺξ σκοτομήνιος, Odysseus freezing in his rags : ρ 25 there is frost
Odysseus cannot face the morning cold ; τ 64, 319 a great deal about piling
up the fire ; φόως ἔμεν ἠδὲ θέρεσθαι ; cf. σ 332. Wilamowitz, *H. U.*, p. 87
also 114. Cf. Carl Fries's *Studien zur Odyssee* (Leipzig, 1910, 1911) : also
Seeck, *Quellen*, pp. 53 ff., 265 ff. On Ithaca cf. A. B. Cook, *Zeus*, i, p. 328
[2] The cattle of the Sun are in seven herds of fifty each, total 350. Hippo
crates divided the year into seven seasons (Galen, vol. xvii, I, p. 19 ; Kuhn
Comm. in Epidem. 7), and Aristotle recognized the 350 as the days of the
lunar year. See Eustathius, *ad loc.*

a staff by Odysseus. He was the ugliest man in the Greek army, bald, and hump-backed, with one leg longer than the other. Let us remember that; and then notice what Odysseus threatens to do with him. He will strip him naked and drive him away from the company of men (ἀγορῆθεν) with blows. Does it not remind one at once of the *pharmakos* or scapegoat, the ugliest man in the community, who was made into a sin-offering and driven out from the city? But let us look further.

The name Thersîtes has all the appearance of a fiction. It is derived from *Thersos*, the Aeolic form of θάρσος, 'courage' or 'impudence'. And the poet of B evidently meant the name to have this latter meaning. It is rather a surprise to find that Thersîtes is really an independent saga-figure outside Homer with a life of his own and very distinguished relations. He was a son of Agrios, the savage Aetolian king, and first cousin once removed of the great Diomedes. His mother was Dia, a name which suggests a goddess. Returning to Homer, we find that Thersîtes was (B 220) 'to two of the Greeks especially most hateful, Odysseus and Achilles'. Odysseus' enmity needs no further explanation: Odysseus beat him. But why should Achilles be his enemy? Because Achilles, in the ordinary story, killed him. It happened in this way. When Achilles was fighting with Penthesilea the Amazon, and had given her a mortal wound, he was suddenly struck with remorse and love as he looked upon her dying face. Thersîtes saw this and grossly jeered, so Achilles very properly slew him, some say by a spear-thrust, others, by a heroic box on the ear. He was purified for this manslaughter by Odysseus. Diomedes, however, Thersîtes' kinsman, took up a feud against Achilles in consequence.[1]

Another story is given in the old chronicle writer Pherekydes (fr. 82) and the poet Euphorion (fr. 131). Thersîtes took part in the hunt of the Calydonian boar, and, for showing cowardice, was thrown by his cousin Meleager over a rock. (He is made to

---

[1] So the *Aithiopis*: followed by Chairemon's tragedy, *Achilles Thersito-ctonos*. Hence Apollodorus, &c. Cf. Istros about the man called Pharmakos who was stoned ὑπὸ τῶν περὶ τὸν Ἀχιλλέα, Harpocrat. s. v. For the feud with Diomedes see Tzetz, *Posthom.* 199, 206: also Lycophr. 999, Quint. Smyrn. i. 767; Schol. Soph. Phil. 445, Dictys Cret. iv. 3. This late Latin book goes back to ancient sources. An earlier Greek version of Dictys has lately been discovered, dating probably from the second century A. D. Tebtunis Papyri.

recover, much injured, in order to be slain again by Achilles.)
Throwing from a rock, it may be remembered, was one of the
regular modes of getting rid of a *pharmakos*.

The evidence so far points towards some connexion with
a human sacrifice of the *pharmakos* type, that is, a purgative
sacrifice to cleanse the community; also to some special connexion with Achilles. Can we take it a step further?

Professor Usener, the author of that stimulating book,
Götternamen, points out a more strange coincidence.[1] Thersites
is found as a name elsewhere in Greece : and derivatives of the
same stem are common, Thersias, Therson, and the like. Now
in the Lacedaemonian [2] dialect this word would probably take
the form Thêrîtas, Θηρίτας: as Περσεφόνεια becomes in
Laconian, Πηρεφόνεια. And Thêrîtas in Lacedaemon is a god
of whom we know something. Pausanias saw his temple
between Amyclae and Therapnae. Pausanias says that he was
the same as Ares ; Hesychius, perhaps more accurately, says he
was Enyalios—another war-god. He had a nurse—or mother—
called Thêro.

Now the old sacrifice of the human scapegoat had in Sparta
died down to a curious form, to which, however, there are many
parallels elsewhere. It became an annual fight in a plane grove
between two bodies of Ephêbi, or Spartan youths. They fought
with no weapons : only fists and feet. The plane grove was
surrounded by a moat, and they threw the defeated, if they could
manage it, into the water—another regular way of disposing of
the *pharmakos*.[3] And before this annual battle the Ephebi
performed *a sacrifice to Enyalios* at a place called the Phoibeion,
and *a sacrifice to Achilles* at his temple on the road to Arcadia
(Paus. iii. 19. 7; 20. 2; 20. 8; battle of Ephebi, 14. 8). If
Enyalios is Thêrîtas, as Hesychius tells us, we have here the
ritual form of the old battle of Achilles and Thersîtes. What
that battle in its primitive religious significance really was lies

---

[1] *Der Stoff des gr. Epos*, in *Sitzungsber. Wiener Akad., phil.-hist. Kl.*
1898, p. 47.

[2] In strict Spartan Σηρίτας. Θηρίτας would be the Doricized 'Achaian'
dialect of the Perioikoi, if Meister is right. See his *Dorer und Achäer*,
pp. 24 ff.

[3] In the Thersîtes-Penthesilea story in Dictys, Diomedes has Penthesilea
thrown, still living, into the water.

beyond our scope. Usener thinks of the common annual rites of
the slaying of Winter by Summer, or of one vegetation god
by another.

Different, again, is a hero like Telamonian Aias. He has no
tribe, no home, no belongings. Only a shield which no one else
can bear, and a father whose name is Telamôn, 'Shield-strap'.[1]
The lines connecting him with the island of Salamis are of the
latest description. But he has another characteristic. Himself
an immense man and fabulously strong, he constantly goes about
with a companion, as brave as himself but small. The two
together are called 'Aiante', 'the two Aiases'. The name of the
other varies. As the *Iliad* now stands, this companion is generally Aias's half-brother, by name Teukros: sometimes he is Aias
the Less, a Locrian and son of Oileus.[2] These persons require,
of course, separate study. One of them at least, Teukros, seems
to be a real saga-figure. But, like the more shadowy son of
Oileus, he has been pressed into service as the Great Aias's lesser
twin. The Aiante are figures of folk-lore, and no doubt of
primitive worship, parallel to the other sets of divine twins, the
Tyndaridae, the Aphareidae, the Dioscuri, the Anake, the
Leucopôlô, the Aktoriône Molîone. It is worth noticing that
Fick considers this twin-worship as characteristic of the Leleges:
Salamis and Locris are both Lelegian centres. And the name
Oileus is referred to the Lelegian language.

Take again the case of Diomêdês. He seems to be a tribal
god or hero, connected with Aetolia and the Aetolian settlements
on the north coast of the Peloponnese, though in the Catalogue
he belongs to Argos and Epidaurus. Originally perhaps an
Achaean, he has been affected by association with these wild
Aetolian tribes, who came from Illyria and expelled the Achaeans,

---

[1] It has been suggested by P. Girard, *Rev. des Études Grecques*, xviii.
(1905), pp. 1–75, that Τελαμών ('Supporter'), as the father of Aias, is originally not a shield-strap, but a door-post or pillar. This is good in point of
religion, and would suit excellently with the conception of the Aiante as twins;
and an inscription (fifth cent.) from the Argive Heraeum uses τελαμών as =
'pillar'. It is also a Roman use—'Telamones', like 'Caryatides'. See
Herwerden, *Lex. Supplet.* But to the writers of the *Iliad* Aias is obviously
a shield-hero.

[2] This suggestion was first made by Wackernagel, *H. U.* 247[11]. Cf. Eur.
I. A. 192 κατεῖδον δὲ δύ Αἴαντε συνέδρω, τὸν Οἰλέως Τελαμῶνός τε γόνον.

reducing Aetolia in historical times to savagery. His kinsman
is ' Agrios ', ' Savage '. His father Tydeus would have been
made immortal, owing to his many merits, had not his own tribal
war-goddess, Athena, seen him eating an enemy's head on the
battle-field, and after that preferred to let him die. However
that may be, we find in Greek tradition two ostensibly distinct
persons bearing the name of Diomedes. There is this hero,
mentioned in the *Iliad* and *Odyssey*, the Epigoni and the
Alkmaeonis, by birth an Argive, but a traveller to Aetolia, Troy,
Italy, and Cyprus. He is a fierce and fiery young warrior, much
associated with horses, but decidedly, if I may borrow a convenient phrase from the language of the theatre, ' sympathetic '.
That is to say, we are wont to be on his side, not on that of his
enemies. But there is also another ' unsympathetic ' Diomedes,
a ruffian and a savage ; a son of the Thracian war-god Ares, and
King of Abdêra in Thrace. This Diomedes, who fed his fierce
white horses with human flesh—an evident trace of human
sacrifices—was suitably destroyed by Heracles, and his horses
taken away. Now, as Eric Bethe has pointed out, these two
heroes are probably in origin the same. As soon as you
scratch the Argive Diomedes you find under his Hellenic surface
the mark of the Thracian. In the most diverse localities we find
him connected with the same horses and the same uncanny sacrifices. In Cyprus to the far south-east he was worshipped with
human victims. To the far north-west the Venetians sacrificed to
him white horses. In the *Iliad* Diomedes has been cleared of
his cannibal tendencies, and is left one of the most attractive
figures in the poem, peculiarly brave and modest and wise in
counsel. Yet incidentally we are constantly coming across his
Thracian connexions. In *K* he slays the King of the Thracians,
Rhêsus, and carries off his famous white horses. In *E* also, I
would suggest, he fights and routs the god of the Thracian
aborigines, Ares : Ares flies to heaven, leaving no horses behind.
But we find that, just before, Diomedes has fought Aeneas and
his mother Aphrodite, and carried off Aeneas's matchless horses.
Aeneas is the son of Aphrodite, and Aphrodite is the goddess
belonging to Ares. Originally, it would seem, a war-goddess
and wife of the war-god, she has passed through the crucibles of
Greek imagination, and emerges identified with a half-oriental

love-goddess, a creature who has no business in battles, and is merely the paramour of the warrior god (see Schol. on Φ 416). Also her son in this case has Anchises for his father, not Ares. This probably is the result of mythological changes and poetic adaptations. One suspects that originally the hero conquered by Diomedes, and robbed of his horses, and immediately afterwards succoured by both Aphrodite and Ares, was a true son of Ares. Thus the story of Diomedes in *E* becomes an exact parallel to that of Diomedes the Thracian tyrant. For, in the processes of ancient mythology, to conquer a son of the Thracian Ares and despoil him of his matchless horses is exactly the same thing as to be a son of the Thracian Ares who is so conquered and despoiled. In the one story Diomedes has the passive part, in the other the active. It is like Dionysus the Bull-Slayer, and Dionysus the slain bull; Apollo the wolf, and Apollo the averter of wolves.

So many and various are the elements of saga and tribal history which have taken shape in the heroes of the *Iliad*. Of course we may admit freely the possibility that in any particular hero there may be traces of a real individual. The legends of the Middle Ages are full of historical names. And the names Paris or Hector or even Agamemnon may have belonged originally to as definite a person as those of Charlemagne or ' Virgil the magician', Attila or Dieterich of Berne. Professor Bury has remarked that the name and personality of a great foeman are apt to remain fixed in a nation's memory. Had nineteenth-century England been still in the saga-making stage, she would certainly have mingled ' Boney' with her ancestral demi-gods. But, if any of the persons are historical, we cannot identify them. And if the names are real, it does not follow that any part of the story really happened to the bearer of the particular name. None of the mediaeval magician-stories happened to the real Vergil.

THE BACKGROUND OF THE ILIAD: THE 'BIRTH OF HOMER'

IN the spring of 1923 a man brought to the experts of the Natural History Museum, South Kensington, a strange object which he wished identified. 'It looks,' he said, 'exactly like a petrified mammalian stomach'; and so it did, with a well-marked pylorus and other details. 'You may be sure,' said the expert, 'that if it was a petrified mammalian stomach it would not look like one.' It proved in fact to be a stone ginger-beer bottle which had collapsed before baking.

I think that, in the search for historical facts among the poetical traditions of Greece, the warning of that expert should be borne in mind. Any real historical fact which was in the poetical tradition by 1000 B. C. would pretty certainly be transformed out of all likeness by the time it had passed through the hands of several hundred bards and formed a *ficelle* in innumerable different poems. Of course we often find that new discoveries 'confirm' or at least 'explain' some epithet or phrase in the poems of which readers had taken no heed. The 'horse-taming Hector' and the Trojans 'mounters of swift horses', the sack of Troy by Heracles ἕνεκ' ἵππων Λαομέδοντος, receive new light when we learn from Professors Myres and Peake that Ilion II was very likely destroyed in the third millennium by an invasion of hordes from the steppes of Russia, who had just discovered that they could ride horses as well as drink the milk of mares. The horse-folk no doubt established themselves on the plain of Troy, and Ilion remained for long a special centre of the horse industry.[1] It throws light on Hector's war-cry

Τρῶες καὶ Λύκιοι καὶ Δάρδανοι ἀγχιμαχηταί,

[1] See F. Sartiaux, *Troie*, 1915: Peake, *Racial Elements concerned in the First Siege of Troy*, 1916: Myres, *Cambridge Ancient History* (1923), p. 82: and especially Macurdy, *Troy and Paeonia*, which I have been privileged to see before publication.

when we are taught by Professor Macurdy that the Dardans and other Thracian tribes in historical times seem to have originated the dense infantry formation known as the Macedonian phalanx.

In these cases history is preserved in the implications of an epithet; it may equally be preserved in myths or proper names, without the knowledge of those who told or spoke them. What does not seem to occur is a plain statement about the act of an individual or tribe in which both the names and the facts are unchanged. So much we have seen in several of the examples taken in the last chapter. If we throw our net rather more boldly and look not for the direct record but the indirect evidence or implication, we shall have a better prospect of obtaining some tangible catch. As so often in these problems of early history, we may be able to divine not indeed the exact thing that did happen, but the sort of thing that must have happened.

Consider the historical background of a case like the following. There is a fine passage of some seventy lines in *Iliad* E 627-98 which narrates the slaying of Tlepolemus of Rhodes, a son of Heracles, by the Lycian Sarpêdon. The passage interrupts the context. It is never referred to afterwards. The Heracleidae are nowhere else mentioned in Homer. And for divers reasons editors have marked the passage as a foreign insertion. But where does the insertion come from? The Heracleid of Rhodes has no place in the Trojan circle of legends. When one sees that his adversary is a Lycian, that is, a chieftain of the mainland just opposite Rhodes, where the Rhodians were constantly attempting to force a settlement, one can guess what may have happened. A local legend of battle between the Rhodian and the Lycian has been torn up from its natural context and inserted into the midst of the fighting about Troy. The song is a fragment of the history of Rhodes and Lycia.[1]

---

[1] The Sarpedon passages generally bear the marks of being in some sense foreign matter, either invented later or transferred from a different context. For instance, the Sarpedon who was buried in the famous grave-mound in Lycia must have been slain in Lycia, not in Troy. This was remarked in antiquity. The passage (Π 668 ff.) where Sarpedon's body is carried from Troy to Lycia by Sleep and Death was considered 'spurious' by Zenodotus, with whom Didymus agreed (Schol. *ad loc.*). Eustathius also (p. 1069, 29) makes the very plausible surmise that Homer, knowing of the historical

In searching for fragments of real history, like this, in the Homeric poems, it is probable that our best hunting-grounds will be in the little backwaters of narrative, where the plot interest is weakest and the details least important. That is to say, the poet will have left the history most unchanged in those places where he had the least motive to falsify it ; and conversely. In the case of Diomedes which we have just considered, for instance, the narrative is in the front plane of interest. Consequently the original story—if we were right in our suggestions—is hidden away under a mass of ornament and addition. Not only has the place of Diomedes' battle with the war-god and his spouse been moved from Thrace to Troy, but the name of Aeneas has been substituted for some other name.   When a story is mere background, and does not need to be made interesting, it is less tampered with.

In the same book (43 ff.) we have the following passage :—

> Then Idomeneus despoiled Phaestus, son of the Maeonian, even of Borus who had come from deep-soiled Tarne. Him spear-famed Idomeneus stabbed with his long lance as he was about to mount upon his chariot, through his right shoulder. And down from the chariot he crashed and a horror of darkness laid hold on him.

Idomeneus is the King of Cnossos in Crete, and Phaestus is otherwise only known to history as the next most famous town

grave-mound in Lycia, invented these lines in order to combine it with his own story that Sarpedon was killed at Troy. It has long since been suggested, on other grounds, that influence was perhaps exerted on the *Iliad* by the princes of Lycia, who derived their descent from Sarpedon and Glaucus.

Sarpedon, however, seems to have Thracian connexions as well as Lycian—even if the latter are not entirely an invention of the said princes, who may well have identified a native ancestor of their own with the famous Sarpedon. A promontory near Ainos in Thrace was called Sarpedon (Strabo, p. 331, fr. 52 ; cf. p. 319), and Ainos is the home of Sarpedon in one of the Heracles legends. Ainos was an Aeolic settlement among Thracians ; hence Sarpedon is the blood-foe of Patroclus. His chosen comrade, Asteropaios (M 102 f.) is a Paeonian, son of the river Axios (Bethe, l. c.). His other comrade, Maris, is otherwise unknown, but suggests Maron. Glaucus himself, one may observe, is guest-friend of the Thracian Diomedes : but Glaucus is a figure with many ramifications. See Macurdy, l. c.

One may notice, as a further mark of something unusual, that the Lycian genealogy given in Z 199 does not agree with the one ordinarily given, from Europa-Minos. And Diodorus says that Sarpedon fought on the side of Agamemnon against Troy ! (v. 79). Perhaps a mere slip.

in the same island.   That is to say, Phaestus *is* the town, or the eponymous hero of the town, and he is asserted to be a 'son' of the Maeonian or Lydian of the mainland.   It reminds us of Zidon the firstborn of Canaan: apparently this was some Maeonian settlement at Phaestus.   We may well have in this passage a record of a local battle or conquest in Crete, torn up from its surroundings and used by the poet to fill in some details of slaughter in a great battle before Troy.

And what sort of a conquest was it?   Idomeneus, if we inquire into his antecedents, appears pretty clearly as a northern invader of Crete.   He is a son of Deucalion, which points to Thessaly. He is a great founder of cities in the north-west, like Diomedes and Odysseus.   The men he fights fall into two groups:[1] Oinomaüs and Alkathoüs—who is in some legends one of the suitors slain by Oinomaüs, in others a son of Pelops the slayer of Oinomaüs—these two take us to the Pelops-group of invaders in the Peloponnese.   The others are what we may call Creto-Asiatic; Asius, from the Asian plain in Lydia, this Phaestus, son of the Maeonian from Lydia, and Othryoneus, a name derived from the Cretan word for a hill ($ὄθρυς$, see Fick-Bechtel, p. 421).

Is there not history here, real history, however fragmentary and adrift from all its moorings?   I think, following a hint of Bethe's, that there is very likely a good deal of historical fact contained in certain passages which look at first sight like mere strings of meaningless names, I mean, the $ἀνδροκτασίαι$, or 'Man-slayings', which constantly fill up the background of a Homeric battle picture.   For instance, at the end of Diomedes' great battle we have (Z 29 ff.) this passage:—

> Then Polypoites, firm in battle, slew Astyalus, and Odysseus smote with his bronzen spear Pidutes of Percote, and Teucros godlike Aretaon.   And Antilochus, son of Nestor, smote Ablerus with his shining spear, and Agamemnon, king of men, slew Elatus. (He dwelt by the banks of fair-flowing Satnioeis, in lofty Pedasus.)   And Eurypylus despoiled Melanthius.   And Menelaus caught Adrastus alive.

And so on.

---

[1] I omit Aeneas and Deiphobus.   They are obviously not inconsistent with the above grouping, but I hesitate to offer an explanation of their meaning in this context.   Orsilochos, Idomeneus' supposed son in ν 260, looks like a fiction.

There may be fiction, and the emptiest kind of fiction, mixed up in this. And probably most of the history is at present untraceable. We will take one case in detail presently. But, first, let us reflect what constituted a man's chief claim to public honour among these primitive northern tribes. The greatest thing, perhaps, was to be *Ptoliporthos*, a Sacker of Cities.[1] Short of that, a hero was chiefly known by the enemies whom he had slain. A curious remnant of this interest is to be found in Hyginus, the mythographer, chapters 112–115. 'Qui cum quo dimicarunt', 'Nobilem quem quis occidit', 'Achivi qui quot occiderunt', and so on. It is a well-known feature of heroic societies. Think of Sigurd Fafnirsbane, Hogni Sigurdsbane, and the rest. Think of the stories of Heracles, Achilles, Diomedes. In each case the main groundwork is a list of the enemies whom the hero slew. In more civilized times we put on the tomb of a general a list of the victories which he won. In earlier times these victories were, or at least were represented as being, personal duels, man-to-man, and were commemorated, at any rate in times of migration, not by inscriptions on tombs, but by paeans or verses current among the tribe. One remembers how the Myrmidons in *Iliad* X march back to the ships singing their paean : 'We have won us great glory, we have slain godlike Hector, to whom the Trojans in their city prayed as to a god.'

The emotion connected with these various victories would of course generally become dim with time, but the verses recording the bare facts would be remembered carefully by the bard of the tribe or group. Indeed their preservation would be the chief part of his business. And I strongly suspect that the lists of men slain by the various heroes in the *Iliad* are, in their origin, these same quasi-tribal records, condensed into mere lists of names and, of course, transferred from their original contexts. In detail fiction may have entered in, and some names may be pure inventions. But in general, if we only interpret the language rightly, I incline to believe that 'Odysseus' did very likely slay 'Pidutes of Percote', and that some people claiming connexion with Agamemnon did very likely take the town of Pedasus in the valley of the Satnioeis. This last point, indeed, we actually know from history.

[1] Cf. Aesch. *Ag.* 472 and Cic. *Ep. ad Fam.* x. 13. 2.

But let us follow the story of the last victim in this 'Man-slaying', Adrastus, who was taken by Menelaus alive and eventually slain by Agamemnon. He appears suddenly, with no name of father or country. But his fate is told at length. His horses took fright, ran into a tamarisk bush, broke the pole of his chariot, and flung him out upon his face. So Menelaus took him, but would have spared his life had not Agamemnon run up and himself stabbed Adrastus in the flank with his spear.

Who is this Adrastus, and where was this battle really fought? The name ('No-escape') is common in myth. It recurs in *B* 830. But we may notice that Pausanias saw a place near Thebes which was called Harma, Chariot; and when he inquired the origin of the name, he was informed that Adrastus, the celebrated King of Sikyon, Leader of the Seven against Thebes, was there cast out of his chariot, which was entangled in a tamarisk bush, when he was flying from the battle at Thebes. This cannot be entirely a fabrication based on the *Iliad*. It is, in part at least, an independent tradition, and we can make a shrewd guess at its source. Adrastus was the leader of the Argives in the *Thebais*, and his defeat and flight one of its crowning incidents. We have found the *Iliad* using the *Thebais* before. (See p. 181 f.) And again, when Agamemnon's kingdom is described in the Catalogue (*B* 572) it includes ' Sikyon, where aforetime Adrastus was king'. That is, this fatherless and floating Adrastus seems—though the reciters of the *Iliad* as a rule did not suspect it—to have been originally the great Adrastus of the Theban War. And what of his slaying by Agamemnon? Does it represent some misty tradition of a real battle? One would think so ; but there is still the likelihood that it may be a mere fiction. In any case, if there is any real history behind it, that history did not take place at Troy.

It seems quite possible that few of these battles of the *Iliad* did. A line of research indicated by Eric Bethe in a brilliant essay on *Die Trojanischen Sagenkreise* tends to establish clearly what many of us had suspected before, that much of the fighting which Homer locates at Troy, in Asia Minor, on the south-eastern shore of the Hellespont, is really a reminiscence of old mainland wars, whose legendary centre, I would suggest, was once not Troy but Thebes. Dr. Bethe's method is this. Those heroes who have a real existence in the tradition, apart from the *Iliad*, can in many cases be traced to their diverse homes or settlements by three trains of evidence: first, their graves and places of worship; secondly, their blood-feuds, for a tribe's blood-feud is usually against a close neighbour; and thirdly, their wives, kinsmen, and the like.

Take the case of Achilles. It is quite clear. Achilles is firmly located in Phthia, in the country between Thessaly and Locris, on the Spercheios river. All his kindred are about him. The temple of Thetis, his mother, is close to Pharsâlos. His father Peleus is associated with Mt. Pelion. His sister was married to the river Spercheios. And in the same neighbourhood we find his blood-foes. Two heroes, celebrated in other contexts, but in the *Iliad* reduced to mere names for filling up an 'androktasia',[1] Dryops and Deucalion, belong to this region. So does his better-known enemy Cycnus, the Swan-hero. More than that, there is quoted from the third-century historian Istros a statement which puzzles Plutarch and directly conflicts with all the Homeric tradition, that Alexandros or Paris was slain by Achilles and Patroclus upon the banks of the Spercheios.

In Homer, of course, Alexandros is a Trojan prince who perhaps never saw the Spercheios in his life, and he is not killed by Achilles, but on the contrary kills him some time after Patroclus is dead. It is startling to find him fighting on the Locrian border. Yet an inquiry into the origin of Alexandros-Paris gives him also a home in the same region as his enemy, Achilles. His sister, who like himself has a double name, Alexandra or Cassandra, was worshipped in historical times in Locris. (The Locrians had some strange connexion with Ilion. As late as the fourth century B. C. they supplied periodically two highly *taboo* priestesses to the temple there. The natives always tried to prevent them coming in, and once killed one of them.[2]) The heroes with whom Paris fights in the *Iliad*, especially those who have no importance in the story, and are therefore not inserted for a fictional purpose, are almost all Thessalians, such

[1] Υ 455, 478.

[2] Timaeus ap. Schol. Lycophr. 1155, 1159: Aeneas Tacticus 31. 24.

as Machaon, Eurypylos, Menesthios.[1]   He is killed at last by the
Malian Philoctetes.

Andromache, the wife of Hector, comes from Thêbê, a town
which is described as Ὑποπλακίη, or in words which explain
that epithet, 'beneath wooded Placos'.   No one in antiquity
knew what or where Placos was, though it was presumed to
be a mountain.   Was it not the mountain above that Thêbê
which lies between Pharsalus and Mt. Pelion, at the northern
boundary of Achilles' realm?   Andromache in one passage of
the *Iliad* (*Z* 397 ff.) is made a Cilician; but in the saga generally
she is connected not with any place in Asia, but with the north
and north-west of Greece.   She is the mother of Molossus, the
eponymous hero of a tribe in Epirus called Molossi.   In another
legend she is the mother of Kestrînos, eponymous hero of the
Epirot territory Kestrînê.   This seems to be the real tradition.
It is then harmonized with the Troy-poems by making some one
bring the Trojan queen back to Greece after the capture of her
city.   In one legend it is Neoptolemus, the son of Achilles, who
so brings her.   In another it is Helenus, her brother-in-law.

And what of Hector himself, the great 'City-holder'?   Did he
always in legend hold the same city?   As Dümmler has observed,
he was worshipped as a hero in Boeotian Thebes.   And if we
examine the list of people whom he kills or fights in the *Iliad*,
their cults and graves and legends crowd round the neighbourhood of Boeotia.   Leïtos (*P* 601) had a tomb in Plataea: Oresbios
(*E* 707) lived in Hylê: Arkesilaos (*O* 329) was buried in
Lebadeia.   As for Hector's comrade, Melanippos (*O* 547-83),
we know that a hero Melanippos was, like Hector himself,
worshipped in Thebes.   Hector was a great 'slayer of men',
and his victims in the *Iliad* make a sort of road from Thebes
upward to the bounds of Achilles' region.   Dr. Bethe mentions
Schedios the Phocian, whose tomb Strabo saw at Daphnûs on
the Euboean Gulf (*O* 515, and again *P* 306: Strabo, ix. 425);
Autonoos, worshipped as a hero at Delphi (*Λ* 301); Orestes,
connected in saga with Phocis (*E* 705) ; Trêchos the Aetolian,
who must be the eponymous hero of Trêchis (*E* 706).   Trêchis
lies at the mouth of the Spercheios on the borders of the realm

---

[1] Cf. Λ 506 ; Λ 580, B 736 ; H 9.

of Achilles. Patroclus, Hector's greatest victim, belongs to the heart of that country. Further north he slew Helenos, son of Oinôps (*E* 707), Epeigeus from the town of Boudeion (*Π* 571), and in some legends also Protesilaos. The road has led us even beyond the blood-foe Achilles, up to Thêbê, the city of Hector's wife Andromache. It is strange. It looks as if forgotten remnants of old Boeotian saga, or even epos, omitted from the canonical *Thebaïs*, which concentrated on the war of The Seven, were used for building up the plot of the 'poetry about Troy'.

Another group of closely united enemies—in these connexions neighbour and enemy are almost interchangeable terms—is to be found in Lacedaemon. If the above was the Achilles-Hector-Alexandros group, this is the Helen group. It consists of Helen, Agamemnon, Menelaus, Alexandros the ravisher of Helen, and Deïphobus her third husband. Alexandros, it will be seen, appears in both groups.[1] Helen of course lived in Sparta. Her husband Menelaus had a grave and a temple at Therapnae: and at the same place, according to the statement of a late though well-informed authority,[2] both Alexandros and Deïphobus received divine honours. Perhaps in this statement Therapnae is a mistake for Amyclae, which suits the geography slightly better. Also Amyclae is the home of a Deïphobus in the Heracles legend (Apollod. ii. 6. 2; Diod. iv. 31; Jahn, *Bilder-chronik*, p. 70): and in Amyclae also lay the sanctuary of Alexandros's sister Alexandra-Cassandra, and beside it her tomb, together with that of Agamemnon.

I will not pursue the subject further. One may well be surprised at the tenacity with which these ancient local worships held their ground through almost the whole lifetime of Greece as a nation. The tribes which instituted them, and through which alone they had reality, had long since passed away both from those particular neighbourhoods and from the face of the earth. They were often in flat contradiction with that other stream of history popularized and made canonical by the *Iliad* and *Odyssey*. At

---

[1] Cf. Agamemnon, of whom the same is true: both Agamemnon and Alexander are famous as 'Lords of Ships'.

[2] The dialogue 'Theophrastus' on the immortality of the Soul, by Aeneas of Gaza (fifth century A. D.), cited in S. Wide, *Lakonische Kulte*, p. 351; Bethe, l. c., p. 16.

a time when all educated people throughout Greece knew from their childhood the Helen of poetry, the fairest of mortal women, the gentle adulteress whose sin is almost forgiven because of her graciousness, old peasants and pietists continued to worship her rude and ugly idol at Sparta, praying for happy marriage or for the health of sick children.   Sometimes the two streams of legend, that of the *Iliad* and that of the local worship, ran on without mingling; more often, of course, ways were invented for harmonizing the two.   That is why, for instance, Cassandra is brought from Troy by Agamemnon, to be buried beside him at Therapnae; why a Locrian hero is made to commit a sin against Cassandra, to be expiated ever afterwards by the Locrians worshipping at her sanctuary.

There is perhaps one point here which calls for special reflection.   It seems to our minds unnatural that such vital poems should be written about mere creatures of the imagination, like gods and tribal daemons.   And Chadwick has convincingly shown that a 'heroic age' is an age of great doings and great individuals.   In the German and Scandinavian legends many of the heroes bear real historical names and represent real persons. Why should this not be the case in Greek legend also?
I think the cause of the difference lies in the vastly greater lapse of time during which the Greek epic grew.   The native epic tradition in Northern Europe was checked and overruled from very early times by the Latin cultural tradition.   The Latin chronicles kept some guard over history.   The rich and accomplished Latin poetry killed out, at least among the literary classes, any effective interest in the struggling vernacular poetry. The Church checked the Pagan imagination.   But the Greek poetic tradition had no elder brother to snub it, no foreign schoolmaster to run a blue pencil through its errors and drive its imagination underground.   It grew in its own soil, luxuriating in invention and building up on its own native lines an ever statelier beauty.
The study of Greek mythology shows beyond serious question the enormous part played by village ritual and custom in forming the great legends.   The aboriginal peasants of Greece seem to have sung and danced about their field-magic, their fertility

cycles, and their Year-Daemons, from the earliest antiquity. Then came the Migrations with their stirring events, their strong-armed magnificent adventurers. The focus of interest was changed. Instead of thinking of the crops and the customs, people talked of the last great deed of some famous *condottiere*, the last great downfall of a Minoan city or castle. The epic lays that then broke into being were doubtless full of these historical persons and events. And if fate had arrested their development about the year 1000 B.C., we might well have had poems as historical as—say—the French epics concerned with Charlemagne. Dr. Chadwick's four stages of Heroic Poetry [1] do not happen to fit the course of Greek literature; but, roughly speaking, Homer seems to represent what Stage II would have grown into, if it had had centuries of free life, and had been perfected neither at Kings' Courts nor at village inns, but at great Pan-European Festivals, like the Panêgyreis of Greece.

The epic developed, but the individuals of the Heroic Age lost their definite settings. The old myths and ritual stories sprang up again and overgrew them. Their real names perhaps remain in fair number; but their deeds are the deeds of mythical beings and they themselves indistinguishable from so many creatures of mythology or fancy.

Even in historical times gods and spirits were present to the minds of the Greek to a degree that we can hardly realize. When they defeated the Persians in the full light of history, their general's comment was: 'It is not we who have done this, but the gods and the heroes' (Hdt. viii. 109). That is not perfunctory piety. It is not even the mark of a specially reverent and beautiful humility; for the speaker was Themistocles, a hard-bitten and scheming man. It is a remnant of the feeling which permeates our record of the warfare of the Heroic Age, and which is found still among primitive peoples. Think how it pervades the Old Testament. Think of the many stories in books of anthropology telling how a savage who has succeeded or

[1] *Heroic Age*, p. 94: 'I. Court poems of the Heroic Age itself. II. Epic and narrative poems based on these. III. The popular poetry of the eighth and following centuries. IV. The German poems of the twelfth and following centuries, when heroic subjects had again come into favour with the higher classes.'

failed in catching his prey explains that his *mana*, or even his *totem*, has been on that particular occasion strong or weak. There is an early inscription extant in which the people of Selinûs celebrate a successful battle, in which presumably various individuals had in the normal ways distinguished themselves. We moderns would have mentioned their names. But the inscription of the Selinuntians runs thus: 'Thanks to the following gods we of Selinûs have conquered: Zeus Nikâtôr, Phobos, Heracles, Apollo, Poseidon, the Tyndaridae, Athena, Mâlophoros, Pâsikrateia, and the others, but especially thanks to Zeus' (*I. G. A.* 515). We know how the gods Castor and Polydeucês fought for Rome at the battle of Lake Regillus, and for the Locrians against Croton. We know how the Greeks before the battle of Salamis sent a ship to Aegina to fetch 'Aias and Telamon and the other Aeacidae', including Peleus and Achilles, to lead them against the Persians (Hdt. viii. 64). They are doubtless included, if not specially meant, in Themistocles' words, attributing the victory to 'the gods and heroes'. The same Aeacidae had been lent by Aegina to Thebes on a previous occasion, about which the less said the better. For the Thebans were defeated, Aeacidae and all (Hdt. v. 80), and told the Aeginetans that next time they would prefer a regiment of men. Now, suppose the battle of Salamis had been fought, not in the full light of Greek history, but in the misty dawn of the Epos, what sort of a story should we have had? Would it have been all about Themistocles and Eurybiades and the Corinthians? I suspect it would have been Aias and Telamon and Peleus and Achilles who defeated Xerxes. That, at least, is the way in which many early Greek traditions seem to have been recorded.

It remains to consider another point. Why do the Homeric battles all refer not to any warfare that was going on at the time of their composition, but to warfare of forgotten people under forgotten conditions in the past? The fact is certain. Even if the analysis made in this essay be all wrong, there will remain just the same problem. For the poems were certainly for many centuries in the hands of Ionian and Attic bards, who are shown by all the evidence to have largely added to them. Yet, with all their additions, they never brought in any celebration of their own immediate present. There is no mention of the Asiatic colonies, of the great Ionian cities, of the later groupings of tribes. The few exceptions to this rule are mere accidents. There is all through the poems a distinct refusal to cheapen epic poetry by the celebration of contemporary things. If men wanted to celebrate the present they did so in other forms of literature.

What shall one say of this? Merely that there is no cause for surprise. It seems to be the normal instinct of a poet, at least of an epic poet. The earliest version of the *Song of Roland* which we possess was written by an Anglo-Norman scribe some thirty years after the conquest of England. If the Normans of that age wanted an epic sung to them, surely a good subject lay ready to hand. Yet as a matter of fact their great epic is all about Roland, a not very important chieftain dead three hundred years before, not about William the Conqueror. The fugitive Britons of Wales made no epic to tell of their conquest by the Saxons; they turned to a dim-shining Arthur belonging to the vaguest past. Neither did the Saxons who were conquering them make epics about that conquest. They sang how at some time long past a legendary and mythical Beowulf had conquered a monstrous Grendel and Grendel's mother and a dragon.

Yet this past of which epic poets make their songs, what exactly is it? It is not the plain historical past. It is the past transformed into something ideal, something that shall be more inspiring or more significant. In the case of the *Iliad* the old traditional fighting is all concentrated into one great war, and that a war for the possession of the very land which the professed descendants of Agamemnon were fighting for in historical times.

1. It is difficult to sum up this scattered evidence, but we seem to find in the historical background of the poems the following elements. There were extant the ruins of a great fortified stronghold at Ilion in the Troad, at least twice destroyed, and a tradition of the moving wars of those peoples from the North who troubled and eventually destroyed Aegean civilization in the third and second millennia B. C. As to dates, the Troad seems to have been invaded by the horse-folk about 2300 B. C., but we hear most about those 'Peoples of the Sea' and others who

raided as far as Egypt between 1300 and 1150 : Akhaiuasha, Danauna, Luka, Dardenni, T'akarai and the like.[1] It follows that this fighting did not all take place at Troy. And it seems almost certain that, as the fame of the Trojan War grew greater, alien heroes were drawn into it, as Atli and Theodoric were drawn into the *Nibelungenlied*.

2. The chief fighters in this warfare, like Menelaus, Odysseus, Agamemnon, bear names apparently Greek, though markedly different in formation from the Greek names of historical times ; others bear regular Greek names, but of types that in later ages occur chiefly in Macedon, Thrace, and Epirus.[2] It seems likely enough, after Dr. Chadwick's work on the subject, that under some of these names lie the names of real Heroic Age adventurers, while others belonged originally to divine or mythical beings. This is a question only to be solved by external evidence, and no external evidence is to be had, but it seems clear that even where these names once belonged to real men, their sagas had by the sixth century been covered over by a vast growth of myth and even of folk-lore, to say nothing of pure fiction.

3. The poet is always conscious of a great difference between his own age and that of the heroes, and maintains with few lapses a remarkably consistent convention of what the Heroic Age was like. We must conclude that there was a fairly continuous tradition from the Heroic Age downward, kept alive no doubt in part by the ruins of Mycenaean castles, by ancient gems and jewels such as are still discovered, by the ancient armour and other relics which we know to have been preserved in temples, but also by sagas and lays. At any rate it is certain that in the poems as recited in the fourth century this heroic convention is preserved and consciously protected. Any lapse from it is noticed in the Alexandrian scholia. Yet the Heroic Age must have been over by about 1100 B.C.

4. It must always be remembered that the *Iliad* and *Odyssey* are not poetic chronicles ; they are elaborate and highly wrought

---

[1] Cf. Ἀχαιϝοί, Δαναοί, Λύκιοι, Δάρδανοι, Τευκροί. The terminations -sha and -na seem to be the same as occur in Lycian. Hall, *Oldest Civilization*, pp. 178 ff. Cyprus was raided by Lukki about 1400 B.C. For other records of these tribes see Breasted, *Ancient Records*, iii, pp. 136, 157 : Cowley, *Hittites* (1920), pp. 13–23.

[2] See Bury in *Quarterly Review*, July 1922 ; also Macurdy, l. c.

works of fiction using traditional material. The material is often very old, the finished poem in its present state comparatively late. For example, the ram-adventure of Odysseus in *Odyssey ι* is depicted on an early Cretan gem and must have been current about 1500 B.C.; whereas the reunion of Odysseus and Penelope after Meton's *eikosieteris* implies an astronomical discovery which is attributed to the year 430 B.C. or thereabouts. (See p. 211.)

5. Into this legendary past were projected the wars of the Greeks who in historical times established themselves in the region called Aeolis, just south of Troy, and perhaps a real historical meeting of hosts from the Peloponnese with hosts from South Thessaly—of Agamemnon with Achilles; while at a later time again the whole tradition was reinspired by the great war of all Hellas against Persia and the East, and knit up with the Spartan ritual myth of the beloved Helen, for ever ravished and rewon.

If we consider this fifth observation more closely, we ought to receive some light upon that question which so vexed antiquity, the birthplace of Homer. Ilion is a fixed and known place; the Aeolian tribes also belong on the whole to a definite area. They were driven from South Thessaly across the North Aegean by a direct bridge of islands: Ikos, Skyros, Lesbos—and there was the south-west extremity of the Troad immediately in front. The meeting of Achilles and Agamemnon, if we could be sure what it meant, would be more conclusive still. Achilles, though he had worship in the Peloponnese, is mostly Thessalian: Agamemnon, though he had Thessalian connexions, is mostly Peloponnesian: and if we look for some great traditional meeting-place for the people of Agamemnon from the south, and the people of Achilles from Thessaly, the first place to suggest itself is the island of Lesbos. It was also about a ' girl of Brisa ' in Lesbos that the chiefs quarrelled. The fourth point is hardly needed, it points to the same result. If the ravishment of Helen now takes a new direction towards the Troad, that fits in with a movement of Helen's Peloponnesian worshippers towards the same place. The time and place which originally provided the main strands of the framework of the Troy-saga are fairly clear. The time is the Aeolian migration, the place is Lesbos or some early settlement on the shore of Asia. If we take Homer as the author of the Troy-epic

the area known as Aeolis is his first birthplace. This conclusion is
exactly borne out by the ancient Lives of Homer, which, however
apocryphal and romantic, represent at least a tradition.

Further, our historical argument fits with the argument from
language. True, the *Iliad* and *Odyssey*, as given in all our
MSS., appear in a quasi-Ionic dialect. But it is beyond question that the dialect has been in some way changed. The epos
has been worked over into its present Ionic from some other
speech. What that speech exactly was is open to dispute.[1]

Professor Fick, in his epoch-making editions of the two poems,
argued boldly that it was ordinary Lesbian Aeolic, and that both
poems had been definitely translated into Ionic by the rhapsode
Kynaithos of Chios about the year 540 B.C. He showed that
the poems were full of ' Aeolic ' forms in the midst of the Ionic,
and these Aeolic forms had the peculiarity, nearly always, of
being metrically different from the corresponding Ionic forms.
That is : the poems for the most part were simply wrought over
into Ionic word for word, but when the proper Ionic word did
not scan, the older Aeolic form was left. The practice is common,
one may almost say regular, in traditional books. Many English
ballads occur in northern and southern forms, many old French
poems in French of Paris, Norman-French, and Picard. And
this general conception of an ' Aeolic ' stage of the Homeric
poems has been accepted by almost all advanced critics.

Yet it needs an important correction. Fick's full theory, with
Kynaithos and the sixth century included, has had few supporters.
And if we abandon that definite date and person, the linguistic
arguments rather change their character. For the two most
characteristic distinctions of the Ionian speech, the loss of *w*-
sounds and the turning of $\bar{a}$ into η, can be shown to have occurred
later, and perhaps considerably later, than the first foundations
of the cities in Asia Minor. So that the *w* and the long *a* sounds
of Homer were as much the property of Proto-Ionic, if we may
use the term, as of Aeolic. The language of Homer—omitting
for the moment the numerous false forms and modernisms of our
present texts—is markedly based upon an older stage of the

---

[1] To the ancients it was chiefly a question of pronunciation : cf. τὴν ποίησιν
ἀναγιγνώσκεσθαι ἀξιοῖ Ζώπυρος ὁ Μάγνης Αἰολίδι διαλέκτῳ· τὸ δὲ αὐτὸ καὶ Δικαίαρχος
(Osann, *Anecd. Rom.* 5).

Greek language than either the Ionic of Herodotus or the Lesbian of Sappho.[1] This is illustrated, among other facts, by the curious affinities between the Epic dialect and two dialects utterly out of the range of epic influence, Arcadian and Cyprian.[2]

What can there be in common between Arcadia, the central highlands of the Peloponnese, and Cyprus, the remote Greek island in the gates of the Semite? Nothing, one would say, but their isolation. They were both so cut off from the normal currents of progressive Greek civilization that they retained more than other communities of their original speech, as the French in Canada retain peculiar elements of the language of Louis XIV. And consequently they show curious agreements with Homer, whose dialect, for reasons easily intelligible, clung to the oldest form of speech that was capable of being comfortably understood. It is not, therefore, accurate to say *simpliciter* that Homer has been translated from Aeolic into Ionic, if by Aeolic we mean sixth-century Lesbian, or the group of which Lesbian is the type, Lesbian-Thessalian-Boeotian. One has to allow for the existence of an old poetic dialect, ancestral both to the Aeolic of Lesbos and to the Ionic of the 'mixed multitudes', the language of old Greece, 'before the sons of the Achaioi came'.

There is certainly a strong Lesbian element in Homer, as was recognized in antiquity. There are certain forms of words which are definitely Lesbian, and not primitive, dialectical peculiarities which first originated in the Lesbian-Aeolic dialects; falsely formed datives in -εσσι, falsely formed perfect participles in -κων, -κοντος, a preference for κεν over ἄν, and various forms like ἄλλυδις, νύμφα, &c. The Lesbian form ἀγρέω is generally altered to αἱρέω, but in the imperative, where it was not recognized, it is left. Still, the main texture of the earlier Homeric language is not Lesbian-Aeolic, but some earlier and more widely diffused speech. What does this mean in history?

It is just what we should have expected from our analysis of the raw material of the poems. It is the speech of these immensely old tribal or quasi-tribal traditions which, as we have seen, form the ultimate historical content of the *Iliad*. They

---

[1] See the valuable Appendix to Monro's edition of *Odyssey* xiii–xxiv, pp. 455–88. He seems to me to underrate the Aeolic element.

[2] Thumb counts Cyprian as 'Achaean', meaning thereby 'pre-Dorian'.

ome in part from Southern Greece, but mostly from the
ountry traversed by various groups of wandering 'Northmen
. the Heroic' Age, from the Vardar and Struma valleys, from
hrace and Macedon and Thessaly. What took place in Aeolia
: Lesbos was the first collecting of them into a Trojan setting.
. is interesting in this connexion to notice that the scenery of
ne similes is apt to be Thessalian and not Asiatic: that the
[uses come from Olympus and the vale of Pieria in Thessaly,
nd the gods, wherever they may wander, still keep their
Olympian houses'.[1]

And there is this to observe: that however loosely the various
nasses of legend floated, there was in very early times some
eeling that they formed a whole, or at least a series of wholes.
There was some conception of a consecutive saga or history.
Each bard is understood to begin his lay—ἔνθεν ἑλών, or τῶν
μόθεν γε—at some particular point in the great story.[2] There
nust have been some great deed or experience in common, some
mpulse to history writing, some breaking down of family and
ribal barriers. That experience, it seems clear, must have been
he Heroic Age.

The next birth of Homer was certainly in Ionia. We have
een that the colonists of Lesbos had some pretensions to unity
of race. The place from which the exodus came was so close.
The bridge from Mt. Pelion to Aeolis, by Skyros and Lesbos, is
o straight and complete. There may also have been some
unity of race in the extreme south of Asia Minor, where the
group called itself 'Doris'. The Dorian tribes were at any rate

---

[1] The Mysian Olympus may have been regarded locally as the seat of the
gods: but the 'Homeric' gods evidently dwell in the Thessalian Olympus.
The 'Twelve Gods' seem to have been a Thessalian institution; the first
altar to them was built by Deucalion (Schol. ap. Rhod. iii. 1085. Cf. ii. 532
with Schol.).

[2] One would like to know when these lays became (1) continuously metrical
and (2) hexametric. The hexameter as it stands in Homer has been thought
to show traces of having originated in two dactylic trimeters with anacrusis,
what the Greek metrists call Paroimiacs (see Van Leeuwen, *Enchiridion*,
pp. 1-24), and it is curious that the extant Aeolic poets hardly use the
hexameter at all. (Sappho 93, 94, 95, are instances.) The Stesichorean
metre, sets of dactylic trimeters mixed with trochaic (or iambic) metra
–◡◡–◡◡––, –◡––), is perhaps older than the finished hexameter. If
there were evidence to show that the hexameter was specifically Ionic, some
clear conclusions could be drawn. ('There is. It was the metre of the
Paean, and was invented by Olen of Lycia, i. e. at Delos.'—J. A. K. T.)

the leaders of their communities.   But all along the great stretc
of coast between these two little groups there seems to have bee
no definite unity or common descent.   They may have inherite
a good deal from Crete,[1] but every city wall contained
σύμμεικτον πλῆθος, a ' mixed multitude '.   They could merely l
classed together as ' Iawones ', Sons of Javan, and even that nam
is given them by foreigners.

It looks as if these ancestors of the Ionians had in the extrem
stress of their migrations lost hold upon their earlier trad
tions.   At any rate, it was only in later times, and only b
turning to their northern neighbours, that the Ionians obtainec
or recovered, their heritage in the Epos.   It came to them the
as part of a regular process.   For it is just these central settle
ments, these most tribeless and fugitive of the Sons of Javar
that built up the greatest achievements of Greek civilizatio
before the rise of Athens.   In historical times the Ionian Greel
is always prevailing over the Aeolian, ousting him, outstrippin;
him, annexing his cities and his possessions.   The Ionian poe
Mimnermus, early in the seventh century, narrates how a part
of Ionians from Colophon and Pylos set forth and capturec
Aeolian Smyrna.[2]   The same thing can be shown to hav
happened in Chios, though there the memory of the conflic
was forgotten, and the island counts as simply Ionian.   Anc
these cases may be taken as typical.   The Aeolic settlement:
belong to an earlier, ruder, and more chivalric stage of culture
and were superseded by the higher intelligence and practica
adaptability of the Ionians.   And besides their walled cities, th
Aeolians were robbed also of their Homer.

How did this process take place ?   There may conceivably a
some time have been a definite authoritative change of dialect
but it seems more likely that the Epic dialect gradually changec

---

[1] See Prof. Burnet's monograph *Who were the Ionians ?*

[2] Mimn. 9.   He makes no apology ; but we have beside his verses a more
defensive Ionian account of the affair, explaining that they were not the
aggressors.   Strabo, xiv. 634.   The town first belonged to the Leleges ; they
were driven out by ' Smyrnaeans ' from Ionic Ephesus : they were expelled
by Aeolians, but returned with help from Ionic Colophon, and ' regained their
own land '.   The story illustrates first the tendency of Ionia to outstrip and
thrust aside Aeolis ; and secondly, the existence of a certain feeling of shame
in thus expelling a city of brother Greeks.   To drive out Leleges was o
course fair hunting.   Cf. Wilamowitz, *Panionion*, in *Sitzungsber. Berlin.
Akad.* 1906, iii.

s the spoken language changed. As more and more Greek
ties, and those the richer and larger ones, began to drop the
etter Vau and to pronounce Eta instead of long Alpha, the
ards who recited Homer in those cities naturally changed their
ronunciation too. Such a change would be as unconscious as
ie modern English change in the pronunciation of *tea* or *room*.
But there was another and a decisive motive of change. We
ave seen already that, though a short lay may be recited round
 camp fire or a banquet board, a poem at all approaching the
ength of the *Iliad* or *Odyssey* can only be recited on some great
ublic occasion, lasting over several days, and consequently can
nly have been created with that sort of occasion in view. Now
hough our information is imperfect, it seems certain that the
reatest gatherings in the Aegean were Ionian. Bards who
vished to compete at the *Panêgureis* at Delos, at Panionion,
t Ephesus, must almost of necessity recite in Ionic Greek, and
hange their method of pronunciation as the spoken pronuncia-
ion changed. We know that there was a Chorus of Maidens at
Delos which could sing or speak in whatever Greek dialect was
equired of them : each bard or composer 'would say it was
imself speaking' (*Hymn. Apoll.* 163). But it is the audience,
ot the performer, that eventually determines matters of dialect
nd accent. The performer must adapt himself and the audience
eed not. The Olympian Muses, if their ambition insisted upon
 great poem and a great audience, must perforce abandon their
ative accent. And later, when the centre of culture passed on
rom Ionia to Athens, they had to repeat the process.

    Aeolis was left in a backwater. And when it emerged, it
spoke in tones as different from those of its old Homer as can
vell be conceived. Poetry in Lesbos became Traditional Poetry
10 more. We must leave it aside and return to the development
of Homer in Ionia.

X

THE ILIAD AS A GREAT POEM

THE HOMERIC SPIRIT AND THE GREATNESS
OF THE ILIAD

WE still stand under the spell of the *Iliad*. Amid the deepest
strands that are woven in the thread of our Western civilization
there is more than one which is drawn originally from Greece and
Greek literature. And at the fountain-head of Greek literature
there stands, naturally enough, the dateless traditional book, not
indeed sacred as in other lands, but still unapproachable, and
far removed from the possibilities of human competition. This
was the position of the *Iliad* in Alexandrian Greece. Rome
took over the conception, and it has passed on, for the most part
to be part of the intellectual heritage of the Western world.

Criticism has, of course, in some respects, shattered the
Alexandrian view to pieces. Instead of the primaeval and all-wise
poet, Homer, we are left with a kind of saga-figure, similar
to that of Achilles or Agamemnon, or the mighty flashing-
helmeted Son of a Shield-Belt. The name Homêros may conceivably be a name once borne by a living person. But if so, we
know nothing of him, except indeed that he did not, in any
complete sense, write the *Iliad* and *Odyssey*. It seems on the
whole safest to regard Homêros as the name of an imaginary
ancestor worshipped by the schools of bards called Ὁμηρίδαι or
Ὁμήρου παῖδες, a name parallel to Ion, or Doros, or Hellen, or
even Amphictyon.[1] The exact form of theory which we accept

---

[1] This line of thought has been brilliantly and to my mind conclusively
developed by Prof. J. A. K. Thomson in Chapter x of his *Studies in the
Odyssey*. The *Aoidos*, or Bard, and afterwards the *Poiêtês*, is evolved from
the *Exarchon* or Leader of the magico-religious dance. Homeros is especially the ideal *Aoidos* or *Exarchon* of the Delian Maidens, as Apollo is of the
Muses. They sang (Hes. *Theog.* 39) φωνῇ ὁμηρεῦσαι; Homeros is a ritual
name, generated from this ' homereia ' and the ' Homeridae ' or ' Homeristae '.

s of little moment. There is a broad general agreement between most of the followers and correctors of Wolf and Lachmann. I wish in the present lecture to advance no theory of my own, but merely to consider what effect this scientific analysis has, or should have, upon our general enjoyment and understanding of the *Iliad* as a great poem.

Mr. Mackail, in his *Life of William Morris*, remarks in passing that in the *Iliad* we have a second-rate subject made into a first-rate and indeed incomparable poem by the genius of a great poet. I think this view would probably be widely accepted. Many scholars would agree, with a pang, that the subject of the Wrath was not quite in the first rank of nobleness. The Wrath against Hector after Patroclus' death may be a great subject. But the Wrath with Agamemnon about a personal slight is not. The fact that in the loss of Briseïs it is almost entirely the personal slight, not the loss of a beloved being, that matters to Achilles, puts all the emotion several degrees lower. So much many scholars would admit, and then console themselves by asserting the splendid perfection of the poem and the genius of the incomparable poet.

Now over this incomparable poet there is much high feeling and, in my opinion, some confusion of thought. He certainly did not write the whole *Iliad*: so much I may take as generally admitted. (Though if even that were denied, one might ask what is meant by 'the whole *Iliad*'. Is it the Oxford text? Or is it the text of our earliest papyri, probably some thousands of lines longer? Or is it the text of Zenodotus or Aristarchus, some thousands of lines shorter?) What then exactly did he write that is so vastly better than the work of his collaborators and followers?

The Alexandrians proceeded by the method of 'obelizing' certain lines, passages, or whole books. These were 'spurious': all the rest was the work of the one Homer. Is this a satisfactory method?

No one would now analyse the Pentateuch by cutting out as 'spurious' the parts that cannot have been written by Moses, and leaving Moses author of all the rest. No one would cut out all the psalms that cannot have been written by David, and leave

David author of all the rest. One cannot even apply such a method to Isaiah, where it would be much more legitimate Isaiah is a definite historical figure. We know when and where he lived. We know his circumstances and his policy. We have some criterion for telling what he wrote. Yet even in his case this method has completely broken down. The processes through which the Book of Isaiah has passed are far too complex for a mere division into 'genuine' and spurious'.[1] Yet this method at its crudest is still apt to be applied to the *Iliad*.

As soon as one has grasped the idea of a Traditional Book, it is clear beforehand that mere 'obelizing' will lead to no good result. It means stripping off one by one the contributions of all the poets who have worked at the *Iliad*. It is like the old attempts at restoring the original language of the original kernel, only far, far more desperate. And in practice, too, it refuses to work. For as you analyse the poem back towards its source, it proves not to have one source but many. The Catalogue and the Doloneia are almost universally recognized as coming into the *Iliad* from elsewhere; the *Embassy*, the book of all others which is most quoted in antiquity and seems most to have impressed the imagination of Greece, is also one of the parts most markedly foreign to its present framework. I will not multiply instances. Very little reflection is needed to convince us that a mere process of stripping off the 'non-original' will not automatically leave us with the pure work of the incomparable poet. If we want to discover him we must search for him.

And how shall we search? What criteria have we? In the case of Isaiah we have that prophet's date, his residence, his recorded political activity. What have we for Homer? The tradition supplies us with plenty of competing birthplaces, with a date which fluctuates between the twelfth century and the sixth, and half a dozen confessedly mythical lives. It is hard to make much use of these. If we try to discover criteria of our own, well, Fick considers that Homer was an Aeolian, and only those parts which will turn back into Aeolic are his genuine work. Some old English scholars thought he lived in Thessaly, and got a criterion out of that. Neither criterion has been successful, for

[1] See, for instance, Prof. Kennett's *Composition of the Book of Isaiah* (British Academy), 1910; or Box's *Isaiah* (1908).

reasons which we need not go into here. One reason was that they chose as their field of operation the supposed first origin of the poems, where our knowledge is almost nil. Obviously that is not a sound method. Beginning at the later end, where there is more hope of a safe result, Wilamowitz has forcibly suggested that one definite individual can be discovered in Θ. He wrote Θ, the *Broken Battle*, in order to make room in the *Iliad* for the *Embassy* and the *Doloneia*, I and K. If we accept that result, we have at any rate one poet whom we can isolate. Bethe, again, has come near to persuading us that the man who wrote the Converse (Z) also wrote the Ransoming (Ω), and did a great deal towards the general shaping and arranging of the *Iliad*. Such a view would perhaps come near to satisfying Miss Stawell; and such a poet, if one felt sure about him, might almost deserve the name of 'Homer'. Yet not quite. He would be a magnificent poet: of that there is no question. But would he be incomparably better than various others? Than the author of the *Embassy*, for instance? Or can we confidently say that the man who put the Bellerophon passages—or the Sarpedon passages, or the Shield-making—into our *Iliad* was incomparably better than the unknown persons who seem to have originally written them for different contexts? Can we say that the *Iliad* owes incomparably more to him than to them? I confess that in the present state of our knowledge all such confident language about the Poet seems to me unwarranted. We have got the Poem, and we can puzzle out a good deal about its probable manner of formation. We have not discovered any one historical poet. He is at best only a hypothesis. There may of course have been a man called Homeros, as there doubtless was a man called David. But we know nothing about him, not his date nor his birthplace nor what he wrote. And the Homer of our imaginations is not he, but a projection of our own feelings, a result of our habit of always thinking in terms of persons, a mythical Maker to account for the thing made. What we really know is not a man but a poem; let us focus our thoughts upon that and try to understand its greatness. I believe we shall find among the causes of that greatness something nobler and more august than the genius of any individual man.[1]

[1] Compare the case of the *Heracleia*. There were evidently many versions

I wish first to consider patiently this difficulty. It is, I suppose
quite clear that the *Iliad* is a good poem. Most people have
only to read it to feel quite sure of the fact : and if any particular
reader does not feel sure by his own instinct, there is enough
authority on the subject to convince any but the most self-
confident that his doubts are ill-grounded. Now why is it that
the *Iliad* is a good poem when it has so many of the characteristics of a bad one ?

In the first place, as we noticed above, the subject is second
rate. The horrid phrase which describes Achilles as ' sulking in
his tent' is not very far from the truth. And sulking is not
a noble, nor yet a poetical, state of mind. Achilles, again, is not
a very sympathetic hero. His eloquence is amazing, and we are
ready to believe in his dauntless courage and prowess and swift-
ness of foot. But, if it were not for his mere misery and repentance at the end of the poem, I think that most readers would
actually dislike him for his crude pride and self-absorption, his
cruelty and lack of love. Even his love for Patroclus never
impresses one as having unselfishness about it : it is not like the
love of Orestes and Pylades.

Again, there is a test which most people apply instinctively to
a modern work of fiction, and which is most powerful in separating the good from the bad. I mean the amount of finish and
conscientiousness in the more hidden parts. What we call
' showy ' or ' flashy ' work is generally work in which the

of that epic, and their ' Homer' is sometimes referred to as ' he who made '
sometimes as ' they who made' the *Heracleia*. (Eratosthenes ap. Strabo
p. 688 οἱ τὴν Ἡρακλείαν ποιήσαντες. It means, I suppose, ' the various people
who put the Heracles-saga into verse'. Cf. Schol. V on π 57 οἱ τῶν Κυπρίων
ποιηταί.) But the interesting thing is that among them we know of three
distinct individuals : Pisander of Rhodes, Peisinoös of Rhodes, and Panyassis
of Halicarnassus. There were doubtless others as well. Now Paul
Friedlaender (*Philologische Untersuchungen*, vol. xix) has made a brilliant
study of the *Heracleia* problem. By analysis of the myth and the local data
he succeeds in tracing several stages in the development of the Heracles-
saga : an epic poem, the *Dodecathlos*, made not in Argos nor yet in Boeotia
but in Rhodes, with the Rhodian goddess Alektrona-Electryone as the hero's
mother; an expanded Rhodian form; and a later Samian and Coan
reshaping. These three stages correspond fairly well with the three authors,
two Rhodian and one from Halicarnassus; and if the *Heracleia* were extant
we could probably separate and appraise their respective contributions. We
have no such data for the *Iliad* and *Odyssey*. A good attempt at finding
personal qualities in the poems in Cauer, *Grundfr.*[3], pp. 548 ff. Also, though
with too much dogma, in Rothe, on Repetitions and Contradictions.

momentary effect of particular scenes is strong, but which will not bear looking into. If you look close you find weaknesses, inconsistencies, contradictions. Now, notoriously, this is the case with the *Iliad*. The wall round the Greek camp alone, though the writing about it is always good and stirring, will provide half a dozen glaring instances of this sort of inner flaw. It is built at the end of *H* in the tenth year of the war. Yet a phrase in the description of the camp later (Ξ 31) implies that it was built—as it naturally would be—in the first. In *M* 10–33 it remains ' steadfast' (ἔμπεδον) till the end of the war and is then destroyed by floods; but in *O* 361, before the death of Patroclus, it is swept away by Apollo like a child's castle of sand on the sea-shore. Its towers had been broken in *M* 399. In *M* and *N* the wall is sometimes present and sometimes absent. Also two separate heroes, Hector and Sarpedon, are mentioned in different places, and in exactly the same words, as being the first to get over it (*M* 438, Π 558). There is a fearful fight when the Trojans are attacking the wall to get to the ships: when they retreat in panic there is generally no wall there. All this is explained in detail in Dr. Leaf's commentary.[1] It is pretty clear that there were two versions of the fighting extant, one in which the camp was unfortified, and one in which it was provided with a wall and moat. And brilliant episodes are borrowed from one or the other as the minstrels pleased.

Again, there is the cardinal instance of the contradiction between Books Π and I. In Book Π, Achilles, as he sees the routed Greeks, breaks into a splendid complaint that if only Agamemnon would seek his friendship and offer him amends the Trojans would soon fly and ' choke the trenches with their dead '. He sends Patroclus forth to help the Greeks, but warns him not to go too far in pursuit, lest Agamemnon should feel too secure and should fail to offer atonement.

Obviously, then, Agamemnon has not offered atonement. Yet there is a book before this which is occupied from first to last entirely with Agamemnon's offers of princely atonement! One sees what has happened. Both passages lay before some com-

---

[1] The late Professor Earle—anticipated, I find, by Hermann—shows reason to suspect that Thucydides used an *Iliad* which did not contain the account of the Wall-building in H. Earle, *Collected Essays*, pp. 142 ff. See Chapter XII, p. 295 n.

piler of the *Iliad*. They were not consistent, but each was too
good to lose. He put both in, sacrificing, like a bad artist, the
whole to the part.

Thirdly, there is the same sort of fault running through many
of the descriptions. Even the battle scenes, vivid as they are
will sometimes not bear thinking out. As we saw in the case o
the breastplate, the poet has not fully thought out the words he
was using. It sounds well. It is exciting. But it is not real
It is like a battle composed by some romantic poet, who furnishes
his warriors with gleaming morions and resounding culverins
but is not quite sure what things they are.

Apply the same test even to the language, the miraculous
heaven-sent language which has been the wonder and the awe
of all poets afterwards. Is it not full of such 'morions' an
'culverins'? Do you not find upon every page fair-sounding
words, whose meaning seems to have been far from clear to the
poets themselves who used them? Of course it is rare to find
a definite substantive of which the meaning is quite unknown
though even such occur: for instance, in the case of epithets
of the gods. Ἑρμείας ἀκάκητα, διάκτορος ἀργεϊφόντης, not one
of the epithets is understood. There are also a few words which
are used in two senses, of which we can fairly say that one
is a mistake.[1] But it is more often the form of the word or
sentence that shows a lack of understanding. There are crowds
of words which, as they stand, are no words but only mistakes
old forms first miswritten and then wrongly recorrected so as
to fill up the metre. There are words first wrongly divided
like νήδυμος, and then wrongly explained.

---

[1] For example, δουπῆσαι means 'to make a noise' (= ψοφῆσαι say the
Lexica), but owing to the phrase δούπησεν δὲ πεσών, 'he crashed as he fell'
the old Glossographi, who explained the hard words in Homer in pre-
Alexandrian times, interpreted it as simply 'to die'. Aristarchus has to
correct them (οἱ γλωσσογράφοι τὸ δουπῆσαι ἐν ἀνθ᾽ ἑνὸς ἀντὶ τοῦ ἀποθανεῖν)
But the writer of Ψ 679 uses the phrase δεδουπότος Οἰδιπόδαο for 'when the
son of Oedipus (?) was slain', τεθνηκότος. That is, he misunderstood the old
usage, just as the Glossographi did. (See Lehrs, *Aristarchus*, p. 103 f.; o
course there are ways of escape suggested by the grammarians.) Again, the
word στεῦται, στεῦτο, looks as if it meant 'stands, stood', but really mean
'intended', or perhaps 'boasted'. So Aristarchus (Lehrs, p. 98 f.). But in
λ 584 it is used as 'stood', στεῦτο δὲ διψάων, πιέειν δ᾽ οὐκ εἶχεν ἑλέσθαι. And
Aristarchus can only condemn the lines: ἵστατο νῦν ἐπὶ ποδῶν· κέχρηται δὲ τῃ
λέξει ὁ διασκευαστὴς παρὰ τὴν τοῦ ποιητοῦ συνήθειαν is Aristonicus's note
These are not isolated phenomena.

Now, of course, a great deal of this is mere ' surface corruption'.   Many mistakes are only due to the latest rhapsodes, who
recited the Ionic poem in Attica, and thus inevitably introduced
Attic elements into the language, and even misunderstood the
older Ionic forms.   You can largely remove the Atticisms and
obvious errors.   Editors like Van Leeuwen and Platt and Rzach
have corrected them by the hundred, with most useful and
instructive results.   But the process of correction is never complete.   Clear away the Attic surface and there rises beneath
another surface with another set of corruptions, where Ionic
rhapsodes have introduced just the same elements of confusion
into an Aeolic, or at least a pre-Ionic, language.   The confusion
of tongues is deep down in the heart of the Homeric dialect, and
no surgery in the world can cut beneath it.

Of course one must not judge a poet as one would a grammarian.   Yet this confusion of tongues has a certain weight as
evidence.   It seems to be part of a general vagueness of treatment, a lack of precision and of grip.

We often find, too, that descriptive phrases are not used so as
accurately to fit the thing described.   They are caught up ready-
made from a store of such things : perpetual epithets, front
halves of lines, back halves of lines, whole lines, if need be, and
long formulae.   The stores of the poets were full and brimming.
A bard need only put in his hand and choose out a well-
sounding phrase.   Even the similes are ready-made.   There
must have been originally some poet who saw the spring of some
warrior in battle, and was struck by its likeness to the leap of
a lion.   But that was long before our *Iliad*.   The poets of our
Iliad scarcely need to have seen a lion.   They have their stores
of traditional similes taken from almost every moment in a lion's
life : when he is hungry, when he is full, when he attacks the
fold, when he retires from the fold, when he is wounded, when he
is triumphant, when he is scared with torches, when he walks
ravening in the wind and rain.   Every simile is fine, vivid, and
lifelike ; but a good many of them are not apposite to the case
for which they are used, and all have the same ready-made air.

Consider in detail this fine simile (*M* 41) :

As in the midst of hounds and men that are hunters,
a boar or a lion wheels, glaring in his strength ; and they

set them like a wall (πυργηδόν) and stand against him, and the spears fly fast from their hands ; yet his proud heart trembles not nor flees, till his daring is his death, but swiftly he turns and turns, making trial of the lines of men ; and wheresoever he charges, the lines of men give way.

The description of the boar or lion is splendid : but what situation does it seem to describe ? A hero left alone, hard pressed by enemies but refusing to retreat ? That is what one thinks of. That is probably the situation for which it was originally written. But, as the passage stands, the Greeks are flying and Hector pursuing them back beyond their wall. The passage continues : 'Even so Hector, going up and down the throng, besought his comrades, urging them to cross the trench.' Hector, urging on his conquering comrades, is really not particularly like this surrounded and baffled lion, ' whose daring is his death '.

Now at a point of the action immediately before this—there is a digression between—in Λ 551, there is a hero very like indeed to this boar or lion, to wit, Aias, who has been up to the last moment standing alone against the advance of the Trojans and protecting the Greek retreat. At the end Zeus sent into him also a spirit of flight.

> He moved backward, searching with his eyes as a wild beast searches, back toward the throng of his comrades, half turning again and again, slowly changing knee for knee. Even as a red lion draws back from a yard of oxen, frighted by hounds and husbandmen keeping vigil all night long, who suffer him not to take out the fat of the oxen ; and hungering for flesh, he charges but wins nothing ; so fast fly spears from brave hands to meet him, and flaming torches, which he shrinks from for all his fury ; and at dawn he goes away alone with misery in his heart : so then did Aias go back from the Trojans, unwilling and with misery in his heart. For he feared for the ships of the Achaeans.

There follows instantly another simile, slightly strange perhaps to our conventional taste, but very vivid and good :

> Even as an ass going beside a field overpowers the boys who drive him, a dull ass about whose back many a staff is broken ; and he enters the standing corn and ravages it, and the boys smite him with sticks, but their strength is feeble, and scarcely do they drive him out when he has had

his fill of the corn. So then about Aias the tall, son of Telamon, high-hearted Trojans and allies famed afar followed thrusting, &c., &c.

Now think of our first simile, the lion or boar surrounded and confronted by a wall of men and hounds, but refusing to retire. Does it not seem to belong here rather than to its present context? Did it not perhaps describe the state of Aias just a moment earlier, while he still stood alone and Zeus had not yet sent into him that ‘fear for the Achaean ships’? I think, agreeing with Leaf and others, that this must have been the original place for which the simile was written. The rhapsode who was composing our eleventh and twelfth book found in various MSS., that came somehow into his hands, no less than three different similes applied to Aias covering the Greek retreat. He put two of them straight in together, the midnight lion and the ass in the corn. The other was far too good to lose, so he kept it by him to use at the first opportunity. Early in the next book came the mention of a wall, which checks for a time the rush of the Trojans; it so happens that the hounds and hunters of the simile were said to be like a wall. That place will do. The incongruity will be decently masked. So he puts it in there; and at present the triumphant advance of Hector is compared to the stubbornness of a baffled boar or lion refusing to retreat.

Does this explanation fail to carry conviction? Demonstration is, of course, impossible in these questions of criticism. But take another case in the same book. When the Trojans (*M* 131 ff.) are charging at the gate of the Greek wall, they find there *standing in front* of the gate *two heroes* of the race of the Lapithae, Polypoites and Leonteus.

> They two in front of the high gate were standing like high-crested oaks on a mountain, which abide the wind and the rain through all days, firm in their long roots that reach deep into the earth.

A moment after we are told of these same two men :—

> Out then they charged and fought in front of the gates, like wild boars on a mountain, who abide the oncoming throng of men and hounds, and charging side-long break the underwood about them, tearing it root-wise up, and through all else comes the noise of gnashing tusks.... So

came through all else the noise of the bright bronze upon their bodies, smitten with shafts in front.

People who stand firm in front of a gate, like oaks, are not very like wild boars that rush out and tear up the undergrowth, making a noise with their tusks. This may sound captious : but the difficulty is quite real, and was felt in ancient times. Different solutions are offered, for instance, by Porphyry and Hephaestion. Did not the last compiler of *M* find in two different books two different accounts of this fight at the gate ? In one the two Lapithae alone stood like oaks. In another a mass of Greeks charged out, led very possibly, but not certainly, by the two Lapithae. Both similes were too good to lose. He followed the story of the oaks, yet he was reluctant to lose the wild boars. So observe his mode of procedure. He puts in the wild boars, and then, at the end, soothes the imagination of any hearer who is puzzled at the lack of resemblance, by explaining that the point of similarity lies in the noise. The contradiction is masked. Boars' tusks make a noise, and so do shields struck with spears ! [1]

Another simile, fifteen lines later, makes of this hypothesis almost what in this atmosphere of conjectures may be called a certainty. Asius, who is leading the Trojan attack, cries out that 'these men are like a swarm of bees or wasps who have built their nests beside a rocky path, and pour out to fight with hunters to protect their young'. That comparison can scarcely have been invented to describe two solitary heroes standing in front of a gate. It may well have described a great mass of Greeks pouring out through the gate. But that was part of the rejected story. It belonged to the same version as the rushing wild boars.[2]

---

[1] An idiom by which 'a mere detail in the original scheme of the simile is made the base of a fresh simile' (Leaf) has many parallels in Homer, but hardly in such an extreme degree as this. The passage O 618 ff. is very similar, and probably has a similar history. Hector's onset is compared (1) to waves falling on a rock, which stands immovable ; (2) to a wave crashing down upon a ship, which is badly shaken ; then comes v. 629, 'even so was the spirit of the Achaeans shaken within their breasts.' I suspect that these two similes come from separate sources ; the minstrel felt them to be not quite consistent, so he added v. 629. It is worth remarking that the five lines just preceding are inconsistent with their present context, and were condemned by Zenodotus and Aristarchus.

[2] Bréal, l. c., p. 115, traces the double names in the languages of gods and

These are mere illustrations. The force of the argument, of course, depends upon the number of such cases.

The conclusion is hard to resist, and it is one that seems to detract enormously from the high value of the poems as original poetry. Even the similes, the very breath of life of the poetry of Homer, are in many cases, indeed usually, adopted ready-made. Their vividness, their closeness of observation, their air of freshness and spontaneity, are all deceptive. Nearly all of them are taken over from older books, and many of them were originally written to describe some quite different occasion.

All these qualities, which we have arrayed in a catalogue, have one common characteristic, and that one which is generally considered fatal to any art which claims to be what we call 'original' or 'individual', a thing created by a particular man. I do not say that Homer has no other flaws. But as to these already mentioned, I venture to think that we only find them vicious because we are judging by wrong standards. We are applying to a traditional poem, the creation of whole generations of men, poets and hearers, working through many ages, canons which only apply to the works to which we are accustomed in modern literature, original poems, made at a definite date by a definite self-conscious author.

The subject is a difficult one, and I am not sure that I see clearly through it. But I will try to give the result of my thoughts.

First of all, I think that we are apt to confuse originality with a much less important thing, novelty. A story about motor-cars or wireless telegraphy possesses, or once possessed, novelty ; but whether it ever possessed originality depended entirely on qualities in the author's mind.

Of course, there was originality in conceiving the notion of bringing the motor-car or the wireless telegraph into the realm of art. A very small modicum of originality, but still some. And I would not say that such originality was contemptible, because one of the ways in which art advances is by the opening

of men to the same multiplicity of sources. One source said Βριάρεως, another Αἰγαίων (A 404). So also Mülder, *Quellen*, pp. 65, 139, 223.

up of new regions to its influence, or, in other words, by the discovery of beauty or interest in new places. Also, the man who conceives or executes a thing for the first time is no doubt apt to do so with a freshness and intensity which make his work not only novel but original. But the difference between the two qualities is clear. Mere novelty is a thing external and accidental. It depends upon dates. It wears off. For instance, the *Hippolytus* seems to have been the first love tragedy in European literature. In that sense it was novel, but its novelty has worn off during these last two thousand three hundred years. Yet its originality is living still and felt vividly.

Origo means a spring, a rising of water. And, though it is generally a mere waste of ingenuity to tie the sense of a word down to its supposed derivation, I suspect that the most fruitful way of understanding the word 'originality' may be to remember this meaning. We do call a work of art original when it produces the impression of a living source, so that one says: 'Here is beauty or wisdom *springing*; not drawn through long pipes nor collected in buckets.' This spring-like self-moving quality is a thing which does not depend on novelty, and therefore cannot grow stale. I remember examining in Florence a MS. of Euripides, which was very hard to read, blurred with age and sea-water and exposure to the sun. And as I pored over it, there gradually showed through the dusty blur the first words of a lyric in the *Alcestis*. It was as old as the hills, and I had long known it by heart. Yet the freshness of it glowed through that rather stale air like something young and living. I remember a feeling of flowers and of springing water.

This quality has not much to do with novelty. Probably it does imply that the poet has in some sense gone himself to the fountain-head, that his emotion is a real first-hand emotion, self-moving and possessed of a life of its own, not merely a derivative emotion responding to the emotion of another. Yet I doubt if even so much can be fairly demanded, that a poet, to be original, must himself go to the fountain-head. The words are ambiguous. It would be preposterous to demand that a writer shall experience personally all that he writes about. And it is very noteworthy how many great poets seem to have drawn most of their inspiration not directly from experience, but derivatively from experience already interpreted in other men's poetry. Think of Burns's songs. There is almost no poetry so original in the impression it makes. And yet we have detailed evidence that a great deal of Burns's most beautiful and spontaneous work is really a working up of old traditional material. He thought over the words and rhythm of an existing country song while his wife sang the air, and thus gradually he modified the existing verses and added others, till a song was produced, a song both new and old, derivative and yet highly original. I suspect that the mistake which we are apt to make is to apply a merely external test to something that depends on the most intimate workings of a man's imagination. The thing that is of importance in a poem, given the necessary technical power, is not mere novelty, nor yet personal knowledge or experience, but simply the intensity of imagination with which the poet has realized his subject. And that intensity may be the product of a thousand things; of which personal experience may, but need not, be one. Almost the first characteristic which one notes in what we call a 'man of genius' is his power of making a very little experience reach an enormous way. This sounds very different from Carlyle's definition of genius as an infinite capacity for taking pains. But in reality that capacity for taking pains is itself dependent on an intense and absorbing interest. So long as you are really interested, you cannot help taking pains. As the interest fades, you first begin to be conscious of the pains, and then cease to take any more.

In the same way, when we blame a work of Art as 'conventional' or 'laboured' or the like, we are often using language loosely. A laboured work is of course not a work on which the man has worked hard: it is a work in which the labour is more manifest than the result, or in which one is somehow conscious of labour. Pains have been taken, but some other factor of success is not there. A conventional work is not a work composed according to the rules of some convention or other. All art is that. It is a work in which other qualities are lacking, and the convention obtrudes itself.

Intensity of imagination is the important thing. It is intensity of imagination that makes a poet's work 'real', as we say;

spontaneous, infectious or convincing. Especially it is this that creates an atmosphere; that makes us feel, on opening the pages of a book, that we are in a different world, and a world full of real beings about whom, in one way or another, we care. And I suspect that ultimately the greatness of a poem or work of imaginative art depends mostly upon two questions: how strongly we feel ourselves transported to this new world, and what sort of a world it is when we get there, how great or interesting or beautiful.[1] Think of the first scene of *Hamlet*, the first page of the *Divina Commedia*, the first lines of the *Agamemnon*; how swiftly and into what wonderful regions they carry you! And if you apply this same test to the *Iliad* or *Odyssey*, the response is so amazing that you understand at once why these poems have so often and in such various ages been considered absolutely of all the greatest. Open the book anywhere (A 33). 'So spake he, and the old man trembled and obeyed his word; and he went in silence by the shore of the many-sounding sea, and prayed alone to the Lord Apollo, whom fair-haired Leto bare.' Turn the pages (Σ 573). 'And a herd he wrought thereon of straight-horned kine. The kine were wrought of gold and of tin, and lowing they wended forth from the byre to their pasture, by the side of a singing river, by a bed of slender reeds.' Turn again (X 356). 'I look upon thee and know thee as thou art. I could never have moved thee, for the heart is iron within thy breast. Therefore beware lest I be to thee a wrath of god, on that day when Paris and Phoebus Apollo shall slay thee in thy valour at the Scaean Gates.'[2]

---

[1] Of course, in proportion as art becomes more realistic the 'new world' in question becomes more and more closely the present world more vividly felt and understood.

[2]
Ὡς ἔφατ', ἔδεισεν δ' ὁ γέρων καὶ ἐπείθετο μύθῳ·
βῆ δ' ἀκέων παρὰ θῖνα πολυφλοίσβοιο θαλάσσης·
πολλὰ δ' ἔπειτ' ἀπάνευθε κιὼν ἠρᾶθ' ὁ γεραιὸς
Ἀπόλλωνι ἄνακτι, τὸν ἠΰκομος τέκε Λητώ. (A 33 ff.)

Ἐν δ' ἀγέλην ποίησε βοῶν ὀρθοκραιράων·
αἱ δὲ βόες χρυσοῖο τετεύχατο κασσιτέρου τε,
μυκηθμῷ δ' ἀπὸ κόπρου ἐπεσσεύοντο νομόνδε
πὰρ ποταμὸν κελάδοντα, παρὰ ῥοδανὸν δονακῆα. (Σ 573 ff.)

Ἦ σ' εὖ γιγνώσκων προτιόσσομαι, οὐδ' ἄρ' ἔμελλον
πείσειν· ἦ γὰρ σοί γε σιδήρεος ἐν φρεσὶ θυμός·
φράζεο νῦν, μή τοί τι θεῶν μήνιμα γένωμαι
ἤματι τῷ ὅτε κέν σε Πάρις καὶ Φοῖβος Ἀπόλλων
ἐσθλὸν ἐόντ' ὀλέσωσιν ἐνὶ Σκαιῇσι πύλῃσιν. (X 356 ff.)

How irresistibly do the chance words bear one away, and to
what a world! We can stand apart and argue and analyse, and
show that the real world portrayed in the poems was one full
of suffering and injustice, and that the poet was sometimes over-
lax in his moral judgements. Yet the world into which he
takes us is somehow more splendid than any created by other
men. Where were there ever battles or heroes like these, such
beauty, such manliness, such terror and pity and passion, and
such all-ruling majesty of calm? There are many strong men
and fair women in other stories; why is it that, almost before a
word is spoken, we feel in our bones the strength of these
Homeric heroes, the beauty of these grave and white-armed
women? You remember, in the Old Testament, the watchman
who stood upon the tower in Jezreel, when they saw men and
chariots approaching in the distance, and sent out one horseman
after another to inquire their purpose. 'And the watchman
answered and said: He came even unto them and cometh not
again. And the driving is like the driving of Jehu the son of
Nimshi; for he driveth furiously.' We knew nothing about the
driving of Jehu before. We hear no word more about it afterwards. But the one sentence has behind it just that intensity of
imagination which makes thoughts live and vibrate like new
things a hundred, or a thousand, or two thousand, years after
their first utterance. And that is the quality that one finds in
Homer.

Think how the beauty of Helen has lived through the ages.
Like the driving of Jehu, it is now an immortal thing. And the
main, though not of course the sole, source of the whole conception is certainly the *Iliad*. Yet in the whole *Iliad* there is
practically not a word spoken in description of Helen. As
Lessing has remarked in a well-known passage of the *Laokoon*,
almost the whole of our knowledge of Helen's beauty comes
from a few lines in the third book, where Helen goes up to the
wall of Troy to see the battle between Menelaus and Paris. 'So
speaking, the goddess put into her heart a longing for her
husband of yore and her city and her father and mother. And
straightway she veiled herself with white linen, and went forth
from her chamber shedding a great tear. . . .' The elders of
Troy were seated on the wall, and when they saw Helen coming,

' softly they spake to one another winged words : " Small wonder
that the Trojans and mailed Greeks should endure pain through
many years for such a woman. *Strangely like she is in face to
some immortal spirit.*" [1] That is all we know. Not one of all
the Homeric bards fell into the yawning trap of describing Helen,
and making a catalogue of her features. She was veiled ; she
was weeping ; and she was strangely like in face to some
immortal spirit. And the old men, who strove for peace, could
feel no anger at the war.

Now this intensity of imagination can be attained by many
writers at their most exalted moments. Their imagination can
follow the call of their emotions. But one of the extraordinary
things in the *Iliad* is the prevalence of this intensity all through
the ordinary things of life. ' As riseth the screaming of cranes
in front of the sunrise, cranes that have fled from winter and
measureless rain, screaming they fly over the streams of
ocean, bearing unto the dwarf-men battle and death.' [2] Who
that can once read Homer freely, untroubled by difficulties of
language, can ever forget the cranes ? And not only the cranes,
but the swarming bees, the flies about the milk-pails, the wolves
and boars and lions and swift dogs, and the crook-horned swing-
footed kine ? It is a fairly wide world that the poets lay open to
us, and every remotest corner of it is interesting and vivid,
every commonest experience in it, the washing of hands, the
eating of food, the acts of sleeping and waking, shares somehow in the beauty and even in the grandeur of the whole.
Mr. Mackail [3] has observed how full the poems are of images
drawn from fire : the bright armour flashes like fire, the armies

---

[1]
Ὣς εἰποῦσα θεὰ γλυκὺν ἵμερον ἔμβαλε θυμῷ
ἀνδρός τε προτέροιο καὶ ἄστεος ἠδὲ τοκήων·
αὐτίκα δ' ἀργεννῇσι καλυψαμένη ὀθόνῃσιν
ὡρμᾶτ' ἐκ θαλάμοιο τέρεν κατὰ δάκρυ χέουσα. (Γ 139 ff.)

Ἧκα πρὸς ἀλλήλους ἔπεα πτερόεντ' ἀγόρευον·
" Οὐ νέμεσις Τρῶας καὶ ἐϋκνήμιδας Ἀχαιοὺς
τοιῇδ' ἀμφὶ γυναικὶ πολὺν χρόνον ἄλγεα πάσχειν·
αἰνῶς ἀθανάτῃσι θεῇς εἰς ὦπα ἔοικεν." (Γ 155 ff.)

[2]
Ἠΰτε περ κλαγγὴ γεράνων πέλει οὐρανόθι πρό,
αἵ τ' ἐπεὶ οὖν χειμῶνα φύγον καὶ ἀθέσφατον ὄμβρον,
κλαγγῇ ταί γε πέτονται ἐπ' Ὠκεανοῖο ῥοάων,
ἀνδράσι Πυγμαίοισι φόνον καὶ κῆρα φέρουσαι. (Γ 3 ff.)

[3] In one of his lectures as Professor of Poetry at Oxford.

clash, 'even as destroying fire that falls upon a limitless forest ';
a hero's 'hands are like unto fire and his wrath unto red iron ';
and the men 'fight together, a body of burning fire '.   The whole
poem is shot through with this fire, which seems like a symbol
of the inward force of which we have been speaking, a fiery
intensity of imagination.   Given this force within, and the
Homeric language as an instrument for its expression, a language
more gorgeous than Milton's, yet as simple and direct as that of
Burns, there is no further need to be surprised at the extraordinary greatness of the *Iliad*.

But now comes a curious observation.   We who are accustomed to modern literature always associate this sort of imaginative intensity with something personal.   We connect it with an
artist's individuality, or with originality in the sense of ' newness '.
It seems as though, under modern conditions, an artist usually
did not feel or imagine intensely unless he was producing some
work which was definitely his own and not another's, work
which must bear his personal name and be marked by his personal
experience or character.   One element at least in the widespread
admiration of such authors as Browning, Meredith, and Walt
Whitman, has been, I think, a feeling that their work must somehow be particularly real and spontaneous, because they have
insisted on doing it in a way in which, according to most well-
constituted judges, it ought not to be done.   And conversely,
poets like Tennyson or Swinburne have been in certain circles
despised as a little tame, conventional, uninspired, because they
seemed to be too obedient to the ideals which poetry had
followed before them.   I do not specially wish to attack this
modern prejudice, if it is one.   I largely share in it : and its
excesses will very likely disappear.   But I do very greatly wish
to point out that artistic feeling in this matter has not always been
the same.   Artists have not always wished to stamp their work
with their personal characteristics or even their personal name.
Artists have sometimes been, as it were, Protestant or Iconoclast,
unable to worship without asserting themselves against the
established ritual of their religion : sometimes, in happier circumstances, they have accepted and loved the ritual as part of the
religion, and wrought out their own new works of poetry, not as

protests, not as personal outbursts, but as glad and nameless offerings, made in prescribed form to enhance the glory of the spirit whom they served. With some modifications, this seems to have been the case in Greece, in Canaan, in Scandinavia, during the periods when great traditional books were slowly growing up. Each successive poet did not assert himself against the tradition, but gave himself up to the tradition, and added to its greatness and beauty all that was in him.

The intensity of imagination which makes the *Iliad* alive is not, it seems to me, the imagination of any one man. It means not that one man of genius created a wonder and passed away. It means that generation after generation of poets, trained in the same schools and a more or less continuous and similar life, steeped themselves to the lips in the spirit of this great poetry. They lived in the Epic saga and by it and for it. Great as it was, for many centuries they continued to build it up yet greater.

What helped them most, perhaps, was the constancy with which the whole race—to use a slightly inaccurate word—must have loved and cherished this poetry. Amid the chaos that followed μετὰ τὰ Τρωικά, when the works of art, the architecture, the laws of ordered society, the very religions of the different centres, were all lost, for the most part never to return, the germs of this poetry were saved. The fugitives left their treasures, their gods, and their wives behind, but the sagas were in their hearts and grew the richer for all their wanderings. They carried their poetry as other nations have carried their religion. How strange and significant a thing, after all, is that which we speak of as either 'the Epic style' or 'the Epic language'. It seems more than a style, though, as we have seen, it cannot quite be treated as an organic spoken language.

For many hundreds of years this wonderful mode of speech was kept alive to serve nothing but the needs of poetry. The ordinary audiences must have understood it as well as, for instance, our audiences understand the authorized version of the Bible, though the differences between Jacobean and Victorian English are utterly trifling compared with those between Homer and the prose speech of classical Ionic inscriptions. And how wonderfully the poets themselves knew it! Even under the microscope of modern philology the Epic dialect appears, in the main, as a

ort of organic whole, not a mere mass of incongruous archaistic
orms.   Van Leeuwen and Monro can write consistent grammars
f it.   And this language has been preserved and reconstructed
yy generations of men who never spoke it except when they
ecited poetry.   It was understood by audiences who never
eard it spoken except when they listened to poetry.   And not
. man among them had any knowledge of the laws of language;
hey had only a sense of style.

But to meet the special difficulties raised above, let us consider
specially the later generations of these bards and the task
hat lay before them.   They were poets, 'makers' as well as
singers'; but, much more than that, they were *Homêridae*, or
Tomêrou Paides, the sons and servants of the greatest of the
ooets.   None of them dreamed of vying with Homer; only of
xalting and preserving him.   Other people no doubt might
vish for a new style of poetry, for lyrics, for elegies, for iambic
.nd personal verse.   The old Epic language was becoming less
cnown and more remote.   The meanings of some of the words
vere taught in schools, others had been forgotten.   And the
ast bards had before them various books, not very many, it
eems, telling the great legends.

I am not looking for the work of any particular compiler or
iarmonizer; I am merely trying to understand the spirit in
vhich any one of these later poets—how great or how small a
ooet matters little—seems to have set about his task.   He could
iave written an epic poem himself, of course: but who wanted
iim to write one?   How should he dare to?   The world was
iot yet reduced to such straits as that.   There was plenty of the
ild poetry still in his power.   He knew it by heart, and he
oossessed scrolls of it, poetry of men far greater and wiser than
ie, voices of those who had talked with gods.   Diligently and
everently he wove it together.   He had before him—let us
magine—a Wrath in which Agamemnon offered no atonement,
.nd he found besides a lay telling of the Embassy to Achilles;
or he had before him some battles around an unwalled Greek
:amp and found another version with the storming of a wall; or
oerhaps he merely found fragments of other epics too good to
ose and not too firmly rooted in their context to transfer.
)iligently and reverently, with a good deal of simple cunning,

he arranged his scheme so as to make room for all. He put inconsistent passages far apart; he altered a few words to mask awkwardnesses and get rid of stark contradictions. He added lines, when he needs must, to connect or to explain; always unobtrusive lines, making no dissonance, borrowed word by word, phrase by phrase, from the old poems themselves. And amid all this gentle and lowly service, when he rehearsed his great recitation, when he went over the lines of some tremendous passage that shook all his being, then, it would seem from the evidence, there came into him the spirit of the ancient men, and a voice as of Homer himself. The lines that he spoke became his own. He had always belonged to them, and now they belonged to him also. And in the midst of them and beyond them he too had freedom to create.

And we critics, we mete to him a hard measure. When he creates, we call it interpolation. When he preserves with careful ingenuity all the fragments that he can save of his ancient Homer, we call attention to the small joints in his structure, the occasional incongruity of a simile which he loved too well to let die. If we knew his name, I suppose we should mock at him. But he has no name. He gave his name, as he gave all else that was in him, to help, unnoticed, in the building up of the greatest poem that ever sounded on the lips of men.

There is, outside and beneath the ordinary rules of art, a quality possessed by some great books or pictures and denied to others, a quality of attracting sympathy and causing the imagination of the reader or spectator to awake and co-operate with that of the artist. It is a quality that sometimes irritates a critic, because it acts fitfully and often depends upon accident. It puts the efforts of art at the mercy of prejudice. Yet, in a clear air, when prejudices can be laid aside and forgotten, this quality is seen to be, despite its occasional connexion with very third-rate things, itself a great thing, like the power of attracting or not attracting love. And in the last analysis, I suspect, one will find that this sympathy, like love in general, mostly goes to the man who both wants it and will duly pay for it. A poet who strikes his reader as perfect—of course none ever are so—who makes the impression of having entirely succeeded in saying what he meant to say, so that he requires no help from others, is apt to be treated with some respectful indifference. If he actually seems self-satisfied, then it is much worse. The reader becomes lynx-eyed for weaknesses, anxious to humiliate, like Ruskin, for instance, in his criticisms of Guido and the later Renaissance painters. And there are other poets or artists whose work has the power of appeal; the nameless charm and wistfulness of a thing not perfectly articulate, which means more than it can ever say, possesses more than it can ever impart, envisages more than it can ever define. It is the beauty of the ruin, suggesting the wonderful building that once was; of the unfinished statue, suggesting the splendour that should have been.

Of course this conception must not be used as an excuse for bad workmanship. It is in the essence of the contract, so to speak, that this appeal to the imagination of others only begins to act when the artist himself has taken all the pains he can. It is only the intensity of his imaginative effort which kindles ours into action. And that intensity will, under normal circumstances, have made him work his best. Only it so happens that the greatest imaginings and desires of the human mind are beyond the greatest powers of words or paintings to utter. And the best artist, when he has used the very utmost of his skill, is left at last dependent on the sympathetic imagination of others. If that fails him, he dies with his meaning unexpressed.

It is in this spirit of sympathetic imagination that we should read most ancient traditional books. And, as a matter of fact, we generally do so. They are all markedly imperfect, but we hardly notice the imperfections. How few of us, for instance, ever noticed that there were two different accounts of the Creation in Genesis before we were compelled? How few scholars were troubled by discrepancies between *Iliad* I and II? How little we resent the half-inarticulate quality of ancient vocabulary and syntax? Nay, we admire them. For the best things that these books are trying to express are not to be reached by any correct human words. With all the knowledge in the world at our disposal, we must needs sooner or later throw ourselves on the sea of imaginative emotion in order to understand or express these greatnesses. And the reason why we are willing to do so in these cases, and not in others, is, I think, ultimately the intensity of the imagination behind. The driving of Jehu, the weeping face of Helen : these have behind them not the imagination of one great poet, but the accumulated emotion, one may almost say, of the many successive generations who have heard and learned and themselves afresh re-created the old majesty and loveliness. They are like the watchwords of great causes for which men have fought and died; charged with power from the first to attract men's love, but now, through the infinite shining back of that love, grown to yet greater power. There is in them, as it were, the spiritual life-blood of a people.

IONIA AND ATTICA

THERE is a well-known list of the seven cities which claim to be the birthplace of Homer. There are always seven; but the names vary so that the actual claimants mentioned amount at least to ten. 'Smyrna, Chios, Colophon, Salamis, Ios, Argos, Athenae'; but instead of 'Ios' we find 'Rhodos' and 'Pylos', instead of 'Salamis' sometimes 'Ithake'. Now, without going into the rather transparent pretensions which have placed some of these cities on the list, we may notice two points. First, antiquity in general is quite agreed in regarding Homer as an Ionian, and it knew the poems only in the Ionian dialect. Secondly, the two cities which have, in the mere statement of the tradition, the strongest claim, are also the two of which we know that they were first Aeolic and only long after Homer's time Ionian: Smyrna and Chios.[1] In both of these Homer was worshipped as a local hero. Thirdly, the two chief Ionian cities, Miletus and Ephesus, are never mentioned in the list of birthplaces. That is to say, the chief Ionian birthplaces prove, on examination, to be not Ionian at all; and the tradition, even while it received and read its Homer in Ionian form, instinctively felt that the spirit of Ionian civilization at its ripest development was alien to the spirit of Homer.

The traditional birthplace of Homer floats from Ithaca to Colophon. His date varies from 1159, given by some authorities quoted in Philostratus, to 686, the year assigned by the historian

---

[1] The evidences for Chios are: Pind. *Nem.* ii. 1, and Schol. (Ὁμηρίδαι); the *Hymn to Apollo* τυφλὸς ἀνήρ, οἰκεῖ δὲ Χίῳ ἐνὶ παιπαλοέσσῃ; cf. Thuc. iii. 104; Simonides, ἐν δὲ τὸ κάλλιστον Χῖος ἔειπεν ἀνήρ, meaning Homer and quoting *Iliad*, Z 146; the anonymous *Life of Homer*. For Smyrna: a local sanctuary (Ὁμήρειον) and statue; Strabo, p. 646; Cic. *pro Arch.* 8; a native tradition which showed (and still shows to-day) the cave by the river Melês where Homer was born. See Proclus, *Vita Hom.*, and 'Plut.' *Vita Hom.*, Paus. vii. 5. 6, and cf. the name Μελησιγένης.

Theopompus.   But he is never born in either of the two greatest
Ionian cities at the time of their power.

The rise of the Ionian civilization is in many ways the most
wonderful phenomenon in Greek history.   Every kind of intellectual advance seems to have its origin in Ionia.   The greatest
works of colonization and commerce, the first banks, the first
maps, and the first effective Greek fleets come from there.   The
first prose[1] historian mentioned by tradition is ‘Cadmus of
Miletus’;   the first who has real substance and influence is
Hecataeus of Miletus.   The first Greek philosopher is Thales
of Miletus, the second and third are Anaximander and Anaxi-
menes of Miletus.   Consider for a moment the strangeness of this
figure of Thales.   Before the end of the seventh century, while
the Ionic portions of our *Iliad* are still taking shape, Ionia
seems to have been ringing with the fame of this new kind of
great man, not a king nor a warrior, nor even an adventurous
merchant prince, only a σοφὸς ἀνήρ, a wise man : a philosopher,
who has quietly rejected all the myths about gods and theogonies ;
an engineer, able to divert the river Halys from its course ;
a mathematician and an astronomer, able to predict the eclipse
which occurred on May 28, 585 B. C.   And this man is not
persecuted like Galileo or Priestley, not dependent on powerful protection, like Leibnitz or Descartes.   He is an acknowledged leader of his people, a man to consult in crises, when
other nations performed a human sacrifice or took the inarticu-
late and dangerous advice of a sacred snake.   A generation
or so later, about 540 B. C., just about the time when the *Iliad*
and *Odyssey* were taken over to Athens to be recited at the
great national festival, we meet another strange Ionian figure,
a Colophonian this time.   Xenophanes is a professional reciter
of his own poetry, whose zeal for the expurgation of ‘Homer’
has become so great that he traverses Greece denouncing the
falseness and immorality of the very poems from which his own
performances were originally drawn.   All the myths are false.
There is only one God, infinite, all intellect, without bodily parts.
Homer and Hesiod ‘tell lies, attributing to the gods all that
among men is a shame and a rebuke, thievings and adulteries,

[1] See Radermacher in *Philol. Wochenschrift*, 1907, No. 10.

and deceivings one of another'. And another philosopher, not otherwise sympathetic to Xenophanes, remarks in passing that 'Homer and Hesiod ought to be whipped'.

Now one must not suggest that the tone of these Philosophers represents the ordinary state of mind of the educated Ionian public. Thales and Xenophanes, and still more Heraclitus, were exceptional men. But the existence of an extreme view or a great advance of thought among a few people is nearly always good evidence for the prevalence of a more moderate view or a feebler advance among a much larger number. Before Xenophanes arose to denounce the moral atmosphere of the Epos altogether, there had probably been others improving that atmosphere from within. The spirit of expurgation, which we studied in the fifth lecture, had already begun its long work of removing the traces of primitive cruelty and brutishness from the heroes of Homer.[1] It could not make its work quite complete.

[1] The limits of date within which expurgation went on are hard to determine. Some bold Paleian might argue that all the expurgation is a late Attic process, on these lines: (1) We find it still going on in the time of Zenodotus (see p. 124 note); (2) Attic tragedy, being early, mostly follows the unexpurgated versions of the sagas; (3) The argument below, that Aeschylus *seems* more primitive than Homer, may be interpreted as simply showing that Aeschylus *was* so, and that the 'Alexandrian' treatment of the Gods in Homer really is Alexandrian—i. e. belongs in date to the fourth or third century, and that Zenodotus was right in considering the passages in which it occurs as spurious. To this we may answer: (1) Expurgation is a normal and constant process, always acting when the next teller or hearers of a story have any different standard of sensitiveness from the last. There is no reason it should stop until the text is fixed firm. We find as early as Xenophanes not only a spirit which must have produced expurgation, but a standard of ethical criticism so exceedingly high and severe that it can scarcely have been the first, or anything like the first, of its kind. I mean: before people got to complaining that Homer's gods were in human shape, they must in all probability have complained of more obviously objectionable things. (2) This is important, but easily answered. Attic tragedy is in a different convention. It takes its legendary material comparatively unexpurgated because its characters are (comparatively) unidealized. Achilles can torture Hector in the *Ajax* or the *Andromache*, Odysseus and Agamemnon can slaughter Iphigenia in the *Agamemnon* or the *Iphigenia Taurica*, because those heroes are not set up as models of chivalry; in many cases they are definitely meant to be 'unsympathetic', and within limits, the wickeder they are the better. The *Iliad*, on the other hand, was the 'mirror of chivalry', a recognized instrument of moral education because it represented an idealized heroic age. Agamemnon in the *Iliad* could not sacrifice Iphigenia, just as Tennyson's King Arthur could not burn Guinevere alive or tear her between wild horses, whatever the old legends might say in either case. Such deeds would be out of the convention, and shocking. (3) The frivolous treatment of the gods in serious or romantic literature is a convention which probably, like much else, comes to Alexandria from Ionia.

Yet if it had done for the gods what it did for the human beings
there would not have been much ground left for the indignation
of Xenophanes.

But there seems to be always a limit to these processes of
expurgation and reform from within. A progressive nation
with a rich legendary tradition must from time to time wake up
to look upon its legends with fresh eyes. They are regarded as
something authoritative, unquestioned, indisputably edifying.
And yet in them there are here and there details which seem
hard to believe, harder still to admire. They are explained,
allegorized, altered, expurgated. For the moment all is well.
And then quickly there appears another crop of difficulties
requiring the same treatment. The process is repeated. The
amount of hard thinking and of emotion which mankind has
again and again expended—perhaps wisely—in trying to patch
the fragments of some great system of false beliefs, which often
has nothing valuable about it except the emotion with which it
happens to be regarded, is one of the most profoundly characteristic things in human history. It was widely prevalent in
Greece, especially after the classical period. But a moment is
apt to come, sooner or later, at which men begin to wonder
whether after so much jettison there is really anything true to
save, whether a bridge so extremely full of rotten planks is worth
such repeated mending. The point at which this stage is reached
seems to depend on a certain proportion of qualities in the minds
of the persons affected, the proportion between their critical
intelligence and boldness on the one hand, and their reverence
and depth of emotion on the other. Now Ionia in the sixth
century was full of intelligence and daring ; it was adventurous,
critical, scientific, rationalist, and self-confident. It was not, like
Thrace, Crete, Athens, South Italy, a centre of religion or
reactionary dreaming. It produced indeed some mysticism ; but
a peculiar scientific and speculative mysticism of its own, more
concerned with the properties of the Infinite ($\tau\grave{o}$ $\mathring{a}\pi\epsilon\iota\rho o\nu$) than
with the traditional anthropomorphic gods.[1]

(Aristophanes is of course quite different.) This subject is too large to
discuss here. But we know that Zenodotus and Aristarchus regarded the
frivolous scenes as $\mathring{a}\pi\rho\epsilon\pi\mathring{\eta}$; that is, they were *not* natural and suitable
according to Alexandrian taste.

[1] See Schulz, *Ionische Mystik*. Also *Die Götterwelt Homers* by Paul
Meyer, *Jahresber. über d. K. Klosterschule zu Ilfeld*, 1907.

This scientific and critical temperament among the people of Ionia was met by a special weakness in the Homeric religion. It was not really religion at all. The beautiful Olympians whom we find in Homer forming a sort of divine family, and whom we know from statues, do not represent the Gods worshipped by any particular part of early Greece. They represent an enlightened compromise made to suit the conveniences of a federation. Each local god had been shorn of his mystical or monstrous characteristics; of everything, that is, that was likely to give offence. And it is nearly always the mystical or monstrous elements of a belief which seem to have excited the keenest religious emotions of an ancient people. The owl Athena, the cow Hera, the snake-man Cecrops; the many ghosts and shapes of terror; the mystic bull Dionysus, who *is* in some strange sense the beast which he himself tears to pieces alive, and from whose blood our souls are made: these things are cleared away from Homer's world, or else humanized and made to tone in with his general serene anthropomorphism. This anthropomorphism happened to suit the art of sculpture, which became highly important in Greece, and for that reason among others the Homeric gods have dominated the later tradition. But the real worship of Greece before the fourth century almost never attached itself to those luminous Olympian forms. There were many ecstasies of enthusiasm and outbreaks of superstition in Greece, but they all depend on deities of quite a different sort. There was enthusiasm for Orpheus and Dionysus: enthusiasm for the mysteries of the Mother and Maid at Eleusis. There was religious feeling about the local pre-Hellenic festivals, like the Thesmophoria. There was superstitious terror in Athens about the mutilation of the Hermae. But those Hermae were no images of the handsome young Homeric god; they represented the old divine boundary stone, whose unedifying form has been entirely expurgated from the Homeric epos. The failure of Nikias in his retreat from Syracuse was due to reverence for no Homeric Artemis, but for the ancient and unhumanized holiness of the Moon. Even the goddess who led Pisistratus back to Athens, Pisistratus τὸν Ὁμηρικώτατον, was originally not so much the Homeric daughter of Zeus as the ancient pre-Homeric 'Athenaia Korê'. And the temple of Zeus, which the same Pisistratus, in the

spirit of his Homeric policy, proceeded to build with so much
pomp, was left all through the classical times unfinished. All the
treasures of Athenian building went to Athena and Poseidon,
the native Earth-Maiden and the native Sea. Of course Athens
may have been a specially 'Pelasgian' community: but *mutatis
mutandis* the same observations could probably be made of any
Greek town of which we possessed adequate records.

One can see then what was likely to happen to the Homeric
gods. They had been made, up to a certain standard, very
beautiful, highly anthropomorphic, not in the least poverty-
stricken, barbarous, or grotesque. But in the process they
had lost their special hold on the worship of any particular
community. They had forfeited the powerful support of un-
critical local superstition: and, after all, in the eyes of an
educated and sceptical Ionian, would they quite bear thinking
about? This serio-comic Olympian family, with its permanent
feud between the husband and wife, in behalf of which we can
but lamely plead that the wife's unamiability is the natural
result of the husband's extreme unfaithfulness, and the husband's
unfaithfulness almost excused by the wife's monstrous unamiability? The lame son at whom the other gods laugh? The
pretty daughter, always in scrapes and tears? To a reverent
spirit these things can be allegorized. To a scientific historian
they possess an historical origin and explanation. But to the
critical Ionian, whose eyes are no longer blinded by the sacred
past, who patronizes while he loves, they tended to take a curious
form. It is a form hard to characterize or to understand, unless
perhaps it is an imitation by the taste of a refined and sceptical
age of the simple-minded burlesque of sacred things which is
often found in primitive 'ages of faith': the form which reaches
its highest, or perhaps I should say its lowest, point in Ovid, or
before Ovid in the Alexandrians. [The gods are not by any
means rejected. They are patronized, conventionalized, and
treated as material for ornament. Their traditional characteristics, roughly speaking, are preserved; Zeus is royal, and
Apollo is musical, and Athena is a warrior or a spinster: and
the late Ionian poets believe in them not much more effectively
than Pope believed in the sylphs who tire his heroine's hair in
the *Rape of the Lock*. There is a depth of unbelief profounder

than any outspoken denial. Pope would not have troubled to deny the existence of sylphs. When you take the gods in such a spirit as this it is not worth while to furbish up their moral characters. They are more amusing as they stand; they may even be, in a certain external and shallow sense, more beautiful.

I think that in this matter of the Homeric or Olympian gods one can notice three distinct stages. There is a primitive stage, represented best by the earliest strata of Hesiod's *Theogony*: a stage in which, for one thing, men did not use their critical faculties at all on this sort of material, and, for another, a great many of the myths which afterwards became shocking or ridiculous still preserved some remnant of their original meanings. At such a time, for instance, the quarrels between Zeus and Hera may still have been felt consciously as part of the old and respectable feud between the conquered native goddess and the invading patriarchal god.[1] Secondly, there is a long middle stage of expurgation, of rejection, of humanizing. When it began we can hardly guess, nor how the expurgations gradually came to be accepted and canonized in the official texts; but the process must, in some form or other, have lasted through a great part of the life of the poems. Thirdly, there is the late Ionian stage of which we have just spoken, in which the Olympians have ceased to have any genuinely religious significance, but serve to provide expedients to the story-teller, and afford material for a kind of half-licentious humour.

Presently, I think, we shall see reason to add a fourth stage, that of the acceptance of the Homeric system by non-Ionian Greece, a stage in which the more primitive Greek communities, beginning to feel uneasiness at the muddle and crudity of their own local superstitions, receive with reverence and enthusiasm the comparatively orderly and civilized system of Homer. In the sixth century, when Ionian culture spread in a great wave to the mainland of Greece, Ionia was probably already *blasée* to the theology of which she was the chief centre. And the Zeus whom Aeschylus accepted from Ionia and Homer was a widely different being from the Zeus of whom the men of Miletus made merry tales.

[1] J. E. Harrison, *Primer of Greek Religion.*

At the very outset of that interesting branch of literature which culminated in the Greek Novel, we hear of the Milesian Stories. Light tales they seem to have been, much in the style of Boccaccio. A typical one is the tale of the inconsolable widow of Ephesus, who used constantly to frequent her husband's tomb—from mixed motives; partly from devotion to his memory, partly because there was a fascinating young soldier on guard there. The first collector of such stories whose name is known to us, Aristides, belongs to an uncertain but much later date. But two or three tales in Herodotus bear the same stamp: among them some, like that of the wife of Candaules, which were certainly not first told by Herodotus. And besides, the very fact that Aristides called his collection 'Milesian Stories' seems to mean that the type of story was already recognized as Milesian. It was a name like 'Contes gaulois'. And I think one can see this spirit, a mocking, half-licentious, Boccaccio-like spirit, already at work in the later, and not the very latest, parts of the *Iliad*.

We will take two detailed instances. But first, let us be clear about the issue. As we have seen before, the human beings in Homer always maintain their dignity and self-respect. No hero is a liar[1] or a coward. None is drunken or loose-lived or vicious. None tortures his enemy. But the gods: that is quite a different matter. They are capable of anything. They not only practise torture—the gods of most nations have had a weakness in that direction—but they lose their dignity. They are cheated, beaten, imprisoned. They lie and are found out. They are routed by human beings. They howl when wounded. Their father 'bangs' them 'about the house'. That, you may say, is characteristic of all simple and primitive religions. Does not Ouranos swallow his children and again vomit them up? Does not the Babylonian Apsu, in the primaeval chaos, cut his wife Tiamat in two, to make one half of her into heaven and the other into earth? Yes. Those are simple and savage stories, visibly allegorical, dependent in part on the mere helplessness of primitive language. The Homeric passages in question are

---

[1] Of course a disguised hero in the course of a dangerous adventure tells the necessary lies to avoid detection. That is in the essence of all romances of adventure.

totally different from that. They are not primitive, but smooth and sophisticated. They mock with easy scepticism at the indecorousness of the primitive beliefs.

But let us take our two instances. There was in Greece a widespread tradition of the Wars of the Gods. Zeus somehow holds his power by conquest over other beings, vaguer, older, and darker shapes, belonging to some old order, or, perhaps, to the chaos that preceded all order. We hear of many treatments in early epic of the Titanomachia, Theomachia, Gigantomachia. And in our Hesiodic collection we have preserved, imperfectly and with many repetitions, due apparently to a conflation of two sources, a long fragment of a Titanomachia. It tells how Zeus gained the victory over the Titans by freeing and calling to his aid certain primitive beings whom the Titans and Ouranos had oppressed (*Theog.* 617 ff.).[1]

> Briareôs and Kottos and Guês, their father Ouranos conceived hatred of them in his heart, being afraid at their wild valour and their looks and tallness, and he bound them in bondage deep beneath the wide-wayed earth. And there they dwelt in anguish under the ground at the ends of the great world, seated on the verge of things, a very long time, amazed and with great mourning in their hearts. But Zeus and the immortal gods, by the counsel of Earth, brought them again to the light.

Zeus asked them to help him in the long war against the Titans, and they consented. The gods stood on Olympus and the Titans upon Othrys; and they had fought already for ten years. So they joined battle:

> And the Titans opposite had made strong their lines, and both sides put forth their might. And there was a terrible cry from the boundless sea, and shattering of the earth, and the broad sky groaned, and high Olympus was shaken from his foundations with the rush of immortal things: and the quaking and the noise of feet upon the steeps came down unto cloudy Tartarus. . . . And the armies met with a great shout, and Zeus held back his fury no more. Down from Olympus and heaven he came in one sweep of thunders

---

[1] If Briareos is a fifty-oared ship, as seems likely, he must have been introduced later into this story. But perhaps the Fifty-oar was rather identified with an already existing Briareos, and thus Briareos identified with Aigaion.

that ceased not : and the bolts went winged from his mighty hand, and the life-bearing Earth cracked with the burning, and around him the fathomless forest roared in fire. . . . And foremost in that bitter stirring of battle were Kottos and Briareôs and Guês, unsated of war, who cast from their hands three hundred great stones, one on another, and darkened the Titans with their castings, and drave them down and bound them in bitter bondage, for all their pride, as far beneath the earth as the sky is above the earth. For a bronzen anvil cast from heaven would fall nine nights and days, and on the tenth night would come to the earth. And from earth a bronzen anvil would fall nine nights and days, and on the tenth night would come to cloudy Tartarus : whereabout there is driven a bronzen fence, and around it Night is shed, Night in three floods. And over it the roots are planted of the earth and the unharvested sea.

Now the exact merit of this as poetry may be a matter of dispute. It may be a little incompetent, a little bombastic. But it is at least genuine and reverent. If we are to describe these primitive battles of gods, that is the kind of way in which to conceive them.

Now turn to the battle of the gods in a late part of the *Iliad* (Φ 391 ff.) :

It was shield-piercing Ares who began, and sprang upon Athena with his bronzen spear, and uttered a word of insult : 'Wherefore again, thou dog-fly, dost drive the gods to strife ? Rememberest not the day when thou didst let loose Diomedes to wound me, and thyself in sight of all didst grasp the spear and drive full at me and tear my fair flesh ? Now I warrant me thou shalt pay for all thy doings ! ' So saying he made a lunge at her aegis tasselled and terrible, which not the thunder of Zeus can make to fall. There bloody Ares lunged with his long spear. But she started back and caught up in her stout hand a stone lying upon the plain, a big black jagged stone, which men of old had put to be the boundary of a field ; and she hit Ares on the neck with it, and his limbs gave way. He reached over seven furlongs as he fell, and his hair was filled with dust and his arms rattled about him. And Pallas Athena laughed aloud, and boasted over him with winged words. 'Fool, hast thou not learned yet how far I am thy better, that thou wilt dare to match thy strength with mine ? That is the way to fulfil thy mother's curses, who plans anger and mischief against thee for deserting the Greeks.'

Presently Aphrodite, who was in love with Ares, came and took him by the arm to help him up, while he made a great groaning, and began gradually to come to. Hera saw, and called to Athena :

> 'Here is that dog-fly '—the poet has an affection for that word—' coming to help Ares. Chase her!' So Athena, rejoicing in her heart, flew at Aphrodite, and drove her in the chest with her stout hand, and her limbs and her dear heart gave way beneath her. And there the two of them lay together on the many-nurturing Earth.

Later on, towards the end of the battle, Artemis is facing Hera :

> To her in wrath spake the reverend spouse of Zeus : 'What seekest thou, shameless she-dog, standing against me ?'. . . So spake she, and with her left hand gripped both the hands of Artemis by the wrist, while with her right she took the bow and arrows off her shoulders ; then with the bow and arrows whipped her about the ears, and laughed as she dipped her head this way and that. And the arrows kept dropping from the quiver. And the goddess full of tears fled like a wood-pigeon.

'One of the few passages in the *Iliad*,' says Dr Leaf, ' which can be pronounced poetically bad.' True, yet the badness lies entirely in the taste, not in the execution. The verses are admirably written, incomparably better than those of Hesiod's *Titanomachia*. But the poet was not writing about anything that he felt as real or as mattering much to anybody's feelings. He was almost writing parody or mock-epic. And he made it quite pretty!

Let us take another instance. Among the old traditional subjects of semi-religious Epos was one which our extant remains of Greek literature leave rather obscure, the mystic marriage of Zeus and Hera. This may have been in its origin a sort of marriage of Heaven and Earth, or of the two greatest divine beings, from which all things arise. It may conceivably have symbolized the union of the two races and two religions—the patriarchal Zeus of the Northerners, being united with Hera, the Argive Korê. It may have been one of those naïve recognitions of the mystery and divinity of the processes of life, which often shed such high dignity upon the external grossness of primitive religion. Whatever its origin, it was a subject treated by divers poets with reverence and mystery, as we can tell by the allusions in Pindar, Aeschylus, and Euripides.

Now, how is this subject treated in the Fourteenth Book of the *Iliad*? Absolutely in the spirit of Boccaccio: I might almost say, of a Palais Royal farce. The passage is sometimes much praised, and is certainly admirably written: 'radiant with humour, grace, and healthful sensuousness,' is the criticism of Dr. Leaf. But what is the story? Its name is almost enough: it is called by ancient writers *The Tricking of Zeus*.

The father of gods and men was sitting on the top of many-fountained Ida, watching the war. The gods had offended him by giving secret help to the Greeks, and he had arranged that the Trojans should win the present battle. So he went himself to sit on Mount Ida, and see that all proceeded as he desired. His wife Hera, a partisan of the Greeks, saw him sitting there—στυγερὸς δέ οἱ ἔπλετο θυμῷ—'and thought how much she disliked him!' She determined to outwit her lord and master. So she went to her room, washed, anointed, and scented herself, and put on her best immortal raiment, including ear-rings with three stones in them. Next she went to Aphrodite and begged for the loan of her Cestus, or embroidered girdle, which acted as a love-charm. She explained—falsely, of course—how she wished it in order to reconcile an old married couple dwelling at the end of the world, who had unfortunately quarrelled—Okeanos and mother Tethys, in fact. Having obtained the Cestus, she proceeds to find the Spirit of Sleep, and with some difficulty bribes him to come and be ready to charm the eyes of Zeus at a critical moment. The bribe has to be high, since Sleep had done her the same service once before, in the old *Heracleia*, and had suffered in consequence. Finally, she repairs to Mount Ida, to ask in most dutiful language the permission of Zeus to make her expedition to Okeanos and mother Tethys. She does not like to go so far without her lord's approval. Remember that all this edifying story began by her thinking how much she disliked Zeus! I can find no dignified word to describe adequately her provocative conduct towards her victim. However, she succeeds in entirely engrossing his attention, and so rouses his

passionate admiration that he compares her favourably with no
less than seven other females towards whom he has entertained
similar feelings. He quite forgets the war. He goes to sleep
in her arms. And Hera sends a message to her allies that they
can do what they like now : Zeus is safe!

Now, were I required to subscribe half a crown to save
Aristides of Miletus and all his children from everlasting death,
I do not say that I would outright refuse. In its own place
this kind of literature has a certain value, and seems to have
served as a stimulus to better work in others. But not all the
riches of Egyptian Thebes could, I think, ever atone for the
injury done to the human race by the invasion of this Milesian
spirit into what is perhaps the greatest poem of the greatest
nation of poets that the world has known. It has defiled its own
beautiful world. It has 'slain the image of God, as it were, in
the eye'. For the poets who actually wrote these passages there
is a great excuse. Their cause was, perhaps, on the whole,
rather a good cause than a bad. But historical circumstances
combined to catch and stereotype the epic at the moment when,
perhaps just after the zenith of its glory, it had caught this
mocking infection. Rightly sceptical towards the authorized
gods and their legends, it had not the serious courage simply to
seek truth and reject falsehood in what are generally regarded
as the highest regions of human thinking. It neither denied its
gods nor remade them. It degraded them further, and used
them for ornament and amusement, to make a good tale the
merrier. I had almost written, to make a good tale into a bad
one. When once this infection has crept into its blood, the Epos
as a form of living and growing poetry was doomed.

Consider what that meant for the history of Greek literature.
Greek literature starts from an immense wealth of Saga traditions,
and the need of an instrument for expressing them ; to meet that
need it created the Epos. It had been a costly and a rare
creation ; a metre, a style, a whole language almost. And now
that part of the Greek people which had done all this for the sake of
the Saga had outgrown the Saga, and was beginning to parody
what it had formerly adored.[1] Had Ionia been the whole of

---

[1] Monro allows quite a large place to the mock-heroic in the second part
of the *Odyssey*, Telemachus' sneeze which σμερδαλέον κονάβησε (ρ 542), the

Greece, not only the Epos, but the whole heroic tradition, might have died during the sixth and fifth centuries.   But Ionia was not the whole of Greece, and the Saga found a new utterance in Attic tragedy.

I always hesitate to use the antithesis of northern and native, or Hellenic and pre-Hellenic, as applied to the whole of any concrete fact.   The rule is that everywhere you find northern and native elements, but nowhere do you find a purely northern or purely native community.   Yet in contrasting the Epos with tragedy that antithesis cannot but occur to one's mind.

When the ancestors of the Aeolians and Ionians fled across the seas—a mixed set of races, often under Achaean leaders—they were compelled, as we observed in the second lecture, to leave behind them their sacred places, most of their tribal and family institutions, and notably the graves of their fathers.   The prestige of the Achaean chiefs, the partial return to migratory life, the convenience of the Northern institutions of the Saga and the Bard, combined to give to the Epos its prevailing Achaean tone. But on the mainland of Greece during all this time, even where the northern occupations were most tyrannous, there remained always some fragments of the old population, peasants and serfs and outlaws for the most part, who still clung to their old objects of worship, their Earth-Maidens and their harvest magic, especially their tribal initiations and their sacred tombs.   A downtrodden people they must have been for many generations, worshipping by stealth and in fear.   But as the populations became more mixed, which was the case everywhere on the mainland, the result was that the old pre-Hellenic stratum of beliefs and emotions re-emerged.   How the initiation rites led to the formation of an initiation-god Dionysus, the Zeus-Child who

pigsty described in language borrowed from Priam's palace (ξ 13 ff.), the πότνια μήτηρ of the beggar Irus (σ 5), &c.   He gives some fifteen alleged instances in the index under 'Parody'.   Mülder goes much further, *Quellen*, pp. 287 ff., 347 ff.

Exactly the same spirit occurs in the *Pèlerinage de Charlemagne*, which, however, belongs to a quite early and good period.   See G. Paris, *Poésie du M. A.*, i. pp. 119-49.   It can be shown on other grounds to be connected with the neighbourhood of Paris (e. g. it mentions no towns except St. Denys, Paris, Chartres, and Châteaudun, with no word of Aix or Laon), and the critic regards its heroi-comic character as 'le plus ancien produit de l'esprit parisien'. Perhaps the Demodocus lay, which looks exceedingly ancient, occupies the same place in 'l'esprit milésien'.

lied and rose again, the God who showed the candidates for
initiation to their dead ancestors and led his rout of masked and
dancing ghosts; how this worship of Dionysus, combined with
the old custom of performing rites round the tomb of a dead
hero, narrating his deeds and sufferings and invoking his return
to his people: that story is too long and intricate to attempt
here.   In even the latest works of Attic tragedy the Masquers of
Dionysus are rarely dissociated from some sacred tomb.   In this
severe, earnest, keenly emotional atmosphere, touched with
mysticism by the shadow of present death, the Greeks of the
mainland kept up in their separate cities and villages their own
local fragments of the heroic saga.

Now about this time of the decay of the Epos, Athens had
thrown off her ages of Pelasgian slumber and was just coming
into intimate contact with Ionia.   To her young and groping
genius the high civilization and intelligence of Ionia, the magnificent form of the Epos, the broad sweep of Homeric pan-Hellenism, the clean and lordly northern spirit, came as a world of
inspiration, and quickened the ancient ceremonials of worship at
the tomb to the splendid growth of Attic Tragedy.

Turn from that late Homeric story of the *Tricking of Zeus*
to the earliest, crudest, most incompetent tragedy which we
possess, though, in its way, one of the most beautiful, the
Suppliant Women of Aeschylus.   It is not only that there is
a marked change of atmosphere, but it seems like a change
backward, not forward, towards an older, a simpler and a
grander, world.   The very first words of the play strike a key-
note: Ζεὺς μὲν ἀφίκτωρ, 'Zeus the Suppliant'.   Would any of
those clear-headed Homeric bards have ventured on that ancient
phrase?   They knew of a Zeus who, on a far-off mountain
throne, observed and avenged suppliants.   But this Zeus of
Aeschylus is himself the suppliant; the prayer which you reject
is his very prayer, and in turning from your door the helpless or
the outcast you have turned away the most high God.   The
belief was immemorially old.[1]   It was doubtless in a thousand of

[1] The discovery of the Hymn of the Kouretes enables us exactly to understand Ζεὺς 'Αφίκτωρ.   He is a 'projection' of the rite of Supplication; a
conception generated from the band of human suppliants just as Zeus Kouros,
or simply ὁ Μέγιστος Κοῦρος, is generated from the band of Kouroi, Silenus
from the Silenoi, Pan from the Panes, or, a very clear case, Amphictyon from

its ramifications foolish and absurd. And the Ionic Epos had
made all its beliefs sensible.

I will venture to read you a strange Aeschylean lyric about
a deed of this same Zeus. It is a story far too primitive and
monstrous for Homer: the tale of Io, the Argive maiden beloved
of Zeus, who was turned into a cow, forsooth, and watched by
the hundred-eyed Argos, and driven over the world by a gad-
fly! A cow-shaped, or even a cow-headed, maiden! And a
cow-headed maiden beloved by Zeus! To a cultivated Ionian
such conceptions must have belonged to the very lowest regions
of 'Pelasgian' folly. They had been expurgated from Homer
generations before. Yet out of that unpromising material
Aeschylus extracts something which is not only genuine religious thought, but, to my feeling, even somewhat sublime
thought. The love of Zeus leads its object through unearthly
shame and suffering to a strange and overwhelming reward.
We cannot understand. But Zeus is bound by no law but his
own supreme will. He has always his own great purpose, and
he moves towards it by inscrutable ways.

I should explain that to the mythologist Io is probably one of
the many shapes of the horned Moon, the wanderer of the sky.
She was identified by the Greeks with the Egyptian Isis, and her
son—conceived miraculously by the touch of the hand of Zeus—
with Apis, the sacred Egyptian bull. The speakers are the
daughters of Danaus, descendants of Io, returned to her native
land, Argos, and praying protection from their pursuers, the sons
of Aegyptus (*Suppl.* 524 ff.) :

> Lord of lords, blessed among the blessed, of perfection
> most perfect strength, O happy Zeus, hear us, and let it be
> Shield us from the pride of man, whom thou righteously
> abhorrest, and whelm in the dark-blue deep our black
> prison-house.[1] Look upon the woman's cause; look on
> the race born of old from the woman whom thou didst love
> and make new the joyous tale. Be a rememberer of many
> things, O thou whose hand was laid on Io. Lo, we are
> beings born of thy race, though sent from this land to dwell
> afar.
>
> I walk again in the print of ancient feet, where our

the Amphictyones. See references on p. 76, note. 'Le dieu est le désir
(collectif) personnifié,' Doutté, *Magie de l'Afrique du Nord*, p. 601.

[1] i. e. the ship of their pursuers.

mother was watched, moving among the flowers; the
meadow of kine, whence Io fled, sea-tossed by a burning
pain, knowing not her desire, to pass through many tribes
of men. . . .

Her wide wanderings are then described, across the Hellespont, through Asia southwards, till she reaches at last ' the all-
pasturing garden of Zeus, the snow-fed meadow visited by the
whirling giant of the desert-sand, and the water of Nile un-
touched by sickness '.

Do you observe how deeply and simply serious it all is?
Aeschylus accepts the whole story. But because he is simple-
minded and great-minded, and has not a grain of lewdness
anywhere in him, this old, barbarous, pre-anthropomorphic
superstition has become to him a great and strange thing; and
the spirit passes from the poet himself to his reader. He throws
no veil over the cow-shaped heroine. The transformation is
part of the mystery, and he emphasizes it. The poem continues:

And men that had then their habitation in the land, their
hearts were shaken with fear at the strange sight, a Being
agonized half-human, part of the race of kine and part of
woman. They marvelled at the mystery. Who was it that
brought her peace in the end, her the far-wandering, the
afflicted, the gadfly-goaded Io?

He who ruleth through ages of unresting life, Zeus [to
whom years are as yesterday]. The unwounding strength
of a hand, the breath of a god, gave rest to her, and her
heart flowed in a sad tenderness of tears. The word of true
promise became a divine seed within her, and she bore a
blameless child, through ages long perfect in happiness.

Whom of gods shall I praise for works more justified?
Father, planter of the garden, worker with the hand, and
Lord, thinker of ancient thought, great builder of our race,
Zeus, whose breath maketh all accomplishment!

He hasteth not at the command of another. Being
stronger than all, he maketh great the weak. None sitteth
above him, and he honoureth none. And the deed and the
word are present as one thing, to dispatch that end whereto
the counselling mind moveth.

The story which Homer rejected has become the vehicle of a
theology higher than Homer's, or, if not higher, at least based on
deeper thought and involving the reconciliation of vaster conflicts.
The mind of Aeschylus was possessed by one of the problems,

perhaps the most dreadful problem, of human evolution. He sees the higher asserting itself gradually over the lower in the process of years; but he sees also, what many people blind their eyes against, that the so-called higher often achieves its end at the price of becoming something more evil than the wild beasts. It is good that the white man should supersede the red and the brown; but what things the white men have done in the process! For Aeschylus the contest was probably present in two forms: a conflict, externally, of Greek against barbarian, and in Greece itself, of what we may call Achaean or Olympian against 'Pelasgian'. Zeus was in each case the spirit of the higher power; and, to Aeschylus, probably, if anything on earth specially typified Zeus, the new conqueror and orderer of heaven, it was the new Dominion of the Athenian Empire.

It was unlike a Homeric bard to have such thoughts at all. It is still more unlike him to express them in the language of the Saga. He was a trained artist, and would not dream of so violating his convention. He kept his poetry in one compartment; his speculation, if he had any, in another. But for Aeschylus they are both one. Two of Aeschylus' earliest trilogies seem to deal explicitly with this subject. Both trilogies are represented to us by one play each, the *Suppliant Women* and the *Prometheus*. In the two isolated plays which remain, the sympathy is entirely on the side of the weaker; it is for the suppliant women against their pursuers, and for Prometheus against Zeus. Yet we know from other sources that in the complete trilogy the ultimate judgement was for the stronger, so soon as the stronger would consent to merge his strength in love. The story of Io is prominent in both plays. It is only loosely connected with the main plot, but it typifies in each case the religious meaning of the whole. Zeus did to Io what seemed like monstrous wrong; professing to love her, he afflicted her and ceased not, and the end was that he brought her to a perfect joy which—so she is perhaps at the end willing to believe—could not be attained otherwise. And even while Prometheus and Io are mingling their griefs against Zeus, it is shown that a child descended from Io is to be also the deliverer of Prometheus (*Prom.* 772, 871 ff.). That too is part of Zeus' purpose.

We know Shelley's magnificent treatment of the Prometheus Saga. Shelley was too passionate a friend of the oppressed ever to make terms with a successful tyrant, be he man or god. In Shelley's *Prometheus Unbound* the prophesied catastrophe which is to hurl Zeus from his throne actually occurs, and the tormented Universe, awakening to a life of peace and love, finds uncontrolled that inward perfection of order which leaves no place for external government. But in Aeschylus we know that the end was different. Zeus the all-ruler must always rule. Does not each one of us know, as a matter of fact, that Zeus and not Prometheus is now governing the world? But Zeus, who came to his throne by violence,[1] learns as the ages pass that violence is evil. For all his wisdom he grows wiser still. Nay, it seems that even from the beginning, in his cruelty to Prometheus, as in his cruelty to Io, he had a great purpose in the depth of his mind, and that purpose was peace. Prometheus is unbound, not by a turning of the tide of war, but by the atonement, after ages of pain, after the suffering by which alone wisdom is born, of a noble rebel and a noble ruler. The Zeus who could be himself a suppliant, who even in the most ancient legends forgave and set free his conquered Titans, was capable of this crowning strength also. I do not suggest that this solution is ultimately tenable or satisfying. But it at least represents intense thought, and thought naturally expressing itself in the medium of poetry. It is just this which Ionia never gave us. It is peculiarly the gift of Athens.

We have tried to follow, in a very imperfect and sometimes inconsequent manner, the life of Traditional Epic Poetry in Greece. We have seen the first fragments of what was afterwards the Greek race gathering behind their bare walls on islands and desert capes in the Aegean; we have caught glimpses of ancient and diverse memories of tribal history, of great deeds, of rich palaces and mysterious kings, meeting and parting and re-joining again into the numerous heroic poems now lost, and the two, more highly wrought than the others, which still survive. We have noted how, of these two poems, one again was more ' Homeric' than its companion; more carefully purified and

[1] Cf. Verrall on *Ag.* 192 ff.

expurgated, more tensely knit and gorgeously worded, while at the same time the heroic and ancient atmosphere was more sedulously protected from the breaths of commoner or more recent life. We have looked as best we could, much helped by Hebrew parallels, into the strange processes of growth and composition which have made the *Iliad* what it is, and have tried to analyse some part of its poetical greatness. Lastly, we have seen how the races which built up ' Homer ' at length outgrew him, and found other subjects than the Heroic Saga in which to express their ideals and satisfy their intellectual thirst. Homer did not die ; on the contrary his greatest fame, his most secure enthronement among poets, was still before him. We shall see in the next chapter something of what Athens did for Homer, and shall perhaps be forced to recognize that the text which we possess is not a thing of pre-Pisistratid, almost pre-Ionian, antiquity, but actually, as a text, less ancient than the *Agamemnon* or even the *Bacchae*. But whatever work Athens may have done for the *Iliad* and *Odyssey* it is extraordinary how strictly she kept up the old Homeric convention, the old language, the old manner, the old subjects and rules of thought. The preservation of the Ionic Epos in Athens throughout the fifth century is a cardinal instance of that sensitiveness to style and tradition which is one of the deepest characteristics of all Greek art. But, after all, it was tradition rather than creation : when we seek the great creative work of the fifth century we find it in other paths, with which Ionia has little to do.[1]

We have moved into a sterner land, more interested in truth and less in romance ; into a language less beautiful, more intellectual, more highly differentiated ; a language which has elements of hard prose mixed with its poetry, and has lost that splendid and careless gleam by means of which Homer was accustomed to set all themes in the world aglow. Homer's poetry was so easy, the sympathy was so clear, the imagination was roused so instinctively, that we must leave it with a sigh. And this new poetry is of a kind which will not yield its

[1] Professor Wheeler of Columbia University calls to my notice the very similar contrast between the mocking boisterousness of the Ionic vase-paintings and the severity of the early Attic. See also Mr. Cornford's remarks in *Thucydides Mythistoricus* on the difference between the Ionic Herodotus and the Attic Thucydides.

treasures without hard thinking, without somewhat intense and vigilant use of the imagination. The poets, for the most part, are no longer merely singing to please us, according to methods which have been tried for generations and proved effectual. They are men not exactly less cultured—intellectually they are far greater—than the Ionian bards; but they are less accomplished. They are imaginatively nearer to the primitive earthborn tangle of desires and wonders. Their feet are set in places lower than Homer's feet; their thoughts strive towards heights and obscurities which his poetry dared not penetrate. They have fought at Marathon, and their hands are reshaping the world. The bitterness of truth is mingled with their dreams of beauty: the passion of men searching gleams through the stiffness of their majestic conventions. Conquerors of the Mede; builders of free Athens; first makers to the world of tragedy and of comedy: it is a rare combination.

But there begins the second great chapter in Greek literature.

XII

THE TEXT OF HOMER

FROM KNOWN TO UNKNOWN

THE main exposition of this book has proceeded in historical order, starting in times of extreme darkness and working slowly towards the beginnings of clear and well-lit history. Of necessity, therefore, the argument has rested cheifly on analogies and general considerations, not on documents : it has had to be very cautious, aiming at probability, not certainty, constantly suggesting, not professing to demonstrate. It will, I think, be convenient now, at the end of the book, to reverse this process, and trace briefly such actual recorded facts as we possess about the history of the poems backward from the known to the unknown. The two inquiries will just meet in the middle. I have hopes that this chapter, if not very inspiring to the general reader, may be of some use to students, helping them perhaps to clarify their conceptions of the whole Homeric problem and free their minds from the fatal glamour of false knowledge diffused by the printed text.[1]

We start from what we may call the modern vulgate, that is, the text as ordinarily printed at the present day apart from the special views of any particular editor. This text is remarkably uniform, almost as much so as that of Vergil, far more so than that of Shakespeare. Also it is based upon an extremely large number of MSS. True, no complete copy is older than the tenth century A. D., but there are large fragments much earlier, and indirect evidence carries the Vulgate back a little before the Christian era.

---

[1] For good remarks on the habits of ancient scholars in dealing with their books, and the remains of fluidity even in the mediaeval MSS. of Homer, see T. W. Allen, *The Text of the Odyssey*, Papers of British School of Rome, V (1910).

We also find in the Scholia, or ancient commentaries, a great deal of information about the texts published or approved by certain Alexandrian scholars, especially Aristarchus (fl. 160 B. C.) and Zenodotus (fl. 285 B. C.). It would almost be possible, from the statements of the Scholia, to reconstitute the whole text according to Aristarchus, and Dr. Roemer at one time promised to do so. For Zenodotus our knowledge is not nearly so full, but we can make out much about his critical method.

It is significant that these two critics invented for their editions certain special signs. Zenodotus apparently used only one, the obelus (−), to mark lines as spurious. Of Aristarchus's signs the two commonest are, first the obelus, then the diplê (>), which is merely a mark for reference like our asterisk. Other signs denoted that lines were repeated more than once in the poems, and that in some places they were right, in others wrong. Others probably showed where the genuine Homer left off and where he began again, the part in between, as far as we can make out, being spurious. Aristarchus had also one sign which meant that he was referring to a note already made by Zenodotus.

When you think of the pressing need there was, according to our ideas, for the invention of a decent punctuation and proper divisions between words, it becomes the more striking that the first need these scholars actually felt was for signs to mark spuriousness. Except for the *diplê* almost the whole apparatus of signs seems devised for the casting out of spurious matter.

Now Aristarchus's own rejections are by our standards extremely vigorous : he rejected, for instance, all the last book of the *Odyssey* at a blow. But, compared with Zenodotus, he was celebrated for his περισσὴ εὐλάβεια, his ' excessive caution'. Some critics indeed have maintained that Aristarchus never under any circumstances made a conjecture of his own, but always had some MS. authority for even his smallest deletions. I do not agree with this view, but the question does not for the moment affect us.[1]

The method of Zenodotus was by the standards of a modern critical editor amazing in its vigour. He hacked away like a woodman clearing an overgrown forest ; and it is clear that he

[1] See Cauer, *Grundfragen*, ed. 3, pp. 57 ff.

relied largely on his personal feelings. We can see that he regarded the texts of his day as containing, in every part of the poems, whole masses of stuff that was not 'Homer'. He collected many MSS., but seems not to have had any that he considered authoritative. He is the author of the traditional division of the poems into twenty-four books denoted by letters of the alphabet, the *Iliad* having capital letters, the *Odyssey* small. Being himself an epic poet he used his critical faculty and rejected much merely because it was 'unseemly'; it is possible that he even rewrote some passages out of his head. The freedom of the old bards was not entirely dead in the first of the critics.[1]

Thanks to the brilliant pioneer work of Zenodotus, Aristarchus was able to proceed with more caution. The ground had been cleared for him, and, besides, the Ptolemies had been for some generations zealously collecting MSS. But it is noteworthy that when Aristarchus does cite a MS. authority for some reading, he never shows knowledge of any particular authoritative MS. nor of any widespread and authoritative tradition. His authorities are such as ἡ Σινωπική, ἡ Μασσιλιωτική, ἡ κατὰ Ῥιανόν, ἡ κατ' Ἀντίμαχον, αἱ κοιναί, αἱ δημώδεις, αἱ χαριέστεραι, τινὲς τῶν παλαιῶν κτλ. One of these, ἡ κοινή, it may be said, is exactly 'the Vulgate'. Possibly; but, if so, the 'vulgate' of that day differed demonstrably from ours, and what is more important, was regarded by Aristarchus with some contempt. He speaks of αἱ κοιναί or αἱ δημώδεις as one might speak of 'the cheap editions'.[2]

This seems to show that (1) Zenodotus found the text in a state of great disorder, and (2) neither he nor Aristarchus had any authoritative MS. tradition by which to correct it. The one recension which Aristarchus thought worthy of a special critical sign was not an ancient vulgate but the edition of Zenodotus.

This conclusion is vehemently opposed by many conservative critics. Obviously those who wish to maintain that our present *Iliad* and *Odyssey* were written, approximately as they stand, by

---

[1] Literature in Susemihl, *Alexandr. Literatur.* i. 333; see especially Roemer. I omit the work of Aristophanes (fl. c. 200 B.C.) for the sake of simplicity. Susemihl, i. 428–48.

[2] Ludwich, *Homervulgata*, p. 49.

one great poet in the eleventh century B.C., cannot possibly admit that the text was still in a very fluid state so late as the third century.   The position of Ludwich, for instance, is that, roughly speaking, our present vulgate was in existence as an authoritative text from the very earliest ages, and passed unscathed through the illiterate centuries of early Greece, through the creative ferment of the fifth century, through the chaos of the pre-Zenodotean texts, and lastly through the fires of Alexandrian criticism, always unmentioned but universally recognized, to emerge in triumph in our post-Christian MSS.

Observe that there are two questions at issue.   First, did there exist at all in pre-Alexandrian times a text like our traditional one?   Second, was this text, if it existed, an authoritative vulgate?   To the second I think the answer is a confident No: as to the first I can find no conclusive evidence.   But let us consider what there is.   We shall find it in two places.   First, in such fragments of MSS. as have come down to us from the times before Aristarchus; secondly, in the quotations made from Homer by classical writers.   In the history of this controversy the evidence of the quotations came first.   The great Wolf, who entirely denied the existence of any text like ours in pre-Alexandrian times, mentions as a certain fact,

> quod apud Hippocratem Platonem Aristotelem et alios istius aetatis scriptores non solum singulorum verborum varietates, sed etiam plures insignes versus legimus, quorum nec in textu nostro nec in Eustathio veterrimisque et doctissimis scholiis ullum indicium superest. (*Prolegomena*, p. 37.)

It might have been more prudent to write *Aeschinem* instead of *Platonem*, but in the main I consider this statement just in itself and signally confirmed by recent discoveries.

But quotations are slippery witnesses.   It will be best to start with the more positive evidence, that of the pre-Aristarchean papyri.   We should remark at the outset that in the case of Euripides and Plato, and, one may say, practically every classical author except Homer, the early papyri, where they exist at all, confirm to an extraordinary degree the accuracy of our MS. tradition.   In no case are there any large differences.   How does the case stand with Homer?

I. 1. There are altogether, according to Dr. Hunt's estimate, some two hundred fragmentary papyri of the Homeric poems, the *Iliad* being about twice as well represented in them as the *Odyssey*. Of these eight were written earlier than 150 B.C., and therefore have a direct evidential value for the present question.

The first of these to be discovered was the Flinders Petrie papyrus (Dublin, 1891) in two fragmentary columns, which contained Λ 502–37, the ends of 502–17 in the first column, the beginnings of 518–37 in the second. The main conclusions are given thus by Ludwich. Of the ends seven out of twenty are different from our vulgate, of the beginnings four out of nineteen. There are altogether thirty-nine lines instead of the thirty-six of the vulgate, the number being made up by the addition of four lines, hitherto unknown, and the omission of one.

This extraordinary result was accepted by some scholars as showing that our vulgate text was merely a product of Alexandrian criticism ; by others it was brushed aside as the accident of a single eccentric or ‘wild’ MS. Such a MS., they held, could not be a fair specimen of the pre-Alexandrian texts. Since that time, however, our specimens of such papyri have been slowly growing both in number and size,[1] and they all show in varying degrees the same general features. They all tend to have additional lines and to leave out some lines that we know. And where the lines coincide with the vulgate, the readings inside the line, as far as we can judge from the fragments, seem often to have been different. The papyri in question are as follows : the sign + denotes additional lines found in the papyrus, – denotes lines omitted. The number in brackets is that given in the *apparatus criticus* of Mr. Allen’s Oxford critical text of Homer.

I. (8 Allen) P. Petrie, beginning of second century B.C., containing Λ 502–37 (39 verses : +4 – 1 ; at least 11 variant readings).

II. (5) P. Genavensis, early second century. Λ 788–M 11 (70 verses : +13 – 0 ; many variant readings).

III. (41) P. Grenfell II, 3, and Hibeh I, 20. Parts of $\Gamma \Delta E$ (66 verses : +1 – 3 : ‘differed widely from the vulgate ’).

---

[1] Dr. Hunt informs me of three more early papyri : one a fragment of Z, which approximates to our text [now published as Pap. Ox. 1388] ; two of ϵ, both wild.

IV. (7) P. Grenfell II, 2, and Hibeh I, 21, Θ 17–258 (97 verses :
+28–0 : between Θ 52 and 66 there are+21).

V. (12) P. Grenfell II, 4, and Hibeh I, 22.   Between Φ 387
and Ψ 281 (190 verses : +certainly 11, perhaps 20 ; —?).

VI. (40) Hibeh I, 19.   Between B 174–830 and Γ 277–371
(105 verses : +13 : many variants).

VII. (19 in *Odyssey* list) Hibeh I, 23, ν 41–68 (30 verses :
+3–1).

VIII. Rylands 49.   Beginnings of Π 484–9 ; six beginnings,
one of them different.

Lastly, two Heidelberg fragments, known to me by the kindness of Dr. Gerhardt, the learned editor of *Phoinix of Colophon*,
who has since published them :

Heid. IV. Θ 191 ff., 16 lines, from the same MS. as IV (16
verses +4).

Heid. V.   183 lines from Φ X Ψ, from the same MS. as IV
(roughly something making the average about +7–2 per cent.
This is the nearest to the vulgate that has been found).

Rather later in date but similar in character is a papyrus of the
first century B.C. in *Berliner Klassikertexte*, v, p. 18, containing
the end of Σ, with the description of the shield of Achilles.
This is so instructive that I cite it in full.

Σ 596–602 agree with the vulgate : then it runs :

603   πολλὸς δ' ἱμερόεντα χορὸν περιΐσταθ' ὅμιλος
604–5 τερπόμενοι· δοιὼ δὲ κυβιστητῆρε κατ' αὐτοὺς
606   μολπῆς ἐξάρχοντες ἐδίνευον κατὰ μέσσους.
606ᵃ   ἐν δ' ἔσσαν σύριγγες, ἔσαν κίθαρίς τε καὶ αὐλοί.
607   ἐν δ' ἐτίθει ποταμοῖο μέγα σθένος Ὠκεανοῖο
608   ἄντυγα πὰρ πυμάτην σάκεος πύκα ποιητοῖο.
608ᵃ   ἐν δὲ λιμὴν ἐτέτυκτο ἐανοῦ κασσιτέροιο (*Aspis* 207–8)
    ᵇ   κλυζομένῳ ἴκελος· δοιὼ δ' ἀναφυσιοῶντες (209–11)
    ᶜ   ἀργύρεοι δελφῖνες ἐφοίνεον ἔλλοπας ἰχθῦς. (212)
    ᵈ   τοῦ δ' ὕπο χάλκειοι τρέον ἰχθύες· αὐτὰρ ἐπ' ἀκταῖς (213)

(I accept the editors' restorations : they are generally pretty
certain and do not affect the argument.)

Observe : 604–5 are run together. In our vulgate they
stand

      τερπόμενοι· μετὰ δέ σφιν ἐμέλπετο θεῖος ἀοιδὸς
      φορμίζων, δοιὼ δὲ κτλ.

But our vulgate has here behaved oddly. Editors have forsaken the MSS. and inserted a phrase from the *Odyssey* (δ 17–18) on the evidence of Athenaeus (p. 180 c), who says that the lines in question originally belonged to Σ and not to the *Odyssey*.

606ª is a new line. 608ª ᵇ ᶜ ᵈ are not known to us in Homer, but a passage closely similar, though slightly longer, stands in our text of Hesiod, *Aspis* 207–13 describing the shield of Heracles.

What is the meaning ot such a phenomenon as this? A passage known to our tradition as part of the Hesiodic Shield of Heracles appears in this MS. as part of the Homeric Shield of Achilles. It is clearly not the mistake of a copyist. It is, as Diels and others have seen, the deliberate variation of a rhapsode, who preferred his 'Shield' in that form. He shortened the expression a good deal and he got in the description of a harbour with plunging dolphins. Whether his judgement was wise may well be disputed; the point is that apparently he thought he had a right to make it. The text of this passage was not absolutely fixed as canonical even by the time this MS. was written—when Aristarchus had perhaps been dead fifty years.[1]

The same explanation seems to me to apply to all the facts about these pre-Alexandrian MSS. The text was still very fluid, at any rate in places. For, as Grenfell and Hunt have pointed out, the additional verses are not scattered evenly all over the

---

[1] This is not an isolated phenomenon. The Townley Scholia on Ω 804, the last line of the *Iliad*, mention that instead of

ʽΩs οἵ γ' ἀμφίεπον τάφον ῞Εκτορος ἱπποδάμοιο

some MSS. read

ʽΩs οἵ γ' ἀμφίεπον τάφον ῞Εκτορος· ἦλθε δ' Ἀμαζών,
῎Αρηος θυγάτηρ μεγαλήτορος ἀνδροφόνοιο.

That is, they ran on from the end of our *Iliad* to another story, the *Aethiopis*, about the Queen of the Amazons. And in some cases such a mixture of sources has actually become canonical. The end of the *Theogony* in all our MSS. is mixed up with another poem, The Catalogue of Women who were loved by gods. The MSS. of our Shield of Heracles have attached that poem to one of the ἐοῖαι, or used the ἐοίη, so to speak, as a peg. See also the striking Fayûm fragment (Allen 53) giving the Chryseis episode (A 486 ff.) in the words of the *Hymn to Apollo*, 503 ff. Cauer, *Grundfr.*³, pp. 44 ff. Cf. Bolling in *A.J.P.* 1914, pp. 125 ff.

poems, but are concentrated in particular parts. They come
where the texture of the narrative is loose: where inorganic
verses can easily be added, or whole formulae of two or three
lines inserted. To put the same fact from a different point
of view, some parts of the poems were specially well known and
canonical; others were still fluid and indefinite—the less
interesting, the merely transitional, the parts perhaps which were
not often chosen for recitation, though they had to exist in any
professedly complete text.

There is, for instance, perhaps no part of the poems which has
been more 'suspected' by scholars than Θ. According to
Wilamowitz it was largely composed very late in order to make
room in the *Iliad* for *I* and *K*. And a glance at the list above
will show the extraordinary ' wildness' of the three fragments of
the papyrus containing Θ. We shall find a similar wildness
about Θ in the quotations.

We may also observe that the new lines seem generally, though
not always, to be made up of lines or half-lines or phrases which
occur elsewhere in the poems; very few seem to have been
original or vital poetry. The Alexandrian critics were wise in
the use of their obelus.

2. Let us now take the quotations.

At the first blush we can see one thing. There are a good
many small fragments quoted from Homer by various authors
which do not occur in our text. Of fifth-century authors, Pindar
observes that Homer says that a noble messenger gives dignity
to any business. Our Homer never gets nearer to that than to
say that it is a good thing when a messenger is tactful. Hippocrates mentions that Homer knew that cattle suffered in winter;
that is why he wrote ὡς δ' ὁπότ' ἀσπάσιον ἔαρ ἤλυθε βουσὶν
ἕλιξι. Our Homer writes nothing of the sort. In the fourth
century Aeschines says that 'Homer says several times in the
Iliad φήμη δ' ἐς στρατὸν ἦλθε ': the phrase never occurs in our
Iliad. Xenophon cites from Homer the phrases γάνυται δέ τ'
ἀκούων and πυκινὰ φρεσὶ μήδεα εἰδώς, which do not occur.
Aristotle, who uses Homer a great deal, quotes quite a number
of lines unknown to our texts;[1] πὰρ γὰρ ἐμοὶ θάνατος, ″Εκτορα

---

[1] Pind. *Pyth.* iv. 277, cf. O 207 ; Hippocr. περὶ ἄρθρων iii, p. 146 K. (p. 62,

δ' αἰδὼς εἷλε, "Εκτωρ κεῖτ' ἀλλοφρονέων, μῦσεν δὲ περὶ βροτόεσσ'
ὠτειλή, Ζεὺς γάρ οἱ νεμέσασχ' ὅτ' ἀμείνονι φωτὶ μάχοιτο.
Besides these completely unknown lines, he quotes known
passages in a strange shape; he found δίδομεν δέ οἱ εὖχος ἀρέσθαι
not in Φ 297 where we have it, but in β 15; he found δ 567 in a
shorter form; he found our lines μ 219 ff., or something very
like them, in a speech of Calypso; he found part of our description of the Cyclops in the ninth *Odyssey* as a description of the
Calydonian Boar in the tenth *Iliad*: he expressly says that
Odysseus' story to Penelope (Ψ 310–41) occupied ' only sixty '
lines: in our text it occupies thirty-three. In *Ethics*, p. 1116
b 24, there are four phrases quoted from ' Homer ', two incorrect
and two unrecognizable. It is also worth noting that Aristophanes
says that Homer describes Iris in words which in our text apply
not to Iris but to Hera and Athena; or that Plato read μήτηρ
instead of "Εκτωρ in Z 402, making a change not only in wording
but in a statement of fact.

This list is not complete, but, even apart from the evidence of
the papyri, it seems to me quite conclusive. There must have
been current in the fourth century texts of Homer very different
indeed from ours. Make handsome allowance for slips of memory
and the like, the testimony of these unknown lines is not to be
overthrown, and cannot even be shaken by any but the most
overwhelming evidence on the other side.

That evidence Ludwich has tried to produce. He collects
a great list of Homeric quotations in authors of the fourth
century or earlier, covering some 480 lines, and urges us not
to concentrate our attention on the ' wild ' lines which reject our
text, but on the great majority of ' tame ' lines which conform to it.

Let us consider this plea. The evidence of quotations is
always hard to use, as certainly an editor of Euripides is not
likely to forget. The quoter may err in memory; he may adapt
the words of the poet to his own purpose; he may intentionally
omit lines. He will quote chiefly what is striking and interesting. In the special case before us, what we have to make out is

Erm.); Aeschin. i. 128 (Blass); Xen. *Symp.* 8. 30; Aristot., pp. 1285 a 10,
1230 a 18, 404 a 29, fr. 167 Rothe, 1387 a 32; 162 b 7, 943 b 21, 1109 a 30,
578 b 2, 1417 a 12; Ar. *Av.* 575; Plato, *Crat.* 392 b. See also fragments in
Allen, vol. v, pp. 146 ff.—Hippocrates and Pindar may have used ' Homer ' in
a wider sense, see p. 298.

whether each quotation in the ancient authors seems most likely to come from a text practically identical with our vulgate or from one like the pre-Aristarchean papyri.

Now, in the first place, single lines or bits of lines which agree with our text prove nothing. They doubtless also occurred in the 'wildest' papyri. Conventional phrases and epic runs prove nothing for the same reason. Even if there were a general tendency not to quote the 'additional' lines much, that would prove nothing, because the additional lines are seldom striking or quotable. Mere descriptions of facts or abbreviations of long passages seldom prove anything, because the differences between the papyri and the vulgate would scarcely show in them. Slight variations in language, on the other hand, do not prove much, nor do omissions of lines. They may be mere mistakes of the quoter. Such things are common in the quotations from Euripides. Out of the great list of quotations given by Ludwich, covering some 480 lines of the *Iliad* and *Odyssey*, more than half fall away at once as non-evidential.

If we take only the quotations of more than three consecutive lines we have some approach to firmer ground. We may class them as follows: *Agreeing but not conclusively, two passages*:

A 17–42, referred to by Plat. *Rep.* iii. 393 d, in a fairly close indirect description, with many lines omitted.

B 671–4: three half-lines cited in *Ar. Rhet.* iii. 12, p. 1414 a 2.

Disagreeing but not conclusively, five:

I 497–501 in Plat. *Rep.* ii. 364 d, one line omitted; wording slightly different.

I 308–14 in Plat. *Hipp. Min.* 364 e (cf. 370 a), one line omitted.

Δ 446–50, roughly cited in Ar. *Pax* 1273: not much evidence, but a much-suspected breast-plate line is omitted (σὺν δ᾽ ἔγχεα καὶ μένε᾽ ἀνδρῶν χαλκεοθωρήκων).

τ 109–13 in Plat. *Rep.* ii. 363 b, one line omitted.

υ 351–7 in Plat. *Ion* 538 e, one striking line omitted and wording slightly different.

Clearly agreeing, perhaps twelve (occasionally with some verbal variation): Z 289–92 in Hdt. ii. 116; *Odyssey*, δ 227–30 in Hdt. ii. 116 (cf. Theophr. *de Plant.* ix. 15. 1); O 494–9 in Lyc. *in Leocr.* § 103 (differences); Σ 324–9 in Aeschines, i. § 143; ζ 42–5 in Ps.-Aristot. *de Mundo*, 6, p. 400 a 6; I 357–63 in Plat. *Hipp. Min.* 370 b (cf. Crito, 44 b); *I* 650–5, ibidem, 371 b; *M* 200–7 in Plat. *Ion* 539 b; Ψ 335–40 in Plat. *Ion* 537 a (cf. Xen. *Sympos.* 4. 6); ω 6–9 in Plat. *Rep.* iii. 387 a; ι 112–15 in Plat. *Legg.* iii. 680 b; Ξ 96–102 in Plat. *Legg.* iv. 706 d (slight differences).

Conclusively and markedly disagreeing we find seven at least :

B 188–202 in Xen. *Mem.* i. 2. 58; six verses omitted, probably not by accident, as they were counted spurious by Aristarchus.

B 391 ff. in Arist. *Pol.* iii. 14 (p. 1285 a 10), with an unknown half-line added, πὰρ γὰρ ἐμοὶ θάνατος.

Σ 95–9 in Aeschin. i. 150, markedly different wording.

Ψ 77–91, ib. 146, with two new lines, one line inserted from elsewhere, and several differences of wording.

Ω 10–12 in Plat. *Rep.* iii. 388 a, considerable differences of wording.

Ω 527–32, ib. ii. 379 c, with one strange line substituted for one of ours.

Θ 548–52 in the Platonic *Alcibiades* ii, p. 149 d, with *four* completely new lines added.

The proportion is just about what it ought to be. The quotations, where they are long enough to afford a fair test, instead of lifting a loud protest against the evidence of the papyri, simply and clearly confirm it.

There is one point more. Grenfell and Hunt, in their masterly discussion of this question in the introduction to Pap. Hibeh 19, have shown that if a dividing line be drawn at 150 B.C. all MSS. earlier than that date differ 'enormously' both from our vulgate and from Aristarchus, and all tend to be longer except possibly Hibeh 20.[1] After 150 B.C. the tendency of MSS. to differ from the vulgate diminishes rapidly, and by the beginning of the Roman period 'the numerous Homeric fragments published in recent years very rarely contain new verses, and serve to illustrate only too well the overwhelming predominance of the vulgate'. Zenodotus had laid the foundations

---

[1] This exception is considered by Dr. Gerhardt, in his introduction to the new Heidelberg fragments, to melt away in the light of later evidence.

of criticism about 280 B.C. Aristophanes and others followed him. The floruit of Aristarchus, most successful and universally acclaimed of Homer scholars, is 160 B.C.; the triumph of the vulgate begins about 150 B.C. The dates speak for themselves. The predominance of a much-castigated and purified text was due directly or indirectly to the great critics of the Alexandrian age. Can we go further than this, and pronounce it definitely the work of Aristarchus? That view, put forward by Wolf and Nauck, and probable on general grounds, has hitherto seemed to break down on the detailed evidence of the scholia, but is now almost proved to be right by the acute researches of Professor G. M. Bolling of Ohio.[1] He has collected in the vulgar tradition— both in the MSS. and the post-Aristarchean papyri—all the lines of doubtful authenticity, and finds that all the directly attested differences between the vulgate and Aristarchus are due to interpolations in the vulgate, while, conversely, no line which is an interpolation in the vulgate can be shown to have been in Aristarchus' text. That text contained about 15,600 lines, to which some 93 have been added by interpolation in the course of the last two thousand years.

But, granted that the present vulgate had in pre-Alexandrian times no central and dominant position—and most scholars have been convinced by Grenfell and Hunt—one question still remains. Did our vulgate exist at all in classical times, or is it, very much as Wolf thought, a later creation altogether, a text hammered out for the first time by the impact of Alexandrian criticism upon a fluid but rather obstinate tradition?

The point is a doubtful one, and depends mainly on the quotations in Plato. They, as may have been seen above, resemble our text pretty closely.

On a rough analysis, there are twenty-three [2 a] quotations in Plato which definitely agree with our text; there are eigh-

---

[1] *A. J. P.* xxxvii (1916), pts. 1 and 4; cf. *Modern Philology*, xvii. 3 (1922). Cf. Cauer, l.c., chap. 3.
[2] a Agreeing, sometimes with slight variations:—

A 15 f.	*Rep.* iii. 393 a.	M 200–7.	*Ion* 539 b.
A 599 f.	*Rep.* iii. 389 a.	P 446 f.	*Axioch.* 367 d.
E 127 f.	*Alcib.* ii. 150 d.	Σ 23 f.	*Rep.* iii. 388 b.
I 357–63.	*Hipp. Min.* 370 b.	T 92 f.	*Sympos.* 195 d.
I 644 f.	*Cratyl.* 428 c.	X 414 f.	*Rep.* iii. 388 b.
I 650–5.	*Hipp. Min.* 371 b.	Ψ 103 f.	*Rep.* iii. 386 d.

teen [b] of no evidential value, being too short, too vague, or containing mere epic phrases which might come anywhere ; there
are seven [c] which omit lines in the middle ; four that vary considerably in wording and three that vary very slightly ; [d] there are
seven which definitely differ from our text by additional lines or
conflated lines ; [e] and there is lastly the perfectly 'wild' quotation from Θ in the post-Platonic *Alcibiades* ii. It needs a bold
man to argue from this that Plato's text was our text. Still it is

Ψ 335–40. *Ion* 537 a.

Ω 80–2. *Ion* 538 d.

α 32–4. *Alcib.* ii. 142 d.

γ 26–8. *Legg.* vii. 804 a.

ι 112–15. *Legg.* iii. 680 b.

λ 489–91. *Rep.* iii. 386 c, vii. 516 d.

ο 245 f. *Axioch.* 368 a.

ρ 347. *Charm.* 161 a.

ρ 485 f. *Rep.* ii. 381 d.

υ 17 f. *Phaedon* 94 d ; *Rep.* iii. 390 d
       iv. 441 b.

ω 6–9. *Rep.* iii. 387 a.

[b] Agreeing, but non-evidentially :—

A 17–42. *Rep.* iii. 393 d.

B 813 f. *Cratyl.* 392 a.

E 221 f. *Cratyl.* 407 d.

Z 235 f. *Sympos.* 219 a.

Θ 14. *Phaedon* 112 a.

Π 112 f. *Rep.* viii. 545 d.

Π 856 f. (phrases). *Rep.* iii. 386 d.

Σ 108 f. *Phileb.* 47 e.

Υ 64 f. (phrases). *Rep.* iii. 386 c.

Φ 308 f. *Protag.* 340 a.

X 506 f. *Cratyl.* 392 a.

Ψ 100 f. *Rep.* iii. 387 a.

Ω 15 f. *Rep.* iii. 391 b.

Ω 525 f. *Axioch.* 367 d.

λ 633 f. *Sympos.* 198 c.

ρ 383 f. *Rep.* iii. 389 d.

τ 395 f. *Rep.* i. 334 b.

χ 1–4. *Ion* 535 b.

[c] Omitting lines :—

I 308–14 (om. 1). *Hipp. Min.* 365 a ; ib. 370 a.

I 497–501 (om. 1). *Rep.* ii. 364 d.

Σ 96–104 (om. 6). *Apolog.* 28 c.

X 15–20 (om. 4). *Rep.* iii. 391 a.

τ 109–13 (om. 1). *Rep.* ii. 363 b.

τ 173–9 (om. 3). *Minos* 319 b.

υ 351–7 (om. 1). *Ion* 539 a.

[d] Different in wording :—

Ξ 96–102. *Legg.* iv. 706 d.

α 351 f. *Rep.* iv. 424 b.

ι 8–10. *Rep.* iii. 390 a.

ρ 322 f. *Legg.* vi. 777 a.

Λ 169–71. *Hipp. Min.* 370 c (slightly).

Π 433 f. *Rep.* iii. 388 c (slightly).

X 168 f. *Rep.* iii. 388 c (slightly).

[e] Different by additional or conflated lines, &c. :—

Γ 8 + Δ 431. *Rep.* iii. 389 e.

Δ 218–19. *Rep.* iii. 408 a.

Z 402 (μήτηρ). *Cratyl.* 392 b.

Λ 639 + 630. *Ion* 538 b.

Ξ 295 f. *Rep.* iii. 390 b.

Ω 10–12. *Rep.* iii. 388 a.

Ω 527–32 (new line). *Rep.* ii. 379 d.

Θ 548–52 (+4). *Alcib.* ii. 149 d (wild).

clear that Plato's quotations are much closer to our text than
those of any other fourth-century writer.

The simplest conclusion would be to assume that Plato used
a text very like ours. Yet perhaps that would be a mistake.
Among the writings of the first disciples of Aristarchus we find
one by Ammonius, περὶ τῶν ὑπὸ Πλάτωνος ἐξ Ὁμήρου μετε-
νηνεγμένων, ' On Plato's quotations from Homer '. The purpose
of the book was textual recension. That is, the quotations in
Plato were a recognized authority for the text of Homer in
Alexandrian times. There was a whole small literature on Plato's
relation to Homer. He shared with Herodotus the title of
Ὁμηρικώτατος, and exercised a quite special influence on the
Alexandrian school. Is it, perhaps, not Plato who agrees with
our vulgate, but our vulgate which, wherever it had the evidence,
tried deliberately to follow the readings of Plato? It is curious,
at any rate, that the writer whose quotations, few as they are,
come next to Plato's for conformity with our text, is the other
recognized ' Homerikôtatos ', Herodotus.[1]

II. The verbal text, then, was still fluid and subject to change
as late as the fourth and third centuries B.C. What can we be
sure of as fixed? The whole main structure, one would suppose,
the incidents and the order in which they followed one another.
Yet even here one cannot feel absolute confidence, at any rate for
the fourth century and earlier.

For instance, to take an observation made by the late
Professor M. L. Earle of Columbia University: Thucydides,
i. 11. 1, writes about the Greeks at Troy: ' When they landed
they must have won a battle; otherwise they would not have
built the fortification round the camp.'[2] This shows that
Thucydides (1) knew of the wall round the camp so frequently

---

[1] See Sengebusch, *Dissert. Prior.*, pp. 118-24; Ludwich, p. 141, note. In
the next generation Trypho wrote περὶ τῆς ἀρχαίας ἀναγνώσεως, which Sengebusch interprets ' On the readings of Homer shown in the ancient quotations in
general '. Sengeb., p. 124. Cf. Susemihl, *Alexandr. Litter.*, pp. 154 and 212.
See also Howes, *Harvard Studies in Cl. Phil.* vi (1895), pp. 153 ff.

[2] Ἐπειδὴ δ' ἀφικόμενοι μάχῃ ἐκράτησαν· δῆλον δέ· τὸ γὰρ ἔρυμα τῷ στρατοπέδῳ
οὐκ ἂν ἐτειχίσαντο. Thiersch ἐκρατήθησαν, ' lost a battle ', which Earle accepts.
The reading does not affect the present argument. The same suggestion, it
is interesting to find, was made long ago by Hermann; *Opuscula*, vol. viii,
p. 387 (371). See Prof. Earle's *Collected Essays*, pp. 142-4.

mentioned in our *Iliad*, and (2) surmised that it must have been built at the beginning of the war, after the first battle.

Now in our *Iliad* (H 337 ff., 436 ff.) the building of this wall and the exact circumstances which led to it are fully described, and are not what Thucydides conjectures they ' must have been '. It was built in a great rush and in picturesque conditions during a scanty truce in the tenth year of the war. It is noteworthy that the particular passage in *H* has been marked by Köchly and many other critics as ' recentissima '.[1]

The view we take of this bold suggestion will obviously depend largely on the presence or absence of other symptoms pointing in a similar direction. It is always hard to get out of our minds the associations of printed books, which appear in definite editions in a complete form, all the copies identical. But let us look at the direct evidence.

There are still extant many MSS. which omit the Catalogue in *B*, though, curiously enough, they give the series of similes with which it is introduced. That is, even at the time when the vulgate became predominant, the Catalogue was not definitely established as a necessary part of the *Iliad*.

There are no MSS. now which omit *K*, but a note in the very valuable Townley scholia informs us: ' They say that *K* was originally placed apart by Homer and is not part of the *Iliad*, but was put into it by Pisistratus.'[2] The statement is repeated in the learned scholia to Dionysius Thrax and in Eustathius, who ascribes it to ' the ancients '. That is—to put the case at its lowest—there was an ancient tradition which knew of, or believed in, the existence of *Iliads* without *K* as well as *Iliads* with.

We also know that Aristarchus thought the last book of the *Odyssey* (ω) spurious, and that both he and Aristophanes of Byzantium considered ψ 296 as ' the end of the *Odyssey* '. This does not necessarily imply that he knew of MSS. without ω or without the end of ψ, but it does show that the canon was still far from certain.

If such large stretches of the poem were not definitely estab-

---

[1] Plato's citation of H 321 in *Rep.* v. 468 d does not of course affect the question.

[2] Φασὶ τὴν ῥαψωδίαν ὑφ' Ὁμήρου ἰδίᾳ τετάχθαι καὶ μὴ εἶναι μέρος τῆς Ἰλιάδος, ὑπὸ δὲ Πεισιστράτου τετάχθαι εἰς τὴν ποίησιν. Schol. T on K 1. Eustathius says φασὶν οἱ παλαιοί, evidently referring to the same source.

lished even in Alexandrian times, it is obviously quite possible
that a passage like the Building of the Wall was not definitely
established in the time of Thucydides.   We must not be indignant
merely because such a result would show a conjecture of many
modern critics to be probably right.

Is there any other test that we can apply?   Only one has
occurred to me, rather a curious one.

It is well known that, for some reason, the Attic tragedians in
choosing their subjects made it a careful rule to avoid the main
subjects and incidents of the *Iliad* and *Odyssey*.   We know, I
suppose, the subjects of some two hundred tragedies by the three
great writers, and the rule is well kept up.   There is, indeed,
one great exception, a lost trilogy of Aeschylus (*Myrmidons*,
Nereids, *Phrygians*) which dealt directly with the subject of *Iliad*
I–Ω.   Its date is unknown; but it comes very early in the
history of Greek tragedy, and, apparently, the experiment it
made was never repeated.   In Satyr plays the rule did not hold.
You could burlesque ' Homer ', as in the *Cyclops* and in Sophocles'
Washing Girls, or Nausicaa.[1]   But you avoided attempting to
treat again in the high style at the Dionysia subjects which your
public already knew in the Recitations at the Panathenaea.   I
can only make out two certain exceptions.   One is the *Rhesus*,
which treats in full detail the story of Dolon, *Iliad* **K**; the other
is a Catalogue of the Greek ships in the *Iphigenia in Aulis*
(164–302).   The Doloneia and the Catalogue!   Just the two
parts of the *Iliad* which we know to have been uncanonical!

On the whole it seems to me probable that Thucydides used,
or learnt at school, or heard recited at the Panathenaea, an *Iliad*
without the account of the Wall-building, Euripides an *Iliad*
without the Catalogue, the author of the *Rhesus* an *Iliad* without **K**.   There is a good field here for further research.

III. In the age of Euripides and Thucydides, then, it would
seem from the evidence that the *Iliad* and *Odyssey* differed from
our vulgate not only in the matter of exact words and lines, but
even in large portions of the story.   ' Homer ' meant to them, as

---

[1] I agree with Valckenaer, *Diatribe* 209, and Lessing.   Welcker, building
on the far from clear passage in Eustathius, *Iliad*, p. 381, thought the Πλύντριαι
a tragedy (*Gr. Trag.* i. 227), and his view has been commonly accepted.   It
was a not unusual subject for comedies.

to us, 'the author of the *Iliad* and the *Odyssey*', but we cannot
be sure that either *Iliad* or *Odyssey* was exactly what we mean by
those words.   If we go a century further back, however, we find
that the meaning of 'Homer' also is different.   His name covers
not only the *Iliad* and the *Odyssey*, but much wider and vaguer
masses of epic writing as well.   Let us take the quotations.

Kallinus, our earliest witness, in the eighth or seventh century
B.C., cites the *Thebaid* as Homer's (Paus. ix. 9. 5.).   Simonides
—either the great Simonides of the early fifth century or he of
Amorgos in the seventh—quotes a proverbial line that comes in
our Z 146 as the work of 'a man of Chios': probably meaning
'Homer'.[1]   The great Simonides quotes 'Homer and Stesichorus' as describing how Meleager 'surpassed all the young
men in spear-throwing across the wild Anauros'.   This does not
come from our Homer; possibly it came from that old Meleager
epos which is a supposed source for *Iliad* I.   Pindar quotes the
Odyssey in *Nem.* vii. 20; he quotes the unknown line about the
messenger in *Pyth.* iv. 277;[2] in *Isthm.* iii. 53 he seems to say
that Homer has told 'all the virtue of Aias', including his death.
This could scarcely refer to our *Iliad*.   In fr. 189 he mentions
that Homer wrote the *Cypria* and gave it for his daughter's
dowry.   Herodotus himself, when he says that Cleisthenes in
his anti-Argive policy silenced the rhapsodes in Sicyon 'on
account of the poems of Homer, in which the Argives and
Argos are generally glorified in every way', has been considered
with some probability to refer to the *Thebais*.   Lastly, when
Aeschylus described his tragedies as merely 'slices from the
great banquets of Homer', it is perfectly clear that he did not
mean that they were taken from the *Iliad* and *Odyssey*—which
they markedly avoid.   When we hear that 'Sophocles rejoiced
in the Epic Cycle', and when Proclus tells us, quite correctly,
that 'the ancients attributed also the Cycle to Homer', we can
understand the situation.   The 'cycle', as Wilamowitz and others
have shown, was a compendium of epic history made up out of
various early masses of poetry.   Sophocles and Aeschylus both
'rejoiced in' and took 'slices out of' that same great body of
poetry, all of which was 'Homer'.[3]   They did what the vase-

---

[1] Callinus 6, Simonides 85, 53, in Bergk's fourth edition.
[2] See above, p. 289.   [3] Hdt. v. 67 ; Ath. 347 e; ib. 277 e.

painters did : these also probably considered that they drew their subjects from Homer, but, with few exceptions, they do not take them from the *Iliad* or the *Odyssey*.

The first of our authorities to reject any of this work as non-Homeric is Herodotus. He argues that the *Cypria* are not by Homer because they contradict the *Iliad* (ii. 117). He is not sure whether Homer wrote the *Epigonoi*, a sort of sequel to the great *Thebais* (iv. 32). By about 350 B.C. the name 'Homer' is normally used in our traditional sense, for the author of the *Iliad* and *Odyssey* and no other epics besides. Yet there are still isolated exceptions, as when Antigonus of Carystus cites the *Thebais* as Homer's,[1] or Simmias—possibly—the 'Little Iliad'. A great bas-relief full of scenes of epic tradition from the War of the Titans onward, intended for educational purposes and composed by one Theodorus in the first century B.C., is superscribed Θεοδώρειον μάθε τάξιν Ὁμήρου.[2] Even as late as that, in certain phrases at any rate, the whole epic tradition could be called ' Homer '.

IV. How is this change to be explained? What force was working between, say, the years 500 and 400 B.C. to put the *Iliad* and the *Odyssey* in a separate and privileged position, as the only true works of 'Homer', and thus far greater and better known than the rest of the epic traditional poetry? One cause suggests itself at once : the public Recitation at the Panathenaea. Let us sift the statements of our authorities on this subject.

First, we know for certain that Homer *was* recited at the Panathenaea. The orator Lycurgus (*in Leocr.*, p. 209) says : ' Your ancestors considered Homer so noble a poet, that they made a law that every four years at the celebration of the Panathenaea his poems *and his alone* should be recited by rhapsodes. '[3] There is a similar statement in Isocrates attributing

---

[1] See Wilamowitz, *Homerische Untersuchungen*, 350 ff., from whom most of this argument is taken. An attempt to overthrow part of it by Hiller, *Rh. Mus.* N. F. xlii, pp. 321-61.

[2] Jahn-Michaelis, *Bilderchronik*.

[3] Lycurg. *in Leocr.*, p. 209 [§ 102, Bekker] βούλομαι δ' ὑμῖν καὶ τὸν Ὅμηρον παρασχέσθαι ἐπαινῶν· οὕτω γὰρ ὑπέλαβον ὑμῶν οἱ πατέρες σπουδαῖον εἶναι ποιητήν, ὥστε νόμον ἔθεντο καθ' ἑκάστην πενταετηρίδα τῶν Παναθηναίων μόνου τῶν ἄλλων ποιητῶν ῥαψῳδεῖσθαι τὰ ἔπη. Cf. Isocr. *Paneg.*, p. 74 οἶμαι δὲ καὶ τὴν Ὁμήρου ποίησιν μείζω λαβεῖν δόξαν, ὅτι καλῶς τοὺς πολεμήσαντας τοῖς βαρβάροις ἐνεκωμίασε,

the institution to 'our ancestors'.   The fact, therefore, is certain :
there was a long-established rule at the Panathenaea of reciting
' Homer and Homer only '.

But what does ' Homer ' in this context mean ?   Is it the whole
epic tradition or is it the *Iliad* and the *Odyssey* ?   I think pretty
certainly the latter.[1]

The conclusive evidence lies in the words of Lycurgus.   He
says 'Homer and Homer only', and no one will dispute that
in his time (*c.* 331 B. C.) that meant the *Iliad* and the *Odyssey*—
unless possibly trifles like the *Margites* were admitted also.
The language of Isocrates is almost equally clear.   And such
indirect evidence as we have points in the same direction.   The
rhapsode Ion, for instance, in Plato's dialogue about him, speaks
definitely of reciting the *Iliad* and *Odyssey*, and never suggests
reciting anything else.   Further, some of our witnesses state
particularly that the law ordered the recitation to be 'in order',
one reciter beginning where the other left off.   It is obvious from
the state of the text in the fourth century that this ' order ' was
not interpreted very rigorously.   The very idea of exactitude in
such matters is a product of a later age.   But it is certainly easier
to understand a rule that the *Iliad* and *Odyssey* should be recited
in order, than to imagine any such attempt made upon the whole
mass of epic saga.

If then we take Lycurgus's words in their natural sense,
the whole development becomes intelligible.   During the fifth
century ' Homer ' gradually gets to mean the author of our two
epics and no others; the chosen poems are known in a fixed
order and gradually acquire a fairly fixed text; the other epics
gradually fall out of general knowledge, and are used mainly as
quarries of tradition from which the dramatists and others can
carve their works.   The rejected epics deteriorate in style and
retain all their barbarities.   The chosen two, still fluid and
occupying a central position in an age of splendid and exuberant
poetical creation, tend still to become better and better written,
and morally more and more idealized.

καὶ διὰ τοῦτο βουληθῆναι τοὺς προγόνους ἡμῶν ἔντιμον αὐτοῦ ποιῆσαι τὴν τέχνην ἔν
τε τοῖς τῆς μουσικῆς ἄθλοις καὶ τῇ παιδεύσει τῶν νεωτέρων.

[1] The other view is upheld by Dr. Verrall in *The Bacchants of Euripides*,
pp. 175 ff.   With almost all of Dr. Verrall's argument in this essay on ' The
First Homer ' I cordially agree.

Can we make out at all why these two should have been selected? A certain kind of critic is ready with his answer, an enthusiastic description of the incomparable poetic merits of these two poems and their immense superiority to all the other poetry of which we know nothing. But the public acts of statesmen are not often swayed by considerations of poetry. If these two poems were felt in some special way to represent in public opinion the crown of the old Ionic poetry, that would be a real motive. If there was in them already some moral superiority, that would be a real motive. They were constantly used for purposes of edification. But I incline to suspect that Isocrates instinctively discerned the main reason:

> I believe that the poetry of Homer won greater glory because he nobly praised those who warred against the barbarian, and that this was the reason why our ancestors conceived the desire to make his art honoured both in the contests of the Muses and in the training of young men. (*Paneg.*, p. 74.)

Isocrates was, no doubt, thinking chiefly of the *Iliad*: but the *Odyssey* has its national character too. The *Iliad* typifies the national heroes who warred with the Mede, the *Odyssey* the national colonists and adventurers who, trusting only to their brains and their courage, searched strange seas from Panticapaeum to Tartessos.

V. We can perhaps make out a little more about the text used at this official recitation.

The first thing to notice is that to some extent the surface of Homer has in our tradition been Atticized. To what extent it is hard to say, since the actual spelling which has come down to us has passed through a further influence, that of the post-classical *Koinê*, or Common Greek. But in any case there are numbers of lines which run perfectly when the Ionic forms are restored, and are visibly wrong as they stand at present. The poems were generally recognized in antiquity as Ionic poems. Yet all our MSS. and the Alexandrians behind them unite in giving us the Attic forms. There is no suggestion in the Scholia of any other view. There are also some few obvious 'Athenian interpolations', and no doubt many more that are not obvious. But though some scholars in antiquity suspected them, there is no statement that any old MSS. left them out. What does this mean? Of course a great predominance of Athenian MSS. would surprise no one; the literary supremacy of Athens would ensure that. But this is much more. It means that when the Alexandrians were searching for ancient MSS. by which to correct the text, and collecting copies of various sorts in places ranging from Marseilles to Sinope, they could not apparently find a single Ionic MS. worth their notice. The Attic versions had completely superseded the Ionic. We can understand why the great collector of MSS., Aristarchus, decided that Homer himself must have been an Athenian.

Zenodotus was an Ionian, and Ionian influences were strong in Alexandrian literature. Yet we have to admit that either there were no Ionic texts of Homer at all, or, if there were, they were so unlike and so inferior to the current Attic texts that critics would not consider them. Either case confirms our previous conclusion that the Athenian recitations exercised an immense influence. Cauer, indeed, argues that perhaps there never had been any Ionic texts at all; that epic poems had never been written down till they came to Athens. But this supposition is difficult in detail. There is much detailed work in both *Iliad* and *Odyssey*,[1] which one cannot imagine a poet carrying through except by careful comparison of different MSS. And the fate of the Samaritan scriptures shows us how completely, in the days before a reading public, a book might be killed. We need only suppose that the MSS. used in Ionia were still the half-secret possessions of professional bards, and that none amounted to a complete Iliad or Odyssey, in our sense.

There is lastly a curious phenomenon about which it is hard to form a confident judgement. We find in the Scholia a clear tradition, backed up by a number of fairly certain corrections of the text by modern scholars, that at some time or other the poems were transliterated from the Old Attic[2] alphabet into the

---

[1] See Seeck's *Quellen der Odyssee*, Verrall's essays in *The Bacchants of Euripides*, and pp. 175 f., 179, above.

[2] Why Attic, it may be asked? Why not some primitive Ionian alphabet, of the days before Pisistratus?—Athens had been the home of the poems for the last three hundred years; the MSS. in the hands of the Alexandrians seem, as we have seen, all to represent the Attic recension; and no Ionian

new.   The new is the Greek alphabet that we know : the old —
to speak roughly—used no double letters, made no distinction
between the three *E*-sounds or the three *O*-sounds, and used *H*
to denote the aspirate.[1]

Now this tradition is only mentioned by the scholiasts in order
to support conjectural changes, and it may be a conjecture itself.
But it looks rather as if it were a true one.   It does explain with
perfect simplicity some confusions that are otherwise difficult.
And if it is true, we are led to a curious and interesting result.

It has been made out pretty clearly that, though Athens did
not adopt the new alphabet for official documents till 404 B.C., it
must have been in use in literary circles very much earlier,
probably as far back as the days when letters were exchanged
between Solon in Athens and Mimnermus in Ionian Colophon.
For literature at that date was an Ionian accomplishment, and
the new alphabet was the Ionian alphabet.   How then could it
happen that, at a time when the new Ionian alphabet was already
used in Athens for literary purposes, the great Ionian book
should be deliberately rewritten back into the awkward old
Athenian script?   There is only one obvious explanation.   It
was written in the official script as an official text for the performance at the Panathenaea.

An official text dating back probably to the sixth century B.C.:
yet we saw that in the third there was apparently no official text!
The critics can appeal to none such.   The papyri and the
quotations show that the poems were still fluid.   Is this not
a contradiction?

Not necessarily, I think, for two reasons.   In the first place,
granted there was an official text made for the Panathenaea in
the sixth century, I think it in the last degree improbable that at
that date a reciter would be kept to it.   It might be stored up,
it might be used for show and for reference.   But the whole
notion of keeping a rhapsode to his written text, instead of

---

alphabet known to us satisfies all the conditions.   The very earliest Ionian
inscriptions all have H for long E and nearly all have ω for the long open O.
Doubtless at an earlier date there may have been a rudimentary Ionian
alphabet, but, as far as I know, the Alexandrians never show any knowledge
of it.   To them the ʻIonic alphabetʼ means the ʻnew alphabetʼ.   See Cauer[3],
p. 126, and Fick in *Bezzb. Beitr.* 30 (1906), p. 297, there cited.

[1] As Wilamowitz puts it, ΕΝΔΕΟΙΚΟΣΙ might mean ἐν δ᾽ ἐοικόσι, or ἦν δὴ
οἰκῶσι, or ἐν δὲ οἰκοῦσι.   See Appendix I.

letting him give you the best he has in him, was in my judgement
an invention of the second half of the fourth century, and would
have seemed a stark absurdity in the sixth. But apart from that,
if there was in sixth-century Athens a government strong enough
and academic enough thus to strangle the poetical powers of the
bards at the Panathenaea, we know that that government did
not survive the year 510 B.C. The Tyrants' authoritative text
may well have fallen with the Tyrants.

But have we any right to suppose that the recitation and the
supposed recension, either or both, were the work of the
Tyrants? Well, if there were no tradition at all, that is the conjecture most people would make. The Panathenaea was probably founded, at the least it was restored in special splendour,
by Pisistratus. The policy of making Athens the head of Ionia
was especially that of Pisistratus. And, apart from the Pisistratidae, the choice is really not large among sixth-century
statesmen. But, as a matter of fact, we have at this point the
help of a definite tradition, the oldest trace of it coming from
Dieuchidas of Megara in the fourth century B.C., the clearest
from some good authorities of the Roman period. Unfortunately there is a lacuna in the quotation from Dieuchidas, so we
do not know what he said. We only know that he somehow
connected Pisistratus and Solon with the text of Homer. Our
earliest full witness is Cicero, a particularly well-informed man
of letters writing in the second great period of ancient scholarship. He speaks of the literary fame of Pisistratus, ' who is said
to have arranged in their present order the works of Homer,
which were previously in confusion '. And the tradition is
mentioned by many writers of the early empire.[1] I see that

---

[1] Düntzer, *Jahrb. f. Philol.* xci, pp. 738 ff., argues that Cicero's authority
was Dicaearchus, a first-rate witness. I subjoin the chief texts: cf. Wolf,
Prolegomena, Cap. xxxiii.

Cic. *de Orat.* iii. 34 ' Quis doctior iisdem illis temporibus, aut cuius
eloquentia litteris instructior fuisse traditur, quam Pisistrati? qui primus
Homeri libros, confusos antea, sic disposuisse dicitur, ut nunc habemus.'

Pausanias vii. 26. 13 Πεισίστρατος ἔπη τὰ Ὁμήρου διεσπασμένα τε καὶ ἄλλα
ἀλλαχοῦ μνημονευόμενα ἠθροίζετο.

Vitae Homeri IV and V in Westermann, Βιογράφοι (= Allen, v, pp. 245, 248).
Τὰ δὲ ποιήματα αὐτοῦ τὰ ἀληθῆ σποράδην πρότερον ἀδόμενα, Πεισίστρατος
Ἀθηναῖος συνέταξε.—Περιιὼν τὰς πόλεις ("Ομηρος) ᾖδε τὰ ποιήματα· ὕστερον δὲ
Πεισίστρατος αὐτὰ συνήγαγεν, ὡς τὸ ἐπίγραμμα τοῦτο δηλοῖ, Ἀθήνησιν ἐπιγεγραμ-
μένον ἐν εἰκόνι αὐτοῦ τοῦ Πεισιστράτου·

these writers are called 'late authorities'. But there is very little of our grammatical record that has more ancient credentials: a strong tradition in the age of Didymus or Herodian, a faint trace in the age before the Alexandrians.

If we inquire into the probable sources of Cicero and the other Romans, the indications point to Crates, the head of the Pergamene school and the great rival of Aristarchus. He had gone on an embassy to Rome about the year 168 B. C., on behalf of Attalus II. We happen to know that—fortunately enough, as it turned out—he fell into a drain near the Palatine and broke his leg, which detained him in Rome longer than he intended, and 'throughout all the time both of his embassy and his illness he gave constant lectures and industriously explained his views'.[1] It is perhaps curious that the remains of Aristarchus make no mention of Pisistratus, nor of any Attic recension. The remains are not nearly full enough to justify us in assuming that he never wrote of the question at all. But he had less need than most people to speak of it because he held the theory that Homer was himself an Athenian, not an Ionian, and that consequently the crudest Athenian forms needed no explanation.

The testimony is not quite uniform. Most of the authorities agree with Cicero. One text speaks of Hipparchus, the son of Pisistratus. This is hardly a contradiction: the policy was the

Τρίς με τυραννήσαντα τοσαυτάκις ἐξεδίωξε
   δῆμος Ἐρεχθειδῶν, καὶ τρὶς ἐπεσπάσατο,
τὸν μέγαν ἐν βουλαῖς Πεισίστρατον· ὃς τὸν Ὅμηρον
   ἤθροισα, σποράδην τὸ πρὶν ἀειδόμενον.
ἡμέτερος γὰρ κεῖνος ὁ χρύσεος ἦν πολιήτης,
   εἴπερ Ἀθηναῖοι Σμύρναν ἐπῳκίσαμεν.

Diog. Laert., i. 57 τά τε Ὁμήρου ἐξ ὑποβολῆς γέγραφε ῥαψῳδεῖσθαι, οἷον ὅπου ὁ πρῶτος ἔληξεν ἄρχεσθαι τὸν ἐχόμενον. μᾶλλον οὖν Σόλων Ὅμηρον ἐφώτισεν ἢ Πεισίστρατος, ὥς φησι Διευχίδας ἐν πέμπτῳ Μεγαρικῶν· . . . ἦν δὲ μάλιστα τὰ ἔπη ταυτί· οἱ δ' ἄρ' Ἀθήνας εἶχον καὶ τὰ ἑξῆς. (A well-known Athenian interpolation, B 546 ff.)

Ps. Plat. Hipparch., p. 228 B (Ἵππαρχος) τὰ Ὁμήρου ἔπη πρῶτος ἐκόμισεν εἰς τὴν γῆν ταυτηνί, καὶ ἠνάγκασε τοὺς ῥαψῳδοὺς Παναθηναίοις ἐξ ὑπολήψεως ἐφεξῆς αὐτὰ διιέναι, ὥσπερ νῦν ἔτι οἵδε ποιοῦσιν.

Aelian, V. H. xiii. 14 Ὕστερον Πεισίστρατος συναγαγὼν ἀπέφηνε τὴν Ἰλιάδα καὶ τὴν Ὀδύσσειαν.

Suidas, v. Ὅμηρος: Ὕστερον συνετέθη καὶ συνετάχθη ὑπὸ πολλῶν, καὶ μάλιστα ὑπὸ Πεισιστράτου, τοῦ τῶν Ἀθηναίων τυράννου.

Eustathius p. 5 Ὅτι ἐν μέν τι σῶμα συνεχὲς διόλου καὶ ἐναρμόττον ἡ τῆς Ἰλιάδος ποίησις· οἱ δὲ συνθέμενοι ταύτην, κατ' ἐπιταγήν, ὥς φασι, Πεισιστράτου τοῦ τῶν Ἀθηναίων τυράννου . . . κατέτεμον αὐτὸ εἰς πολλά (i. e. divided it into books).

[1] Suet. Gramm. et rhet. ii, p. 100.

policy of the Pisistratid family.   But Dieuchidas says it was Solon
who ordained the recitation, and 'thus threw more light on
Homer than did Pisistratus who . . .' and there comes the gap in
the text.   The words imply some knowledge of the Pisistratus
tradition, and apparently some criticism of it, and they attribute
the recitation law to Solon.   On the face of it this does not seem
probable.   In Solon's time there was very likely no such thing
as the Panathenaea ; pretty certainly there was not yet an
authoritative Pan-Ionian policy ; and we must remember that the
name of Solon, as ' the lawgiver ' *par excellence*, had a habit of
attracting to it the credit for all good laws whatever.[1]

On the whole, the Pisistratus tradition stands its ground.   It is
by no means certainly true ; it is not very clear in its statement.
But it accords with the general probabilities of history ; it is fully
as clear as a sober scholar would expect in a tradition about
mere literary history in an age before the annals of literature
had begun.   And I am bound to say that the more I study the
traditions of the good Scholia or the Grammatici of Roman
times, the less am I inclined to suspect them of gross carelessness
or wilful invention.   In the history of Drama we give credence
to many texts far later and less strongly attested.   In any case,
the Pisistratus tradition marks the utmost limit of our Homeric
record.   That last little glimpse of firm land may, of course, be
only an illusion.   Beyond it, at any rate, we must steer our best
on a sea without a shore.

The study of these great poems is still involved in confused
and sometimes in curiously bitter controversy.   This means, of
course, that no advanced critic has yet completely solved the
problem before him ; probably no wise critic ever for a moment
imagined that he had.   It may be that the most helpful solution
will be something which no one has yet thought of.   But in the
meantime, without expecting agreement about results, we might,
I think, try to agree about our approach to the Homeric Question.
We might distinguish the data from the problem.

[1] The romance about the travels of Lycurgus of Sparta, in which he meets
Thales and Homer and collects the wisdom of the Egyptians and the secrets
which Rhadamanthys learned from Zeus, ought not by any critical scholar
to be brought into this connexion.   Strabo, p. 482 ; it has the compromising
support of Heraclides Ponticus, *Pol*. ii. 2 (= F. H. G., ii, p. 210).

The Homeric Question can never be solved by starting from the question, Who was Homer and when did he live? 'Homer' is a hypothesis and not even a clear hypothesis. The *Iliad* and *Odyssey* are known facts, and it is from the facts that we should start. The *Iliad* and *Odyssey* are two poems dealing with ancient heroic material selected for public recitation in Athens at the great festival of the Panathenaea, at or just about the foundation of that festival by Pisistratus, and after that time regularly recited every four years during the classical period. So much we can say with reasonable certainty, without going beyond the bounds of our evidence; and if we grasp this first fact firmly we shall find a great deal of light thrown upon many remoter problems.

We have seen that the Homeric poems 'and no others'[1] were recited at the great Panathenaea in the generations before and after Plato. We are definitely told that Pisistratus was the founder of the great Panathenaea, and have evidence[2] to the effect that either Pisistratus, or his son Hipparchus—who was much given to poetry and the arts—instituted the recitation, and fixed the order in which the poems were to be recited. Before that the poems were 'preserved by memory', and were 'different in different places', so that Pisistratus may be said to have 'arranged in their present order the books of Homer which before were in confusion'.

The law commanded the poems 'ῥαψῳδεῖσθαι', to be 'treated by rhapsodes', and the word rhapsode was generally interpreted as a 'song-stitcher' or, in Pindar's paraphrase, a 'singer of stitched lays'. That is, the songs or lays were already in existence, but the rhapsode 'stitched them together' into wholes, longer or shorter according to the occasion and the time available. These lay-stitchers were also called Homeridae, 'sons of Homer', or Homeristae, 'Homerizers', and presumably specialized in the works of their 'divine ancestor'. But it needed a very special effort of lay-stitching to produce out of their old epic material unities so large and finely knit as the *Iliad* and *Odyssey*.

That the *Iliad* and *Odyssey*, and not the *Thebais* or the poems of the so-called Cycle, were the 'Homeric Poems' selected for

---

[1] But see below, p. 309.   [2] See p. 304 f. note.

the Panathenaea, may be taken as practically certain.[1] And the
selection of these two poems for the Panathenaea seems to be
the simplest explanation of their survival, in complete form, when
all the rest of the abundant epic literature perished. Lastly,
this hypothesis alone seems to explain the otherwise astonishing
fact that Attic tragedy, while drawing almost all its material from
the heroic saga, carefully abstains from using the *Iliad* and
Odyssey. These two poems were performed at the Panathenaea ;
consequently the performances at the Dionysia had to take other
subjects.

It is quite possible that the name is actually preserved of the
chief rhapsode who worked up the *Iliad* and *Odyssey* into their
present shape. There is a note by a certain Hippostratus,
a chronicler of the Alexandrian age, quoted in the valuable
scholia to Pindar, *Nemea* 2, 1. 'The name Homeridae was
first applied to Homer's descendants who performed his poems
in succession to him in Chios, but afterwards to other rhapsodes
who did not claim descent from Homer. Distinguished among
them was the school of Kynaithos (οἱ περὶ Κύναιθον), who are
said to have interpolated much of their composition into Homer's
poetry. Kynaithos was a Chian, and is supposed to have made
the Hymn to Apollo which bears Homer's name. This
Kynaithos was the first person to perform (ῥαψῳδεῖν) Homer's
poems at Syracuse about the 69th Olympiad (504 B. C.).'

I am disposed to think that this is probably true. Kynaithos
'made' the Hymn to Apollo in the sense in which Athenaeus
speaks of 'all those who have made the *Heracleia*'; that is, he
did a poetical version, a ποίησιν, of it. If 'much' of our Homer
is the 'composition' of him and his school, perhaps it was they
who put together for Pisistratus the present shape of the *Iliad*
and *Odyssey*. When the Pisistratidae fell, in 510 B. C., Kynaithos
sought refuge elsewhere, and in a few years' time is found
reciting at Syracuse, doubtless at some great festival, the
Iliad and *Odyssey* which he had once recited for Pisistratus.
In this he was doing the normal work of a rhapsode, though
a specially distinguished example of it. For, as the same
scholion proceeds to say : 'At a time when the poetry of Homer
was not yet brought into one body, but dispersed, variable, and

---

[1] See above, p. 300.

divided in parts, the rhapsodes who produced it at performances
did something equivalent to "joining "and " stitching "when they
brought it into a unity.   That is how Pindar understands the
word.'   And a little later : ' They knew by heart and repeated
the poetry of Homer in its scattered state ; and they did great
violence to it '—that is, altered it greatly as they worked it up
into new unities.

We saw above that this action of Pisistratus falls excellently
into line with his general policy.   He wished to assert the
claim of Athens to be the Mother-City of all the Ionians and the
champion of Hellas against the Orient.   It is significant that the
only poem which ever received the glory of being recited, or
read aloud, at the Panathenaea together with Homer was the
Persêis, or epic of the Persian War, by Choirilos.[1]   And,
secondly, he wished to make Athens the centre of Ionian
culture in place of Miletus and the other Ionian cities which had
recently fallen a prey to Croesus of Lydia (about 560 B. C.).
The Panathenaea served both ends.

This, then, is the recorded history, in itself consistent and
credible.   Is it of any help towards understanding the *Iliad* and
Odyssey ?   In the first place it solves the most pressing of all the
problems : it tells us at last what the two poems are.   They are
not court-poems, nor yet folk-poems : they are panêgyris-poems,
a kind which does not exist anywhere outside Greece.   The
puzzle has always been to understand what the *Iliad* and
Odyssey were meant for, or how such immense poems came to
be composed.   To be read ?   But there was no reading public ;
and the tradition always speaks of them as ' sung ' or recited.
To be recited as wholes ?   But, by ordinary standards, they are
enormously too long.   To be recited in bits, like lays ?   But they
do not fall apart into lays.   One of the most certain results ot
Homeric criticism since Lachmann is that all attempts to divide
the poems into recitable lays have ended in complete failure.
The *Iliad* and *Odyssey* are unities ; elaborate, well-constructed
unities, composed with infinite pains out of discrepant materials.
All those pains were not only wasted but were positively self-
defeating if the poet's object was to recite his poem in parts
round the camp-fire or in the banquet-hall.   If he had to do

---

[1] The *Persêis* σὺν τοῖς Ὁμήρου ἀναγιγνώσκεσθαι ἐψηφίσθη.   Suidas, s. v. Χοιρίλος.

that, it was lays he wanted: lays about the length of an ordinary tragedy, those very lays in fact which he had just spoiled in building his two great works of art! The two facts given us are: first, that the *Iliad* is a poem originally meant for recitation; second, that it does not fall into separate lays and that the whole would take some twenty-four hours to recite. Conclusion: the poem must be intended for some extraordinary occasion, demanding even greater enthusiasm and powers of endurance than the annual celebrations of tragedy at the Dionysia.

The same consideration solves another of the principal problems over which controversy has raged since the time of Wolf. The old practice, still largely current, was to divide Homeric critics into Unitarians and Separatists. It was a wrong division; because both views are right. The poems are unities; while various parts of the unity are discrepant in substance, and divergent in date and style. For several generations Homeric scholars tried to treat this problem by supposing that the unity came first and the discrepancies were 'late additions' or 'interpolations'. There was an original poem of manageable length by 'Homer', containing no flaws or contradictions; then came interpolating rhapsodes and diaskeuasts, added to it and spoiled it. The method may be seen at its best in Dr. Leaf's great commentary. But even at its best it has always failed. For one thing, no amount of excision has ever resulted in producing the required uncorrupted poem, not even if allowance is made for supposed omissions. For another, it has generally been possible to show that wherever a passage was inconsistent with the rest of the poem conscious pains have been taken to explain away or bind together the discordances.[1] Again, it was often difficult to understand the motive of an 'interpolator' in adding something of his own which simply made trouble. For these and other reasons, scholars have been driven to try the alternative hypothesis: that the discrepant versions were there first, and the unity has been imposed upon them by the 'song-stitcher'. It is not a new hypothesis. It is simply that described in the scholia to Pindar. The 'work of Homer'—and all epic poetry was the

---

[1] e.g. the scruple of Diomede in Z 129 lest Glaucus should be a god, after the assurance of Athena in E 124-32. See the long note by Porphyry in Schol. Ven. B.

work of Homer—was 'scattered' and 'different in different places', recited from memory by 'Homeridae'; and the song-stitchers put them together, 'doing great violence to the poems' in the process.

For example, Book I of the *Iliad*, in which Agamemnon beseeches Achilles to accept atonement and is refused, seems inconsistent with certain statements and situations, especially in Book II, which imply that Agamemnon had made no such offer. If we say that Book I is a 'later addition', we do not explain at all why the maker of the addition should go out of his way to compose a lay contradictory to the rest of the poem. But if we suppose that the 'song-stitcher' found in his store some good material which implied one situation and some which implied another slightly different, and that both versions were good in themselves and both already dear to parts of his audience, it is only natural that he should wish to use both. Again, in our present *Odyssey* there is a motive twice repeated in which the disguised Odysseus is injuriously treated by one of his own servants. In one part, σ and τ,[1] the treacherous servant is a maid Melantho, daughter of Dolios; in another,[2] ρ, υ, and especially φ and χ, it is a man, Melanthios or Melantheus, son of Dolios. The Melantho part never mentions Melanthios; the Melanthios part never mentions Melantho, not even when it comes to the hanging of the wicked handmaids in χ 470 ff. It is surely most unlikely that one is original Homer, and the other a 'late addition'. Who would deliberately add such a monotonous doublet? If both were varying versions, current in different schools or in the stock of the same school of poets, one can readily see how the stitcher took in both, and sewed them together.[3]

On the other great problems also light is thrown by the same conception: they all show new use of old material. The Homeric

---

[1] σ 321-40, τ 65-92.
[2] ρ 247, 369; υ 173, 255; φ 176, 181, 212, 265; χ 142, 152, 159, 161, 182, 195, 474.
[3] In the same way there are three cases where Odysseus has something thrown at him by the suitors: in ρ 462 Antinoos hits him hard with a stool (θρῆνυς), in σ 394 Eurymachus misses him, but fells a cupbearer, with a stool (σφέλας), in υ 299 Ktesippus misses him with a cow's foot. The passages do not form a climax and seem to have no relation to one another. Independent stories have apparently been combined.

language is very old Greek, some of it actually unintelligible to Attic ears, worked over and over by Ionic and Attic rhapsodes, or in the last instance by Ionic rhapsodes and Attic copyists. The Homeric culture and civilization are not the naïve presentations of a primitive age by a primitive poet, but the conscious descriptions of an idealized heroic age by one to whom that age is far past. This is proved by the fact that various modern objects are mentioned in similes, but not in the body of the poem (p. 121 f.). And this heroic past as described in Homer has two marked characteristics, which at first sight seem contradictory: it shows, with some lapses, remarkable unity and consistency, as if it were the description of a real historic age, and, on the other hand, it entirely refuses to correspond with any historical age known to us. It is not Minoan or Mycenaean; it is not, within the limits of our knowledge, post-Mycenaean. It is an idealized past, when men were heroes and lived, ate, dressed and talked as heroes should. The unity is not an original fact, marred and confused by subsequent interpolations; it is a unity subsequently imposed on confused materials by conscious art.

The amount of Attic influence actually visible in the poems has been variously estimated. It seems to me just what one might expect: quite comparable, except in the matter of dialect, to the amount that is visible in such a purely Attic creation as tragedy. In tragedy for the most part we find the great myths of the heroic tradition treated simply for their artistic value: Agamemnon, Orestes, Oedipus, Ajax, Heracles are not made into material for patriotic propaganda any more than Hamlet is by Shakespeare. At the most we find a few local Attic myths chosen as subjects, one or two praises of Athens in the choral odes, an occasional appearance of Theseus where a non-Athenian poet might not have thought of him.

Even the dialect shows more than the mere mistakes of Attic copyists. Forms such as ἥλιος by ἠέλιος, ἕπεσθαι by ὀπάζειν, ὅπως &c. for Aeolic ὀκκ- and Ionic ὀκ-: ἀμόθεν γε, βεβῶσα, ἦντο, ἐκεῖντο seem to reveal the hand of Attic poets. And is it not significant to meet the form ἑωσφόρος in the description of a dawn which '*rises over the sea*'? Significant also that in the *Odyssey* in its present form the adventures of Odysseus are turned into a contest between Poseidon and Athena, a contest which forms one of the most central and characteristic of Athenian myths, and, as in the Attic myth, Athena is the true friend and has the best of it; that Athena is extraordinarily prominent in what seem to be the later parts of the poem, so that Odysseus is, as it were, annexed by the Athenian Korê; that a sympathetic minor character who protects and helps Telemachus is actually called 'Pisistratus' and is made the son of the aged Nestor—from whom Pisistratus of Athens claimed descent; that, in order to prevent any mistake, when Athena leaves Odysseus and goes home, we are told that she flies straight off to the 'strong House of Erechtheus'—in which she lived on the Athenian acropolis! Such instances can be multiplied.[1]

It is the same with the *Iliad*. Take, for example, the Catalogue of Ships in *B*. By general agreement that is a document of respectable antiquity, not composed for its present place, but inserted there at some time when the *Iliad* was nearly complete, and by additions, omissions, and alterations, accommodated to its surroundings. If we compare it with the rest of the *Iliad*, taken as a whole, two classes of peculiarity strike us. First, there are peculiarities of origin. It is in the style of the Boeotian school, and magnifies the Boeotians; it also divides Greece on a principle quite different from that usual in the poem. Then, secondly, there are peculiarities of revision: additions made to the original text or omissions from it. If we consider the spurious additions, most of them are merely editor's alterations to fit the Catalogue into its context, but some are markedly Athenian. There is the startling statement that Menestheus, the obscure Athenian chief, was the best general, for both horse and foot, in the whole Greek army; the significant single line, covering apparently a large omission, which states that Ajax, the hero of Salamis, drew up his ships among those of the Athenians. Salamis had just been conquered and annexed by Athens in the time of Pisistratus.

The omissions, so far as we can trace them, point the same way: Thebes, Aegina, Megara are omitted entirely; Salamis is suppressed, Corinth belittled. These five cities are the principal enemies of Athens. It is also worth noticing that in the account

---

[1] ἑωσφόρος Ψ 226, cf. Ω 12. See p. 191 n. Erechtheum η 80 f: Pisistratus γ 36 ff. &c.

of the Athenian contingent no town in Attica is mentioned except Athens. There is no word of Eleusis or Marathon or Acharnae or Brauron: that must be the work of an Athenian, writing long after the synoikismos of Attica. The result is much what might be expected—except indeed by those who talk always of Attic 'forgeries' and 'Athenian vanity' and imagine that those are the motives by which great poetry is produced. The Athenian colour is present, but it is not gross or crude. One handsome mention of the troops of Athens, and some not very conspicuous silences about the glories of her principal enemies.

There is one further difficulty which is solved, or greatly reduced, if once we grasp the circumstances of the Panathenaic Recitation. If the text of the *Iliad* and *Odyssey* was fixed by Pisistratus, and an official copy written out in the official script,[1] how comes it that the text fluctuated so greatly afterwards? How, for instance, can we account for the great divergences between our text and Aristotle's or Aeschines' quotations, and the 'wildness' of the early papyri? Let us remember that the Pisistratean text was made for a great recitation, which occurred only once every four years. Such a recitation would influence but could not dominate the ordinary tradition, which would continue to be formed by the frequent everyday recitations or public readings of Homer, in lays or episodes or extracts. The complete continuous text would not become impressed on people's minds until two influences had time to work: the teaching in boys' schools and the rise of an educated reading public. It is quite conceivable, though not very probable, that the Vulgate Text of Homer is really an attempted restoration of the Pisistratean. But at least we can see why that text was not likely to fix immediately the text of the ordinary recitations.

We may observe two further consequences that flow from a clear acceptance of this tradition. It changes the Homeric Question from a question of genuine and spurious, of original and interpolated, to a question of Sources. All poems have sources: and all poems in nations where there is no widespread reading public are apt to use their sources just as they please, with no scruples about what we call 'originality' or 'literary property'.

---

[1] See above, p. 302 f.

The rhapsodes of our *Iliad* and *Odyssey* used the *Thebais* and the *Nostoi* without disguise or shame, as doubtless the rhapsodes of the *Thebais* or the *Nostoi* used their *Iliad* and *Odyssey*. This simplifies in one way the process of criticism, while on the other hand it makes necessary much greater caution in using the poems as historical documents. There has been, and still is, a regrettable tendency among historians to use any part of the poems, unless it is definitely condemned as 'spurious' or 'a late addition', as being 'real Homer', and therefore a first-hand authority of about the tenth century B. C. This must be given up. We can only say of any average Homeric statement: This was accepted in the sixth century B. C. as belonging to the Heroic Tradition'; though, of course, in certain cases we can proceed to argue about its original date. One is reminded of the problems of Deuteronomy. A sober critic no longer treats Deuteronomy as a work written by Moses but interpolated by the priests who 'found it in the Temple' in the year 621 B. C. He treats it as a work 'found' in the year 621, which contains ancient material from different sources, both Hebrew and Babylonian.

And the beauty of the poetry? Is that affected one way or another? I confess that, as explained in Chapter XI, the beauty of the *Iliad* as poetry has to me that touch of the infinite, that strictly incomparable quality which results when a beautiful object is confessedly imperfect and inevitably suggests a beauty beyond itself. 'Thus I deliver my message, but ah, if you had heard my master!' I have noticed that readers of Homer who have no theories of their own have the habit of freely 'thinking away' pieces which they do not like—Athena's treachery in *Iliad* X for example, or the superfluous transformations and re-transformations of Odysseus in the later books of the *Odyssey*. There is an instinctive sense that the real poem is somehow more perfect and beautiful than this version that we happen to have; perhaps the same instinct that sent all the early critics searching for spurious lines which were 'unworthy of Homer'. And it is a perfectly sound instinct. I do not suggest that, if we had all the library of Kynaithos open before us and all his memory as well, we should find any given version which would satisfy us as being absolutely complete and uncorrupted Homer.

Any traditional poem or drama—whatever may be true of a 'original' one—exists only in a series of performances or versions each of which is an attempt to represent better and better a ideal which is never reached.   This is no high aesthetic doctrine but plain fact.   *Hamlet* only exists to the full when performed yet *Hamlet* is obviously something much greater than an particular performance by Garrick or Irving or, for that matter by Burbage and Shakespeare.   The *Iliad* is greater than an given version of the *Iliad*.   Kynaithos, let us say, did his best and Kynaithos was evidently a brilliant poet with a wide knowledge of the epic literature.   But Kynaithos knew that nothing that he could re-create could ever be the full thing that was meant And it seems as if some effluence of that knowledge still reached us as we read, and as if the rhapsode had thereby added to the poem something which could not have been present in any really original work by a self-conscious creator.   He has added to it that touch of spiritual hunger which creates a beauty beyond visible beauty Whether 'Homeros' is a mythical ancestor of poets, like Amphictyon or Hellen, or whether there was once a bard called 'Homeros' who acquired a mythical reputation, the Homer to whom Kynaithos ascribed the *Iliad* and *Odyssey*, but a more perfect *Iliad* and *Odyssey* than could ever afterwards be recovered, belongs now to the company of his own heroes, not born in Chios or Athens or Smyrna, but ὧν ἀεὶ ἐν οὐρανίῳ τόπῳ

APPENDIX A

THE PHARMAKOI AND HUMAN SACRIFICE

As there has been a tendency of late, perhaps started by Rohde *Psyche*, p. 367, n. 4), to make out that the pharmakos rite was a real human sacrifice in the full sense, it may be well to give verbatim the more important texts on which Rohde based his opinion.

I. *Ancient Texts.*

(*a*) Hipponax, several fragments: especially

4. πόλιν καθαίρειν καὶ κράδῃσι βάλλεσθαι.

5. βάλλοντες ἐν λειμῶνι καὶ ῥαπίζοντες
   κράδῃσι καὶ σκίλλῃσιν, ὥσπερ φαρμακόν.

6. δεῖ δ' αὐτὸν ἐς φαρμακὸν ἐκποιήσασθαι.

7. κἄφη παρέξειν ἰσχάδας τε καὶ μᾶζαν
   καὶ τυρὸν οἷον ἐσθίουσι φαρμακοί.

9. λιμῷ γένηται ξηρός, ἐν δὲ τῷ θυμῷ
   φαρμακὸς ἀχθεὶς ἑπτάκις ῥαπισθείη.

37. ὁ δ' ἐξολισθὼν ἱκέτευε τὴν κράμβην
    τὴν ἑπτάφυλλον, ἣν [ᾗ MSS.] θύεσκε Πανδώρῃ,
    Ταργηλίοισιν ἔγχυτον πρὸ φαρμακοῦ.

These in any case prove nothing about Athens. Hipponax was over a century earlier than Aristophanes, and Ephesus was a town much exposed to barbarian influences. But, even as to sixth-century Ephesus, the fragments prove only: (1) that the Pharmakos-sacrifice was a known ceremony, as for instance, breaking on a wheel, hanging, drawing, and quartering, &c., are known to us, but that Hipponax *has to explain it.* (2) That some ceremony or other still went on which could be described as a 'beating of the pharmakoi', like our own burning of Guy Fawkes. (3) It is worth remarking that all these phrases seem to occur in one context, and the same is true of the passages in Attic Comedy. They are all comic or rhetorical curses. Now in such curses it is on all grounds more comic, and more effective, to invoke an obsolete and imaginative punishment on your victim. The curses in Aristophanes illustrate this. (Those invoked *Eq.* 928 ff., *Ach.* 1156 ff., or the threats of *Ran.* 473 ff. have nothing to do with real life.) (4) No fragment

speaks of killing a pharmakos, and fr. 37, obscure as it is, speaks quit*
clearly of *the dough figure in place of a pharmakos*. Ἔγχυτον = 'a cak*
in a mould'; one of the regular substitutes for a real victim.

(*b*) Aristophanes, *Ranae*, 732 οἷσιν ἡ πόλις πρὸ τοῦ | οὐδὲ φαρμακοῖσι
εἰκῇ ῥᾳδίως ἐχρήσατ' ἄν. This merely shows knowledge of the existenc*
of such a custom πρὸ τοῦ, 'once upon a time.'

(*c*) *Eq.* 1135 ff. τούσδ'... ὥσπερ δημοσίους τρέφεις... εἶτα... θύσα*
ἐπιδειπνεῖς. It is strange that any one should take this as evidence fo*
a pharmakos-sacrifice. Who would 'cook and dine on' a pharmakos*
The Scholiast (V) explains rightly that δημόσιοι are animals kept an*
fattened at the public expense.

(*d*) Eupolis, *Demoi*, 120 (K):

> ὃν χρῆν ἔν τε ταῖς τριόδοις κἂν τοῖς ὀξυθυμίοις
> προστρόπαιον τῆς πόλεως κάεσθαι τετριγότα.

Merely a comic curse; perhaps a literary reminiscence of Hipponax*
In any case it proves nothing about contemporary practice.

(*e*) Lysias vi. 53. 'The right thing would be ἀπαλλαττομένου*
Ἀνδοκίδου τὴν πόλιν καθαίρειν καὶ ἀποδιοπομπεῖσθαι καὶ φαρμακὸ*
ἀποπέμπειν'.—Comic abuse, as before. But observe that Lysias think*
of the pharmakos not as killed, but as 'sent away', or banished.

II. *Explanations of Grammarians.*

A. Much the oldest, Ister: in Harpocration, s. v. φαρμακός. Δύ*
ἄνδρας Ἀθήνησιν ἐξῆγον, καθάρσια ἐσομένους τῆς πόλεως ἐν τοῖς Θαργηλίοις,
ἕνα μὲν ὑπὲρ τῶν ἀνδρῶν ἕνα δὲ ὑπὲρ τῶν γυναικῶν. [Originally a man*
named Pharmakos had stolen cups from Apollo and ὑπὸ τῶν περὶ τὸ*
Ἀχιλλέα κατελεύσθη.] καὶ τὰ τοῖς Θαργηλίοις ἀγόμενα τούτων ἀπομιμή-
ματά ἐστιν. Ἴστρος ἐν α' τῶν Ἀπόλλωνος ἐπιφανειῶν.

Observe: they did not 'kill', they 'led out' two people in a*
procession; and the ceremony was an '*imitation*' of stoning to death.*
Such 'imitation' ceremonies were as common as can be in Greece.*
(On the Achilles question see Lecture VIII on Thersites.)

B. Helladius, *ap.* Phot. *Bibl.* 1593 ἔθος ἦν ἐν Ἀθήναις φαρμακοὺς
ἄγειν δύο, τὸν μὲν ὑπὲρ ἀνδρῶν τὸν δὲ ὑπὲρ γυναικῶν πρὸς καθαρμὸν*
ἀγομένους. καὶ ὁ μὲν τῶν ἀνδρῶν μελαίνας ἰσχάδας περὶ τὸν τράχηλον εἶχεν,
λευκὰς δ' ἅτερος· σύβακχοι δέ, φησίν, ὠνομάζοντο. It was an ἀποτροπιασμὸς
νόσων in atonement for the death of Androgeos the Cretan.

This writer agrees with Ister, except that he does not happen to add
that it was a μίμημα. He probably took that for granted. The
imitation cannot have been very close, one would think, if some took it

for a stoning, others for banishment, others for burning. Androgeos was killed in an ambush on the road to Thebes. We may conjecture that he in some way βαλλόμενος ἀπέθανε. This would give the stoning, with κράδαι and σκίλλαι: then the banishment would be the running away of the real man; the burning would be the burning of the ἔγχυτον or effigy.

C. Tzetzes on the Hipponax passages: Tzetz. *Chil.* v. 726, in case of special calamity, τὸν πάντων ἀμορφότερον ἦγον ὡς πρὸς θυσίαν | εἰς τόπον δὲ τὸν πρόσφορον στήσαντες τὴν θυσίαν | τυρόν τε δόντες τῇ χερὶ καὶ μᾶζαν καὶ ἰσχάδας, | ἑπτάκις γὰρ ῥαπίσαντες ἐκεῖνον εἰς τὸ πέος | σκίλλαις¹ συκαῖς ἀγρίαις τε καὶ ἄλλοις τῶν ἀγρίων, | τέλος πυρὶ κατέκαιον ἐν ξύλοις τοῖς ἀγρίοις. | καὶ τὸν σποδὸν εἰς θάλασσαν ἔρραινον εἰς ἀνέμους. ὁ δὲ Ἱππῶναξ κτλ. (fr. 4–9).

I do not feel sure what object Tzetzes meant to be supplied to κατέκαιον. Did they burn 'him' or only 'it', sc. τὴν θυσίαν, i.e. the ἔγχυτον or effigy? It seems to be distinguished from ἐκεῖνον, the man who 'was led out' ὡς ἐπὶ θυσίαν, 'as though to sacrifice'. But perhaps Tzetzes did not really understand the source which he was quoting: he seldom did, being an inaccurate writer, and 1500 years later. So far, then, there is no single statement that the pharmakoi even at Ephesus, much less at Athens, were really sacrificed. But now we have two such statements.

(*a*) Schol. *Equites*, l. c. The first part of the note given in the best MSS. explains quite rightly δημοσίους· λείπει βοῦς ἢ ταύρους. The second says ἔτρεφον γάρ τινας Ἀθηναῖοι λίαν ἀγεννεῖς καὶ ἀχρήστους καὶ ἐν καιρῷ συμφορᾶς τινος ἐπελθούσης τῇ πόλει, λοιμοῦ λέγω ἢ τοιούτου τινός, ἔθυον τούτους ἕνεκα τοῦ καθαρθῆναι τοῦ μιάσματος. And presumably ate them, as we remarked above !

This note (1) is absent from R and V, the two good sources: (2) shows itself by its language as belonging to a bad period of scholia, e. g. the λοιμοῦ, λέγω, ἢ τοιούτου τινός: (3) is obviously wrong as an explanation of the passage to which it refers.

(The note in the good MSS. runs: λείπει βοῦς ἢ ταύρους ἢ ἄλλο τι τοιοῦτον θῦμα. | δημοσίους δὲ τοὺς λεγομένους φαρμακοὺς οἵπερ καθαίρουσι τὰς πόλεις τῷ ἑαυτῶν φόνῳ | ἢ τοὺς δημοσίᾳ καὶ ὑπὸ τῆς πόλεως τρεφομένους. Of these three explanations, the first is obviously right. The second, 'the so-called *pharmakoi*, who cleanse cities with their blood', is quite vague, as well as wrong. It also occurs in Suidas, and probably did not begin life as a note on this passage. The third is right as far as it goes.

¹ Probably not the garden squill, but the wild bulb.

(*b*) Schol. *Ranae*, 733, one inferior MS., C, has a note : τοὺς γὰρ φαύλους καὶ παρὰ τῆς φύσεως ἐπιβουλευομένους εἰς ἀπαλλαγὴν αὐχμοῦ ἢ λιμοῦ ἤ τινος τῶν τοιούτων ἔθυον, οὓς ἐκάλουν καθάρματα. Exactly what one expects in inferior scholia which abbreviate their sources ! He says ἔθυον for short, because he was careless. He may have found ἐξῆγον ἐπὶ θυσίαν or ἦγον ὡς ἐπὶ θυσίαν. It is not necessarily false as it stands, since no subject or date is given to ἔθυον ; but even if it said ἔθυον τότε οἱ ᾿Αθηναῖοι it would be worthless.

The general result is to show that (1) the ancient texts all come to the same type : 'He ought to be tied on a cart and burnt in a bonfire like a Guy.' They imply that a pharmakos-sacrifice was known to have existed at some time somewhere : they suggest that some μίμημα of it lived on.

(2) The best grammatical tradition explains that this μίμημα did exist, and partly what it was like.

(3) The worst and latest grammatical tradition, dropping the qualifying clauses as its manner is, says that 'they sacrificed very ugly people'.

Even without the general considerations of probability advanced in the text of Lecture I, this evidence clearly points to the Thargelia ceremony being a μίμημα. [Cf. also Stengel in *Hermes*, xxii. 86 ff., and especially Farnell, *Cults*, iv. 270 ff.]

We give in full the Pelopidas story, which has actually been used as evidence that the Greeks of the fourth century had no objection to human sacrifice.

Plutarch, *Pelopidas*, xxi. (Before the battle of Leuctra, 371 B. C. Pelopidas was encamped near the grave of certain Virgins who had been, according to the tradition, violated by Lacedaemonians. They had died, and their father had committed suicide upon their grave. A fearful and haunted place !)

'Pelopidas dreamed that he saw the Virgins wailing about their tombs and uttering curses upon the Spartans, and their father commanding him to sacrifice to the Virgins a fair-haired Maiden if he wished to conquer the enemy. The shocking and unlawful (δεινὸν καὶ παράνομον) command started him from his sleep, and he consulted his prophets and officers. One party insisted that the dream should not be neglected or disobeyed, producing precedents from ancient times, Menoikeus, son of Creon, and Macaria, daughter of Heracles' [both of these devoted themselves voluntarily], 'and in a later generation Pherekŷdes the wise, who was flayed by the Lacedaemonians and his skin preserved by the kings, according to a certain oracle' [a mythical divine king, like

Frazer's Marsyas], 'and Leonidas, who in a sense sacrificed himself for Hellas by the command of an oracle, and further the men sacrificed by Themistocles before Salamis to Dionŷsus Ômêstes. These actions had all been approved by subsequent success. On the other hand, Agêsilaus had led an army from the same place as Agamemnon and against the same enemies; the goddess demanded of him the sacrifice of his daughter, and he saw the vision while sleeping at Aulis, but refused, and through softness disbanded the expedition, which was inglorious and incomplete.

'The others opposed such a view. No superior and more than human beings could be pleased with so barbarous and unlawful a sacrifice. It was not the legendary Typhons and Giants who ruled the world, but one who was a Father of all gods and men. As for spirits (δαίμονες) who rejoiced in the blood and slaughter of men, to believe in such beings at all was probably folly, but if they existed, they should be disregarded, as having no power. Weakness and badness of nature (ψυχή) was the only soil in which such monstrous and cruel desires could grow and last.'

The arguments on both sides are interesting. The first set shows what was possible to reactionary and superstitious individuals at a time of great fear. The others speak the language of ordinary philosophic Hellenism.

APPENDIX B

TORTURE OF SLAVE WITNESSES

THIS bad business is sometimes misunderstood and grossly overstated. The torture of witnesses who are suspected of concealing important facts has only in comparatively recent times been abolished in England and France. In Athens this sort of torture was forbidden in the case of freemen, but not in the case of slaves. To say that a slave could not give evidence at all except under torture is absurd. He could of course give evidence to a simple fact, e. g. where he witnessed a murder. And, in a complicated case, Isaeus, *Philoct.* 16, seems to speak of a proclamation *inviting evidence* from relations or slaves. The cases where a slave's evidence was not good except under torture were those where the slave had an obvious interest, such as personal complicity or fear of his master. The typical case is where a man is accused of some misdoing which his household must have known about. In such a case the Court cannot seize his slaves and examine them without the

Y

master's consent; but the Accuser can challenge him to hand them over for examination under torture. The master, if he accepts this proposal, can stipulate what tortures are to be used; and if the Court inflicts any permanent injury or any temporary loss of working power on the slave, the Court, or the Accuser, as the case may be, has to pay damages. To Roman or mediaeval torturers such a stipulation would have made the whole proceeding nugatory.

It is worth observing that: (1) This challenge seems generally to have been refused. (2) To accept it implied not only a consciousness of innocence, but a strange confidence in the affection of your slaves. One would expect a slave in such a situation to accuse his master of everything that was desired, especially as he could acquire freedom thereby, if his evidence was believed. (3) I can find no case mentioned where a witness died under torture. Where torture is really severe such cases seem to be frequent, from heart failure and other causes. On the other hand, the Christian use of the word martyr, witness, is terribly significant. To poor folk in Roman times a witness meant one who suffered; but, of course, it was implied that the witness refused to betray his master.

It looks as if this was one of the numerous cases in which Attic Law preserved in the letter an extremely ancient power which was not much used, or at any rate not to its full extent. (The scene in *Frogs* 620 ff. is perhaps instructive. It is unpleasant and of course unjust, but does not suggest much real cruelty.) The article *Servus* in Smith's *Dict. Antiq.* seems very sound.

APPENDIX C

THE THALASSOCRATS

THERE is extant a very curious and ancient Greek document which throws some light directly on this Dark Age which followed the fall of the Aegean empires and indirectly on the growth of the Epos. It is a list of the various powers which have exercised what the Greeks called 'Thalassocratia', or Rule of the Seas, from the fall of Troy up to the founding of the Athenian League. The list is given by Eusebius with slight omissions and discrepancies, both in the *Chronographia* and the *Canones*, and was taken by him from Diodorus.[1] It bears well the tests

---

[1] See the historical reconstruction by J. L. Myres in *J. H. S.* xxvi. 1; also Fotheringham's criticism in *J. H. S.* xxvii and Myres' answer. Winckler's discussion is in *Der Alte Orient*, vol. vii, part 2.

that have been applied to it, and seems to be drawn from authentic sources, perhaps from a list set up in some Aegean temple.

The list starts with the fall of Troy. That catastrophe, by whatever coalition of invaders it was immediately produced, is taken as typifying the final downfall of the old Aegean system, a system which in Greek tradition is represented by the ancient thalassocratia of Minos. But what exactly is meant by a thalassocratia, or control of the seas? It seems to mean something quite definite, not a mere general naval preponderance, because the dates of the various 'controls' are marked off so precisely. And the wars of the Diadochi, in which first Demetrius Poliorcêtês, then Ptolemy, then Antigonus Gonatas are masters of the Aegean, provide a very suggestive parallel. (See Tarn, *Antigonus Gonatas*, 1913.) The explanation is, I think, to be found in the peculiar geography of the Aegean, and in the distinctive character of the great Aegean centres. They were (pp. 36 ff.), generally speaking, fortified toll stations : the various cities of Crete commanding all the southern trade routes ; Troy those of the Hellespont ; Thebes the traffic between its 'three seas' ; and even Mycenae, which seems so remote, some important trade routes between the Aegean and the Corinthian gulf. And the Aegean is so formed that both to the north, the south-east, and the south-west the necessary routes of trade are well marked and narrow. The whole of them together could be controlled by a really strong sea power, though it is not likely that an ancient command of the seas was often so complete as that. When one reflects on the amount of fighting which went on in historical times for the possession of, say, the Hellespont or Naxos, and the constant train of explosive maritime rivalry, ever ready to burst out in commercial wars, such as that between Miletus-Eretria-Athens and Chalkis-Samos-Aegina, the conclusion strongly suggests itself that the prize in each case was the control of one or more of these five or six great passages or toll stations of the Aegean, and that such control constituted 'thalassocratia'. A power became completely 'thalassocratês' as soon as it could establish a guard of ships and forts at, say, the Hellespont, the channels of the Cyclades round Naxos or Delos, the passages on each side of Carpathos, and on each side of Ogylos, together with certain roads of more local trade, like the Straits of Euboea.

Now, if we turn to the List of Thalassocrats, we find at the very outset two phenomena which we might well have expected. First, for a long time after the fall of Troy there seems to have been no thalassocracy at all ; and secondly, it is a very long time indeed, certainly 400 years and perhaps 600, before there is a genuinely Greek thalassocracy. The Fall of Troy was dated by the authors of the list—viz. the tradition represented by Eusebius-Diodorus-Eratosthenes—at 1184 B.C. The list then runs[1]:

Lydi et Maeones	92 years	[Cares	—?] years
Pelasgi	85	Lesbii	—?
Thraces	79	Phocaeenses	44
Rhodii	23	Samii	17
Phryges	25	Lacedaemonii	2
Cyprii	33 or 23?	Naxii	10
Phoenices	45	Eretrienses	15
Aegyptii	60?	Aeginetae	10
Milesii	18		

Now the dates at the bottom of this list can be verified. The Aeginetan thalassocracy certainly ended in 480 B.C. We work from 480 B.C. backwards, and find a considerable though of course a steadily decreasing amount of historical confirmation as we go. There are one or two confusions, notably a grave one at Nos. 10 and 11, the Carians and Lesbians. These two powers have, in the first place, no specific time of duration attached to them; and, in the second place, there seems to be very little room for either. But whatever we do with these confused places, it is practically impossible to stretch out the dates given in the list so as to fill the whole historical period between the fall of Troy and the invasion of Xerxes. On Mr. Myres' arrangement there is a gap at the beginning, directly after the Trojan War, amounting to 128 or 138 years. On any plausible system there is about a century missing.

Now what are we to make of this gap? I suspect that it really is a gap, and that after the fall of the old Aegean empires there was no power strong enough or well enough organized to command much of the Aegean beyond its own shores. Mr. Myres thinks that the Carians have been transposed in the list. They are put tenth, where there is no room for them; they should have been first, where they are wanted. There is evidence in Diodorus for this suggested rearrangement, and it is quite likely to be right. But I would suggest that if we interpret the language properly a Carian thalassocracy at that date is probably the same thing as no thalassocracy at all. These race names are apt to be loosely handled, as we saw in Lecture II. Diodorus and the Greek

---

[1] I take the figures from Mr. Myres' list, marking the more uncertain figures. The textual criticism of the list is highly complicated; see Mr. Fotheringham's article. He considers on purely textual grounds that Eusebius' text gave Aegyptii 43, Cares 61, and Lesbii perhaps 68. The last two figures would then be mistakes on the part of Eusebius or his authority.

historians frequently use the word Carian to denote the aboriginal or pre-Hellenic inhabitants of the Aegean in general. Any rude and weak creatures whom you drove out of an island were roughly described as Carian. Take the most explicit passage, Diod. v. 84:

> After the capture of Troy the Carians increased and became more powerful at sea: getting possession of the Cyclades they seized some for themselves and drove out the Cretans who were settled there, while they occupied others in common with the Cretans who were there before. Afterwards when the Hellenes increased, it befell that most of the Cyclades were colonized, and the barbarous Carians driven out.

I suspect that one might put that statement in other words, thus:

> After the fall of the Minoan or Aegean empires, under the influence of the northern invasions, the first effect was not that the northern invaders began to control the seas. They were not advanced enough for that. It was that the subject populations in the islands began to raise their heads, and especially formed a small piratical power in the Cyclades. The guards of the local Minoan forts, being cut off from their base, were faced with two alternatives. They either resisted to the uttermost and perished. Or they made terms with the natives, and eventually sank to their level. When the Greeks came into existence as a people, they found the Cyclades inhabited by populations who were a mixture of the uncivilized Carian-Lelegian-Hittite natives and the isolated remnants of the Minoan settlements.

The first thalassocracy mentioned on the list is that of the Lydians and Maeones. Possibly some federation of the coast people of Asia Minor arose, under the protection of Lydia, for resisting the piracy of the Carians in the islands. It is nearly a century later that we find the first suggestion of a thalassocracy of Northern invaders, and even that is ambiguous. The Pelasgians, however, are possibly the definite tribe of that name, the tribe which raided Boeotia during the Trojan War, and, taking to the sea, made settlements in Lemnos, Attica, and Crete. They at any rate are succeeded by a real Northern race, the Thracians, who have left traces in the Maeander valley, in Naxos and Attica, as well as in Boeotia and Phocis. From what we know of the Thracians in historical times it is difficult to suppose that their control of the seas amounted to more than vigorous piracy. Next comes the first glimpse of something that seems Hellenic: the Rhodians are thalassocrats from about 800 B.C. for the short space of twenty-three years. But was Rhodes at that time a Hellenic island? The settlement of Rhodes is attributed by Greek tradition to a very early period, perhaps to the end of the eleventh century. Wandering Dorians, people from Megara in two relays, people from Crete and from Argos, seem to have joined hands there. And it is quite likely that when Rhodes began to use its geographical position, holding the south-east gate of the Aegean, it deserved actually to be called a Hellenic power. In any case, it could not long stand, and no other Hellenic power could support or even succeed it. There follow Phrygians, Cyprians, Phoenicians, Egyptians, covering some 160 years. The Cyprians were scarcely Hellenic at this time, and the rest are plain βάρβαροι, though we happen to know that the Egyptian sea-power depended a good deal upon 'Ionian and Carian' ships. The Greeks, it seems, could supply the ships and the fighting material; they could not yet supply the permanent basis and organization. But that step was easy to take. And when Egypt became distracted by the invasion of Nebuchadnezzar in 604 B.C., the centre of gravity changed from the mouth of the Nile to the harbour of Miletus, and the Aegean for many centuries to come remained a Greek sea. Milesians 18 years; Lesbians 4; Phocaeans 44; Samians 17; Lacedaemonians 2; Naxians 10; Eretrians 15; Aeginetans 10; and then the Athenian Empire.

APPENDIX D

HUBRIS, DIKÊ AND HORKOS[1]

THIS central idea of Aidôs has various ramifications in the ethics of early Greek poetry. Most of the Homeric words of disapproval mean something like 'excess', or 'going too far', and imply that there are points where a man should check himself. The wicked are ἀτάσθαλοι, 'outrageous', ὑπερήφανοι, 'overweening', ἄδικοι, 'away from Dikê', justice or law: most of all, wickedness is Ὕβρις. That word is the antithesis of σωφροσύνη and of αἰδώς, and like its antitheses it defies translation into our forms of thought. It unites so many ideas which we analyse and separate: and it has a peculiar emotional thrill in it, which is lost instantly if we attempt to make careful scientific definitions. We can understand it, I think, in this way. Aidôs—or Sôphrosynê, which is slightly more intellectual—implies that, from some subtle emotion inside you, some ruth or shame or reflection, some feeling perhaps of the comparative smallness of your own rights and wrongs in the presence of

---

[1] For a further analysis of these and other ideas of primitive Greek society see Mr. F. M. Cornford's illuminating book, *From Religion to Philosophy*, especially the early chapters: also Glotz, *Solidarité de la Famille*, and *Études sociales et juridiques*.

the great things of the world, the gods and men's souls and the portals of life and death, from this emotion and from no other cause, amid your ordinary animal career of desire or anger or ambition, you do, every now and then, at certain places, stop. There are unseen barriers which a man who has Aidôs in him does not wish to pass. Hubris passes them all. Hubris does not see that the poor man or the exile has come from Zeus: Hubris is the insolence of irreverence: the brutality of strength. In one form it is a sin of the low and weak, irreverence; the absence of Aidôs in the presence of something higher. But nearly always it is a sin of the strong and proud. It is born of *Koros*, or satiety—of 'being too well off'; it spurns the weak and helpless out of its path, 'spurns,' as Aeschylus says, 'the great Altar of Dikê' (*Ag.* 383). And Hubris is the typical sin condemned by early Greece. Other sins, except some connected with definite religious taboos, and some derived from words meaning 'ugly' or 'unfitting', seem nearly all to be forms or derivatives of Hubris.

What relations are there between this group of ideas and the other great conception of 'Justice', Themis or Dikê? Both words have a strong flavour of custom or precedent in them, but their meaning is different. Themis is the Right Custom, the thing that is always done and therefore legitimate, inside the group: Dikê is the dispute between two persons, or between the group and another group, and the Right Decision that is given when such a dispute occurs. A King can utter Themistes or Dooms, merely declaring the right way of behaviour. An oracle is the seat of Themis; where the most ancient fountains of knowledge, the dead ancestors, declare 'what is done' under such and such circumstances. This can occur without any argument or conflict, whereas Dikê is the 'thing done', or the 'right custom', in trying and judging a dispute.

Thus Dikê and Themis are themselves one of the bonds which Aidôs enables you to feel. You feel 'what a man has a right to expect'. If your neighbour takes one of your cattle, you will naturally apply to the judges to make the man give it back, with perhaps something extra for damages. That is what is always done: what you have a right to expect. If the judge, having received bribes from your neighbour, refuses to hear you, then you are aggrieved: that is not Dikê, not the normal course. The judge has no Aidôs. The people, and the gods, will feel Nemesis. 'Dikê' is associated with trials, while 'Themis' seems rather specially to be concerned with the keeping or breaking of Oaths.

False Swearing, though it is not mentioned in Hesiod's list of the five deadly offences, is in general one of the most typical and most loudly cursed of ancient sins. And its relation to Aidôs is very close.

The word *Horkos*, which we translate an oath, really means 'a fence', or 'something that shuts you in'. The process by which the oath becomes important is this. You make to a man some statement or promise, and then he requires some πίστις, some ὅρκος—a πίστις to make him feel confident, an ὅρκος to fence you in. The simplest form of 'Horkos', and according to Medea (Eur. *Med.* v. 21) the greatest, is simply to clasp hands. With more formality you can, both of you, call upon the gods, or the *daimones* who happen to be present in the air about you, to witness the spoken word. Or you can ensure their presence by calling them to a sacrifice. And, instead of being satisfied with the general Nemesis which these divine witnesses and judges will feel if the word is broken, you and your friend can specify the exact punishment which the gods are to inflict upon you if you fail. That is the Horkos, the 'sanction' which binds the speaker. In general, covenant by oath belongs to a form of society which cannot enforce its judgements. It is ultimately an appeal to Honour, to Aidôs. Of course priests and prophets may thunder about the vengeance which the gods will exact for a breach of the covenant which they witnessed: but that sort of vengeance has in all ages of the world remained a little remote or even problematical. The real point of importance is that there is no vengeance by men, and no available human witness. The man who has sworn is really face to face with nothing but his own sense of Aidôs, *plus* a vague fear of gods and spirits, who are for the main part only the same Aidôs personified and wrapt in mythology. The thing that makes the perjurer especially base, or ἀναιδής, is precisely his security from danger. I knew once a perfect case of the simplest Horkos. A certain Egyptian wished an Englishman to take a quantity of antiquities to Europe and sell them for him. The Englishman accepted the trust, and drew up a full catalogue of the articles, with a list of the prices which he might expect to get for each of them. The Egyptian shook his head at all this complication of securities: 'I would like', he said, 'if you will shake my hand, and say you will be my brother.' That handshake was the Horkos, the fence or bond. A man who broke through such a Horkos would be ἀναιδής, a shameless or ruthless man. It is just what Jason did to Medea.

I have not attempted in the text to consider the origin of any of these terms, but Mr. Cornford, in his chapter on *Moira*, has essayed in a very striking manner to trace their ultimate derivation from the spatial divisions of a primitive tribe. Cf. Mauss et Durkheim, 'Formes primi-

tives de classification', *Année Soc.* 1901-2. The Moirai, or Portions, are
the traditional moieties or structural divisions of the tribe : there is a
Dasmos or Distribution of these Moirai (cf. the regular Dasmos of the
Moirai of the gods, Zeus having heaven, Poseidon the sea, Hades the
underworld, &c.) ; the Horkos is the 'fence' or barrier between these
Moirai ; specially important is the Tribal Pasture ; Νόμος, 'Custom',
'Law', is the legitimate power wielded (cf. νέμειν κράτη) within a 'range'
or 'province' (νομός) which is ultimately a pasture or feeding-ground
(νομός and νομή). Nemesis (on Mr. Cook's lines, from νέμος) is connected with the pasture-ground and its rules which must not be
transgressed, and so on. It is interesting to note that in Eur. *Hipp.* 78
Aidôs is connected with abstinence from trespassing on a taboo meadow.

Other primitive moral terms are derived from the order of the Moon
and the Seasons.

APPENDIX E

THE PSEUDO-CALLISTHENES

THE MSS. of the Greek version of the Alexander Romance, attributed
to Callisthenes, the well-known *savant* who accompanied Alexander's
expeditions, fall into three main classes, represented by—

A (Paris, 1711), of the eleventh century. This version practically
    agrees with the Latin translation of Julius Valerius, made
    before A. D. 340, and the Armenian translation made in the
    fifth century.

B (Paris, 1685; bearing date A. M. 6977 = A. D. 1469), abbreviated.
    The good Leyden MS., L, is of this class.

C (Paris, 113 Suppl., bearing date A. D. 1567), greatly expanded.

As a mark of difference we may take the point that A inserts the
Greek campaign between i. 41 and ii. 7, awkwardly making the con-
nexion by inserting κἀκεῖθεν ὥρμησεν εἰς τὰ μέρη τῶν βαρβάρων διὰ τῆς
Κιλικίας.

B and C put the Greek campaign at i. 27, but give different accounts
of it ; they then insert an abbreviated repetition of the same events at
i. 41. The Greek campaign is evidently in both cases an interpolation
from another source, and breaks the connexion.

The differences between these various classes of MSS. cannot be
illustrated except in large extracts. They are tabulated in K. Müller's
introduction, pp. x ff., in his large edition of Arrian and Callisthenes.
Still less can the differences between the various translations. But a

short passage taken from two MSS. of the same class, and thus closely resembling one another, may be instructive.

Subjoined is a passage (i. 18) as it appears in Paris C and Barocc. 17, showing the freedom with which the scribe treats his original. The scribe of Barocc. 17, for instance, prefers to put the chariot race at *Rome* by the temple of *Capitolian* Zeus, instead of *Pisa* and *Olympian* Zeus. And he uses his own fancy in narrating the conversation between Alexander and his father. The passage is fairly typical.

Μιᾷ οὖν τῶν ἡμερῶν Ἀλέξανδροσ μετὰ τῶν συνηλικιωτῶν αὐτοῦ συνών, λόγουσ
Ἐν μιᾷ οὖν τῶν ἡμερῶν   μετὰ τῶν   ἡλικιωτῶν αὐτοῦ συνών, λόγουσ

λόγοισ προτείναντεσ, εἰσφέρεται λόγοσ, ὡσ ὅτε εἰσ Πίσαν ἀρματηλατοῦσιν οἱ
λόγων προτεινόντων, εἰσφέρεται λόγοσ, ὡσ ὅτι ἐν Ῥώμῃ ἀρματηλατοῦσιν οἱ

δοκιμώτεροι τῶν βασιλέων παῖδεσ, καὶ τῷ νικήσαντι ἆθλα διδοῦσιν ἀπὸ τοῦ Ὀλυμ
εὐδοκιμώτεροι τῶν βασιλέων παῖδεσ καὶ τῷ νικήσαντι ἆθλα δίδοται παρὰ τοῦ Καπ

πίου Διόσ· ὃσ δ' ἂν ἡττηθείσ, παρὰ τῶν νικησάντων θανατοῦται. Ταῦτα ἀκούσα
τωλίου Διόσ. Ὁ δὲ ἡττηθεὶσ παρὰ τῶν νικησάντων θανατοῦται.   ταῦτα ἀκούσα

Ἀλέξανδροσ ἔρχεται προσ Φίλιππον   δρομαῖοσ, καὶ εὑρίσκει αὐτὸν εὐκαιροῦντ
Ἀλέξανδροσ ἔρχεται προσ τὸν πρᾱ αὐτοῦ δρομαῖοσ, καὶ

καὶ καταφιλήσασ αὐτὸν εἶπε· Πάτερ, δέομαί σου,   ἐπ
                 λέγει· Δέομαί σου, ὦ δέσποτα, τῶ ἐν ἐμοὶ καταθύμιον πλη

τρεψόν μοι εἰσ Πίσαν πλεῦσαι ἐπὶ τὸν ἀγῶνα τῶν Ὀλυμπίων, ἐπειδὴ ἀγωνίσασθα
ρωσον, καὶ τὸ ἁρμόζων παρασχόμενοσ [1] ἀπόστειλόν μοι ἐν Ῥώμῃ ἀρματηλατῆσα

βούλομαι. Ὁ δὲ Φίλιπποσ εἶπε προσ αὐτόν· Καὶ ποῖον ἄσκημα ἀσκήσασ τούτουσ
         Ὁ δὲ Φίλιπποσ λέγει· ὦ βία ἀπὸ σοῦ, παῖ· [3] οὔπω γάρ σοι ὄγδοον ἔτο

ἐπιθυμεῖσ;   οὐ συγχωρῶ σοι τοῦτο πρᾶξαι.
διῆλθε καὶ ἀρματηλατῆσαι βούλει; οὐ συγχωρῶ σοι τοῦτο πρᾶξαι.

The upper line throughout is Paris C, the lower the Bodleian cod. Barocc. 17. See much longer extracts in Meusel, *Ps.-Callisthenes*, pp. 794 ff.

It is worth remarking that the commonest errors in the Callisthenes MSS. are those which come from mere misspelling. If the pronunciation came right the spelling mattered little. The book was essentially the prompt-book of an oral story-teller.

[1] i. e. give me my share of the inheritance.
[2] Should be τούτου.   [3] 'Via! Far be it from thee!'

I have not met with Nöldeke, *Beiträge zur Geschichte des Alexander-romans* (1890). The Syriac and Ethiopic versions have been edited with great learning by Budge (1889 and 1896 respectively). He points out that much of the material is of immemorial antiquity. For instance, Etanna, a Babylonian hero, rode on an eagle up to the gods. He reached Anu Ea and Bel, rested, and went on towards Ishtar, but the eagle grew faint and fell. This story was then attached to the Assyrian-Accadian Gilgamesh, to Bellerophon, and at last to Alexander. (Ps.-Kall. ii. 41.)

APPENDIX F

STAGES OF OLD FRENCH POEMS: *ROLAND* AND *ST. ALEXIS*

NOTE ON *LA CHANSON DE ROLAND*.

TAKEN chiefly from Gaston Paris's Introduction to his little book of *Extraits* (8th edition, Hachette, 1905). The history of this ' traditional book ' can be made out in more detail and with more definite evidence than that of any ancient Epic, though of course it must not be supposed that M. Paris's results are absolutely final. We find the following stages :

I. *The historical event.* In A.D. 778, Charlemagne, the young King of the Franks, was returning from an expedition in the North of Spain, where he had been received in various cities, but shut out from Saragossa. When his main army had passed the Pyrenees, the rear-guard with the baggage was surprised *by the Basques* in the valley of Roncesvaux and cut to pieces. Among the slain were *the Seneschal Eggihard, the Count of the Palace, Anselm,* and *Hrodland, Count of the March of Britanny.* We know that this disaster became immediately famous, because of the language of an historian who wrote only sixty years after. He mentions the engagement, and adds : ' extremi quidam in eodem monte regii caesi sunt agminis : quorum, quia vulgata sunt, nomina dicere supersedi.' (*Life of Louis I,* in Pertz, SS. ii. 608.) The epitaph of the Seneschal Eggihard has been discovered, and shows that the battle took place on August 15. Apart from the epitaph, Eggihard and Anselm have disappeared from fame. Roland was a Breton, and we often find that the Breton songs have more vitality than others.

Such is the Frankish account, confirmed in most respects by that of the Arab Ibn-al-Athir (thirteenth century, but drawing on ancient sources). He, however, attributes the attack to the Moslems of Saragossa, not to the Basques. It would seem most probable that the Moslems organized the attack, and instigated the Basques. (G. Paris, *Légendes du Moyen Âge*, pp. 3, 4.)

II. *The earliest poetical account, a source which we may denote as RCT.* That is, a state of the poem represented by the common elements in three extant sources. These are (1) the Norman-French poem, *Roland* (R), of the eleventh century; (2) the prose chronicle which bears the name of Archbishop Turpin (T), and narrates these events in chapters xxi–xxix (early twelfth century); (3) a Latin poem, *Carmen de proditione Guenonis* (C), which is of the same epoch, but represents an earlier state of the poem than our extant MSS. (i. e. than any extant form of R).

RCT, then, represents the poem as it was before these various versions had made their different modifications of it. According to RCT:

Charlemagne, *Emperor of the Romans*, has conquered all Spain except Saragossa, which is held by the brothers Marsile and Baligant, under the suzerainty of the 'Admiral of Babylon'. (Babylon seems to mean Bagdad: if so, this is a memory of the very ancient suzerainty of the Eastern Caliphs over Spain.) He sends *Ganelon* to demand their submission. Ganelon is bribed, and promises to betray the best French warriors to the Saracens. He returns to Charles, announces the submission of the brothers, and induces Charles to return to France, leaving behind him, as rear-guard, the best of his barons, including *his nephew Roland, Count of Le Mans and Blaie, Oliver, Count of Geneva,* and 20,000 Christians. These are attacked at Roncesvaux by 50,000 *Saracens,* led by Ganelon. The first army corps of 20,000 Saracens is destroyed by the French. Then a fresh body of 30,000 Saracens destroys the French, except Roland and a hundred men. Roland *blows his horn* and rallies the hundred, who pursue and rout the Saracens. Roland kills Marsile, and then proceeds to die of his wounds. He bids farewell to his peerless sword, Durendal, and tries in vain to break it. It cuts through the marble on which he strikes it. Then, to warn the main army, he blows his horn again, so loud that it bursts the veins of his neck. Charles hears the horn and would return, but Ganelon persuades him that Roland is only hunting. Presently there arrives *Baldwin, Roland's brother,* with news of the disaster. The army returns, to find Roland dead; also Oliver, and others. There is a great lament. Charles pursues the Saracens. Night is approaching, but *a miracle retards the sun,* so that he overtakes them on the bank of the Ebro, and kills all that are left. Ganelon is accused of treason. *There is an ordeal; Pinabel fights for Ganelon, Tierri for Charles.* Tierri kills Pinabel, and Ganelon is torn in pieces. Roland is buried in St. Romain de Blaie, while his horn is left at St. Severin in Bordeaux. Oliver is buried at Belin. Charles returns to Aix and, after a time, dies.

III. *A source RC*, i. e. the story common to Roland and the Carmen, but not to Turpin. Various changes have been introduced. *Baligant has disappeared;* Marsile reigns alone at Saragossa. *Ganelon is provided with a motive* of spite against Roland : it was Roland who recommended the Emperor to send Ganelon on the dangerous mission to Marsile. The battle is even further embroidered, and the description of the country made marvellous. The *Twelve Peers* of Charlemagne are introduced, Roland being their chief. They slay twelve similar Peers of Marsile. After the second battle with the Pagans a *third Pagan army* comes up. The French are reduced to sixty. There is no Baldwin. It is the horn that brings Charlemagne back. Meantime Oliver is slain, and Roland and Turpin are the sole survivors of the French army. The Saracens flee. Roland collects the bodies of the twelve peers, and brings them to the dying Archbishop to receive the last blessing. Roland faints from his wounds. Turpin, in an effort to fetch water, dies. Roland recovers and folds Turpin's hands in a cross upon his breast, and pronounces a *regret* over him. Then he faints again. A Saracen returns and tries to take Roland's sword, Durendal, at which Roland recovers consciousness and breaks the Saracen's head with his *olifant* or horn. He tries in vain to break Durendal ; says a long farewell to all that he loves, dies, and is transported to heaven by angels. There are some slight variations in the final scenes also. Ganelon, for instance, is *écartelé* on the spot.

IV. *The extant Chanson de Roland, or R*, composed shortly after 1066. In this version Marsile is made to take the initiative in offering his submission to Charlemagne, and sending hostages. It is in answer to this embassy that Charles sends Ganelon to Saragossa. Roland offers to go as messenger himself before suggesting Ganelon, who is in this version his *parâtre*—his uncle by marriage—and has a grudge against him in consequence. Ganelon is corrupted by the Saracens on the way to Saragossa. Nevertheless, on arrival he delivers Charles' defiance just as in the old versions, though the defiance has now lost all *raison d'être*. At the beginning of the battle Oliver sees from a hill the vast hordes of the Saracens, and urges Roland to sound the horn. Roland from pride refuses ; a fine scene, which has a pendent later, when Roland wishes to sound the horn and Oliver dissuades him. Oliver is more prominent altogether than in the older versions, and Roland is betrothed to his sister, Aude. When Marsile is taken prisoner and dies, his queen Bramimonde, who, like other Saracen princesses, admires the Christians, is taken back to France and happily baptized. After the burial of Roland, Oliver, and Turpin at Blaie, Charles returns to Aix, and there holds a solemn trial of Ganelon. This part is worked up. Ganelon intimidates and bribes the judges. They acquit him. At last one of them, Tierri—who is now 'Tierri of Anjou'—takes the office of accuser upon himself, fights Pinabel, and hands Ganelon over to his punishment. Charles is about to rest after his labours when the angel Gabriel appears in a dream, and orders him forth to another expedition to the 'land of Bire', to 'succour the king Vivien in Imphe'. So comes the famous ending:

> 'Deus!' dist li Reis, 'si penuse est ma vie!'
> Pleurut des oilz, sa barbe blanche tiret. . . .
> Ci fait la Geste que Turoldus declinet.

V. *A large interpolation in R.* A little later than R, another poet had made a song in which the revenge after Roncesvaux was more crushing. Marsile is the vassal of Baligant—the brother and the Admiral of Babylon of the early sources combined into one person. Summoned to the aid of Marsile, Baligant takes seven years to arrive, and appears just in time to rally the Pagan forces after Roncesvaux. He challenges Charles to a supreme battle between all the forces of Christianity on the one hand and Paganism on the other. This gives rise to a 'Catalogue' of the thirty columns of the armies of Baligant, which forms an interesting parallel to the Homeric Catalogues (*Roland*, 3217-65). The list can be divided into Historical and Imaginary peoples; 'but the Historical peoples are those against whom the Christian powers were fighting, not at the time of the Crusades, but during the tenth and eleventh centuries' (Gaston Paris in *Romania*, ii, pp. 330 ff.; or L. Gauthier's note to *Roland*, ad loc.). That is, the interpolator has not described the Pagans of his own day, but has drawn from an ancient list of Pagans, which happens to be even earlier than the poem to which he was adding. The Christians of course win, and Charles, sustained by an angel, slays Baligant.

The above versions, IV and V, are best represented in the Oxford MS. which affords several curious parallels to the history of the Homeric text. "The Oxford MS. is the work of an Anglo-Norman scribe, and the text which this scribe gives us is a very pure specimen of the French spoken and written in England a hundred years after the Conquest, about the year 1170. But it was long before the year 1170, half a century earlier at the least, that the 'Song of Roland' was composed by the poet, and nothing leads us to think that the poet ever lived, as the scribe did, in England. The Oxford text shows itself at first glance as a late transliteration into Anglo-French of a work first written in a different idiom. If, further, we consider how in course of a long transmission which no doubt had its vicissitudes, many scribes and many revisers, one after the other, may have modified the original readings in the free manner of that age, we are led to suppose that the copy under our eyes is separated from the original MS. of the poet by a gulf more or less considerable and possibly very great indeed. How are we to measure this gulf? Who was the poet, a Norman or a Frenchman of France? At what date did he compose his *chanson*? About the year 1110, as many critics including the present writer maintain, or as others believe twenty or thirty years earlier, well before the Crusade, about 1080? In what language did he write it? In such and such a dialect of Normandy, or such and such a dialect of the Capesian Kingdom? Or in a literary language, more or less tinged by dialectical peculiarities? The answers to these questions vary." (*Chanson de Roland* publiée et traduite par Joseph Bédier: Introduction, p. 3. no date; 1920?)

VI. *The Rimed Version and later forms.* The Chanson is also extant in a Venetian MS. of the fourteenth century, and various translations into Norwegian prose (twelfth century), German verse, Netherlandish verse, &c. But the most important point in the succeeding history of the poem is the Rimed Version of the later part of the twelfth century. The poetical taste of the period had moved from assonance to rime, and the old poems written in assonance were changed throughout. This is the opening of a whole new history, the various rimed *remaniements* reaching down to the sixteenth century.

(In assonance the last accented vowel—and the succeeding vowels, if any—in each line must be the same; in rime the last accented vowel and all succeeding vowels and consonants: thus in assonance we can end successive lines with Turp*ins*, lar*iz*, *dit*, *ci*, mur*ir* (*Roland*, xcv), or *sages*, *armes*, *haltes*, *chevalchent*.)

A further change in form was the adoption of the Alexandrine, or twelve-syllable line divided in the middle, instead of the old ten-syllable. The Alexandrine derives its name from the first French version of the Pseudo-Callisthenes, a metrical romance written in 1184 by Lambert li Tors with the assistance of Alexander of Paris. Examples of the changes in text produced by the introduction of rime and Alexandrine are given below, from the *St. Alexis*.

St. Alexis.

Vie de St. Alexis, poème du XIe siècle, et renouvellements des XIIe XIIIe et XIVe siècles. Gaston Paris et Léopold Pannier, 1887.

This book contains four successive versions of the same poem, showing its growth and its adaptation to varying periods of taste.

I. Eleventh century: assonance: probably chanted in church.

> Bons fut li siecles als tens ancienor,
> Quer feit i ert e justise et amor,
> Si ert credance, dont or n'i at nul prot:
> Tot est mudez, perdude at sa color;
> Ja mais n'iert tels com fut as anceisors.
>
> Al tens Noe et al tens Abraham,
> Et al David, que Deus par amat tant,
> Bons fut li siecles, &c.

This may be translated:

> Good was the world in the time of old,
> Surely faith there was and justice and love,
> So was there belief, whereof now there is no profit (?),
> All is dumb, it has lost its colour,
> Never shall it be such as it was to those of old.
>
> In the time of Noah and in the time of Abraham,
> And of David whom God the Father loved so much,
> Good was the world.

II. Middle of twelfth century: work of a popular *jongleur*. Still in assonance, but greatly interpolated.

> [Signour et dames, entendés un sermon
> D'un saintisme home qui Allessis ot non,
> Et d'une feme que il prist a oissor,[1]
> Que il guerpi[2] pour Diu son Creatour,
> Caste pucele et gloriouse flour,
> Qui ains a li nen ot convercion;
> Pour Diu le fist, s'en a bon guerredon:
> Saulve en est l'ame en ciel nostre signour,
> Li cors en gist a Rome a grant honour.]
> Bons fut li siecles au tans ancienour
> Quar fois i ert et justise et amor, &c. (as in I).

The largest interpolation comes, characteristically, at the romantic moment where Alexis has to relinquish and convert his betrothed—a *persona muta* in the old text; here 30 verses are expanded into 245.

III. Rimed version. Twelfth century. Based on the old text, but assonances changed to rimes. This sometimes causes great disturbance. The opening is very close to its original.

---

[1] oissor = wife.   [2] guerpi = relinquished.

Cha en arriére, au tens anchienors,
Fois fut en tiere et justiche et amors
Et verités et creanche et douchors :
Mais ore est frailes et plains de grans dolors.
Jamais n'iert teus con fut as anchissors.
Ne portent foit li marit lor oissors,
Ne li vassal fianche lor signors. . . .

Au tens Noë et au tens Moysant,
Au tens David cui Dius par ama tant,
Bons fut li siecles, &c.

(Observe *Moysant* instead of *Abraham*, for the sake of the rime.)

IV. Alexandrine version, in monorimed quatrains. Fourteenth century. This version is based on III, and opens at a passage which is about l. 14 of I, l. 45 of II, and l. 20 of III. I say 'about', since the actual line is not in I and II. It is introduced in III in the process of running a *laisse* of assonances in -*a* and -*e* into one long *laisse* of rimes in -*ant*, joining on to *Moysant* above.

The process of turning the ten-syllable lines into Alexandrines is, of course, child's-play.

En l'honor Diu le glorios poissant
Ki nos crea trestos a son semblant, &c.

merely becomes—

Ens en l'onneur de Dieu le pére tout puissant,
Qui nous fourma et fist trestous a son semblant, &c.

The peculiar critical value of the *St. Alexis* is that we have it in four distinct stages corresponding to four styles of French epic taste.

APPENDIX G

EXPURGATION IN THE HYMN TO DEMETER

THIS 'Homeric' expurgation extended to the Homeric Hymns also, as is illustrated by the Orphic papyrus of the second century B. C. recently published by Buecheler in *Berliner Klassikertexte*, v. 1. (See also an article upon it by T. W. Allen, in *C. R.*, xxi. 4.) The papyrus quotes, as ἐκ τῶν Ὀρφέως ἐπῶν, several passages from the Homeric Hymn to Demeter, in a slightly different shape. Notably the following incident.

Demeter, disguised and acting as Nurse in the house of Keleos, is secretly making the child Demophoon immortal by soaking him in fire. The mother, Metaneira, discovers her putting him in the fire, and shrieks with horror. Demeter, *in the Homeric Hymn*, takes the child out of the fire, puts him on the ground (254 f.) and then turns in anger on the Mother : ' Blind and witless are men, knowing not the portion of good when it cometh, nor yet of evil. And thou too hast got thee a huge hurt by thy follies ! So hear me the Horkos of the Gods, the unrelenting water of Styx, I would have made thy son deathless and ageless for all days, and made undying honour to follow him ; but now, I swear, he shall not escape Death and the Slayers ! '

In the ' Orphic ' or non-Homeric version there is nothing about Demeter taking the child out of the fire. On the contrary, when she gets to the words ' he shall not escape Death and the Slayers ', it proceeds : ' So saying, . . . (?) ing the child she burned it and slew it, and proclaimed herself.' (καὶ τὸ παιδίον επι . κ . . . σα (?) καίει καὶ ἀποκτείνει καὶ ὀρθῶς αὐτὴν διαγορεύει.) And exactly the same story is given by Apollodorus i. 4. 5 τὸ μὲν βρέφος ὑπὸ τοῦ πυρὸς ἀναλώθη, ἡ θεὰ δ' ἑαυτὴν ἐξέφηνε.

There can be little hesitation as to which of these versions is the older and more original. The whole myth is based on a ritual not indeed of child-sacrifice, as I conjectured in the first edition of this book, but of child-ordeal, as Mr. W. R. Halliday has shown in *C. R.* xxv. p. 8. The fire-washing was one of those ' rites de passage ' by which the young member of a primitive tribe was initiated or specially fortified against dangers and weaknesses. The typical instance is the flogging of the Spartan *iranes* at the altar of Artemis Orthia. (All these rites were supposed by the Greeks themselves to be remnants of Human Sacrifice.)

The ἱερὸς λόγος connected with the rite naturally told how the goddess herself had instituted it, how the rite, when properly performed and unwatched by outsiders, was infinitely beneficial, but, if interrupted, death-bringing. The interrupted goddess threw the child into the fire, as any primitive deity naturally would. When this idea became repulsive to pious men, the tale was softened. The goddess only puts the child down on the hearth, a very soft-hearted and civilized proceeding. The child so saved is, one may conjecture, the origin of ὁ ἀφ' ἑστίας παῖς so often mentioned in connexion with the Mysteries, ὃς ἀντὶ πάντων τῶν μνουμένων ἀπομειλίσσεται τὸ θεῖον. Porph. *de Abst.* 4. 5. (See Farnell, *Cults,* iii. p. 352, note 209.) The reverse process would contradict all analogy.

This throws light on another point. We have long observed that those parts of the Demeter cult which struck unsympathetic observers as obscene have no place in the Homeric Hymn, while they are quoted from 'Orpheus' by Clement and Arnobius (Abel, *Orphica*, fr. 215). It was just conceivable that they might have come in as a late degradation of a rite which in 'Homeric times' was pure. But now it is pretty evident that they must go along with the primitive barbarity of the child-burning story. They belong to the things expurgated from Homer. (See Mr. Allen (l. c.), who still inclines to the other view. For the probable explanation of Baubo, see Diels, *Arcana Cerealia*, in *Miscellanea di Archeologia dedicata al Prof. Salinas*. Palermo, 1907.)

The expurgations of some ancient critics, especially Zenodotus, for which we generally laugh at them, are merely continuations of the Homeric spirit. E. g. Zenodotus on Π 93-6, and apparently the whole Koinê together with Aristarchus on the Phoenix story, I 458-61, Sosiphanes on 453, &c. They objected to what was ἀπρεπές, which was quite in the spirit of Homer, supposing the standard of 'unseemliness' to be the same.

APPENDIX H

THE EPIC CYCLE

THIS note will do little more than restate in a much shortened form Wilamowitz's criticism on the views of the Cycle current in 1884. I shall not attempt any positive account of the Cycle. Such a work takes one far afield and cannot be essayed with any prospect of success except on the basis of a thorough study of the Mythographi and their methods : see Schwartz and Bethe, as referred to below. I shall merely deal with certain false ideas of the Cycle which affect the preliminaries of the Homeric Question. See also the full and careful account by Monro in his edition of the *Odyssey* (App. pp. 340-84), against which some of my criticism here is directed.

My own view is, roughly speaking, that to call the authors of the *Cypria* or the *Thebais* 'cyclic poets' is very like calling Shakespeare and Milton 'birthday-book poets'. The Greek poets were no more responsible for the Cycle than the English are for the birthday-books. Nay, more : the birthday-books do at least profess to quote the actual words of Shakespeare ; but the Cycle only professed to tell the general mass of epic history, using the old poems as authorities. It seldom gave a quotation and seems freely to have filled in gaps and omitted redundancies, though it sometimes gave variant versions according to different poets.

But to come to the evidence. Our supposed knowledge of the 'Epic

Cycle' is based chiefly on certain extracts from the *Chrestomatheia Grammatikê* or 'Compendium of Useful Knowledge in Literature' made by Proclus—presumably the Neoplatonic philosopher in the fifth century after Christ. The extracts come to us in two forms: (1) A very brief epitome in Photius's *Bibliotheca* (*c.* 850 A.D.); (2) some fuller but fragmentary epitomae of that part of Proclus which dealt with the *Trojan Cycle*, preserved in the Scholia to the *Iliad*. (Dindorf, Vol. I, pp. xxxi–xli : also in Kinkel's *Epicorum Fragmenta*, init.) The view I wish to correct accepts Proclus's account—or the account given by the Scholiast of Proclus's account—practically without criticism.

Photius (p. 319) tells us that Proclus gave a catalogue of the chief epic poets and their biographies: 'he embraces also an account of the so-called Epic Cycle, which begins with the legendary Marriage of Heaven and Earth . . . and goes on through the various myths related by the Greeks about the Gods and some few stories that are true in history; the Epic Cycle, *made complete out of various poets*, ends with the landing of Odysseus in Ithaca, where he is killed by his son Telegonus who does not know him. He says that the poems of the Epic Cycle are preserved and studied generally not for their merit but for the sequence of events (τὴν ἀκολουθίαν τῶν πραγμάτων).'

Such 'cycles' were made by many Grammatici in Alexandrian times, from the κύκλος ἱστορικός of 'Dionysius the Cyclographer' onwards. Even a short study of the mythographical literature shows us how these handbooks were copied word by word one from another with such additions or omissions as suited the aims of the particular writer. For instance, the last sentence cited from Photius above, 'the poems of the cycle are preserved and studied, &c.', has probably been copied verbally together with the rest of its context from handbook to handbook through many centuries. (I agree with most authorities in thinking it almost out of the question to suppose that the old poems themselves were extant in Proclus's time.) The first source cannot be traced; but Bethe has shown that many of Proclus's sentences show marked verbal similarity with sentences in the fragments of Apollodorus's *Bibliotheca*, the author of which pretty certainly used a 'cycle'. (Bethe in *Hermes* xxvi.)

The Epic Cycle is that part of the general Cyclus Historicus which comprises epic, or legendary, history; parts of it again are referred to as the 'Trojan Cycle', the 'Theban Cycle'. The Trojan Cycle in Proclus is given as follows:

1. The *Cypria*, from the Judgement of Paris to the capture of Chryseis and Briseis, the death of Palamedes, and the 'counsel' of Zeus; author, Stasînus of Cyprus (amid other competitors).

2. The *Iliad* by Homer.

3. The *Aethiopis* by Arctînus of Miletus, from the end of the *Iliad* to the death of Achilles. 5 books. The heroine is the Amazon, Penthesilea.

4. The *Little Iliad* by Lesches of Mytilene, from the contest for the Arms of Achilles to the taking of Troy. 4 books.

5. The *Sack of Ilion* by Arctînus. 2 books.

6. The *Nostoi*, or *Homecomings* of the Greek chieftains, by Agias of Trozên. 5 books.

7. The *Odyssey* by Homer.

8. *Telegonia* by Eugammon of Cyrene. 2 books.

Now some scholars, accepting Proclus as he stands, have deduced from him several conclusions which are to my mind unjustifiable.

1. Some have actually argued that the poets themselves (in the seventh century B. C. !) clubbed together to compose a Cycle. This seems to me so contrary to all history and to the words of Proclus as scarcely to need detailed refutation. It is, however, conclusively refuted by Monro, pp. 342–4. Abandoning this extreme suggestion, Monro and others argue from the contents of the poems in Proclus's account of the Cycle that the poems themselves presuppose the existence of the *Iliad* and *Odyssey* and were, in a sense, written to fill up their omissions.

2. They have accepted as canonical the list of six poems, each complete with its author, as given by Proclus.

3. They have accepted for these authors a series of dates based upon the *Chronicon* of Eusebius.

In criticism of this method of treating the question Wilamowitz points out, first, that Proclus is a writer belonging quite to the decline of learning, and that we have not even the statements of Proclus entire, but only in extracts and epitomae; and secondly, that there are earlier and better authorities available, and they use quite different language.

1. We may take first the Tabula Iliaca (No. 1 in Jahn-Michaelis, *Bilderchroniken*, 1873), a large relief illustrating scenes in the history of the Trojan War. It is drawn up on the scheme of a grammarian called Theodorus, and belongs to the first century B. C. While partly agreeing with Proclus, it makes up the post-homeric part of its Trojan Cycle from 'the *Aethiopis* according to Arctinus, the so-called *Little Iliad* according to Lesches of Pyrrha, and *the Sack of Ilion according to Stesichorus*'. That is, the 'Epic Cycle' was not a fixed whole. Theodorus could follow the epico-lyric poet Stesichorus in preference to Proclus's Arctinus. Also, observe Theodorus's language : he uses the *Aethiopis* 'according to' Arctinus, the *Sack* 'according to '

Stesichorus. That is, the *Aethiopis* or the *Sack* is to him a fixed mass of legend, a traditional subject of poetry, which he can give according to any one of its successive composers. He does not think of the *Aethiopis* as a new poem invented by Arctinus ; nor does he think of his own work as a mere exact reproduction of the poems which he cites as authorities. (See e. g. his illustration of *Iliad* Υ.) He writes Θεοδώρειον μάθε τάξιν Ὁμήρου, Ὄφρα δαεὶς πάσης μέτρον ἔχῃς σοφίας. 'Learn Theodorus's arrangement of Homer'—that is, an epitomization of the whole of legendary history—'that, knowing it, you may have the measure of all wisdom' (see above, p. 298 f.).

Further, the Tabulae know of a much greater number of these old poems which could be used to form a 'cycle' than does Proclus or Photius. In the Theban Cycle of the Tabula Borgiaca (VI. K.), where the text is mutilated, we cannot even identify all the poems mentioned. This is very different from the six 'cyclic' poems with one author each, which we get in the epitome of Proclus. We must always remember that, if we had the whole text of Proclus, it might be much less positive. The abbreviator may have simply, in each case, left out all names but one.

2. About the year 225 A. D. we find Athenaeus, a really learned man and dependent on good authorities, recognizing all these poems, but not professing to know their authors or dates.

Ὁ τὴν Τιτανομαχίαν ποήσας, εἴτ' Εὔμηλός ἐστιν ὁ Κορίνθιος ἢ Ἀρκτῖνος ἢ ὁστισδήποτε χαίρει ὀνομαζόμενος (277).

Ὁ τὰ Κύπρια ἔπη πεποηκώς, Ἡγησίας ἢ Στασῖνος ἢ Κύπριος (682).

Ὁ τὸν Αἰγίμιον ποήσας, εἴθ' Ἡσίοδός ἐστιν ἢ Κέρκωψ ὁ Μιλήσιος (503).

Ὁ τὴν Ἀλκμαιωνίδα (460), ὁ τὴν κυκλικὴν Θηβαΐδα (465), ὁ τὴν τῶν Ἀτρειδῶν κάθοδον (281, 399). Once ὁ τὴν Ἰλίου Πέρσιν . . . Ἀγίας, a definite name, but one that happens to contradict the Proclus-epitome.

3. Still more important is Pausanias, writing in the second century A. D. and using largely the historians and mythographers of the first century B. C., contemporaries of Theodorus. He refers several times to the lost epics, but especially has a great burst of quotations in his account of Polygnotus's paintings in the Leschê at Delphi (x. 25 ff.), where he seems to be using some special authority who possessed great knowledge of these poems. (Whether Pausanias himself had seen the epics themselves, or seen them as quoted by his authority, or had never seen them at all, but merely adopted the language of his authority in speaking about them, need not be discussed at the moment. Those who know late Greek literature best seem generally to take the last view.) To Pausanias the *Cypria* and *Little Iliad* are anonymous poems.

The *Sack of Ilion* is by Lescheôs.[1] The *Nostoi* is anonymous, though he knows elsewhere the name of Hêgias of Trozên. The *Minyas* is by 'Prodicus, or whoever else it was'. The *Thebais* is 'perhaps Homer'; the *Oedipodeia* and *Eumolpia* are anonymous; the *Naupactia* are by 'Kinaithon or Kreophylus or Peisandros or Hêgias'.

That is, the good authorities, as compared with the Proclus extracts, know a great many more poems, and do not pretend to know the authors of them.

4. Wilamowitz proceeds to show that this is the usual language of the early Grammatici. The poem is cited without an author: Ὁ τὴν Πέρσιν, ὁ τὴν Μικρὰν Ἰλιάδα, ὁ τοὺς Νόστους ποήσας. Sometimes we find οἱ ποήσαντες. Οἱ τὴν Ἡράκλειαν ποήσαντες, Eratosthenes, ap. Strab. 688; οἱ τῶν Κυπρίων ποιηταί, Schol. v. on π 57. What does this plural mean? It means, I think, that many poets had 'done' or 'made' the Heracles-saga or the Homecomings; consequently you could represent the subjects 'according to' any one of them.

Proclus speaks of the *Cycle* as made up 'out of various poets'. Earlier writers would have said, more correctly, 'out of various poems.' In early times the poem is the datum, the author a matter of conjecture or of indifference. It is exceedingly rare to find an author cited alone without a poem—I mean, to find the statement 'Lesches says', 'Arctinus says', except in one special kind of literature. Such phrases occur freely in Clement's *Stromateis* (especially the sixth book) and Eusebius's *Praeparatio*, always in quotations from the so-called 'Peripatetic Jew', Aristobulus. Aristobulus wrote about 100 B.C. to prove that all Greek philosophers had 'stolen' their wisdom from Moses and Solomon, and in the course of the argument chose to prove that all the ancient poets were habitual thieves. He wrote περὶ κλοπῶν, and says that Homer stole from Orpheus; that Eugammon stole the *Thesprotis* from Musaeus; Panyassis stole the *Taking of Oechalia* from Kreophylus; Peisander stole the *Heracleia* from Peisinoos of Lindos. Aristobulus, in fact, was the first important writer to get hold of these questions by the wrong end, by the conception of literary property, and his misunderstanding haunts us still.

As to the dates commonly assigned to the authors used in the Cycle, they are based on statements drawn, at various removes, from the *Chronicon* of Eusebius, which is known to have fallen early into a state

---

[1] Apparently from a genitive, Λέσχεω Ἰλίου Πέρσις. Pausanias found the name only in the genitive and conjectured a nominative Λέσχεως. We ourselves are in just the same position about the writer Πτολεμαίου τοῦ Ἡφαιστίωνος, quoted in Photius. Is he Ptolemaeus Hephaestio, or Ptolemaeus son of Hephaestio? No one knows.

of confusion, and, even if free from contradictions, would be a shaky basis. It is the authority, for instance, for the following entries (Wilamowitz, l. c., p. 348):

Ol. I. Ἀρκτῖνος Μιλήσιος ἐποποιὸς ἤκμαζεν.

Ol. IV. Eumelus poeta qui Bugoniam et Europiam, et Arctinus qui Aethiopidem composuit et Ilii Persin agnoscitur.

Cinaethus Lacedaemonius poeta qui Telegoniam scripsit agnoscitur.

Ol. IX. Eumelus Corinthius versificator agnoscitur.

Ol. XXX. Λέσχης Λέσβιος ὁ τὴν μικρὰν Ἰλιάδα ποιήσας, καὶ Ἀλκμαίων ἤκμαζε.

Ol. LIII. Εὐγάμμων Κυρηναῖος ὁ τὴν Τηλεγονίαν ποιήσας ἐγνωρίζετο.

Thus the 'Sack of Ilion' is by Arctinus, Lesches, Augias, as well as by Stesichorus. The author of the *Telegonia* is 'Cinaethus' in Ol. IV and Eugammon in Ol. LIII, nearly two hundred years between them. It is not utterly impossible that all these statements may, in a sense, be true: the various traditional poems may have been 'done' by all these poets and others too. But two things are, I think, clear: first, that the evidence of Proclus and Eusebius is too weak to support much superstructure; secondly, weak as it is, it gives no support to the notion that Lesches, Arctinus, &c., clubbed together to write poems to fill the gaps left by Homer. The 'cycle' of the epitomator is only 'made complete out of the works of various poets'. And the evidence of the earlier and better authorities points steadily towards the hypothesis that has generally been urged in this book: that there was a large mass of traditional poetry, which was 'done' by various poets whose names generally remain unrecorded. The legendary matter was then collected in cycles—sometimes perhaps in verse, normally (Clem. Al. *Strom.* vi. p. 267 Sylb.= vol. 3, p. 112, Klotz) in prose—for educational purposes by the scholars of late Alexandrian and Roman times, while the old poems themselves passed out of mind and disappeared.

It is perhaps needless to controvert further the theory that Proclus's account of the Cycle is an accurate account of the old poems out of which the cycle was composed, but two test cases may be taken. (Cf. Monro, l. c., who gives more details.)

1. Herodotus says (ii. 117) that the *Cypria* are not by Homer because the *Cypria* say that Paris reached Ilion on the third day after leaving Sparta, with smooth sea and favouring wind, whereas the *Iliad* says he wandered or was driven out of his course to Sidon. Proclus on the contrary makes the *Cypria* say that Hera sent a storm upon them and Paris was carried to shore at Sidon and took the city.

What has happened? Herodotus's criticism has affected either the

Cypria themselves, or, more likely, the historical 'cycle' which used the *Cypria*. Homer said Alexander went to Sidon, and what Homer said must take rank as true. So the cycle-maker adopts Homer's version. (Several similar cases given in Schwartz, Pauly-Wiss. i. 2879.) Whether Homer's version ever got into the text of the *Cypria*, as an independent poem, or not, we have no evidence.

2. Aristotle, *Poetics*, cap. 23 ad fin., says that out of the *Little Iliad* more than eight tragedies can be made, and suggests ten: *The Judgement of the Arms, Philoctetes, Neoptolemus, Eurypylus, The Begging* (of Odysseus in Troy), *The Laconian Women, The Sack of Troy, The Sailing Away, Sinon,* and *The Trojan Women.* Of these ten the first six only fall inside the *Little Iliad* of Proclus's Cycle; the other four would fall in Proclus's *Sack of Ilion.* That is, the cycle-maker preferred to follow the *Sack of Ilion* rather than the *Little Iliad* for this part of the history. There is no difficulty about that. A difficulty is only created by imagining that the Cycle which was 'made complete out of different poets' was really the work of those poets themselves.

The whole genesis and purpose of these 'Cycles' in early Alexandrian times is admirably expounded in the article on Apollodorus (61st of that name) in Pauly-Wissowa by Schwartz, who understands the mythographical literature if any one does. The object is never to give an exact *résumé* or table of contents of a poem; the object is to tell again, in a full and connected form, for the purposes of general culture, all that the poets or historians have told us of the history of the past. It is concerned not with form or poetical beauty but with the ἀκολουθία τῶν πραγμάτων, the 'sequence of events', and it makes that sequence as clear and complete as it can. A fair instance is to be found in Hyginus, who uses, directly or indirectly, a number of ancient poets, but never attempts to give an account of their contents. He simply tells the story afresh, harmonizing his sources as best he can, and filling gaps by his own imagination or common sense. The cycle-maker of course had the *Iliad* and *Odyssey* before him, and used them as his first and most canonical authorities.

[See especially Wilamowitz, *Homerische Untersuchungen,* pp. 328–80; also Bethe in *Hermes* xxvi, and the articles by Schwartz on Apollodorus (61), Dionysius Skytobrachion (109), and Dionysius Κυκλογράφος (110) in Pauly-Wissowa's *Realencyclopädie.* An attempt to reassert the old (pre-Monro) view is made by T. W. Allen in *C. Q.,* ii (1908).]

APPENDIX I

EVIDENCE FOR TRANSLITERATION FROM 'THE OLD ΛLPHABET'

Cf. Cauer, *Grundfragen*³, pp. 105 ff.

A. Definite tradition in the Scholia :

1. Η 238 οἶδ' ἐπὶ δεξιά, οἶδ' ἐπ' ἀριστερὰ νωμῆσαι βῶν. βῶν most MSS. βοῦν Aristoph. Schol. TV explains ἐν τοῖς παλαιοῖς ἐγέγραπτο ΒΟΝ, ὅπερ οὐκ ἐνόησαν οἱ διορθωταί.

2. α 275 μητέρα δ', εἴ οἱ θυμὸς ἐφορμᾶται γαμέεσθαι, ἂψ ἴτω. Schol. τῇ ἀρχαίᾳ συνηθείᾳ ἐγέγραπτο ΜΕΤΕΡ ἀντὶ τοῦ ΜΗΤΗΡ. τοῦτο ἀγνοήσας τις προσέθηκε τὸ α.

3. [Add α 52 ⟨ΟΛΟΟΦΡΘΝ⟩ ἐγέγραπτο κατὰ τὴν ἀρχαίαν γραφήν, εἶτά τις μὴ νοήσας προσέθηκε τὸ ΟΣ.]

4. Ξ 241 ἐπίσχοιες A and most MSS. in antiquity : nearly all our MSS. have ἐπισχοίης. Schol. A τῷ ἐπίσχοιμι ἀκόλουθόν ἐστι τὸ ἐπίσχοις, τῷ δὲ ἐπισχοίην τὸ ἐπισχοίης. καὶ ἴσως ἔδει οὕτως ἔχειν, παρεφθάρη δὲ ὑπὸ τῶν μεταχαρακτηρισάντων. ἐπισχοίης for ἐπίσχοιες seems to be merely a conjecture of Alexander of Kotyäon, *saec.* II. A.D.

5. Λ 104 ᾧ ποτ' Ἀχιλλεύς. Zenodotus ὅν ποτ' Ἀχιλλεύς. Aristonicus μήποτε πεπλάνηται, γεγραμμένου τοῦ ο ὑπ' ἀρχαϊκῆς σημασίας ἀντὶ τοῦ ω, προσθεὶς τὸ ν.

6. Φ 362-3 ὡς δὲ λέβης ζεῖ ἔνδον ἐπειγόμενος πυρὶ πολλῷ, κνίσην μελδόμενος ἁπαλοτρεφέος σιάλοιο. In the Geneva Schol. Peisistratus of Ephesus and Hermogenes make the correction μελδομένου (with σιάλοιο) instead of μελδόμενος (with λέβης) and proceed : γραφομένου ΚΝΙΣΗΜΕΛΔΟΜΕΝΟ καὶ οὐ προσκειμένου τοῦ υ ὁ μεταγράφων εἰς τὴν νῦν γραμματικὴν οὐκ ἐνόησεν ὅτι ΜΕΛΔΟΜΕΝΟΥ ἦν, ἀλλ' ἄνευ τοῦ υ ἀναγιγνώσκων ἀδιανόητον ἡγεῖτο καὶ ἡμαρτημένον εἶναι, διόπερ προσέθηκε ἀντὶ τοῦ υ τὸ σ ΜΕΛΔΟΜΕΝΟΣ ποιήσας. We know from the Commentary of Ammonius (*Pap. Oxyrh.* 221, col. 17, 30 ff.) that this correction dates from Crates.

B. There are further several pretty certain corrections of the text by modern scholars which rest on the hypothesis of a 'transliteration'.

1. η 107 καιροσέων δ' ὀθονέων ἀπολείβεται ὑγρὸν ἔλαιον. Lobeck

explains rightly as ΚΑΙΡΟΣΕΟΝ for καιρουσσέων, fem. gen. pl. of καιρόεις, καιρόεσσα. An old Milesian inscription has ΤΕΙΧΙΟΣΗΣ ΑΡΧΟΣ, i. e. Τειχιούσσης ἀρχός (*I. G. A.* 488).

2. τ 109 θεουδής supposed to be for θεοδδής (i. e. θεο-δϝής, 'god-fearing') —I should prefer to take it as θεώδης from θεο-ϝάδης, 'god-pleasing' (so Fick): either would be written ΘΕΟΔΕΣ.

3. κ 510 ὠλεσίκαρπος, as Schulze points out, is for οὐλεσίκαρπος: written ΟΛΕ- -.

4. Δ 359, π 203 περιώσιος is for περιούσιος (G. Meyer) from περιεῖναι.

5. θ 408 ἔπος δ' εἴ πέρ τι βέβακται δεινόν, ἄφαρ τὸ φέροιεν ἀναρπάξασαι ἄελλαι. Δεινόν gives a wrong sense : E. Bruhn ΔΕΝΟΝ, i. e. δεννόν (= κακολόγον Hesych.).

6. ναιετάωσαν, ἀρόωσι, δηϊόφεν, δηϊοῶντες all false forms derived from mis-interpretation of ΝΑΙΕΤΑΟΣΑΝ, ΑΡΟΟΣΙ, ΔΕΙΟΟΙΕΝ, ΔΕΙΟΟΝΤΕΣ.

7. Ο 635 αἰὲν ὁμοστιχάει. Schol. Β συμπορεύεται· βάρβαρον δέ φησιν εἶναι αὐτὸ Διονύσιος. Bekker ὁμοῦ στιχάει (ΟΜΟΣΤΙΧΑΕΙ).

8. Ζ 344 and Ι 64 κακομηχάνου ὀκρυοέσσης and ἐπιδημίου ὀκρυόεντος. Payne-Knight saw that the true forms were κακομηχάνοο κρυοέσσης, ἐπιδημίοο κρυόεντος : misinterpretation of ΚΑΚΟΜΕΧΑΝΟΟΚΡΥΟΕΣΕΣ, ΕΠΙΔΕΜΙΟΟΚΡΥΟΕΝΤΟΣ.

9. Η 434 τῆμος ἄρ' ἀμφὶ πυρὴν κριτὸς ἔγρετο λαὸς Ἀχαιῶν and Ω 789 τῆμος ἄρ' ἀμφὶ πυρὴν κλυτοῦ Ἕκτορος ἔγρετο λαός. ἔγρετο means 'woke': Düntzer corrects ἤγρετο, 'was gathered': the MS. text is a misinterpretation of ΕΓΡΕΤΟ.

10. Γ 416 μέσσῳ δ' ἀμφοτέρων μητίσομαι ἔχθεα λυγρά is difficult to understand. Perhaps ΜΕΣΟΙ really meant ΜΗ ΣΟΙ; this involves changing δ' to γ', but is a great improvement.

11. ὠμηστής is perhaps wrong for ὠμεστής (ἀπὸ τοῦ ὠμὰ ἐσθίειν). Of course the analogy of ὀρχηστής is amply enough to account for the η, but it may be pre-Greek (Sanscr. āmād-).

C. The same cause may have helped in many of the common modernizings of Homeric language (εἰργάζετο from ΕΡΓΑΖΕΤΟ, ἐῴκει from ΕΟΙΚΕΙ, ἕως τέως from ΗΕΟΣ ΤΕΟΣ, τεθνειὼς στείομεν εἴαται from ΤΕΘΝΕΟΣ ΣΤΕΟΜΕΝ ΗΕΑΤΑΙ: see Wackernagel in *Bezzenb. Beitr.* iv. pp. 265 ff.), but of course there are quantities of similar moderniza-tions and Atticisms in which no such cause can have helped : ἰέναι for ἴμεναι, μειλιχίοις ἐπέεσσι for μειλιχίοισι ϝέπεσσι, ἤν που for αἴ κεν, &c. See Prof. Platt's texts of the *Iliad* and *Odyssey*, or Van Leeuwen's.

APPENDIX J

THE CATALOGUE AS A 'LEGAL DOCUMENT'

MR. ALLEN in *The Homeric Catalogue of Ships* treats the Catalogue as a sort of legal document, 'an international authority' (p. 28), 'a document constituting a title' (p. 38), and argues that for any one in antiquity to tamper with its text would be like falsifying a will or a charter, 'a forgery made with a material and quasi-legal purpose'. I do not see how such a view can be reconciled with the actual facts of the text of B; for instance, the many variant readings shown in Mr. Allen's own edition; but apart from this difficulty the whole theory appears to me to rest on a misunderstanding.

We all know that the Greeks habitually used the traditional legends as evidence, or at least as ornament, to support political claims. If the legend could be backed by a quotation from Homer or some ancient poet, so much the better, though I know of no instance in which such evidence was accepted by the Court as decisive. Thus in Hdt. ix. 26, 27 the Tegeans and Athenians bring up καινὰ καὶ παλαιά to justify their respective claims to a post of honour, all about the Heracleidae, and the expedition of Polynices and the Amazons. So in Hdt. v. 94 the Athenians argue that the Mytileneans have no more right to Sigeum than any other of the Greek peoples who συνεπρήξαντο Μενέλεῳ τὰς Ἑλένης ἁρπαγάς. Periander decided the dispute by letting each side keep what they had got. In vii. 161 a definite reference to Homer is added to other arguments. The Athenians refuse to yield supremacy at sea to the Syracusans, because (1) they have had for some time the largest naval force in Greece; (2) they are αὐτόχθονες, the only Greeks who have never been driven from their country; (3) 'Homer the poet says that Menestheus was the best marshaller of an army at Troy'. The Homeric reference adds ornament and point to the claim, but is very far removed from being the citation of an 'authoritative legal document'.

It will be noticed that these references to Homer are all made by Athenians. By the fourth century it looks as if the knowledge of our text was more widespread, for the Phocians support their claim to the possession of Delphi at the opening of the Sacred War, 357 B.C., by a definite quotation of B 519, where the Phocians hold 'Kyparissos and rocky Pytho': quite a good argument as it happens, but one which had no effect in convincing the other side.

The Solon anecdote is often misrepresented, as if it stated that in the dispute with Megara about Salamis Solon had produced the sacred text B 558 στῆσε δ' ἄγων ἵν' Ἀθηναίων ἵσταντο φάλαγγες, and the Court immediately bowed to its authority. Its point is quite different. It is that the line, which looks on the face of it like a forgery, was actually forged by Solon or Pisistratus on the occasion of the arbitration about Salamis. No ancient author treats the anecdote very seriously. Strabo does not believe it. Quintilian quotes it merely to illustrate a technical point. Plutarch says that the Athenians consider it 'nonsense' (φλυαρία) and give the real arguments which they allege to have been used by their representative at the arbitration.

The only texts which give any semblance of support to Mr. Allen's view of the 'international title-deeds' are some rhetorical phrases in the Scholia, especially Schol. B on B 494: 'So sweet and gorgeous is the Catalogue that cities use the verses of Homer in their contentions. He it was who presented Calydon to the Aetolians ... the people of Abydos won Sestos from the Athenians by quoting B 836: two lines sufficed to give victory to the Milesians against Priene (868 f.); Solon handed Salamis to the Athenians by adding the line 558.' This may very suitably be termed φλυαρία. For my own part I doubt if, among the innumerable changes which have occurred in the text of Homer between the time of their first commission to writing and the age of Aristarchus, there have been any number worth considering due to the motive of 'deliberate fraud for a material purpose'. Even the passage about Salamis, obviously 'cooked' as it is, is not quite that. It is more like an awkward patch made to cover up a hole. No one could expect the Athenians to enjoy the public recitation of a passage of genuine traditional Homer which showed that Salamis was independent, and their own seizure of it 'unjust'. Hence the original lines about Ajax were omitted. Then the gap had to be filled, as unostentatiously as possible, in such a way as not to annoy the public.

INDEX